LinkedIn®

6th Edition

by Joel Elad

LinkedIn® For Dummies®, 6th Edition

Published by: **John Wiley & Sons, Inc.,** 111 River Street, Hoboken, NJ 07030-5774, www.wiley.com

For general information on our other products and services, please contact our Customer Care Department within the U.S. at 877-762-2974, outside the U.S. at 317-572-3993, or fax 317-572-4002. For technical support, please visit https://hub.wiley.com/community/support/dummies.

Wiley publishes in a variety of print and electronic formats and by print-on-demand. Some material included with standard print versions of this book may not be included in e-books or in print-on-demand. If this book refers to media such as a CD or DVD that is not included in the version you purchased, you may download this material at http://booksupport.wiley.com. For more information about Wiley products, visit www.wiley.com.

Library of Congress Control Number: 2021933662

ISBN 978-1-119-69533-2 (pbk); ISBN 978-1-119-69539-4 (ebk); ISBN 978-1-119-69534-9 (ebk)

Manufactured in the United States of America

SKY10025645_031521

Contents at a Glance

Table of Contents

Introduction

Relationships matter. Ever since the dawn of time, when Fred Flintstone asked Barney Rubble whether there was any work at the quarry, human beings have networked. We're social creatures who like to reach out and talk to someone. As the Internet developed and grew in popularity, people rapidly took advantage of this new technology for communication, with email, instant messaging, personal web pages sharing voice, video, and data, and lots of other applications to keep everybody connected. But how can the Internet help you do a better job with your professional networking? I'm glad you asked! Welcome to *LinkedIn For Dummies,* 6th Edition.

LinkedIn was founded in 2003 by a guy named Reid Hoffman, who felt that he could create a better way to handle your professional networking needs. He saw lots of websites that let you build your own page and show it to the world, extolling your virtues and talents. But a lot of the popular websites that Hoffman came across at that time focused more on the social aspects of your life and not that much on the professional side. LinkedIn changed all of that with its approach of augmenting all the professional networking you do (or should do) daily. You don't have to be looking for a job to use LinkedIn, but if you are looking, LinkedIn should be part of your search. As Hoffman put it, LinkedIn was designed to "find and contact the people you need through the people you already trust."

In short, LinkedIn allows you to coordinate your professional identity on the Internet and make you more effective in your career. The site is designed to make the aspects of networking less time consuming and more powerful, so you can open doors with your professional connections and tap the connections of people you know who make up your extended network. LinkedIn doesn't require a huge amount of time or usage to be effective, and is focused only on providing tools that help your professional career.

Perhaps you've heard of LinkedIn, but you don't understand fully what it is, how it works, and most importantly, why you should care about it. Maybe you received an invitation to join the LinkedIn website. Perhaps you've received multiple invitations, or you keep hearing about it and want to find out more. Well, you're taking the right first step by reading this book. In it, I talk about the *whys* as well as the *hows.* If you're looking to enhance your professional life, I truly believe you need to look at LinkedIn. If you want to go straight to the beach and retire, though, maybe this isn't the book for you!

About This Book

This book covers all aspects of using the LinkedIn site: signing up and building your profile, growing your network of contacts, taking advantage of some of the sophisticated options, and everything in between. I include a lot of advice and discussion of networking concepts, but you also find a lot of step-by-step instructions to get things done. In this sixth edition, I revisit some of the newer facets of LinkedIn, including its extensive settings and privacy options, the mobile app, the news feed, and Companies sections, and I have updated all core processes, from creating your profile to looking for a job.

You can read each chapter one after the other, or you can go straight to the chapter on the topic you're interested in. After you start using LinkedIn, think of this book as a reference where you can find the knowledge nugget you need to know and then be on your merry way. Lots of details are cross-referenced, so if you need to look elsewhere in the book for more information, you can easily find it.

Foolish Assumptions

I assume that you know how to use your computer, at least for the basic operations, such as checking email, typing a document, and surfing the great big World Wide Web. If you're worried that you need a PhD in Computer Operations to handle LinkedIn, relax. If you can navigate your way around a website, you can use LinkedIn.

You may be new to the idea of social networking, or the specific ins and outs of using a site such as LinkedIn, but don't assume that signing up means you'll get a job instantly with zero effort.

This book assumes that you have a computer that can access the Internet; any PC or Mac is fine, as well as Linux or any other operating system with a web browser. All the main web browsers can access LinkedIn. In some parts of the book, I discuss specific applications such as Microsoft Outlook; if you have Outlook, I assume you know how to use it for the purposes of importing and exporting names from your address book.

Icons Used in This Book

As you go through this book, you'll see the following icons in the margins.

TIP

The Tip icon notifies you about something cool, handy, or nifty that I highly recommend. For example, "Here's a quicker way to do the described task."

REMEMBER

Don't forget! When you see this icon, you can be sure that it points out something you should remember, possibly even something I said earlier that I'm repeating because it's very important. For example, "If you are going to do only one of my bullet point suggestions, do the last one because it's the most powerful."

WARNING

Danger! Ah-*oo*-gah! Ah-*oo*-gah! When you see the Warning icon, pay careful attention to the text. This icon flags something that's bad or that could cause trouble. For example, "Although you may be tempted to go into personal details in your profile, you should never post anything that could embarrass you in a future job interview."

Beyond the Book

In addition to what you're reading right now, this book comes with a free access-anywhere cheat sheet that provides steps on building your LinkedIn network, tips for enhancing your LinkedIn profile, advice for getting the most out of LinkedIn, and tips for using LinkedIn to search for a job. To get the cheat sheet, simply go to `www.dummies.com` and search for *LinkedIn For Dummies Cheat Sheet* in the Search box.

Where to Go from Here

You can read this book cover to cover, or just jump in and start reading anywhere. Open the Table of Contents and choose a topic that interests or concerns you or that has piqued your curiosity. Everything is explained in the text, and important details are cross-referenced so that you don't waste your time reading repeated information.

Good luck with LinkedIn. Happy networking!

1

Understanding LinkedIn Basics

IN THIS PART . . .

Explore all that LinkedIn has to offer.

Sign up with LinkedIn and create an account.

Build a LinkedIn profile that details your professional and educational experience.

IN THIS CHAPTER

» Getting to know your networking toolkit

» Understanding the different degrees of network connections

» Discovering LinkedIn features

» Comparing the different accounts

» Navigating the LinkedIn menu system

Chapter 1
Looking into LinkedIn

When I hear the terms "social networking" and "business networking," I always go back to one of my favorite phrases: "It's not *what* you know; it's *who* you know." Now imagine a website where both concepts are true, where you can demonstrate *what* you know and see the power of *who* you know. That's just one way to describe LinkedIn, one of the top websites today where you can do professional networking and so much more.

Social networking has garnered a lot of attention over the years, and while newer sites such as Tik Tok, Instagram, and Snapchat are gaining in popularity, the two sites that most people think of first for social networking are Twitter and Facebook. Let me state right now, in the first chapter, that LinkedIn is *not* one of those sites. You can find some elements of similarity, but LinkedIn isn't the place to tweet about what you had for lunch or show pictures of last Friday's beach bonfire.

LinkedIn is a place where relationships matter (the original LinkedIn slogan). It was developed primarily for professional networking. When you look at its mission statement, LinkedIn's mission is simple: "Connect the world's professionals to make them more productive and successful." This is not a website that requires a lot of constant work to be effective. It's designed to work in the background and help you reach out to whomever you need while learning and growing yourself. The key is to set up your online identity, build your network, and steadily take advantage of the opportunities that most affect you or greatly interest you.

In this chapter, I introduce you to LinkedIn and the basic services it has to offer. I answer the questions "What is LinkedIn?" and, more importantly, "Why should I be using LinkedIn?" I talk about how LinkedIn fits in with the rest of your professional activities, and then I move on to the tangible benefits that LinkedIn can provide you, regardless of your profession or career situation. I discuss some of the premium account capabilities that you can pay to use, but rest assured that LinkedIn has a lot of free features. The last part of the chapter covers basic navigation of the LinkedIn site. I show you the different menus and navigation bars, which you encounter throughout this book.

Understanding Your New Contact Management and Networking Toolkit

When thinking about how people can be connected with each other, it helps to picture a tangible network. For example, roads connect cities. The Internet connects computers. A quilt is a series of connected pieces of fabric. But what about the intangible networks? You can describe the relationship among family members by using a family tree metaphor. People now use the term *social network* to describe the intangible connections between them and other people, whether they're friends, co-workers, or acquaintances.

People used to rely on address books or contact organizers (PDAs) to keep track of their social networks. You could grow your social networks by attending networking events or by being introduced in person to new contacts, and then continuing to communicate with these new contacts. Eventually, the new contacts were considered part of your social network.

As people began to rely more and more on technology, though, new tools were created to help manage social networks. Salespeople started using contact management systems such as ACT! to keep track of communications. Phone calls replaced written letters, and cellular phones replaced landline phones. Then email replaced phone calls and letters, with text messaging increasingly handling short bursts of communication. Today, with the mass adoption of smartphones, laptops, and tablets, Internet browsing has dramatically increased. People manage their lives through web browsers, SMS (Short Message Service) communications, and apps on their smartphones.

Internet tools have advanced to the point where online communication within your network is much more automated and accessible. Sites such as LinkedIn have started to replace the older ways of accessing your social network. For example, instead of asking your friend Michael to call his friend Eric to see whether Eric's friend has a job available, you can use LinkedIn to see whether Eric's friend works for a company you want to contact, and you can then use LinkedIn to send a message through Michael to Eric (or in some cases, directly to Eric's friend) to accomplish the same task. (Of course, this assumes you, Michael, and Eric are all members of LinkedIn.)

In the past, you had no way of viewing other people's social networks (collections of friends and other contacts). Now, though, when folks put their social networks on LinkedIn, you can see your friends' networks as well as their friends' networks, and suddenly hidden opportunities start to become available to you.

Because of LinkedIn, you can spend more time researching potential opportunities (such as finding a job or a new employee for your business) as well as receiving information from the larger network and not just your immediate friends. The network is more useful because you can literally see the map that connects you with other people.

However, just because this information is more readily available, networking still involves work. You still have to manage your connections and use the network to gain more connections or knowledge. Remember, too, that nothing can replace the power of meeting people in person. But because LinkedIn works in the background guiding you in finding contacts and starting the networking process, you can spend your time more productively instead of making blind requests and relying solely on other people to make something happen.

Keeping track of your contacts

You made a connection with someone — say, your roommate from college. It's graduation day; you give him your contact information, he gives you his information, and you tell him to keep in touch. As both of you move to different places, start new jobs, and live your lives, you eventually lose track of each other, and all your contact information grows out of date. How do you find this person again?

One of the benefits of LinkedIn is that after you connect with someone you know who also has an account on LinkedIn, you always have a live link to that person. Even when that person changes email addresses, you'll always be able to send him or her a message through LinkedIn. In this sense, LinkedIn always keeps you connected with people in your network, regardless of how their lives change. LinkedIn shows you a list of your connections, such as the list in Figure 1-1.

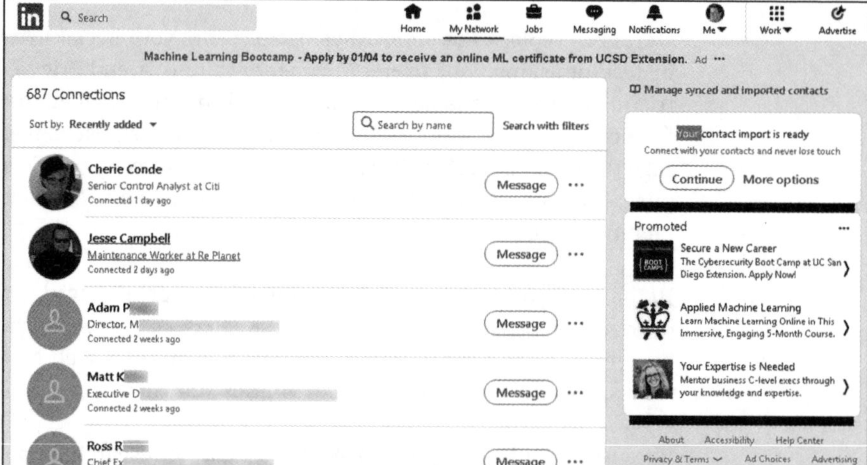

FIGURE 1-1: See all your connections in one centralized list.

Understanding the different degrees of network connections

In the LinkedIn universe, the word *connection* means a person who is connected to you through the site. The number of connections you have simply means the number of people who are directly connected to you in your professional network.

Here are the different levels of connectedness on LinkedIn:

- **First-degree connections:** People you know personally; they have a direct relationship from their account to your account. These first-degree connections make up your immediate network and are usually your past colleagues, classmates, group members, friends, family, and close associates. Unlike Facebook, where everyone you connect to is a "friend," on LinkedIn, you can connect to friends who might not have a work, school, or group connection to you but whom you know personally outside those criteria. Similar to Facebook, though, you can see your list of first-degree connections and they can see yours — provided your settings (and those of your connections) are configured so any connection can see other people's list of connections.
- **Second-degree network members:** People who know at least one member of your first-degree connections: in other words, the friends of your friends. You can reach any second-degree network member by asking your first-degree connection to pass along your profile as an introduction from you to his friend.

» **Third-degree network members:** People who know at least one of your second-degree network members: in other words, friends of your friends of your friends. You can reach any third-degree network member by asking your friend to pass along a request to be introduced to her friend, who then passes it to her friend, who is the third-degree network member.

The result is a large chain of connections and network members, with a core of trusted friends who help you reach out and tap your friends' networks and extended networks. Take the concept of Six Degrees of Separation (which says that, on average, a chain of six people can connect you to anyone else on Earth), put everyone's network online, and you have LinkedIn.

So, how powerful can these connections be? Figure 1-2 shows a snapshot of how someone's network on LinkedIn used to look.

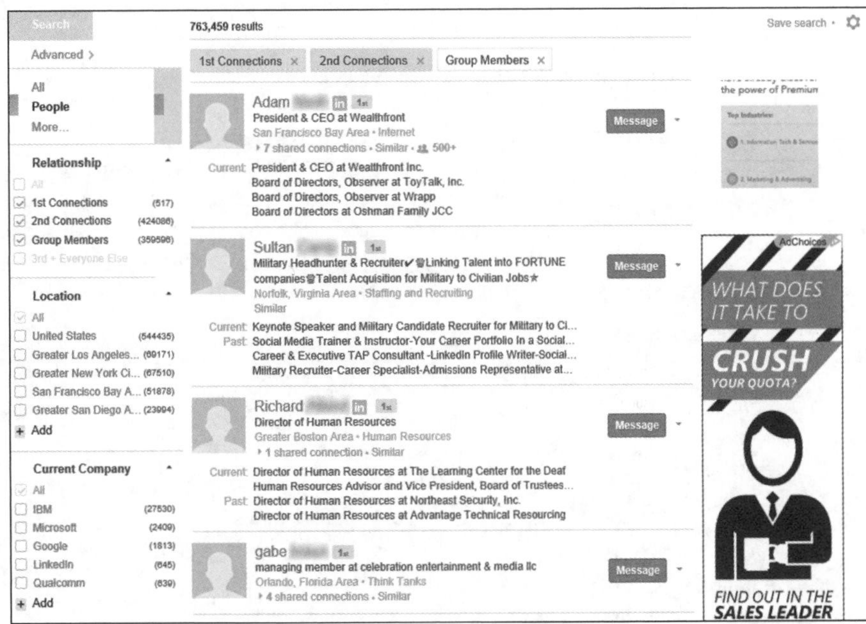

FIGURE 1-2: Only three degrees of separation can give you a network of millions.

The account in Figure 1-2 has 517 first-degree connections. When you add all the network connections that each of these 517 people have, the user of this account could reach more than 424,000 different people on LinkedIn as second-degree network members. Add over 359,000 LinkedIn users who are members of groups that this account belongs to, plus millions of third-degree network members, and the user could have access to millions of LinkedIn users, part of a vast professional network that stretches across the world into companies and industries of all sizes. Such a network can help you advance your career or professional goals — and in turn, you can help advance others' careers or goals. As of this writing, the LinkedIn community has more than 722 million members, and LinkedIn focuses on your first-degree connections instead of your second- and third-degree network members, but the concept is still valid. Your network can be vast, thanks to the power of LinkedIn.

THE DIFFERENCE BETWEEN A USER AND A LION

Given all the power and potential to reach people around the world, some people — LinkedIn open networkers (LIONs) — want to network with anyone and everyone who's eager to connect with them. Their goal is to network with as many people as possible, regardless of past interactions or communications with that person.

One of your most prominently displayed LinkedIn statistics is the number of your first-degree connections. After you surpass 500 connections, LinkedIn displays not your current count of first-degree connections but just the message 500+. (It's kind of like how McDonald's stopped displaying the running total of hamburgers sold on its signs. Or am I the only one who remembers that?) Part of the reason LinkedIn stops displaying updated counts past 500 is to discourage people from collecting connections. Many LIONs have thousands or even tens of thousands of first-degree connections, and the 500+ statistic is a badge of honor to them.

LIONs encourage open networking (that is, the ability to connect with someone you have never met or worked with in the past) by advertising their email address as part of their professional headline (for example, John Doe; Manager firstname@lastname.com), so anyone can request this person be added to his or her network. LinkedIn offers a formal program — Open Profile — for people interested in networking with the larger community. You can sign up for this premium service any time after you establish a premium account. When you enable the Open Profile feature, you can send and receive messages with any other Open Profile member. I discuss this in the upcoming section, "Understanding LinkedIn Costs and Benefits."

I've been asked many times whether it's okay to be a LION and whether there is any meaning or benefit to having so many connections. My answer is that I don't endorse being a LION *at all!* Although some people feel that they can find some quality hidden in the quantity, LinkedIn is designed to cultivate quality connections. Not only does LinkedIn heavily discourage users being a LION to the point of almost banning them, but also the random connections make it next to impossible to tap the real power and potential of LinkedIn.

Discovering What You Can Do with LinkedIn

Time to find out what kinds of things you can do on LinkedIn. The following sections introduce you to the topics you need to know to get your foot in the LinkedIn door and really make the site start working for you.

Building your brand and profile

On LinkedIn, you can build your own brand. Your name, your identity, is a brand — just like Ford or Facebook — in terms of what people think of when they think of you. It's your professional reputation. Companies spend billions to ensure that you have a certain opinion of their products, and that opinion, that perception, is their brand image. You have your own brand image in your professional life, and it's up to you to own, define, and push your brand.

Most people today have different online representations of their personal brand. Some people have their own websites, some create and write blogs, and some create profile pages on sites such as Facebook. LinkedIn allows you to define a profile and build your own brand based on your professional and educational background. I use my profile as an example in Figure 1-3.

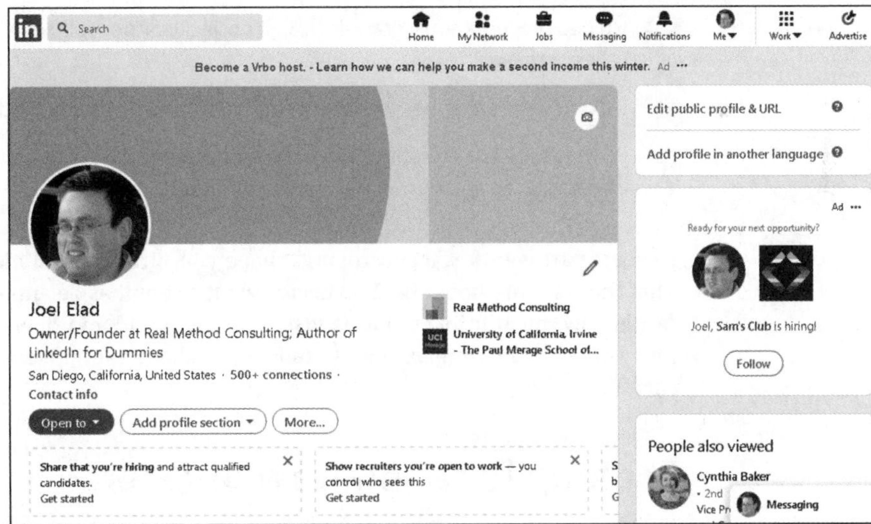

FIGURE 1-3: Create a unified profile page to showcase your professional history.

Your LinkedIn profile can become a jumping-off point, where any visitor can get a rich and detailed idea of all the skills, experiences, and interests you bring to the table. Unlike a resume, where you have to worry about page length and formatting, you can provide substance and detail on your LinkedIn profile, including any part-time, contract, nonprofit, and consulting work in addition to traditional professional experience. You also have other options to consider; for example, you can

- Write your own summary.
- List any groups you belong to.
- Describe any courses you have completed and test scores you have achieved.
- Show any memberships or affiliations you have.
- Cite honors and awards you have received.
- Identify any patents or certifications you have earned.
- Provide links to any publications you've written or published.
- Give and receive endorsements of people's skills. (I discuss endorsements in Chapter 7.)
- Give and receive recommendations from other people. (I discuss recommendations in Chapter 9.)
- Indicate your professional interests or supported causes.
- Upload presentations, graphic design projects, or portfolio examples for others to view.
- Upload videos that demonstrate a particular skill or past project.
- Post website links to other parts of your professional identity, such as a blog, a website, or an e-commerce store you operate.

The best part is that *you* control and shape your professional identity. You decide what the content should be. You decide what to emphasize and what to omit. You decide how much information is visible to the world and how much is visible to your first-degree connections. (I talk more about the power of your profile in Chapters 2 and 3.)

Looking for a job now or later

At some point in your life, you'll probably have to look for a job. It might be today, it might be a year from now, or it may be ten years from now. The job search is, in itself, a full-time job, and studies show that as many as 85 percent of all jobs are found not through a job board such as Indeed or CareerBuilder, or a newspaper classified ad, but rather through a formal or informal network of contacts where the job isn't even posted yet. LinkedIn makes it easy to do some of the following tedious job search tasks:

- **Finding the right person** at a target company, such as a hiring manager in a certain department, to discuss immediate and future job openings
- **Getting a reference** from a past boss or co-worker to use for a future job application
- **Finding information** about a company and position before the interview
- **Enabling the right employers to find you** and validate your experience and job potential before an interview
- **Searching posted job listings** on a job board such as the one on LinkedIn

The hidden power of LinkedIn is that it helps you find jobs you weren't looking for or applying to directly. This is when you're a *passive job seeker,* currently employed but interested in the right opportunity. As of this writing, hundreds of thousands of recruiters are members of LinkedIn, and they constantly use the search functions to go through the database and find skilled members who match their job search requirements. Instead of companies paying big money for resume books, they now have instant access to millions of qualified professionals, each of whom has a detailed profile with skills, experience, and recommendations already available.

This practice of finding passive job seekers is growing quickly on LinkedIn, mainly because of the following reasons:

- **Companies can run detailed searches** to find the perfect candidate with all the right keywords and skills in his profile, and they then contact the person to see whether he is interested.
- **LinkedIn users demonstrate their capabilities** by providing knowledge on the site, which gives companies insight into the passive job seeker's capabilities. Not only does LinkedIn give users the opportunity to share updates and knowledge, but it also hosts an extensive network of groups on the site. Each group runs its own discussion board of conversations, where LinkedIn users can pose a question or start a conversation and other LinkedIn members can provide insight or link to relevant articles and continue the discussion.
- **Companies can review a person's profile** to find and check references ahead of time and interview only people they feel would be a great match with their corporate culture.

» **Employed individuals can quietly run their own searches** at any time to see what's available, and they can follow up online without taking off a day for an in-person or phone interview.

REMEMBER

LinkedIn research shows that "people with more than 20 connections are 34 times more likely to be approached with a job opportunity than people with fewer than 5 connections." Therefore, your connections definitely influence your active or passive job search.

Finding out all kinds of valuable information

Beyond getting information about your job search, you can use the immense LinkedIn database of professionals to find out what skills seem to be the most popular in a certain industry and job title. You can discover how many project managers live within 50 miles of you. You can even find current or past employees of a company and interview them about that job. LinkedIn now has millions of detailed Company pages that show not only company statistics but also recent hires, promotions, changes, and lists of employees closely connected with you. (Read more about Company pages in Chapter 15.)

Best of all, LinkedIn can help you find specific information on a variety of topics. You can do a search to find out the interests of your next sales prospect, the name of a former employee you can talk to about a company you like, or how you can join a start-up in your target industry by reaching out to the co-founder. You can sit back and skim the news, or you can dive in and hunt for the facts. It all depends on what method best fits your goals.

Expanding your network

You have your network today, but what about the future? Whether you want to move up in your industry, look for a new job, start your own company, or achieve some other goal, one way to do it is to expand your network. LinkedIn provides a fertile ground to reach like-minded and well-connected professionals who share a common interest, experience, or group membership. The site also provides several online mechanisms to reduce the friction of communication, so you can spend more time building your network instead of searching for the right person.

First and foremost, LinkedIn helps you identify and contact members of other people's professional networks, and best of all, you can contact them not via a cold call but with your friend's recommendation or introduction. (See Chapters 9 and 6, respectively, for more information.) In addition, you can find out more about your new contact before you send the first message, so you don't have to waste time figuring out whether this is someone who could be beneficial to have in your network.

You can also meet new people through various groups on LinkedIn, whether it's an alumni group from your old school, a group of past employees from the same company, or a group of people interested in improving their public speaking skills and contacts. LinkedIn groups help you connect with other like-minded members, search for specific group members, and share information about the group with other members. (I cover LinkedIn groups in Chapter 16.)

Navigating LinkedIn

When you're ready to get started, you can sign up for an account by checking out Chapter 2. Before you do, however, take a look at the following sections, which walk you through the different parts of the LinkedIn website so you know how to find all the cool features I discuss in this book.

After you log in to your LinkedIn account, you see your personal LinkedIn home page, as shown in Figure 1-4. You'll use two important areas on your LinkedIn home page a lot, and I cover those areas in the following sections.

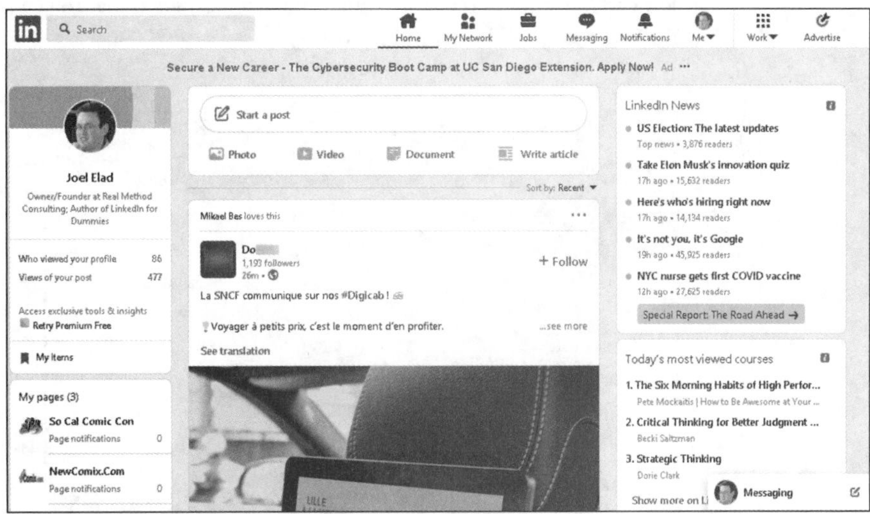

FIGURE 1-4: Your LinkedIn home page.

Touring the top navigation bar

Every page on LinkedIn contains links to the major parts of the site, and I call this top set of links the *top navigation bar* throughout this book. As of this writing, the major parts of the top navigation bar are as follows:

- **Home:** Go to your personal LinkedIn home page.
- **My Network:** View your connections on LinkedIn, add new connections, and import new connections.
- **Jobs:** View the different job searches and postings you can do on LinkedIn.
- **Messaging:** Go to your Messaging inbox to communicate with other LinkedIn members.
- **Notifications:** Go to your Notifications page to see what your LinkedIn connections are doing, reading, and sharing, as well as daily rundowns on news items, the work anniversaries and birthdays of your connections, and suggestions for influencers or companies you can follow on LinkedIn.
- **Me:** When you start your LinkedIn account, you'll see a generic icon in this spot. After you add a profile picture to your LinkedIn account, the icon changes to a thumbnail of your profile photo. When you click the drop-down arrow, you can choose to access your Settings & Privacy page, access the LinkedIn Help Center page, or manage your LinkedIn posts, job postings, or company pages.

You have to click each element in the top navigation bar to go to that direct page. For the Me icon, you need to click the drop-down arrow to see the various options for selection, as shown in Figure 1-5.

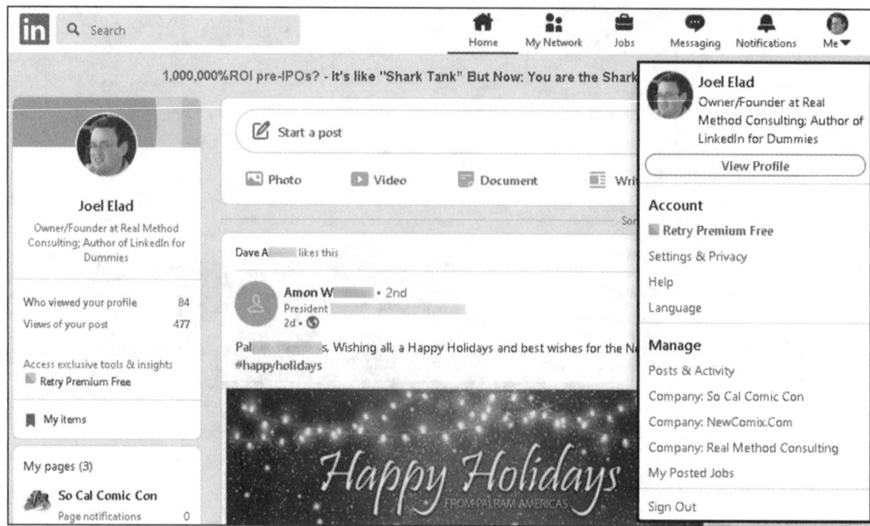

FIGURE 1-5: Click the drop-down arrow to see options for this section.

Finally, other features typically appear along the top right of the screen:

- **Advertise:** This icon takes you directly to the LinkedIn Advertising page. I discuss using LinkedIn Ads in more depth in Chapter 18.

TIP

If you don't see Advertise as its own option, you can find it as an option in the Work drop-down list.

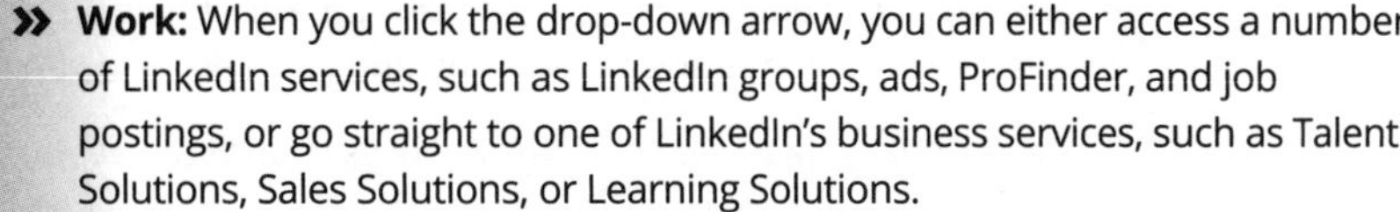

- **Work:** When you click the drop-down arrow, you can either access a number of LinkedIn services, such as LinkedIn groups, ads, ProFinder, and job postings, or go straight to one of LinkedIn's business services, such as Talent Solutions, Sales Solutions, or Learning Solutions.

TIP

At the very bottom of this drop-down list is the Create a Company Page option, where you can build a Company page. You'll be using this link when you explore Company pages in Chapter 15.

Looking at the Settings & Privacy page

If you need to update any aspect of your LinkedIn account, click the Me icon, and then select the Settings & Privacy option. The page shown in Figure 1-6 appears.

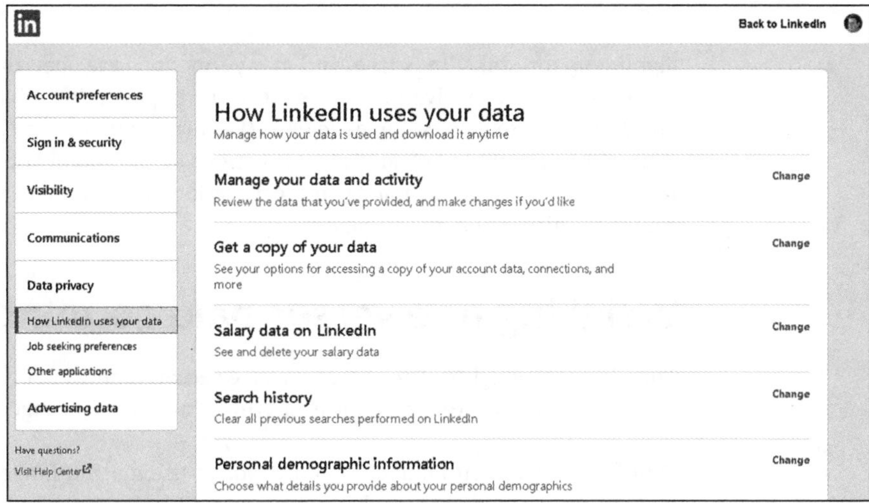

FIGURE 1-6: You can change the details of your LinkedIn account.

Following are the settings you can access from this page:

- **Account Preferences:** Update your profile, language, and security settings; upgrade, downgrade, or cancel your LinkedIn account; connect your LinkedIn account to Microsoft or Twitter, and more.

- **Sign in & security:** Update email addresses, phone numbers, and your password, and enable two-step verification to access your account.
- **Visibility:** Set how much of your profile is accessible by your contacts and how much information you want to make available to your network in terms of profile or status updates. Control your data and advertising preferences.
- **Communications:** Set the frequency of the emails you receive from LinkedIn and which LinkedIn partners can reach you. Select how other LinkedIn members can communicate with you and who can send you invitations.
- **Data privacy:** Manage how LinkedIn uses your data, set your job-seeking preferences, and manage your connection to other functions in programs such as Microsoft Word.

You spend more time on how to properly use these settings for your benefit in Chapter 11. For now, it's important to know where to find the Settings page in case you need to change something about your account.

Understanding LinkedIn Costs and Benefits

Signing up for LinkedIn is free, and many functions are open to all account holders, so you can take advantage of most of the opportunities that LinkedIn offers. You don't have to pay a setup or registration fee, but you can pay a monthly fee for a premium account to get additional functions or communication options. Finally, tailored solutions are available for corporations that want to use LinkedIn as a source for hiring quality candidates.

Weighing free versus paid accounts

There's not much difference between a free account and a paid account on LinkedIn. And the basic (free) account is anything but basic in usage.

Your free account with LinkedIn allows you to use most of LinkedIn's most popular features, including the following:

- Build a network of connections with no limits on size or numbers.
- Reconnect with any member of the LinkedIn network, provided that he or she knows you and agrees to connect with you.

- Create a professional and detailed LinkedIn profile.
- Give and receive an unlimited number of recommendations.
- Join up to 100 or create up to 30 different LinkedIn groups.
- Perform an unlimited number of searches for LinkedIn members in your extended network of first- and second-degree members plus group members.

If you want to step up to a paid account, some of the main features include these:

- Send a message to anyone in the LinkedIn community — regardless of whether he or she is in your extended network — through an InMail messaging service. (***Note:*** You get a limited number of InMail credits depending on your paid account level.)
- View more LinkedIn profile information of people not in your LinkedIn network when you conduct advanced searches.
- See more LinkedIn network profile information when you conduct advanced searches.
- See who has viewed your profile (if those viewers have not configured their settings to be anonymous when viewing profiles) and how they arrived at your profile.
- Obtain membership in the Open Profile program, which gives you unlimited Open Profile messages.

Comparing the paid accounts

LinkedIn offers a few levels of paid accounts, each with a specific level of benefits. For the most up-to-date packages that LinkedIn offers, check out the Free and Paid Accounts Help page at `http://www.linkedin.com/premium/products`, as shown in Figure 1-7. You can also click the Try Premium for Free link at the top right of your screen to see a comparison of the paid accounts.

Every premium account comes with certain benefits regardless of the level you choose. These benefits include

- Open Profile network membership
- Unlimited Open Profile messages
- Ability to see who viewed your profile
- Access to premium content
- One-business-day customer service for your LinkedIn questions

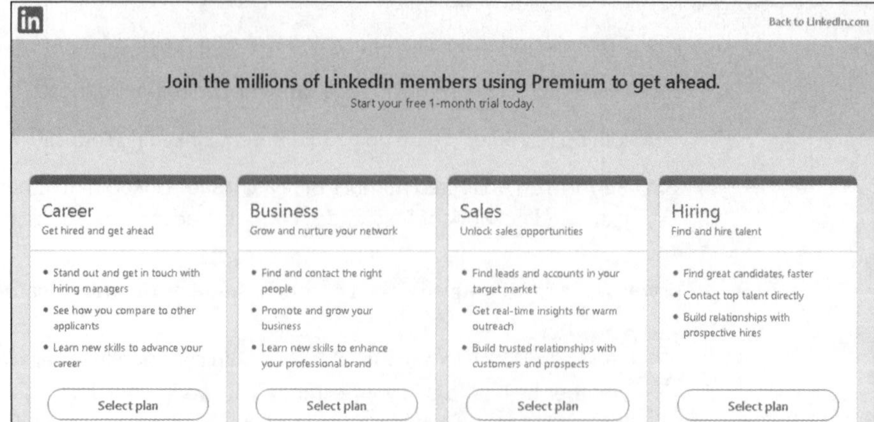

FIGURE 1-7: Learn about different paid account features on LinkedIn.

As of this writing, LinkedIn offers a variety of premium packages targeted at individual users: Premium Career, Premium Business, Premium Sales, and Premium Hiring. Each account level comes with specific benefits:

- **Premium Career:** $29.99 per month, billed monthly, or $239.88 per year when you buy an annual subscription, at a 33 percent savings. This account includes the following:
  - Five InMail credits per month, which allow you to contact any LinkedIn member regardless of whether he or she is in your network, as long as the other member agreed to receive InMail messages
  - Ability to see who viewed your profile in the last 90 days and how they located you

    WARNING

    Even with this feature in a premium account, if the other person has her privacy settings configured to remove her visibility, you won't see her name when you look at who viewed your profile.

    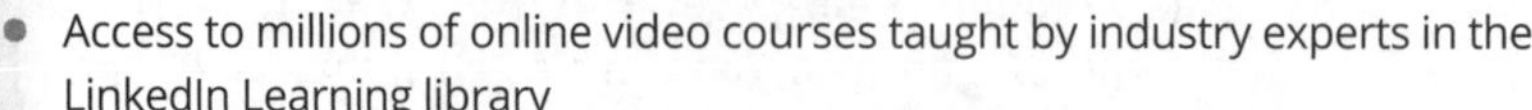

  - Access to millions of online video courses taught by industry experts in the LinkedIn Learning library
  - Salary insights that show you salary details when browsing job listings, without having to share your own personal data
  - Applicant insights to see how you (and your skill set) compare to other candidates for a potential job
  - Featured Applicant status when a recruiter searches for applicants, which means you are moved to the top section of a recruiter's search screen

- **Premium Business:** $59.99 per month, billed monthly, or $575.88 per year when you buy an annual subscription, at a 20 percent savings. This account includes the following:
  - Fifteen InMail credits per month (see Chapter 6 for more on InMail)
  - Ability to view unlimited profiles when you perform a LinkedIn search, including any third-degree network members
  - Ability to see who viewed your profile in the last 90 days and how they located you
  - Business insights that give you the most up-to-date trends and information on how a company's growth rate and hiring trends are projecting, so you can research companies more effectively
  - Many of the benefits of the Premium Career account, such as LinkedIn Learning, and applicant and salary insights
- **Premium Sales (or Sales Navigator Professional):** $79.99 per month, billed monthly, or $779.88 per year when you buy an annual subscription, at a 19 percent savings. This account includes the following:
  - Twenty InMails per month
  - Help in finding recommended leads to reach out to, insight into how to reach out to them, and the ability to save the leads to your account and to create, organize, and keep track of leads and accounts through lists
  - Real-time updates on your leads and accounts when they post updates such as job changes or company growth
  - Lead Builder and Recommendation tools to help you find the right people to close the deal in your sales life
- **Premium Hiring (a.k.a. Recruiter Lite):** $119.95 per month, billed monthly, or $1,199.40 per year when you buy an annual subscription, at a 16 percent savings. This account includes these features:
  - Thirty InMails per month
  - Advanced search engines geared for recruiting to help you find top talent even faster, and a guided search experience to navigate the LinkedIn network efficiently
  - Smart Suggestions tools to help you find potential qualified candidates for your job listing that you may not initially considered
  - Ability to create projects in LinkedIn, where you can track the progress of multiple applicants in a potential pool, categorize people in folders, attach notes to profiles, and set up automated reminders

Upgrading to a premium account

What's the value in getting a premium account? Besides the features listed in the previous section for each account level, premium accounts are designed to give you more attention in areas such as job searches. When an employer lists a job posting and collects applications through LinkedIn, premium account holders show up at the top of the applicant list (similar to the Sponsored result in a Google search) with a Featured Applicant status next to their name. LinkedIn provides special content in the form of emails, video tutorials, and articles that provide job search and professional development tips and advice from leaders in the industry. Finally, you get to see who has viewed your profile, which can be helpful when you're applying for jobs or trying to set up business deals. A premium account is not essential for everyone, so consider what you need from your LinkedIn experience and decide if upgrading is right for you.

TIP

As of this writing, LinkedIn gives you the option to try any premium plan for free during the first month, and it automatically charges your credit card each month afterward for the full amount, unless you bought a yearly plan, for which the charges renew every 12 months.

To upgrade to a premium account, I highly recommend starting by creating your free account and using the various functions on LinkedIn. If you find that after some usage, you need to reach the larger community and take advantage of some of the premium account features, you can always upgrade your account and keep all your profile and network information that you previously defined.

WARNING

If you're in charge of human resource functions at a small, medium, or large company and you are interested in using the Recruiter functions for your company, don't follow the steps in this section. Instead, visit `https://business.linkedin.com/talent-solutions` for more information on its Talent Solutions.

To subscribe to a premium account, just follow these steps. (You must have created a LinkedIn account already; see Chapter 2 for details.)

1. **Go to the LinkedIn home page at** `https://www.linkedin.com`.
2. **Click the Me icon on the top navigation bar, and then click the Try Premium Free For 1 Month link in the drop-down list that appears, below the Account header.**

   In some cases, you'll see a Try Premium Free link on the top navigation bar to the right of the work drop-down menu. Click that link to proceed.

   LinkedIn asks you a series of questions to help recommend a plan.

3. **Answer the questions LinkedIn posts and click Next after each question.**

   The Premium Products page appears.

4. **Click the Select Plan button to display that premium account's specific options, as shown in Figure 1-8.**

   LinkedIn accepts PayPal, Visa, MasterCard, American Express, or Discover to pay for your premium account. If paying by credit card, make sure the billing address you provide matches the credit card billing address on file.

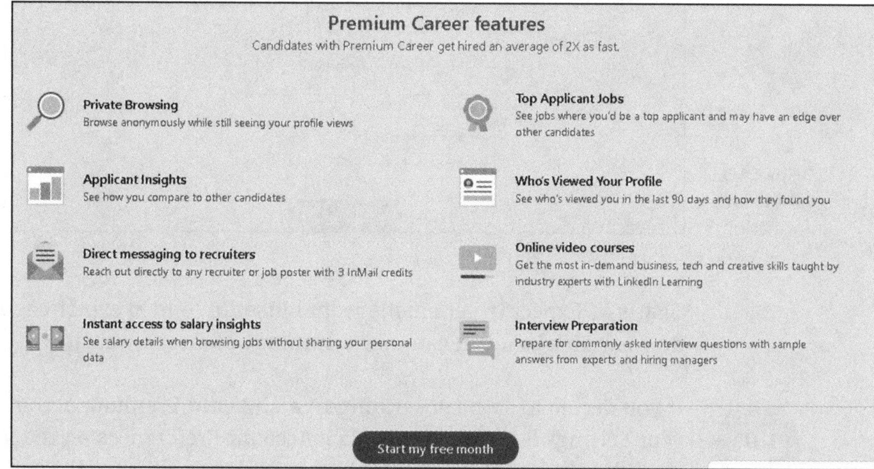

FIGURE 1-8: Review the options for the premium account you are considering.

5. **Click the blue Start My Free Month button for the premium level to which you want to upgrade.**
6. **When asked to confirm if you want monthly or annual billing, click the type you want.**
7. **Select the radio button beside the credit card or PayPal option to bring up the specific payment fields. Fill in the appropriate billing information, as shown in Figure 1-9, and then click the Review Order button.**
8. **Verify the information you've provided, and review the terms in the Review Your Order box.**

   If you want, click the links to review LinkedIn's terms of service, refund policy, and how to cancel.

9. **Click the blue Start Your Free Trial button to complete the process.**

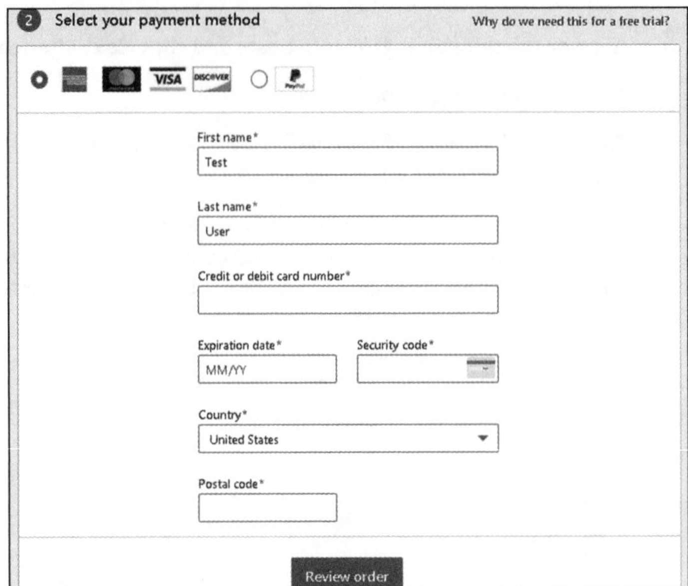

FIGURE 1-9: Enter your billing information.

That's it! Expect to get emails from LinkedIn to help explain and demonstrate the new features that you can take advantage of on the website.

REMEMBER

If you decide to stop subscribing to a LinkedIn Premium account, you must go to your Settings & Privacy page, click Account Preferences on the left, scroll down to the Subscriptions & Payments section, and then either click Switch Plans to change the level of your premium subscription or click the Cancel Subscription link to cancel your premium account. Follow the on-screen instructions to switch or cancel your Premium subscription. (See "Looking at the Settings & Privacy page," earlier in this chapter, for information about how to reach and use this page.)

» Registering and setting your preferences

» Connecting with people you already know on LinkedIn

Chapter 2
Signing Up and Creating Your Account

When LinkedIn first launched, it grew primarily through invitations — you joined only if someone who was already a member invited you and encouraged you to join. However, membership is now open to anyone 16 years or older (as long as the user hasn't previously been suspended or removed from LinkedIn, of course). You can have only one active account, but you can attach multiple email addresses, past and present, to your account so that people can more easily find you.

You'll be presented with some configuration settings during the sign-up process that might confuse you until you're more familiar with the system. Fortunately, you can customize all those settings later, but for now, I suggest some initial settings. In addition, based on your initial settings, LinkedIn recommends people to invite to your network. This chapter touches on the initial recommendation process; in Chapter 5, I discuss the ways you can grow your network more extensively.

Joining LinkedIn

Many people join LinkedIn because a friend or colleague invited them. You can join just as easily without receiving an invitation, though. Everyone joins at the basic level, which is free. (You can opt for different levels of paid membership, as spelled out in Chapter 1.) Being able to start at the basic level makes the sign-up process quite straightforward. Most importantly, the basic level still gives users the ability to take advantage of the most powerful tools that LinkedIn offers.

Joining with an invitation

When a friend or colleague invites you to join, you receive an email invitation. The email clearly identifies the sender and usually has *Invitation to connect on LinkedIn* as its subject line. (There's a chance, though, that the sender came up with a custom header, because LinkedIn now has built-in options for the sender to choose a custom reason for the invitation.)

When you open the message, you see an invitation to join LinkedIn, such as the message shown in Figure 2-1. There might be some extra text if the person inviting you personalized the message. You also see a button or link that takes you back to LinkedIn to create your account, such as the Join to View Invitation button shown in Figure 2-1.

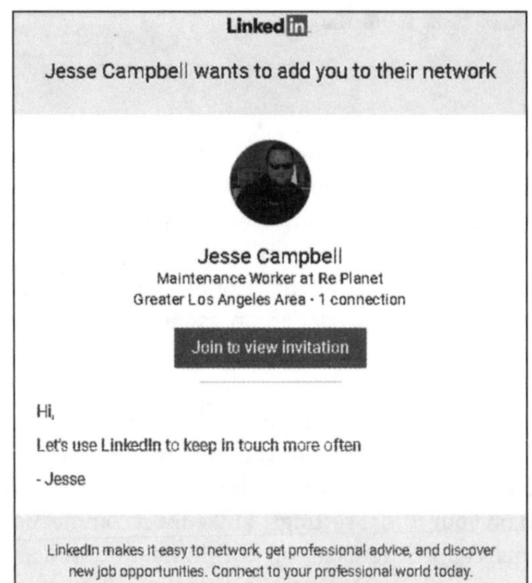

LinkedIn
Jesse Campbell wants to add you to their network
Jesse Campbell
Maintenance Worker at Re Planet
Greater Los Angeles Area · 1 connection
Join to view invitation
Hi,
Let's use LinkedIn to keep in touch more often
- Jesse
LinkedIn makes it easy to network, get professional advice, and discover new job opportunities. Connect to your professional world today.

FIGURE 2-1: An invitation to connect on LinkedIn.

When you're ready to join LinkedIn with an invitation, you'll start with these two steps:

1. **Click the button or link from your invitation email.**

   A new window appears that goes to the LinkedIn website, as shown in Figure 2-2.

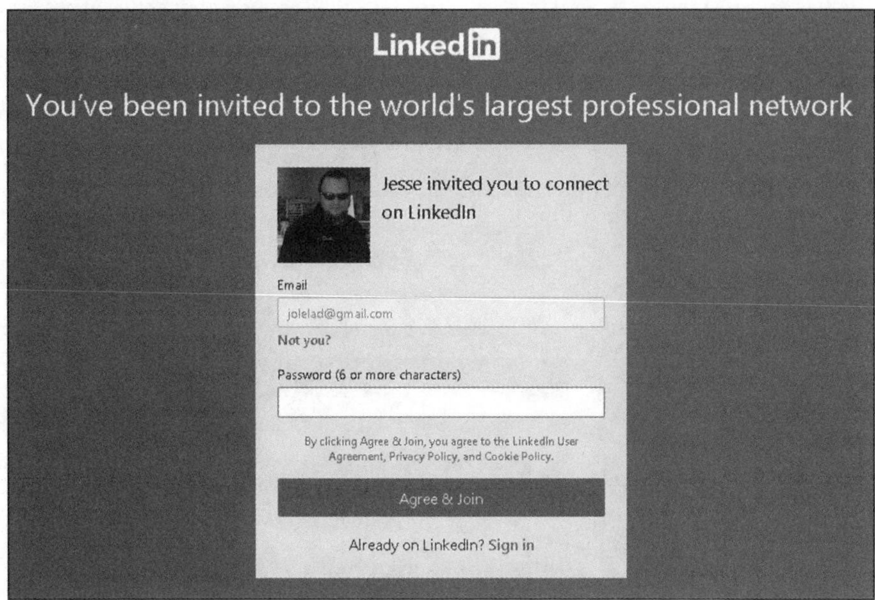

FIGURE 2-2: Provide your name and create a password.

2. **Enter your email address, and create a new password for your account.**

TIP

If you want to use a different email address from the one used for your invitation, you can change the details by clicking the Not You? link below the Email field.

3. **Click the Agree & Join button.**

You are taken to the next part of the sign-up process, where you provide basic information that LinkedIn will use to create your account. I cover the remainder of the sign-up process in "Completing the sign-up process," later in this chapter.

TIP

Try to choose a password that no one else can guess. You should use a combination of letters and numbers, and avoid commonly used passwords such as your name, the word *password*, a string of letters or numbers that are next to each other on the keyboard (for example, *qwerty*), or a password that you use on many other sites.

Joining without an invitation

If you haven't received an invitation to join LinkedIn, don't let that turn you into a wallflower. You can join LinkedIn directly, without an invitation from an existing user. Open your web browser and go to `https://www.linkedin.com`. When you're ready to join LinkedIn, click the Join Now link in the top-right corner to display the page shown in Figure 2-3. Simply provide your email address and enter a password, and then click the Agree & Join button.

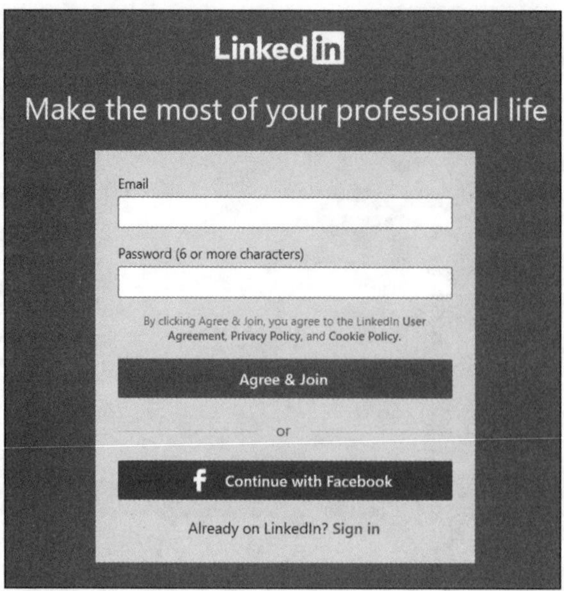

FIGURE 2-3: Join LinkedIn from its home page.

After you click the button, you advance to the next part of the sign-up process, where LinkedIn collects some basic information to create your account.

Completing the sign-up process

Whether you've been invited to join LinkedIn or created an account directly from its home page, LinkedIn requires some basic information beyond your name and email address to finish creating the basic account. When you're ready to complete the sign-up process, follow these steps:

1. **In the Make the Most of Your Professional Life window, enter your first name and last name in the boxes provided.**
2. **Click Continue.**

   The Welcome screen appears.
3. **Select the country where you reside.**

   Typically, LinkedIn will fill in this information based on data from your Internet provider, but you can always update this field if the information is incorrect. LinkedIn also asks for a zip code or a postal code.
4. **Provide your zip code or postal code, verify that the Location within This Area field matches your geographical area (see Figure 2-4), and then click the Next button.**

   LinkedIn starts to build your professional profile by asking about your current employment status and whether you're a student,.

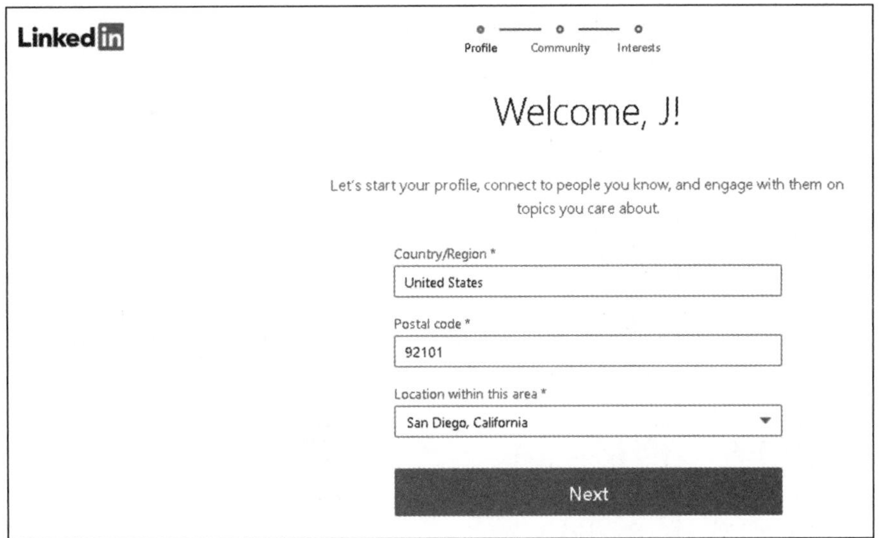

FIGURE 2-4: Tell LinkedIn where you are located.

5. **Complete the fields regarding your most recent job title or student status (see Figure 2-5):**
   - *I'm a Student:* If you're a student and want to move forward in the registration process without providing information on a recent job, click the I'm a Student link instead of completing the Most Recent Job Title text box.
   - *Most Recent Job Title:* If you're not a student, indicate your current job title by typing your answer in the text box provided.
   - *Employment Type:* After you enter a job title, an Employment Type drop-down box appears, as shown in Figure 2-6. Select your employment type from the choices provided, such as Full Time, Part Time, Self-Employment, and Freelance.

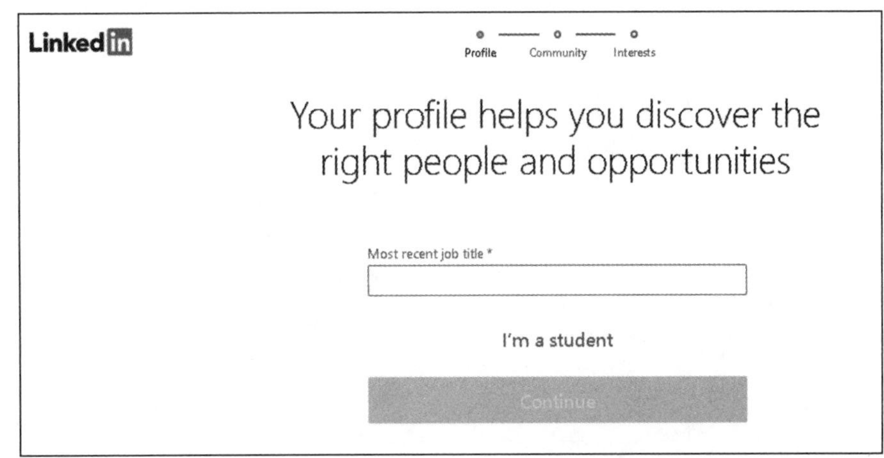

FIGURE 2-5: Tell LinkedIn a little about yourself to create your account.

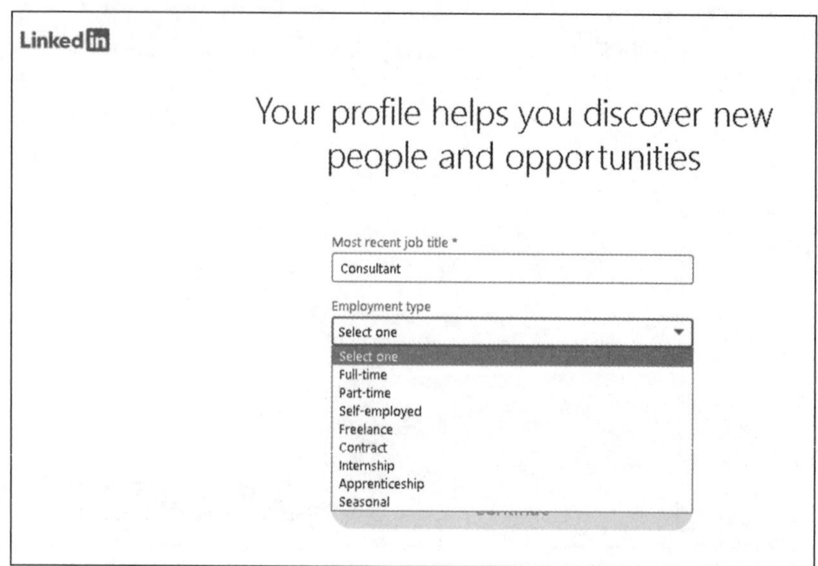

FIGURE 2-6: LinkedIn wants to know your employment type.

- *Most Recent Company:* LinkedIn asks for a company name. As you type the name of your company, you'll see companies in the LinkedIn database, as shown in Figure 2-7.
- *Industry:* After you provide the company name, LinkedIn may automatically assign the Industry field for you. If your company name is not in LinkedIn's directory, or your company isn't fully defined in LinkedIn, you'll see an Industry option. Use the drop-down list to identify which industry you feel you belong to, as shown in Figure 2-8.

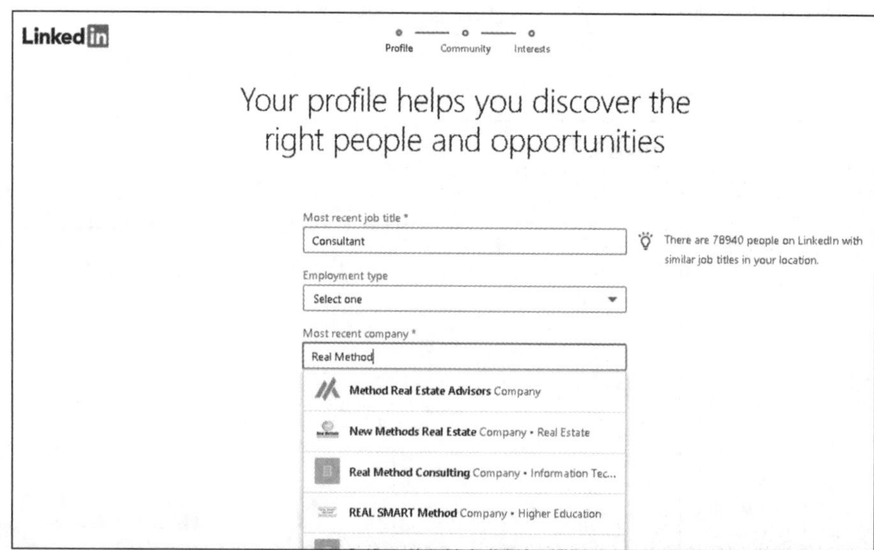

FIGURE 2-7: LinkedIn can help associate you with known companies in its database.

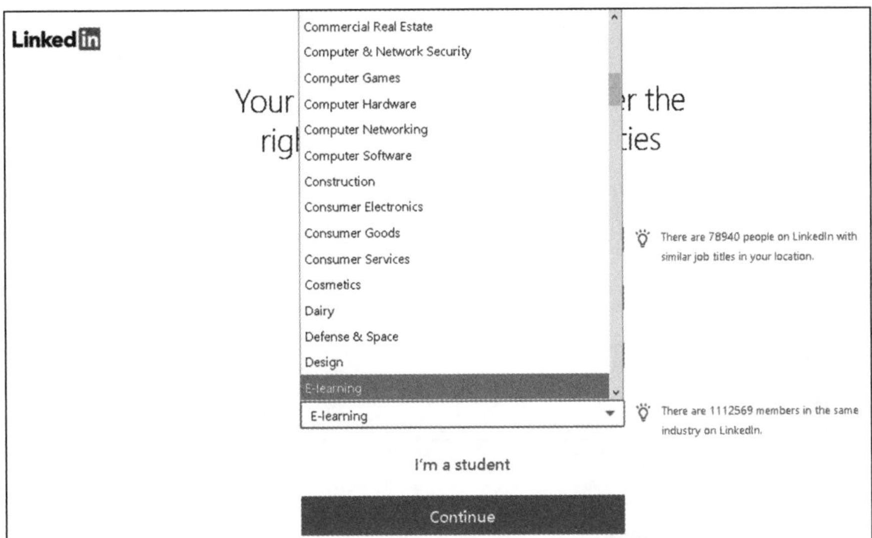

FIGURE 2-8: Choose the industry that best matches your current job.

TIP

If you find it difficult to choose an industry that best describes your primary expertise, just choose one that's closest. You can always change the selection later. If you're employed but looking for another job, you should still choose the industry of your current profession.

6. **Click the blue Continue button to continue.**
7. **If necessary, confirm the email address for your account.**

   If you join LinkedIn without an invitation, it emails you a confirmation with a verification code to help verify the email account you're using. Open your email program and look for an email from LinkedIn Messages with the subject line *(your name), your pin is XXXXXX. Please confirm your email address*. Open that email, and note the verification code. Go back to LinkedIn and enter the verification code in the box provided, as shown in Figure 2-9. Then click the Verify button.

WARNING

If you skip the step of confirming your email with LinkedIn, you won't be able to invite any connections, apply for jobs on the LinkedIn job board, upgrade to a Premium account, or take advantage of most other LinkedIn functions.

8. **(Optional) Start building your network by importing your known contacts, or click Skip to do so later.**

   LinkedIn offers to import your contacts from your email program, as shown in Figure 2-10. You walk through the steps of importing your address book. LinkedIn uses that information to send out invitations so you can connect with existing members of LinkedIn. You can also do these tasks after you create your account by clicking Skip.

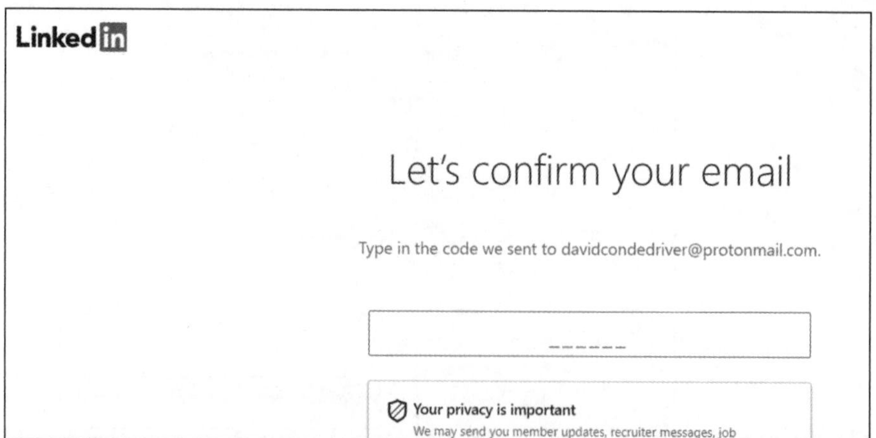

FIGURE 2-9: Confirm your email address with LinkedIn.

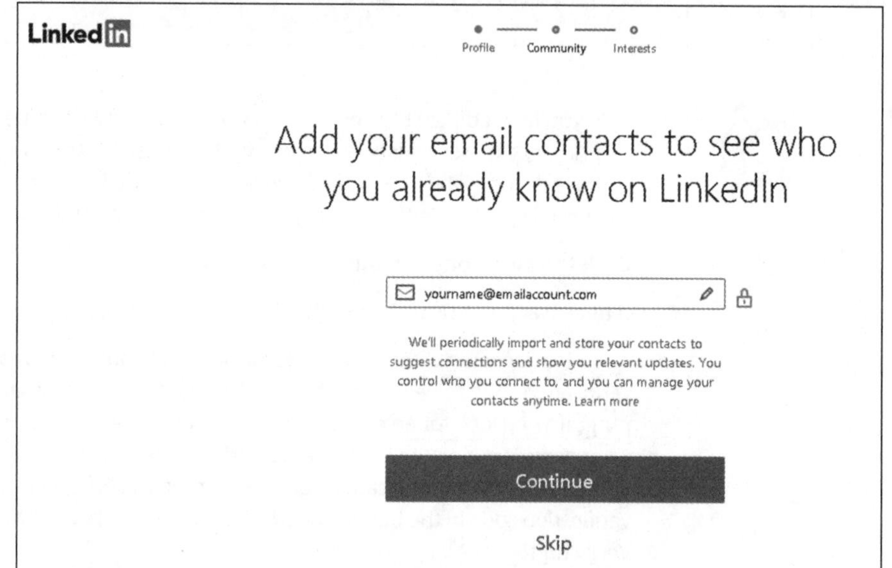

FIGURE 2-10: LinkedIn can help you identify who to add to your network.

TIP

It might be tempting to start inviting friends and colleagues to connect with you right away, but you might want to work on creating your complete and up-to-date profile before flooding people's email inboxes with invitations. You can invite people to connect with you at any time.

9. **(Optional) Select specific people who you can invite as a connection and then click the Add x Connection(s) button. Or click Skip to do so later.**

   Based on the information provided so far, whether it's your current job position or location, or the fact that a LinkedIn member invited you to join the network, LinkedIn knows a little bit about you and offers you a set of current LinkedIn members to whom you can send invitations to connect with you, as shown in Figure 2-11.

To connect with someone, click + in the top-right corner of the person's profile photo. The + changes to a check mark, as seen with my name in Figure 2-11. As mentioned in the preceding step, it's a good idea to work on your profile first before inviting additional people to your network.

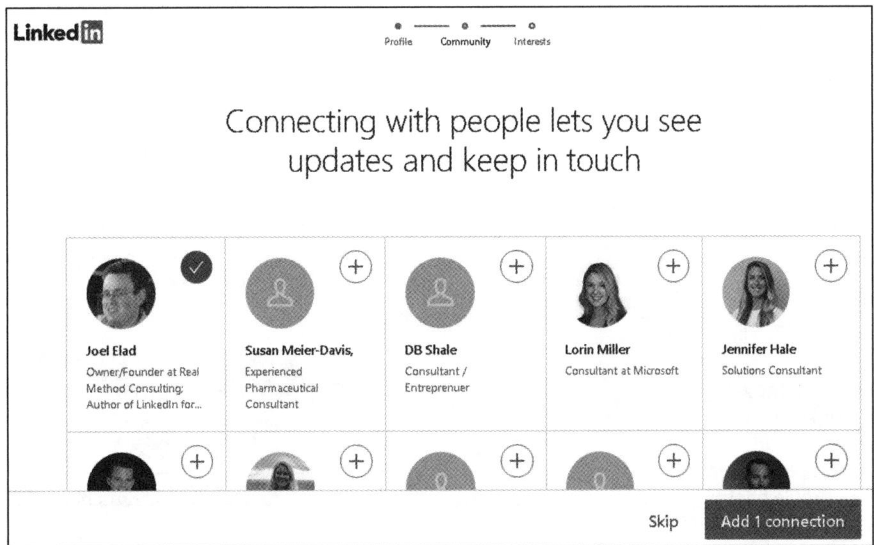

FIGURE 2-11: LinkedIn offers to help you connect with other LinkedIn members.

10. Upload a profile photo.

One of the most important elements of your LinkedIn profile is your profile photo. Your profile photo should indicate that you're a professional and responsible person. (In other words, this is not the social networking site to use to show off your party animal skills.) In Chapter 3, I talk about tips and tricks for choosing the perfect photo, but for now, locate a respectable photo of your face.

a. *Click the Add Photo button, as shown in Figure 2-12, and follow the prompts to select a photo from your computer.* You can instead click the Use My Google Photo button or the Use My Facebook Photo button to automatically bring in a photo from either account. Just be sure that it's a professional photo of your face if you decide to use either of those options.

b. *Rotate or crop your photo, if necessary, to capture your face (and the top of your shoulders if available), as shown in Figure 2-13.* You can also use a variety of filters and photo-editing tools to enhance your photo.

c. *Click Save Photo to upload the photo to LinkedIn.*

d. *Click Continue to assign it to your profile.*

LinkedIn prompts you to receive a link to download its mobile app.

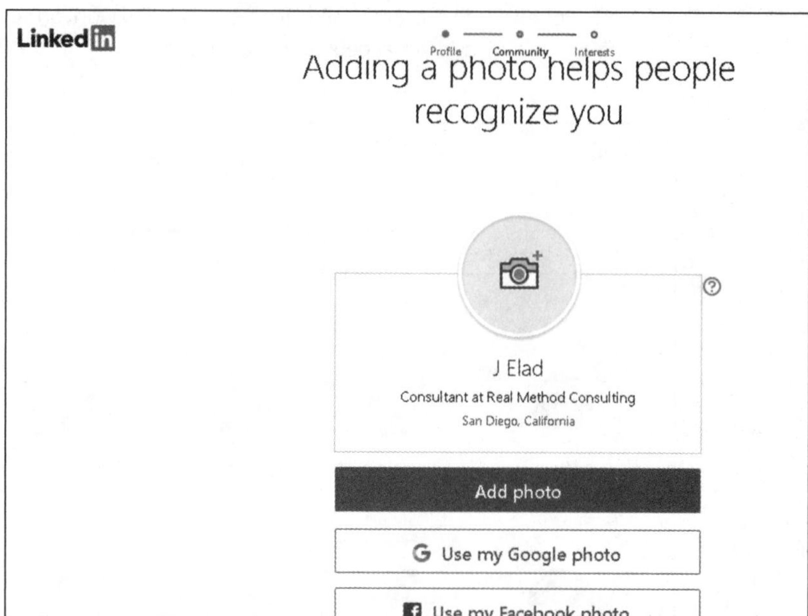

FIGURE 2-12: LinkedIn offers you the chance to upload your profile photo.

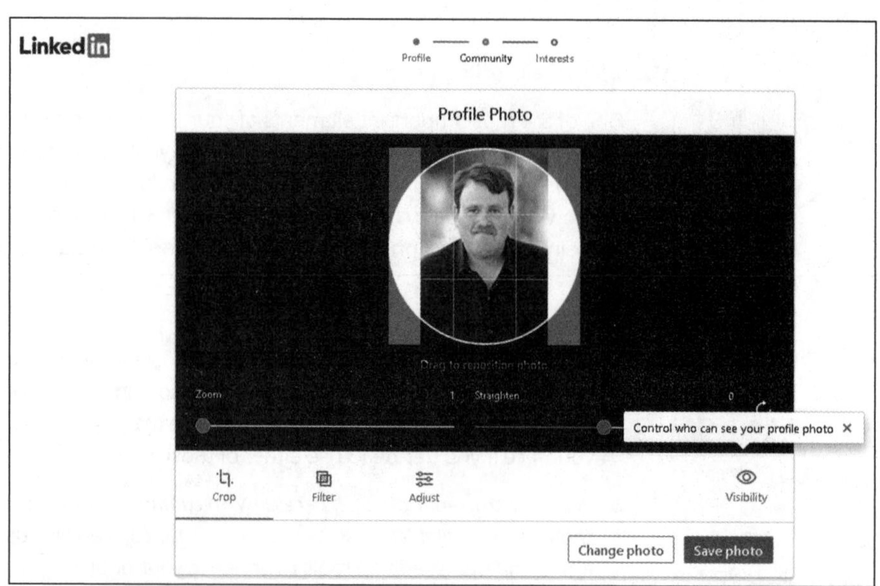

FIGURE 2-13: Use LinkedIn's tools to customize your photo.

11. **Provide your mobile number to receive the LinkedIn mobile app download link, and then click the Text Me a Link button. Or click Skip and install the app later.**

I discuss mobile applications in depth in Chapter 10.

Your LinkedIn home page appears.

12. **Follow the prompts that guide you through the rest of the creation process.**

LinkedIn is focused on having you share and provide content to your network, and encourages you to follow companies, influencers, other people, and even specific hashtags. At this point, you'll see the Follow Recommendations page (see Figure 2-14) and can start following specific people, topics, or companies that will influence your LinkedIn feed.

By default, LinkedIn assigns you to Follow LinkedIn News so that important information disseminated through their News channel will automatically show up in your LinkedIn feed. You can scroll down and peruse the various recommendations based on your job position, location, industry, what's popular on LinkedIn, and more.

I describe your LinkedIn feed in more depth in Chapter 7 and the steps for following different companies in Chapter 15. Revisit the ability to follow people or companies later when you're more grounded and ready to expand your horizons. (LinkedIn recommends that you choose at least five areas to follow, but it's not mandatory.)

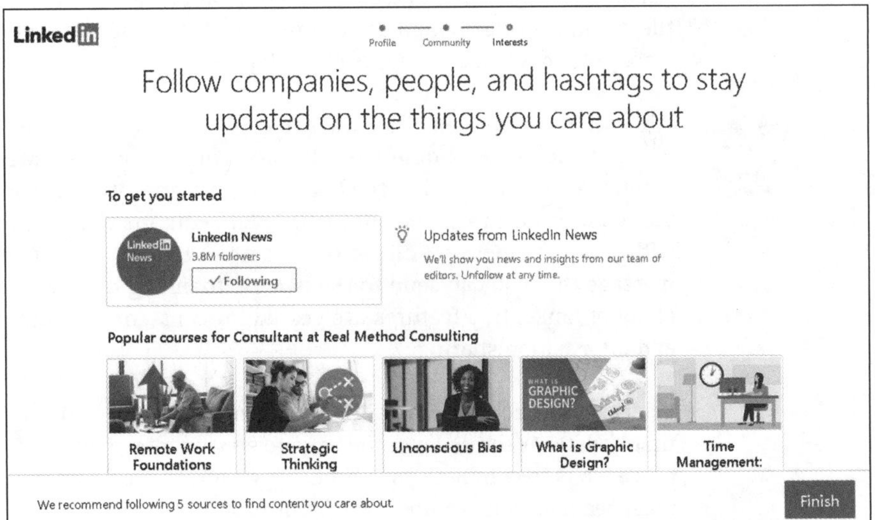

FIGURE 2-14: LinkedIn encourages you to follow different sources for information.

13. **To complete the setup process, click Finish and then complete the series of prompts.**

After you complete the series of prompts, your profile page appears (as shown in Figure 2-15).

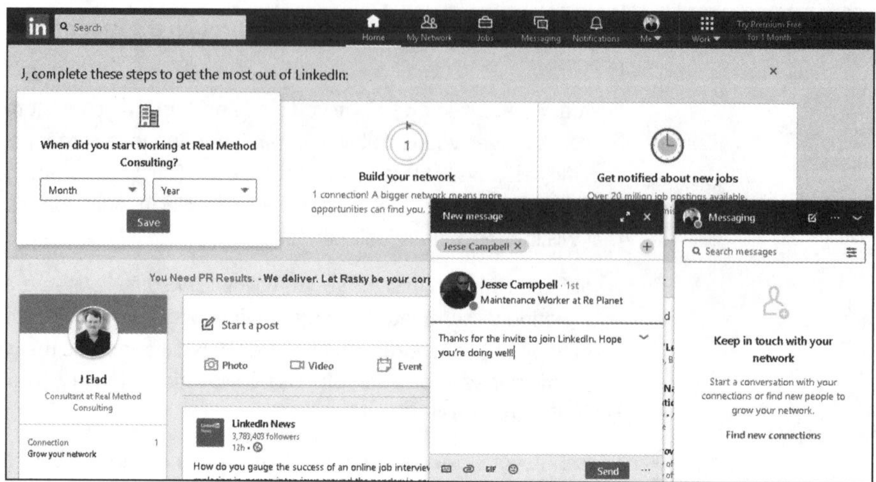

FIGURE 2-15: LinkedIn prompts you to complete your profile.

On your profile page, LinkedIn displays a series of tiles along the top of your screen with the header "*Name*, complete these steps to get the most out of LinkedIn." These steps include establishing work dates for your most current job, building your network, and creating notifications for potential new jobs. Click any tile, fill in the information as prompted, and click the Save button to complete the task. Note that you can always click Skip to save a task for later.

TIP

LinkedIn will offer you other ways to continue adding to your LinkedIn profile or your interaction with others on the site. For example, the Messaging window is automatically expanded in the bottom-right corner (refer to Figure 2-15) in case you want to start reaching out to other LinkedIn members. If you joined LinkedIn with an invitation, as I did in the example, LinkedIn automatically generates a message that you can send to the person, thanking him or her for the invitation. Many of LinkedIn's features are geared for constant and routine communication and information sharing.

You can also click the Start a Post box (in the middle of the screen) to write your first update, or scroll down the page to start reading your feed. However, the best next step is to complete your profile. I go into more detail in Chapter 3 about the main sections you can update on your profile.

Building Your Network

You're ready to look at how to build your network, with tools and forms provided by LinkedIn. Based on the screens and prompts you see, you may think that your first step is to decide whom you want to invite to connect with you on LinkedIn.

However, I recommend that you completely fill out your profile before you start inviting people to connect. Having a complete profile makes it easier to find former colleagues and classmates. After all, if you invite someone to connect whom you haven't spoken to recently, he'll probably take a quick look at your profile before responding. If he doesn't see a part of your professional history where he knows you, he will most likely ignore your invitation.

Your best bet now is to start using LinkedIn with some thought and planning. Here are some common pitfalls after signing up:

- » You feel compelled to start inviting friends and colleagues to connect with you right away, before working on your profile.
- » You get nervous and decide not to invite anybody beyond one or two close friends or family members.
- » You wonder about the value of LinkedIn (or get busy with your career and daily activities) and leave your account alone for a long period of time with no activity.

PRIVACY CONFIDENTIAL

When you give LinkedIn access to your existing contact lists (such as on Gmail or Yahoo! Mail), rest assured that LinkedIn respects your privacy. LinkedIn is a licensee of the TRUSTe Privacy Program. In its privacy policy, LinkedIn declares its adherence to the following key privacy principles:

- LinkedIn will never rent or sell your personally identifiable information to third parties for marketing purposes.
- LinkedIn will never share your contact information with another user without your consent.
- Any sensitive information that you provide will be secured with all industry standard protocols and technology.

I've seen all three scenarios with various people who have joined LinkedIn, so don't feel bad if one of these is your natural reaction.

When you want to start using LinkedIn, begin by navigating to the home page and clicking Sign In. You're asked for your email address and LinkedIn password, which you provided when you joined the site. After you're logged in, your profile screen appears, as shown in Figure 2-16, and you can access any of the functions in the top navigation bar.

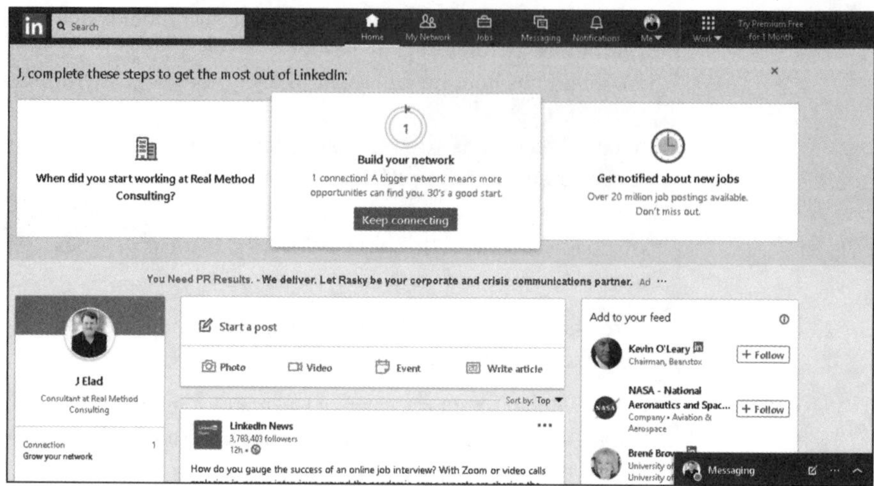

FIGURE 2-16: Continue to work on your profile.

If you want to start thinking about the people you'd like to invite to join your network, even if your profile isn't complete yet, the easiest method is to click the Keep Connecting button under the Build Your Network header. (Note that if you joined LinkedIn without an invitation, the button will say Find Connections instead of Keep Connecting.) A new window appears, as shown in Figure 2-17, displaying people you can connect with, as well as LinkedIn courses you can take to learn more about networking on the site.

A number of tools are available for growing your network, from syncing your email account or address book to uploading contact files. I cover these techniques in greater detail in Chapter 5. I recommend that you first spend time setting up your profile. Then think about the people you want to invite, and use LinkedIn to connect with those individuals.

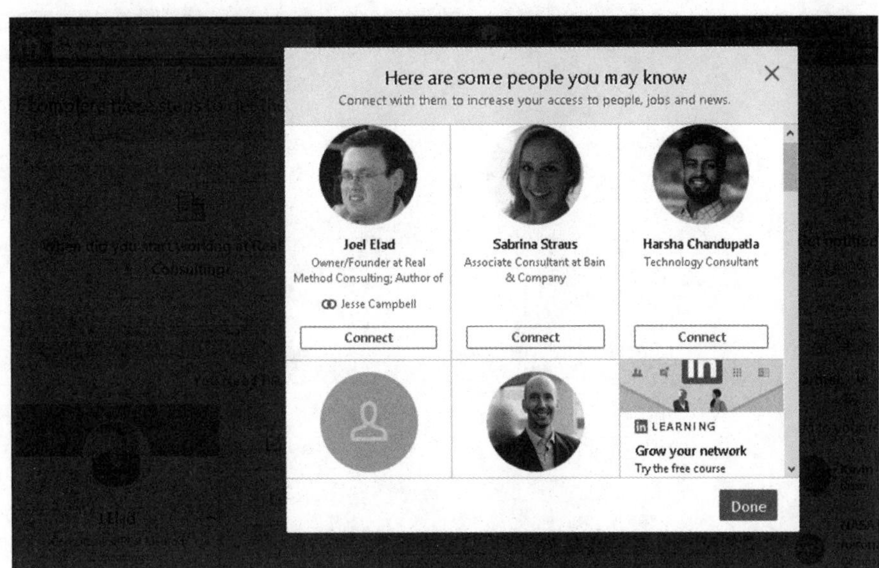

FIGURE 2-17: Add connections to your network.

IN THIS CHAPTER

» Crafting your summary information

» Updating your contact settings

» Adding a position to your profile

» Including your education information

» Customizing your public profile settings

Chapter 3
Completing Your Profile

After you register with LinkedIn and work to build your network by looking outward, it's time to look inward by focusing on your profile. Think of your LinkedIn profile as your personal home page to the professional world: This profile exists to give anyone a complete picture of your background, qualifications, and skills as well as paint a picture of who you are beyond the numbers and bullet points.

In this chapter, I walk you through all the different sections of your profile and explain how to update them and add the right information in a concise and appealing manner. I take you through adding information at each stage so you can update your profile now or down the road (say, when you finish that amazing project or get that spiffy promotion you've been working toward).

REMEMBER

You can access your LinkedIn profile at any time to view or make changes. Simply go to `www.linkedin.com`, click the Me icon in the top navigation bar, and then click the View Profile link.

Adding a Summary and Basic Information

Your LinkedIn profile Summary section, which appears in the top third of your profile, should give any reader a quick idea of who you are, what you've accomplished, and most importantly, what you're looking for on LinkedIn. Some people think of their summary as their elevator pitch, a 30-second introduction of themselves that they tell to any new contact. Other people think of their summary as simply their resume summary, a high-level overview of their experience and job goals.

Each summary is as individual as the person writing it, but there are right ways and wrong ways to prepare and update your summary. Always keep in mind your professional or career goals, and what kind of image, or brand, you want to portray in support of those goals. Those goals should give you direction on how to write your summary.

REMEMBER

Your summary is your best chance of explaining to future employers what you can offer them as a new employee. Specifically, you should describe not only what you can do, but what can you do *for them* (with *them* being the new company). Knowing Microsoft Excel is great, but using Microsoft Excel to automate processes and bring down costs 12 percent while speeding up product development time by 15 percent is a statement that allows employers and recruiters the chance to see why you matter as a job candidate.

To keep your summary easy to read so it can be digested quickly, you could divide the Summary section into two distinct parts:

- **Your professional experience and goals:** This part contains a one-paragraph summary of your current and past accomplishments and future goals. See the later section, "Writing your summary first," for more on how to construct the right paragraph for this part.
- **Your specialties in your industry of expertise:** This part is a list of specific skills and talents. Include specific job skills (for example, contract negotiation or writing HTML software code) as opposed to your daily responsibilities or accomplishments, which you list in the professional experience and goals paragraph. This part not only gives readers a precise understanding of your skill set but also gives search engines a keyword-rich list to associate with you, and it's at the top of your profile.

Other core elements of your LinkedIn profile are stored in the Basic Information section. Be sure to polish these elements so they reflect well on you:

- **Your name:** Believe it or not, defining your name properly can positively or negatively affect your LinkedIn activity. Because people are searching for you to connect to you, it's important that LinkedIn knows variations, nicknames, maiden names, or former names that you may have held, so be sure you correctly fill in your First, Last, and Former/Maiden name fields. Also, LinkedIn allows you to choose a display name of your first name and last initial, in case you want to keep your name private from the larger LinkedIn community outside of your connections. (For details on limiting the display of your name, see Chapter 11.)

TIP

You can also include your middle name in the First Name field. I highly recommended you do so if you have a common name (for example, John Smith); in this way, people can find the "right you" when searching.

- **Your professional headline:** Think of this as your value proposition, or "why am I different from other job seekers?" You are limited to 120 characters. The headline is displayed below your name on LinkedIn, in search results, in connections lists, and in your profile, so you want a headline that grabs people's attention. Some people put their job titles; other people add some colorful adjectives and include two or three different professions. For example, I use

  Author, LinkedIn For Dummies; Owner/Founder, Real Method Consulting

  indicating two of my main professions. Meanwhile, my entrepreneur friend Liz Goodgold currently has her headline as

  Maximizing Brand Results * Boosting Lifetime Value of Customer * Creating Unforgettable Experiences * Keynote Speaking * Virtual Presenter

  Your headline changes only when you update the headline field, so if you add a new position to your profile, your headline doesn't update to show that addition. You have to decide what changes are worth reflecting in your headline.

WARNING

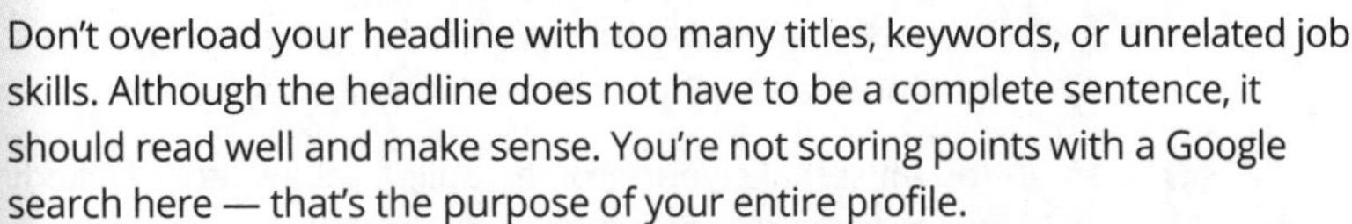

Don't overload your headline with too many titles, keywords, or unrelated job skills. Although the headline does not have to be a complete sentence, it should read well and make sense. You're not scoring points with a Google search here — that's the purpose of your entire profile.

- **Your primary location and industry of experience:** As location becomes a more important element when networking online, LinkedIn wants to know your main location (in other words, where you hang your hat . . . if you wear a hat) so it can help identify connections close to you. Then LinkedIn provides a list of industries you can choose from to indicate your main industry affiliation.

Updating the basic information sections

When people meet you, the most common questions they'll probably ask are, "So, what do you do?" and "Where did you go to school?" However, there's more to you than your jobs and education. LinkedIn includes the Intro and Contact Info section to tie your LinkedIn profile to your real-life identity. This section enables you to provide lots of information in the following areas:

- **First, Last, and Former Name(s):** Your current and former names are important for other people on LinkedIn to reach out and connect with you, as well as stay connected.

- **Current Position and Education Level:** Although I discuss how to add positions and education to your profile in later sections in this chapter, it's important to include your current employer and most recent education in your LinkedIn profile, because these will have prominence for people reading your profile.
- **Location and Industry:** The Internet helps us live with a global network of contacts, but you should still identify your current location, so LinkedIn can help connect you with nearby connections, and your industry, so it can match you with like-minded LinkedIn members to create future connections.
- **Websites:** You can add to your profile up to three website links, such as your personal website, your company website, a blog, an RSS feed, or any other promotional mechanisms you use online.

TIP

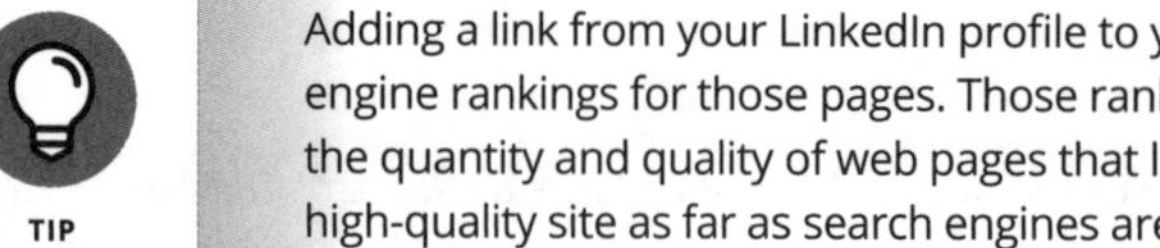

Adding a link from your LinkedIn profile to your other websites boosts search engine rankings for those pages. Those rankings are partially determined by the quantity and quality of web pages that link to them, and LinkedIn is a high-quality site as far as search engines are concerned.

- **Instant Messenger:** As LinkedIn increases its global membership, it has added integration with WeChat, the world's fastest-growing social app, which integrates various messaging, gaming, and social features. When you link your WeChat account with LinkedIn, you'll be able to see which of your LinkedIn connections are currently on WeChat. (You can also specify Skype, ICQ, Google Hangouts, and QQ instant messenger account names.)

TIP

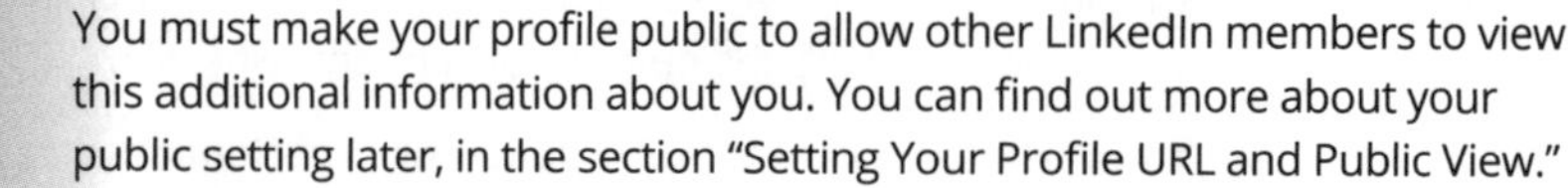

You must make your profile public to allow other LinkedIn members to view this additional information about you. You can find out more about your public setting later, in the section "Setting Your Profile URL and Public View."

When you have an idea of what you want to put in your profile's basic introduction sections, it's time to plug that data into the correct fields. When you're ready, follow these steps:

1. **Log in to LinkedIn at** `www.linkedin.com/secure/login`.
2. **Click the Me icon in the top navigation bar, and then click View Profile from the drop-down list that appears.**

   You're taken to the profile page, as shown in Figure 3-1. Note the pencil icons. You click those to edit the sections.
3. **To update your basic information, click the pencil icon to the far right of your name and profile photo.**

   The Edit Intro box shown in Figure 3-2 appears.

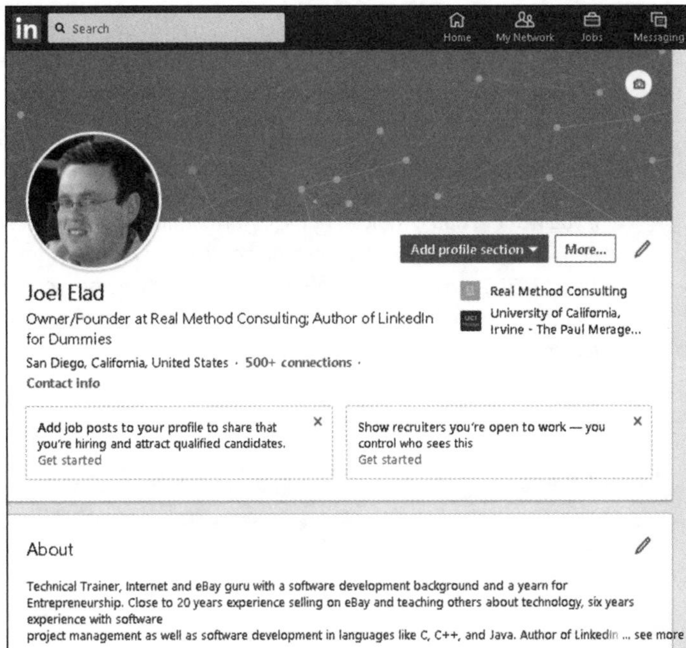

FIGURE 3-1: Display your LinkedIn profile page.

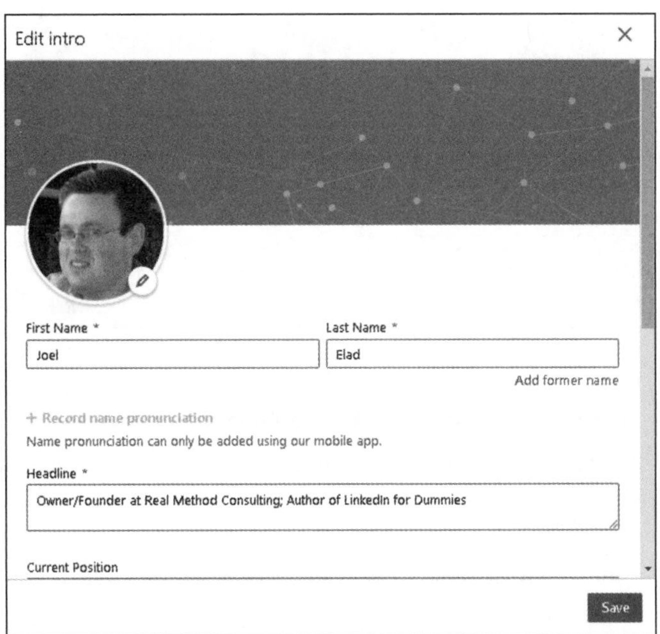

FIGURE 3-2: Define your basic information.

4. **In the First Name and Last Name text boxes:**

   a. *Double-check your name.*

   b. *If you want to add a middle name (or middle initial), type it in the First Name text box.*

   c. *If you want to add a maiden name or former name to your account, click the Add Former Name link and enter the name in the Former Name text box (see Figure 3-3). Then click the Visible link and choose whether your connections or your network (anyone within three degrees of connection to you) will see this former name.*

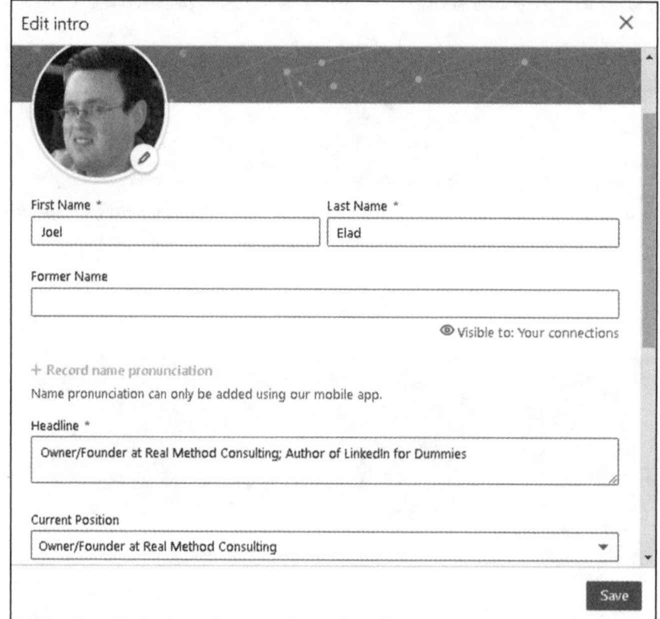

FIGURE 3-3: Add a former or maiden name to your profile.

5. **In the Headline text box, enter your professional headline (main job title).**

   You can put any job title here, but make sure it conveys your main role as you want others to see it. (See the previous sections for what to include in your headline.)

6. **Enter your current position and education:**

   a. *Scroll down to the Current Position box and, if you have more than one current position defined in your LinkedIn profile, click the drop-down arrow and choose which defined current job will be assigned as your Current Position.*

b. Scroll down to the Education box, click the drop-down arrow, and select the most recent education entry as your main Education entry. You can also deselect the Show Education in My Intro check box if you want.

7. **Enter your country, zip code, and location:**

   a. Scroll down to the Country/Region box and click the drop-down arrow to select your current country in the list.

   b. After your country is selected, fill in the postal code box that appears.

   c. Click the drop-down arrow next to the Location box to update your location on LinkedIn.

   In the example shown in Figure 3-4, I selected United States as the country. LinkedIn then displayed a Postal Code text box, where I entered my zip code. I then selected the closest defined area in LinkedIn to my zip code, which is Greater San Diego Area.

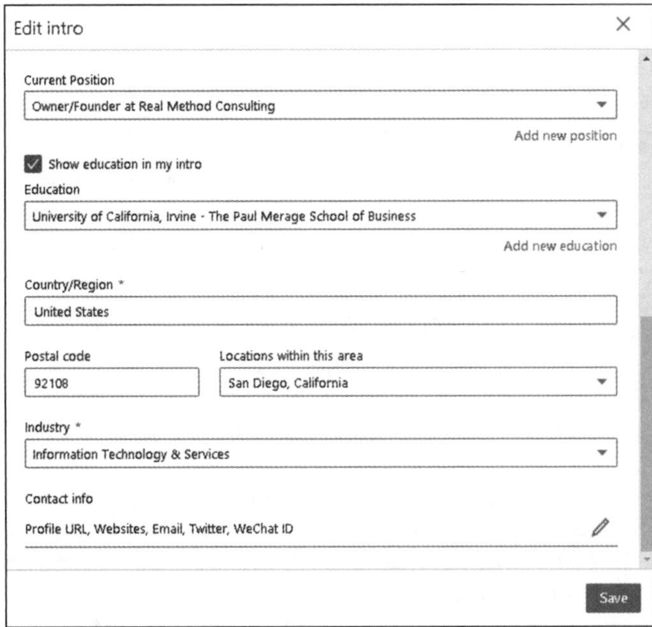

FIGURE 3-4: Define your location.

8. **Click the drop-down arrow next to the Industry field and select the industry you most associate with your career.**

   You can choose from more than 140 designations, so take a few moments to scan the list. Note that some of the industries listed are more specific than others. Choose the best match possible. For example, if you create custom graphics for websites, you could select Internet as your industry, but an even better choice would be Online Media.

9. **Scroll down to the Contact Info section and click the pencil icon to the right of the section under Contact Info.**

   The Edit Contact Information box appears, as shown in Figure 3-5. Ignore the Profile URL for now; you will revise this in a later section, "Setting Your Profile URL and Public View."

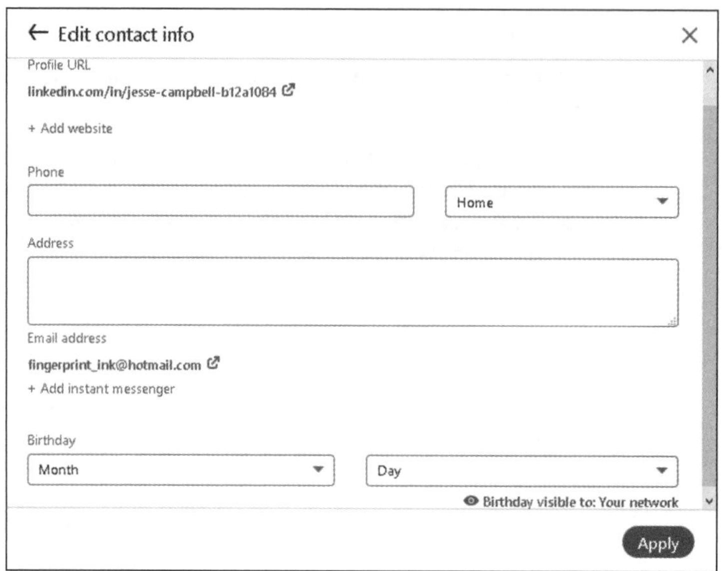

FIGURE 3-5: Update your Contact info section.

10. **(Optional, but recommended) To add a website URL:**

    a. *Click the Add Website link.* The screen shown in Figure 3-6 appears.

    b. *In the Website URL box, type the URL.* You don't need to add the http:// (or https://) part.

    c. *In the box to the right of the Website URL box, click the drop-down arrow and choose a descriptive label.* Choose from the predefined list (Personal, Company, Blog, RSS feed, Portfolio, and Other) or choose Other, as shown in Figure 3-7, and then in the Type (Other) box that appears, type a brief custom description for your website link (such as My E-Commerce Site or the name of your activity). This description will appear in parentheses next to the URL in your profile.

TIP

Search engines look at the text in these links when calculating rankings. So if you want to include certain keywords that will rank your site higher, add them in the link text. For example, you might want to have "Springfield Toastmasters" rather than "My Toastmasters Club."

    d. *Repeat these steps to add up to three website URLs.*

WARNING

People are going to click those links and check out your websites. Sure, that's the point, but do you remember that hilarious but embarrassing picture of yourself that you added to your personal site, or that tirade you posted in your blog about a co-worker or a tough project? Before you link a site, scour it to make sure you won't end up scaring off or offending your contacts.

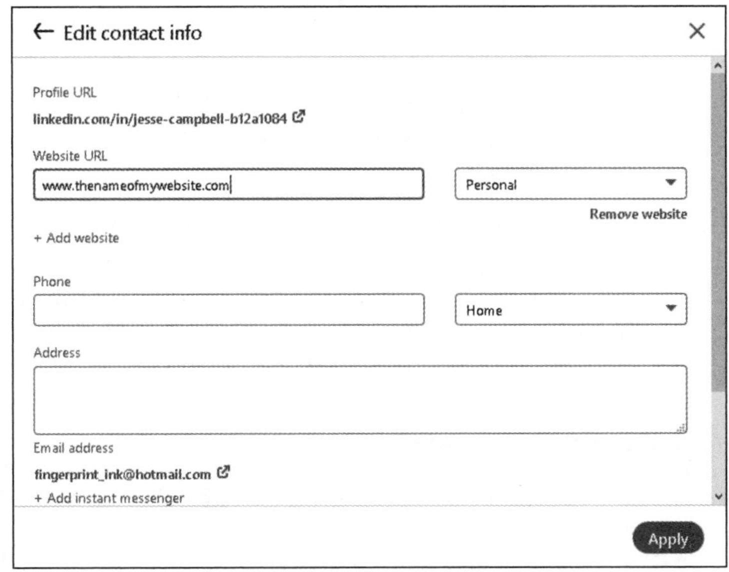

FIGURE 3-6: Add website URLs to your profile.

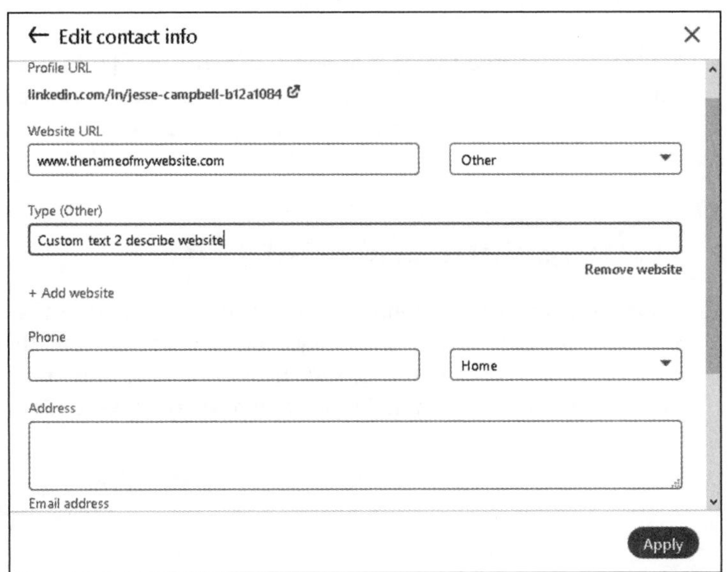

FIGURE 3-7: Give your website link a custom name.

11. **(Optional) Update your contact information: phone, physical address, and email.**

    Use each labeled text box to add the appropriate information (refer to Figure 3-5).

12. **(Optional) If you want to add an Instant Messenger account to your LinkedIn profile, do the following:**

    a. *Click the Add Instant Messenger link.*

    b. *Type your IM account name in the box provided.*

    c. *Select the service from the drop-down list to the right of the Instant Messenger text box.*

13. **(Optional) Add your birthday in the boxes provided.**

    Currently, if you input your birthday information, it will be visible to your network. If you want to change the visibility, click the Birthday Visible to: Your Network link, below the Day field, and change it to your first-degree connections, your network (first-, second-, and third-degree connections), or all LinkedIn members.

14. **Click the Apply button.**

    The Contact Info section in your profile is updated and you return to the Edit Intro window (refer to Figure 3-2).

15. **To save all your changes, click the Save button.**

    Your profile page appears with your updated information.

You've now covered the core of your LinkedIn profile. In the next sections, you find out about the other essential elements to include in your profile, namely your summary, additional information, and your current and past experience and education.

Writing your summary first

Before you update your summary on LinkedIn, I advise writing it using a program such as Microsoft Word. This allows you to organize your thoughts, decide the right order of your statements, and choose the most important statements to put in your summary. Then simply copy and paste the text to LinkedIn.

THE $5,000 PROFILE UPDATE

I have a great example of why you should update your profile. Years ago, Jefre Outlaw's LinkedIn profile focused mostly on his entrepreneur skills and didn't include the more than 25 years he spent as a real estate investor and developer, nor that he obtained a real estate license and joined his cousin Blake's agency, Outlaw Realty. Outlaw was interviewed for the Linked Intelligence blog (`www.linkedintelligence.com/the-5000-profile-update`). "At first I completely forgot about updating my LinkedIn profile," he said. "But I got a request to forward an introduction, and it reminded me that I should probably go update my profile to include my new gig as a Realtor."

He realized a golden opportunity was available to him through LinkedIn. And this turned out to be a valuable update for Outlaw.

Several weeks later, someone from his extended network was using LinkedIn to search for Realtors and saw Outlaw's profile. This person contacted Outlaw about listing a home for sale. Well, the potential client signed up with Outlaw's agency, which was able to sell the house quickly for $170,000. When you do the math, $170,000 home × 3% commission = about $5,000 to the brokerage.

As Outlaw relayed his experience to Linked Intelligence, he wanted his story to be clear. "Let's not overstate what happened," said Outlaw. "Being on LinkedIn didn't get me the business. We [Outlaw's real estate agency] were one of several Realtors the client talked to, and I brought in my cousin, who's a great closer and more experienced than I, to meet with the client. But the fact that I was on LinkedIn, that my profile was up to date, that I have over 20 really good recommendations in my profile — all that put us on the short list."

The moral of the story is simple. Keep your profile up to date — you may never know what opportunities you're missing by ignoring your profile.

The goals of your summary should be the same as your goals for using LinkedIn. After all, your summary is the starting point for most people when they read your profile. As you write your summary, keep these points in mind:

- **Be concise.** Remember, this is a summary, not a 300-page memoir. Most summaries are one paragraph long, with a separate paragraph to list your skills and specialties. Give the highlights of what you've accomplished and are planning to do. Save the detailed information for when you add your individual employment positions to your profile.

- **Choose three to five of your most important accomplishments.** Your profile can have lots of detail regarding your jobs, skill sets, education, and honors, but your summary needs to reflect the three to five items throughout your career that you most want people to know. Think of it this way: If someone were introducing you to another person, what would you want this new person to know about you right away?

  REMEMBER

  Depending on your goals for LinkedIn, the accomplishments you put in your summary might not be your biggest accomplishments overall. For example, if you're trying to use LinkedIn to get a new job, your summary should include accomplishments that matter most to an employer in your desired field.

- **Organize your summary in a who, what, goals format.** Typically, the first sentence of your summary should be a statement of *who* you are currently, meaning your current profession or status; for example, "Software project manager with extensive experience in Fortune 500 firms." The next few sentences should focus on *what* you've accomplished so far in your career, and the end of your summary should focus on your *goals.*
- **Use the right keywords.** Keywords are especially important if you're looking for a new job or hoping to pick up some consulting work. Although you should use a few keywords in your professional experience paragraph, you should use all the appropriate keywords for skills you've acquired when you write the Specialties section of your summary. Potential employers scan that section first, looking for the right qualifications, before making any contact. If you're unsure what keywords are the most important, scan the profiles of people in your industry, see what articles they're posting, or look at job opportunity postings in your field to see what employers want when they hire personnel with your title.
- **Be honest with your skills, but don't be shy.** Some people stuff their Summary section with the buzzworthy skills for their industry (even if the person doesn't know those skills at all) in hopes of catching a potential employer's eye. Typically, a prospective employer can detect this resume skill padding during the interview phase, which wastes everybody's time. Conversely, some people don't include a skill in their Summary unless they feel they're an expert. You should list any skill or specialty that you believe puts you above the level of a novice or pure beginner.

TIP

If you need help coming up with your Summary, look at profiles of other people in similar industries or reach out to your LinkedIn network.

Completing Your Summary

When you're ready to update the summary in your profile, follow these steps:

1. **Click the Me icon in the top navigation bar, and then click View Profile from the drop-down list that appears.**

   Your profile page appears.

2. **Scroll down to and complete the About section:**

   a. *Click the pencil icon to the right of the About section.* The Edit About box appears, as shown in Figure 3-8, where you can update your summary.

   b. *In the Summary text box, enter a paragraph or two that sums you up professionally (as discussed in the preceding section). You can enter your skills and specialties in a separate list or paragraph.* You're limited to 2,600 characters; keep your text concise and focused.

REMEMBER

   If you decide to create a skills list, separate each item with a comma and don't put any punctuation after the last item in your list. You don't need to press Enter or Return between skills.

3. **Click the Save button.**

   This step updates your summary (About section) in your profile.

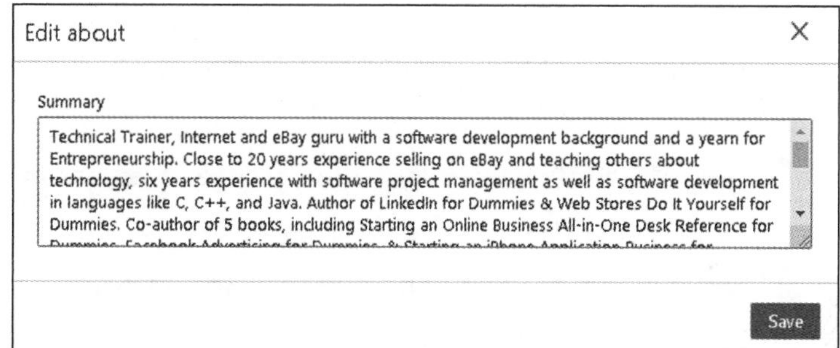

FIGURE 3-8: Update your summary here.

Adding More Profile Sections

LinkedIn continues to add lots of exciting sections so you can highlight your achievements and skills. On your profile page, click the Add Profile Section button to see a list of Featured sections for enhancing your profile, as shown in Figure 3-9. Simply click a section and fill in the appropriate information. In Figure 3-9, I expanded the Featured section, which displays options for adding Posts, Articles, Links, and Media.

TIP

As of this writing, LinkedIn has created a Featured part of your profile for uploading the best examples of your skills and previous work. You can find out more about how to utilize the Featured area by going to LinkedIn's help page at `www.linkedin.com/help/linkedin/answer/117363`.

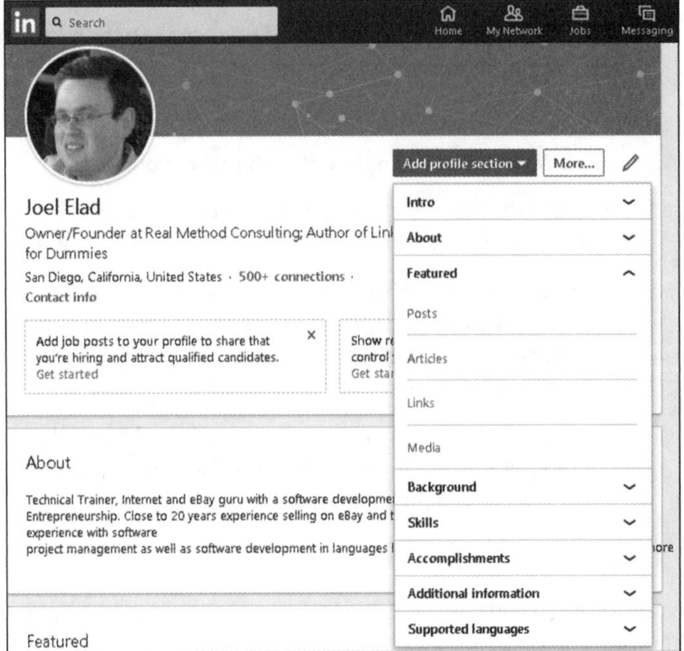

FIGURE 3-9: See what other sections of information you can add to your LinkedIn profile.

For example, to add media (a document, photo, video, or presentation) to your profile, do the following:

1. **Click the Add Profile Section button, click Featured, and then click Media.**

   A browser window appears on your screen.

2. **Browse to find and select the file to upload, and then click Open.**

   The Add Media screen appears.

3. **In the Title and Description boxes, add a title and description of the media item, respectively.**
4. **Click Save.**

If you want to add a website URL as an example of your work to your profile, do this:

1. **Click the Add Profile Section button, click Featured, and then click Links.**
2. **Type the URL in the text box that appears, and then click the Add button.**

   LinkedIn goes to that URL to make sure the link is valid.

3. **In the Title box, add or edit the title of the website referenced in your link.**

   If LinkedIn detects a title from your specified URL, it will autofill this field. You can keep of edit the autofill text.

4. **In the Description box, add or edit the description of the website referenced in your link.**

   Again, if LinkedIn detects a description from your specified URL, it will autofill the field. You can keep the autofilled text or change it.

5. **Click Save.**

   You return to the Edit profile screen.

Adding a Position

One of the most important aspects of your LinkedIn profile is the list of positions you've held over the years, including your current job. This list is especially important if you're using LinkedIn to find a new or different career or to reconnect with past colleagues. Hiring managers want to see your complete history to know what skills you offer, and past colleagues can't find you as easily through LinkedIn if the job they knew you from isn't in your profile. Therefore, it's critical to make sure you have all the positions posted in your profile with the correct information, as long as doing so fits with the brand or image you want to portray to the professional world.

For a company in LinkedIn's directory, you need to fill in the following fields:

- Company name (and display name, if your company goes by more than one name)
- Your job title while working for the company
- The time period you worked for the company
- Description of your job duties

If your company is *not* listed in LinkedIn's directory, you need to fill in the industry and website for the company when you're adding your position to your profile.

TIP

Use your resume when completing this section, because most resumes include all or most of the information required.

To add a position to your profile, follow these steps:

1. **Click the Me icon in the top navigation bar, and then click View Profile from the drop-down list that appears.**

   Your profile page appears.

2. **Scroll down your profile until you see the Experience section, shown in Figure 3-10.**

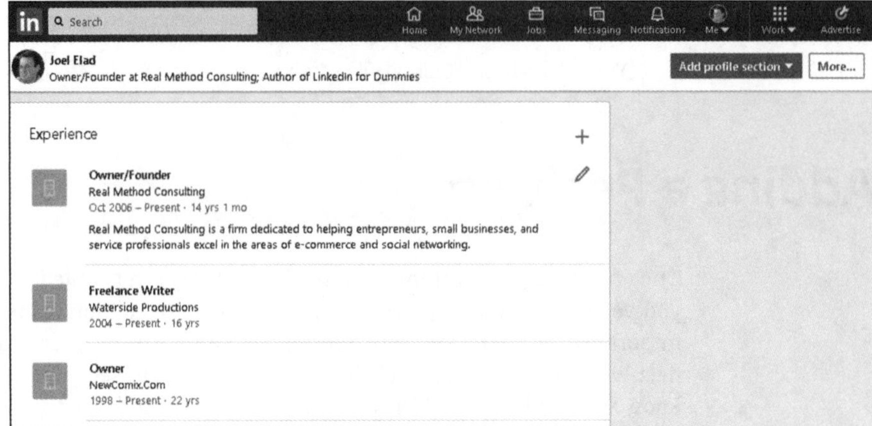

FIGURE 3-10: Start at your Experience section in your profile.

3. **Click the + button to the right of the Experience header.**

   Depending on your web browser, the button may not be visible until you hover your cursor over the Experience header. An Add Experience window appears, as shown in Figure 3-11.

4. **In the text boxes provided, enter the information about your position, including title, employment type, company, location, time period, and job description.**

TIP

   When you type your company name, LinkedIn checks that name against the Company pages of thousands of companies from its records, and you see suggested company names while you type. (An example is shown in Figure 3-12.) If you see your company name in that list, click the name, and LinkedIn automatically fills in all the company detail information for you.

5. **Upload or link any media that was part of this job.**

   For example, you might upload or link a document, photo, presentation, or video.

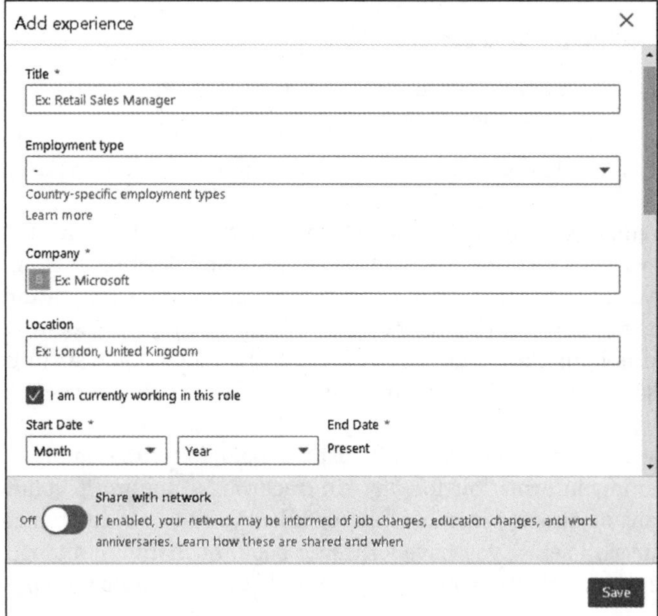

FIGURE 3-11: Enter your job information here.

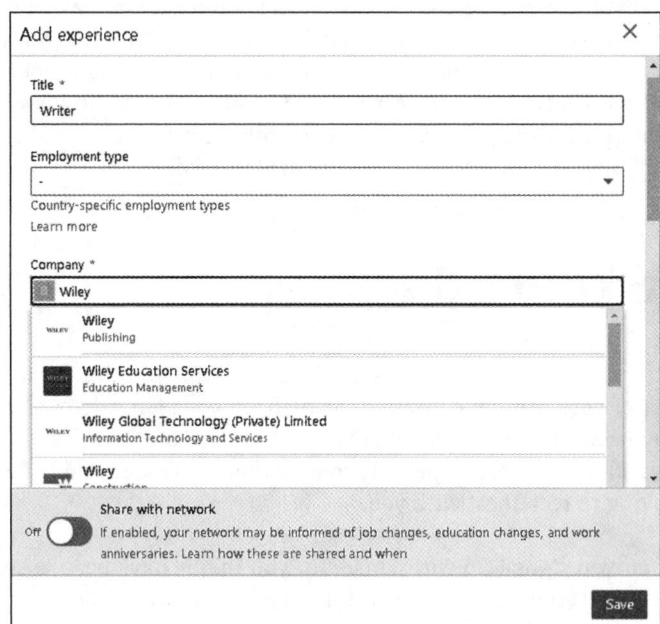

FIGURE 3-12: LinkedIn checks its Company pages for your company listing.

6. **Click the Save button.**

   The newly entered position is added to your profile, and you're taken back to your profile page.

7. **Repeat Steps 2-6 for any additional position you want to enter.**

To edit a position you already listed, click the pencil icon next to that record in the Experience section instead of clicking the Add Position button. In addition, if you have multiple positions in a similar time period, you can rearrange a job's position in the list by hovering your cursor over the job in your Experience section, clicking and holding down the four-lines icon that should appear to the right of the job description, and then moving the cursor to the new position.

REMEMBER

The Experience section isn't just for paid full-time employment. You can add position information for any contract work, nonprofit volunteer assignments, board of director membership, or other valid work experience that increases to your skill set. If you have written a book, or maintain a blog, or write a regular magazine column, you might want to list that as a separate position.

If you have most of the information for a given position but are missing a few details in the description, go ahead and add what you have. (You must provide a job title, company, and time period to save the position in your profile.) You can fill in missing information later. In addition, if you make your profile public (as discussed later in "Setting Your Profile URL and Public View"), make sure any position information you enter is something you don't mind the entire world — including past employers — seeing in your profile.

Reporting Your Education

After you document your past and current jobs, it's time to move on to the next part of your profile: education. Aside from your job, where else do you meet and stay in touch with so many people? At school, of course! Your Education section says a lot about you, especially to potential employers and to former schoolmates looking to reconnect with you.

When you signed up with LinkedIn, you might have been asked to provide your basic education information. Maybe you have more than one school to list, or perhaps you didn't create a full listing for the schools you put down upon registration. In either case, you can go back to make sure that your profile is up to date and lists all your education.

Some people ask how much education to list in their profiles. Although you could theoretically go all the way back to preschool or kindergarten, most people start with high school or undergraduate college. Keep in mind that the more items you list, the greater the opportunity that your past schoolmates can locate and contact you.

REMEMBER

This section isn't limited to high school, undergraduate, and post-graduate education. You should also list vocational education, certification courses, and any other stint at an educational institution that matters to your career or personal direction.

When you're ready to update or add your education information, follow these steps:

1. **Click the Me icon in the top navigation bar, and then click View Profile from the drop-down list that appears.**
2. **Scroll down your profile until you see the Education header, and click its + link.**

   The Add Education window appears, as shown in Figure 3-13.

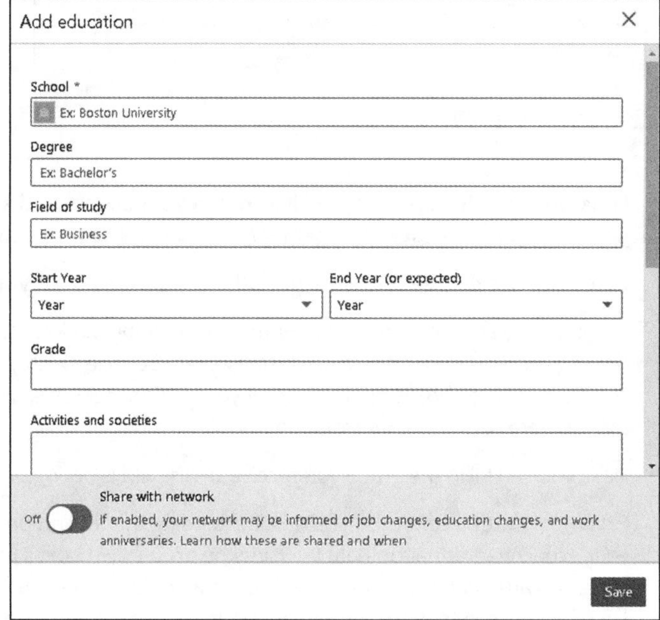

FIGURE 3-13: Enter your school information into the Education section.

3. **In the School box, start entering the school name you want to add to your profile.**

   As you type, LinkedIn displays a drop-down list of schools, as shown in Figure 3-14.

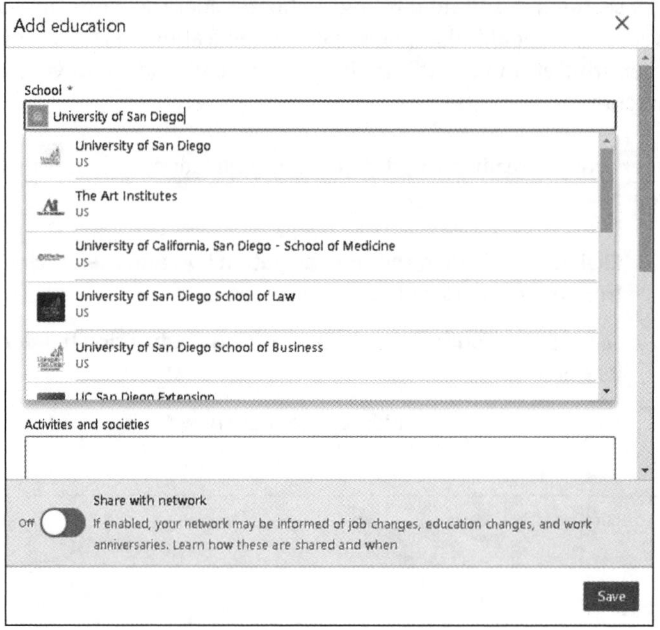

FIGURE 3-14: Choose your school from the list provided, or continue typing the name of your school.

4. **Look through the alphabetized list to find your school and select it. If your school name doesn't appear, just finish typing the name.**
5. **Complete the degree and time period information about your education.**

   For your degree type, you can either provide an abbreviation (BS, BA, and so on) or write the entire degree name (Masters of Science, Doctorate, and so on). The Field of Study box is optional, but if you had a specific major or emphasis, this is where to put that information.

   Next, you can fill in the grade you received; this field is optional.

   Finally, for dates attended, if you're still attending this institution, simply fill in your expected graduation date by using the drop-down boxes to choose the years you attended the institution. If you're an older worker and concerned about age discrimination, you can leave the dates of attendance blank; this is optional information.

6. **Scroll down to the Activities and Societies text box and fill it in.**

   Enter any extracurricular activities you participated in while attending this school. Also list any clubs or organizations you belonged to (including any officer positions you held in those clubs) and any societies you joined or were given membership to, such as honor societies, fraternities, or sororities. Be sure to separate each activity with a comma.

   Decide whether listing these activities will support or enhance your overall professional goals and brand image. Make sure to list any activities, such as current alumni organization activities, that apply to your situation today.

7. **Scroll down to the Description box, and enter any additional information about your education experience.**

   Enter any awards or honors received from this school, as well as any special events or experiences that didn't fit in the Activities and Societies box, such as studying abroad, events you organized, or committees that you served on at this school.

   You can separate each item with a period if you want.

8. **Scroll down to the Media section. Click Upload to add a document, photo, presentation or video to your Education entry, or click Link to provide a URL to link to a media file associated with your Education.**

   If you have a media file that will demonstrate skills you picked up while getting an education — perhaps a graduate or undergraduate thesis, a final project document for one of your classes, or a video of a lecture you gave while pursuing this education — click the Upload or Link button to add this content to your LinkedIn profile. You can add multiple media files to any Education entry.

9. **When you have finished entering information, click the Save button.**

   The education listing is added to your profile, and you return to your profile page.

10. **Repeat Steps 2-9 for any additional education listings you want to enter.**

To edit an existing education record, click the pencil icon, instead of the Add Education link, next to that record in the Education section.

Setting Your Profile URL and Public View

After you fully update your LinkedIn profile, your next goal is probably to share it with the entire world, not just your LinkedIn network. The best way to accomplish this is to set up your profile so that your full profile is available for public viewing.

Setting your profile to full public view gives you several advantages:

- Anyone looking for you has a better chance of finding you because of the increased information tied to your name.
- When you make your profile public, it gets indexed in both the Google and Yahoo! search databases. This makes your online identity accessible and controlled by your access to LinkedIn.
- You give increased exposure to any companies, projects, or initiatives that you're working on by having that credit published on your LinkedIn profile.

When you're ready to set your profile to Public, follow these steps:

1. **Click the Me icon in the top navigation bar, and then click View Profile.**
2. **To the right of your photo, click Edit Public Profile & URL.**

   A new window appears, showing you how your profile page looks to people who are not logged into LinkedIn, as shown in Figure 3-15.

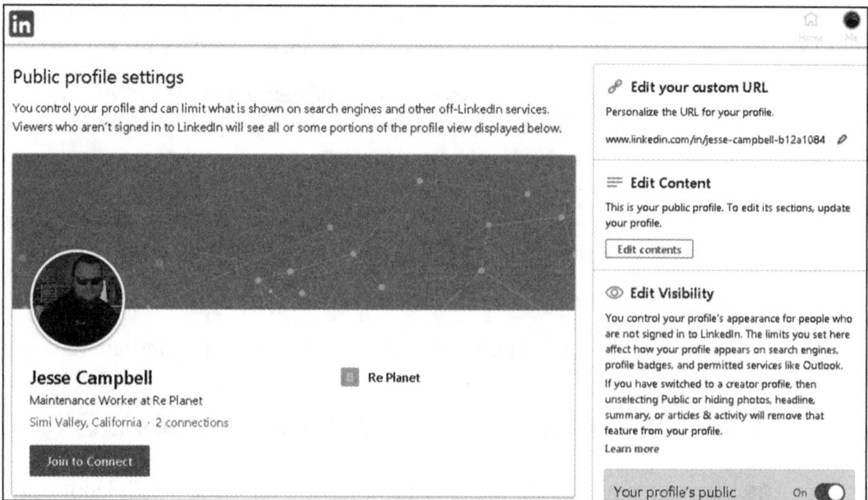

FIGURE 3-15: Edit your LinkedIn profile settings.

3. **To change your public profile URL:**

   a. *Click the pencil icon next to your LinkedIn URL.* Your LinkedIn URL is in the Edit Public Profile URL section (`www.linkedin.com/in/jesse-campbell-b12a1084` in Figure 3-15). A text box appears so you can edit your URL, as shown in Figure 3-16.

b. *Replace the text that appears after* `www.linkedin.com/in/` *with your new text.* You can type 5 to 30 numbers or letters; spaces, symbols, and special characters are not allowed.

c. *Click Save.*

It's much easier to point people to, say, `www.linkedin.com/in/jessecampbell/` than to `www.linkedin.com/in/jesse-campbell-b12a1084/`.

WARNING

Keep your URL changes to a minimum (preferably, just set it once and leave it) so that everyone, especially a search engine, knows how to get to your profile. (If you change your custom URL later, the previous custom URL is no longer valid.) Otherwise, you'll have different versions of your profile with different URLs in different places on the Internet.

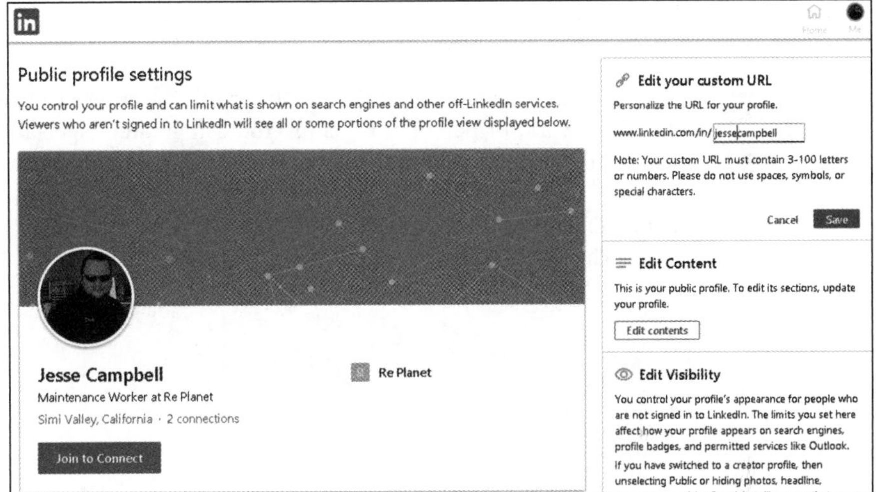

FIGURE 3-16: Create a custom URL for your LinkedIn profile.

4. **Scroll down to the Edit Visibility section and choose the parts of your LinkedIn profile that you want available for public viewing.**

   To reveal a section on your public profile, scroll down and simply select the Show slider next to that section, as shown in Figure 3-17. Your basic information is already selected by default, but you can decide whether to add your education, positions, groups, or any other indicated section. As you add sections, the profile preview on the left side of the page is updated and your changes are saved automatically.

5. **Click the LinkedIn icon in the top-left corner to return to your LinkedIn home page and go about your business.**

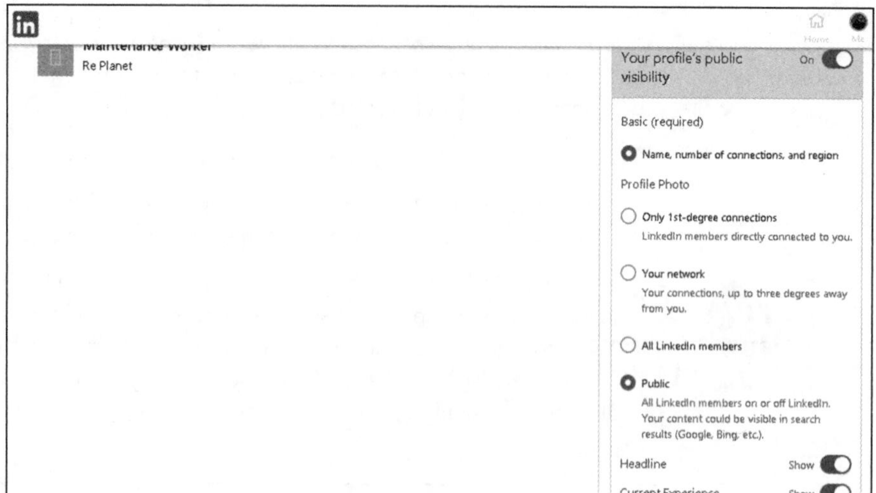

FIGURE 3-17: Decide what to add to your public profile.

TIP

Do you want to promote your LinkedIn profile on other websites, such as a blog, social network, or personal website? You can create a special clickable LinkedIn icon (called a *public profile badge*) and add it to a website to direct people to your public LinkedIn profile. Just scroll down past the Save button, click the Create a Badge link below the Your Public Profile Badge section, and follow the instructions. This process is covered in depth in Chapter 12.

2 Finding Others and Getting Connected

IN THIS PART . . .

Search LinkedIn far and wide for people, groups, or companies.

Grow your network using the LinkedIn built-in tools.

Keep track of your existing network with LinkedIn Messages and expand your network with InMail.

Interact and share knowledge with your LinkedIn network.

Give and receive skills endorsements.

» Using special keywords in your search

» Saving your search requests to run later

Chapter 4 Discovering and Building Your Network

After you sign up for LinkedIn and build your profile (see Chapters 2 and 3, respectively, for more on those topics), it's time to go forth and find connections! As you start searching your own immediate network of your first-degree connections, plus second- and third-degree network members, you can see just how valuable LinkedIn can be to you. LinkedIn is the embodiment of the Six Degrees of Separation concept because, in most cases, you can connect to any other person in the network regardless of whether you already know that person.

In this chapter, I demonstrate the different ways you can search the LinkedIn network, both your ever-growing personal network and the greater LinkedIn member network. I talk about viewing your own network, searching in the second and third degrees of your network, and performing searches on LinkedIn using different types of criteria or search terms.

Searching Your First-Degree Connections

I recall an old saying: "You have to know where you have come from to know where you are going." This holds true even for LinkedIn. Before you start searching throughout the network, it's helpful to understand the reach of your own immediate network and how your first-degree connections' networks add up. The first task is to become familiar with your own LinkedIn network.

To view and search through your own LinkedIn network, just follow these steps:

1. **Log in to LinkedIn. From the top navigation bar, click the My Network button.**

   Your My Network page appears.

2. **Along the left side click either the Connections subheader or your number of connections, which is also a link.**

   A list of your current connections on the Connections page appears, as shown in Figure 4-1.

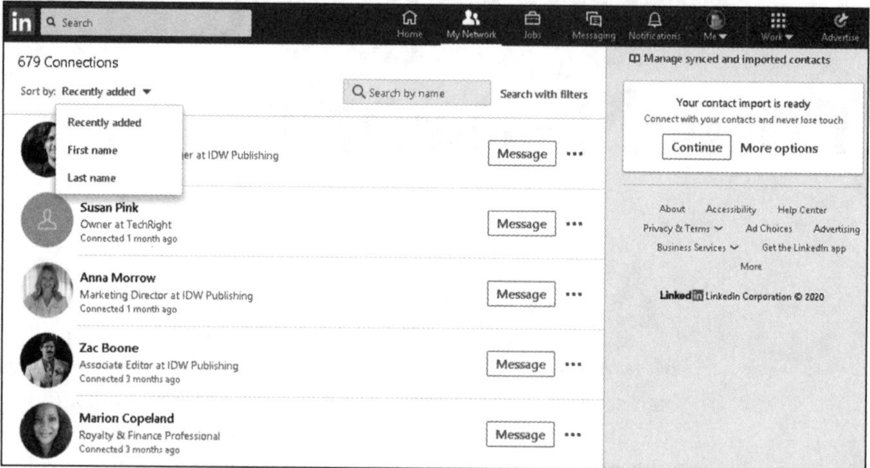

FIGURE 4-1: Sort your connections by last name.

3. **You can either scroll through the list, which is automatically sorted by Recently Added, or click the drop-down arrow next to the Sort By menu and then click the First Name or Last Name option to sort the list of connections in alphabetical order.**

4. **To filter your list of connections, use the Search (by Name) Connections box or the Search with Filters link or both, at the top of the screen.**

   - *To search for someone's name:* Start typing a first or last name in the Search box. LinkedIn automatically shows you all the connections who match the name you're typing. Press Enter after typing to see a filtered list of connections.

- *To search for more than just someone's name:* Click the Search with Filters link to display an Advanced LinkedIn search screen, and then click the All Filters link to display a Filters window, which shows all your filter options as you scroll down. The 1st check box (under Connections) should be automatically selected. If you're looking for, say, professionals who live in San Diego, click *San Diego* in the Locations section (see Figure 4-2), and then click the Show Results button to see a revised list of first-degree connections with this new parameter.

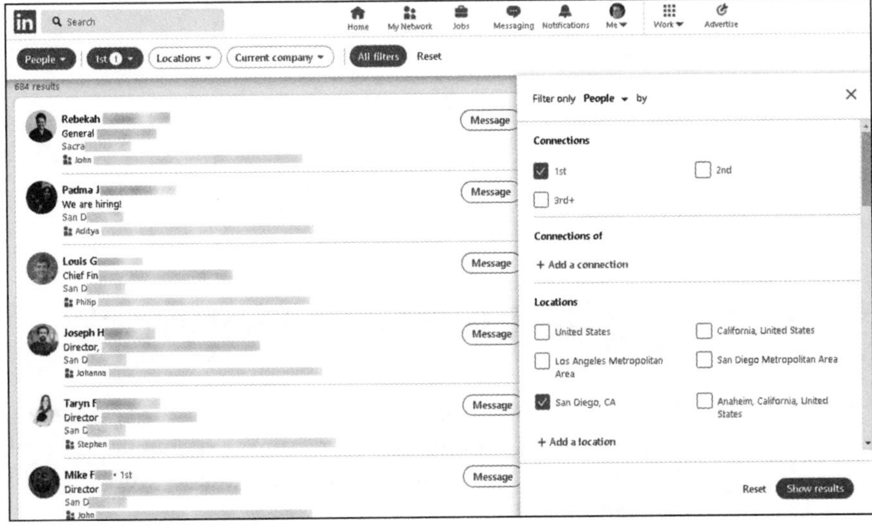

FIGURE 4-2: Generate a targeted list of your connections based on a filter.

5. **Use the other filters, such as Current Company, to view a more targeted set of connections.**

   LinkedIn catalogs a wealth of information about you and your connections, allowing you to run specific searches on your network. Let's say you're looking for connections who have the Walt Disney Company as a current employer and who live in either Anaheim or San Diego. Simply update the Current Company and Locations filters (see Figure 4-3) and click the Show Results button and LinkedIn searches to see the connections in your network who match this query.

   For most filters, you simply type words in a Search box and select your option from a list that LinkedIn displays. That option gets an assigned check box. When you're using the Locations filter, if the location doesn't appear as an option, you select the closest area that LinkedIn has defined in its system to add that location to your search.

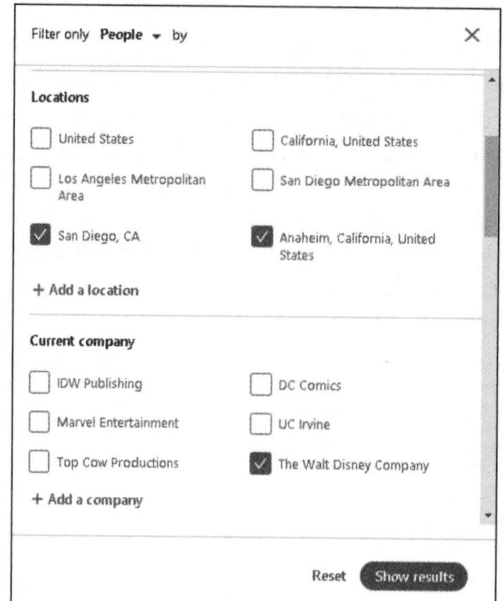

FIGURE 4-3: See a detailed search query of your network.

Searching the LinkedIn Network

When you're ready to find a specific person, use the LinkedIn search engine, which you can use to scan, based on keywords, the hundreds of millions of LinkedIn members. The two main ways to search the network are a basic search and an advanced search.

At the top of every page on LinkedIn is a simple Search box, with which you can run a keyword search via the LinkedIn database. This is your go-to tool if you're searching for a specific name, employees of a particular company, or people with a specific job title.

You'll get a lot of results with the basic search because you're searching each LinkedIn member's entire profile, not just one field, for your keywords. For example, if you type *Mike Jones* in the basic Search box as opposed to searching by the name Mike Jones (see "Advanced searching with filters," later in this chapter), you get a larger set of results because you see every profile where the words *Mike* and *Jones* are anywhere in the profile. (When you search by name, LinkedIn searches only everyone's Name field.) Keep this in mind when you do your search, and choose the method you want based on your goals.

In some situations, though, a simple search just doesn't cut it because you want to specify whether you're searching for someone's name, title, employer, industry, skills, location, or some combination thereof. In those cases, you need LinkedIn's advanced search functionality, which you can access in the following two ways:

- From almost any page on LinkedIn, click the text box at the top of the page, enter some keywords in the box, and press Enter to display the search results page. From this results page, click the headers under the Search box — People, Posts, Companies, Groups, Jobs, Schools, Events, or Courses, as shown in Figure 4-4 — to display advanced search capabilities for your selection.
- If you download the LinkedIn mobile app (as discussed in Chapter 10), you can perform a search from the Search box in that program.

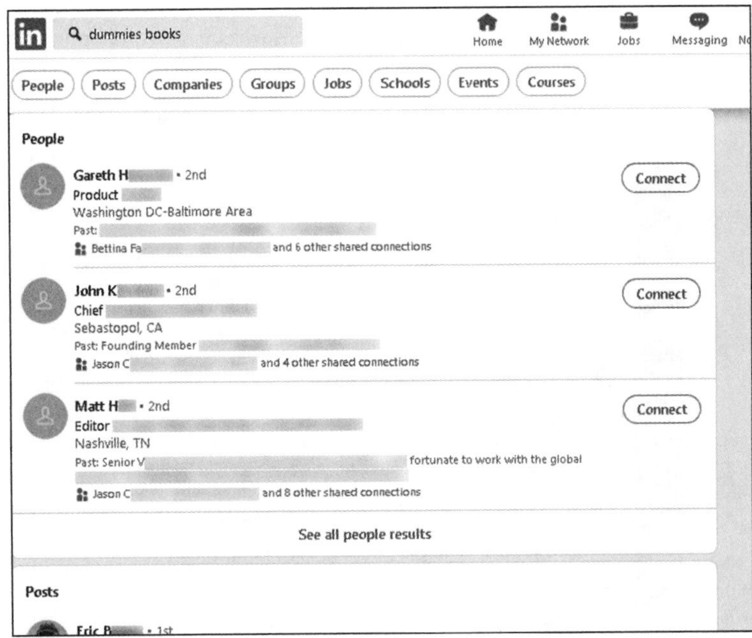

FIGURE 4-4: Access the LinkedIn search results page from by using the text box at the top of the screen.

Starting with basic search options

Quick, do you know someone who can write software code in PHP? Who do you know who enjoys mountain climbing or hiking? Do you know anyone who gives presentations on a regular basis? Well, you can find out if you search by keyword.

In a keyword search, LinkedIn analyzes everyone else's profiles to find the matching word. You can put any sort of skill, buzzword, interest, or other keyword that might be present in someone's profile to see who in your network is a match. To search by keyword, follow these steps:

1. **While logged in to LinkedIn, click the search text box at the top of the page.**
2. **Enter the keyword(s) in the text box.**

   In Figure 4-5, I searched for Six Sigma. If you enter multiple keywords as I did, LinkedIn looks for members, groups, companies, job listings, and schools who have all the keywords in their profile.

   TIP

   I recommend tacking on additional search criteria, such as one or more industries, location information (country and zip or postal code), or perhaps a job title to get a more meaningful search result (for example, Six Sigma San Francisco). Otherwise, your result list will be long and unhelpful.

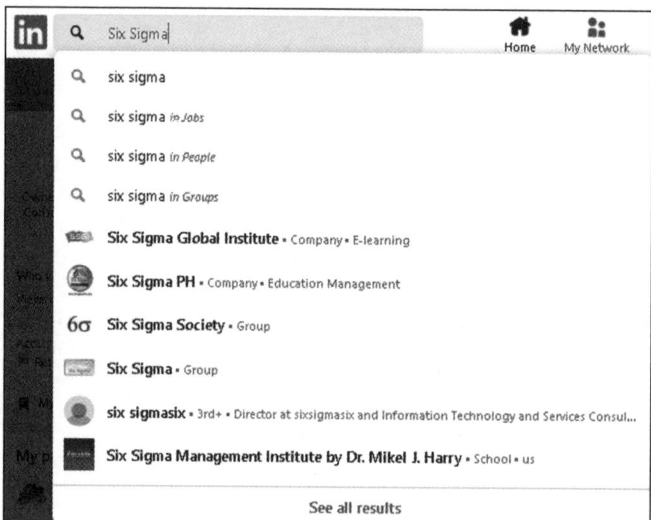

FIGURE 4-5: Search by keywords.

3. **Look through the drop-down list that appears to see whether your desired result is an option on the list.**

   LinkedIn provides you with an assortment of search options based on the keywords you entered. At the top of the list are options to do a basic search with your keywords and one of the filters, such as Jobs, People, or Groups.

Below the top options, LinkedIn prompts you with links to companies, groups, schools, or even people who partially or fully match the keywords you provided. Click one of those links to be taken to the respective LinkedIn page.

4. **If you don't see the result you want from the drop-down list, press the Enter key to display the search results page.**

   When you press Enter, you're telling LinkedIn to run a basic search with just the keywords you entered. LinkedIn presents a search results page (see Figure 4-6), given the keywords you entered.

   If you click a filter (header) below the text box, a more focused search results screen appears. For example, Figure 4-7 shows the screen when the Jobs filter is clicked. Then click a listing for more detailed information. Note that when you click a filter, a new set of additional subfilters appears along the top line so you can refine your search.

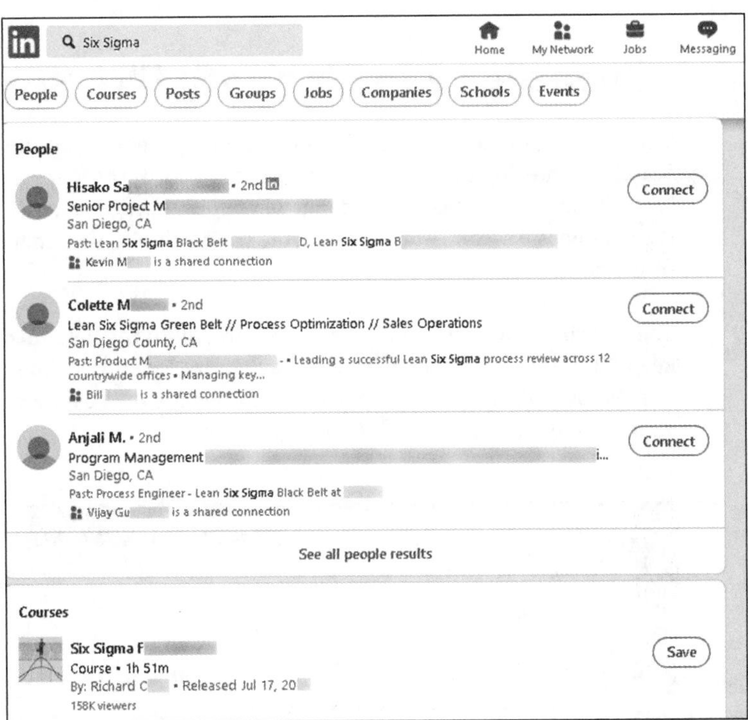

FIGURE 4-6: Display the search results page for more options.

In the next section, you discover how to use the various additional filters on the top of the search results screen to refine your search results by entering more information, such as degrees of connection, job titles, user types, and location information, by selecting the check boxes provided.

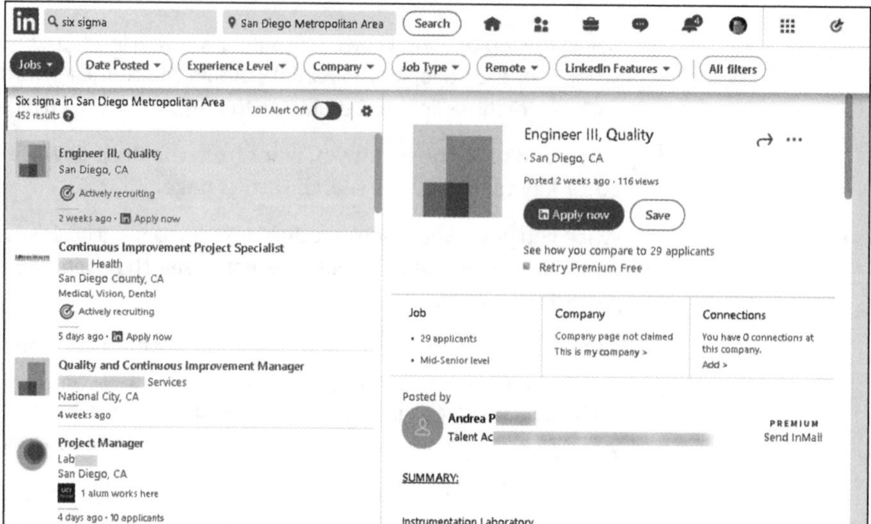

FIGURE 4-7: Narrow your search results by using a main filter, such as the Jobs filter here.

Advanced searching with filters

When you want to find a specific person on LinkedIn, you most likely start your search by entering the person's name. When you start to type a name in the Search box, you see a list of people based on what you've typed so far (refer to Figure 4-5). If someone is a second- or third-degree connection to you, that info shows up next to the name.

You can click any name in the list to go directly to the person's profile, or you can keep typing to update the list. Let's say you're looking for John Smith who works at IBM. By adding *IBM* as an extra search term, you see a new list of John Smiths who work(ed) at IBM, as shown in Figure 4-8.

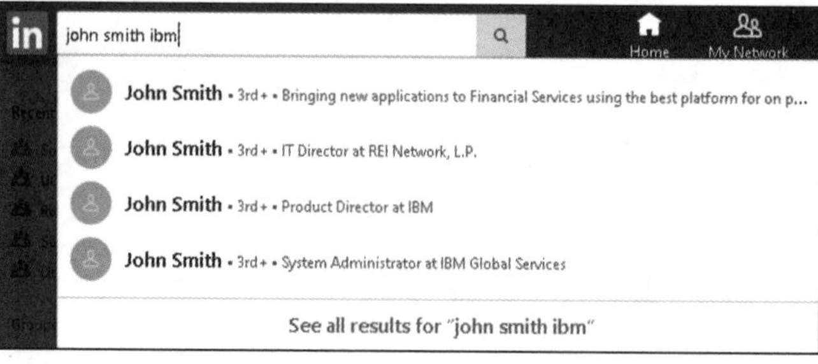

FIGURE 4-8: Search LinkedIn by someone's name and company.

The advanced way to search is to use the additional search filters for a person search to refine the results from LinkedIn's member base of over 726 million members. If you have several details about the person to help refine your search, I highly recommend plugging in that information with the additional search filters to find the person or people with whom you are looking to connect.

REMEMBER

When you search by name, you are required to enter the last name; entering the first name is optional.

When you're ready to perform a detailed search by name, follow these steps:

1. **While logged in to LinkedIn, enter a name in the Search box at the top of the page and press Enter.**

   The search results page appears.

2. **Click the People header, near the top of the screen.**

3. **Click the All Filters link, and use the additional filters to include more information to help find the person.**

   For example, if you know a company where the person used to work or is currently employed, click the drop-down arrow next to Current Companies or Past Companies and select an option from the list presented, or add your own search criteria for that filter by clicking the + Add link and typing your specific criteria in the box that appears, as shown in Figure 4-9.

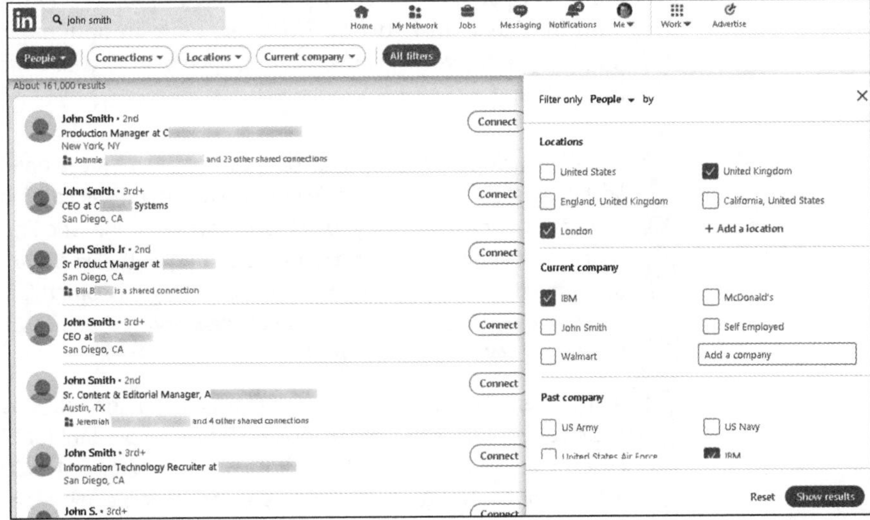

FIGURE 4-9: Provide additional filter information to find your person.

4. **(Optional) If you know the approximate location of the person, use the Locations drop-down list and select one of the prefilled options for a location.**

   After you click the Show Results button when updating a field, LinkedIn refreshes the search results based on the fields you've filled out. You see an updated results list of people, sorted by the relevance of your name search (for example, second-degree network members appear above third-degree network members) and then by additional search filters you entered.

5. **(Optional) For better results, use additional or different filters in your search.**

   If you haven't already done so, add more keywords, a company name, or location information using the filters on the top of the search results screen. You can click the All Filters link to display a dedicated screen of filters, where you can scroll down and choose more specific filters to refine your search results.

TIP

If you've refined your search results too much, the easiest way to start over is to click Reset in the All Filters side window. Doing so wipes out any additional search filters and starts the search with just your initial keywords.

Performing advanced searches

LinkedIn's search screens allow you to perform detailed searches by using check boxes and drop-down lists, so you don't need to know any programming to dig deep into the LinkedIn network. However, built-in options are available if you want to add specific words, called *boolean operators*, to your search. Here are some of your options:

- **OR:** When you do a search that could call for one or more options, but the search *must* contain at least one of those terms, the OR command is incredibly useful. For example, if you're looking for someone who knows how to program in either Java or JavaScript, you can type the words *Java OR JavaScript* to get the desired result. Or when you're looking for something that could be typed as one word or two, such as *Help desk* or *helpdesk*, put OR between the two terms: *Help desk OR helpdesk.*
- **AND:** When your search requires multiple criteria, the AND operator seems essential. Let's say you need a Certified Public Accountant (or CPA) who knows QuickBooks and lives in California. You can search for *CPA AND QuickBooks AND California.* Thankfully, LinkedIn assumes that the AND operator is implied with multiple keywords, so you don't have to type AND. When you type multiple keywords without the word AND between each one, LinkedIn will still look for every keyword, assuming that the word AND is there.

- **NOT:** When your search requires you to exclude a particular term, you can use the word NOT (or a minus sign) in front of the term you want to exclude. For example, if you type *director NOT president,* you're looking for people who work as a director, but not the president of the company.
- **" " (quotation marks):** When your search requires exact phrases instead of a string of keywords (such as the Six Sigma example shown previously in Figure 4-7), you need to add quotation marks around each phrase. That way, when you look for, say, *"Executive Assistant,"* you'll get results for an executive assistant but not for an executive who has a job duty of assistant to the president, for example.
- **( ) (parenthetical searches):** You can take the previous operators and combine them, using parentheses to build complex searches. For example, if you need a software developer or engineer who knows either Java or JavaScript, but who isn't a manager, you can search this by typing:

```
(Java OR JavaScript) AND ("software developer" OR "software
   engineer") AND NOT Manager
```

Saving searches for future use

LinkedIn enables you to save your searches so you can run them later. Let's say you're a recruiter who wants to check her network every week for someone who can fill a specific job opening, or a job seeker who wants to see if the right person pops up in one of the companies she is targeting.

To save your searches to use later, follow these steps:

1. **Log in to LinkedIn and enter your keywords at the top of the home page in the Search box.**

   The search results page appears.

2. **Click the People filter and perform the search you want to save by entering the appropriate keywords in the boxes and selecting the check boxes next to each filter.**

   The search results page appears, similar to the one in Figure 4-10.

3. **Click the Create Search Alert button, near the top-right corner.**

   A Search Alerts window appears, as shown in Figure 4-11. LinkedIn creates a title for your search, based on your keyword search parameters.

TIP

LinkedIn will email you weekly with search results for this saved search as long as you leave the Weekly option selected and the Email check box selected.

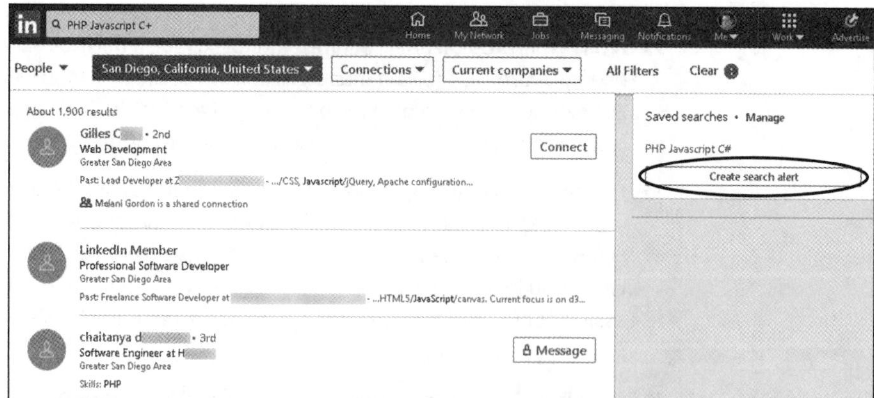

FIGURE 4-10: Perform a search that you want to save for later use.

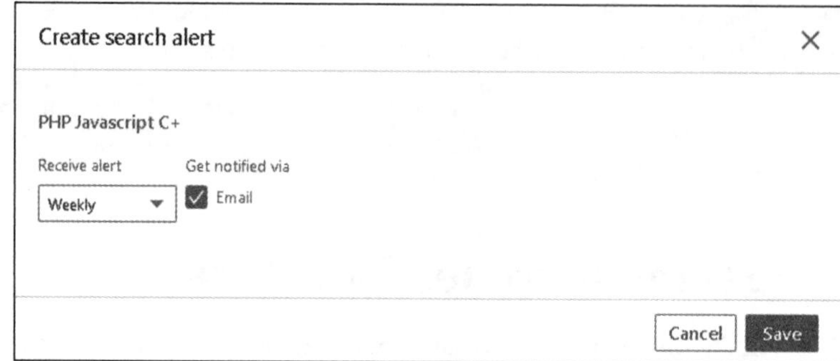

FIGURE 4-11: Set the parameters to save your specific search.

4. **Click the blue Save button to save your search.**

   The search results screen appears and displays the title of the saved search, as shown in Figure 4-12. Your saved searches appear on the right side of the screen, below and to the right of the additional search filters up top.

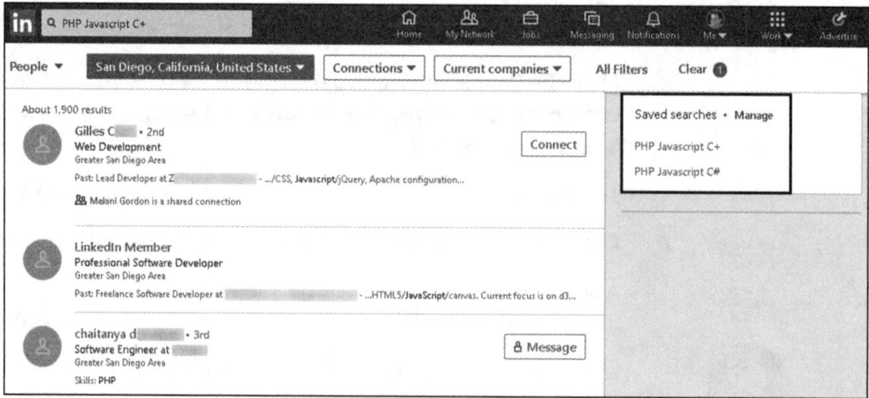

FIGURE 4-12: See your saved searches in a list.

5. **When you need to bring up your saved search, go to the Saved Searches section of the search results page and click the title of your search.**

   When you click the name of the search, you're executing the same search you did before. If you have a basic account, you can store three saved searches. If you have a premium account, you can store more searches, depending on the account level.

» Using the best strategies for expanding your network

» Sending connection requests

» Weeding out connections

» Dealing with invitations

Chapter 5

Growing Your Network

Maybe by now, you've signed on to LinkedIn, created your profile, searched through the network, and started inviting people to connect to you — and you're wondering, what's next? You certainly shouldn't be sitting around on your hands, waiting for responses to your invitations. LinkedIn is designed to open doors to opportunities using the professional relationships you already have (and, with luck, by creating new ones). The best use of it, therefore, is to capture as much of your professional network as possible in the form of first-degree connections to your LinkedIn network so that you can discover inside leads as well as friends of friends who can help you.

In this chapter, I discuss how you can grow your LinkedIn network and offer guidelines to keep in mind when growing your network. I also cover various search tools for you to use to stay on top of LinkedIn's growing membership and how others may relate to you.

To expand your network, you need to know how to send invitations as well as how to attract LinkedIn members and contacts who haven't yet taken the plunge into LinkedIn membership. I cover all that here, too. And finally, this chapter helps you deal with the etiquette of accepting or declining invitations that you receive, and shows you how to remove connections that you no longer want to keep in your network.

REMEMBER

An *invitation* is when you invite a colleague or a friend to join LinkedIn and stay connected to you as part of your network. An *introduction* is when you ask a first-degree connection to introduce you to one of his or her connections so you can get to know that person better. I cover the concept of introductions through messaging in more depth in Chapter 6; invitations are covered right here.

Building a Meaningful Network

When you build a house, you start with a set of blueprints. When you start an organization, you usually have some sort of mission statement or guiding principles. Likewise, when you begin to build your LinkedIn network, you should keep in mind some of the keys to having and growing a professional network. These guiding principles help you decide whom to invite to your network, whom to search for and introduce yourself to, and how much time to spend on LinkedIn.

LinkedIn is different from Facebook and Twitter because it focuses on business networking in a professional manner rather than encouraging users to post pictures of their latest beach party or tweet their latest status update. The best use of LinkedIn involves maintaining a professional network of connections, not sending someone an event invitation or a game request.

That said, you'll find variety in the types of networks that people maintain on LinkedIn. Much of that has to do with each person's definition of a meaningful network:

- **Quality versus quantity:** As I mention in Chapter 1, some people use LinkedIn with the goal of gaining the highest number of connections possible, thereby emphasizing quantity over quality. Those people are typically referred to as LinkedIn open networkers (LIONs). At the other end of the spectrum are people who use LinkedIn only to keep together their closest, most tightly knit connections without striving to enlarge their network. Most people fall somewhere in between these two aims.

  The question of whether you're after quality or quantity is something to keep in mind every time you think of inviting someone to join your network. LinkedIn strongly recommends connecting only with people you know, so its advice is to stick to quality connections. Here are some questions to ask yourself to help you figure out your purpose:

  - Do you want to manage a network of only people you personally know?
  - Do you want to manage a network of people you know or who might help you find new opportunities in a specific industry?

- Do you want to promote your business or expand your professional opportunities?
- Do you want to maximize your chances of being able to reach someone with a new opportunity or job offering, regardless of personal interaction?

» **Depth versus breadth:** Some people want to focus on building a network of only the most relevant or new connections — people from their current job or industry who could play a role in their professional development in that industry. Other people like to include a diversity of connections who include anyone they have ever professionally interacted with, whether through work, education, or any kind of group or association, in hopes that anyone who knows them at all can potentially lead to future opportunities. For these LinkedIn users, it doesn't matter that most of the people in their network don't know 99 percent of their other connections. Most people fall somewhere in between these two poles but lean toward including more people in their network.

  Here are some questions to keep in mind regarding whether you want to focus on depth or breadth in your network:

  - Do you want to build or maintain a specific in-depth network of thought leaders regarding one topic, job, or industry?
  - Do you want to build a broad network of connections who can help you with different aspects of your career or professional life?
  - Do you want to add only people who may offer an immediate benefit to some aspect of your professional life?
  - Do you want to add a professional contact now and figure out later how that person might fit with your long-term goals?

» **Strong versus weak link:** I'm not referring to the game show *The Weakest Link*, but rather to the strength of your connection with someone. Beyond the issue of quality versus quantity, you'll want to keep differing levels of quality in mind. Some people invite someone after meeting him once at a cocktail party, hoping to strengthen the link as time goes on. Others work to create strong links first and then invite those people to connect on LinkedIn afterward.

  This issue comes down to how much you want LinkedIn itself to play a role in your business network's development. Do you see your LinkedIn network as a work in progress or as a virtual room in which to gather only your closest allies? Here are some questions to keep in mind:

  - What level of interaction needs to have occurred for you to feel comfortable asking someone to connect with you on LinkedIn? A face-to-face meeting? Phone conversations only? A stream of emails?

- What length of time do you need to know someone before you feel that you can connect with that person? Or, does time matter less if you have had a high-quality interaction just once?
- Does membership in a specific group or association count as a good enough reference for you to add someone to your network? (For example, say you met someone briefly only once, but she is a school alum: Does that tie serve as a sufficient reference?)

» **Specific versus general goals:** Some people like to maintain a strong network of people mainly to talk about work and job-related issues. Other people like to discuss all matters relating to their network, whether it's professional, personal, or social. Most people fall somewhere in between, and herein lies what I mean by the "purpose" of your network. Do you want to simply catalog your entire network, regardless of industry, because LinkedIn will act as your complete contact management system and because you can use LinkedIn to reach different parts of your network at varying times? Or do you want to focus your LinkedIn network on a specific goal, using your profile to attract and retain the right kind of contact that furthers that goal?

Here are some more questions to ask yourself:

- Do you have any requirements in mind for someone before you add him to your network? That is, are you looking to invite only people with certain qualities or experience?
- Does the way you know or met someone influence your decision to connect to that person on LinkedIn?
- What information do you need to know about someone before you want to add him to your network?

REMEMBER

By the way, this isn't a quiz — there is no one right answer to any of these questions. You decide what you want to accomplish through your network, and how you want to go from there. Also remember that although you might start LinkedIn with one goal in mind, your usage and experience might shift you to a different way of using the site. If that happens, just go with it, as long as it fits with your current goals.

After you establish why you want to link to other people, you can start looking for and reaching out to those people. In the next section, I point you to a number of linking strategies that can help you reach your goals for your network. When you start on LinkedIn, completing your profile (see Chapter 3) helps you get your first round of connections, and you're prompted to enter whatever names you can remember to offer an invitation for them to connect with you. Now you're ready to generate your next round of connections, and to get into the habit of making this a continual process as you use the site.

Importing Contacts into LinkedIn

One of the most popular (and necessary) activities people use the Internet for is email. Your email account contains a record of the email addresses of everyone you regularly communicate with via email. And from your established base of communications, LinkedIn offers a way for you to ramp up your network by importing a list of contacts from your email program.

Importing your email contacts into LinkedIn eliminates the drudgery of going through your address book and copying addresses into LinkedIn. This section shows you how to import your email contacts into LinkedIn to update your connections.

Importing a contacts list from your email system

This section shows you how to use the LinkedIn function to import your email contacts into LinkedIn. To do so, follow these steps:

1. **Click the My Network icon on the top navigation bar to display your network page.**
2. **Click the More options link below the Add Personal Contacts section on the bottom of the screen.**

   The Sync Contacts screen appears, as shown in Figure 5-1. Your email address on file is already entered in the email address text box in the middle of the screen.

   Below your email address is a row of buttons representing Gmail, Yahoo! Mail, Outlook, and AOL, an email message icon (for inputting a list of email addresses manually), and an upload icon (for uploading a file of email addresses).
3. **Click Continue to use the prefilled address, replace the email address by typing a new email address and then click Continue, or click one of the buttons to select an email system from which to import your contacts.**

   The Sign In window appears for your email account, as shown in Figure 5-2.
4. **Follow the prompts to connect your email account with LinkedIn.**

   At the end of the prompts, you'll be asked to allow LinkedIn to access your email contacts, as shown in Figure 5-3.

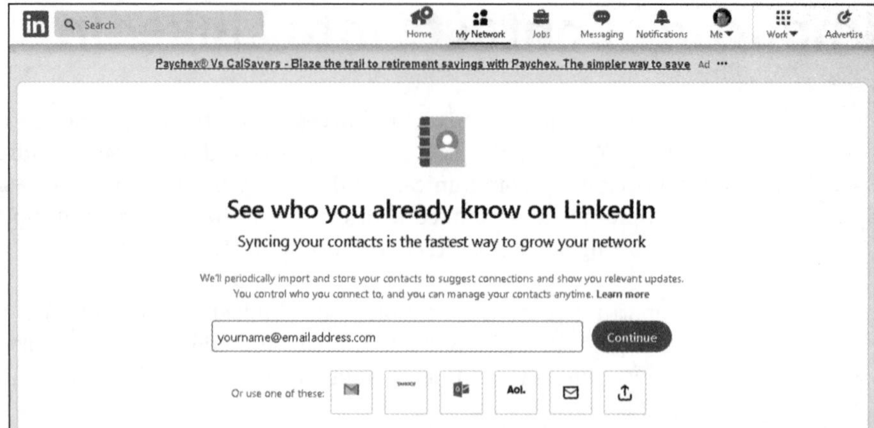

FIGURE 5-1: Sync your email contacts with LinkedIn.

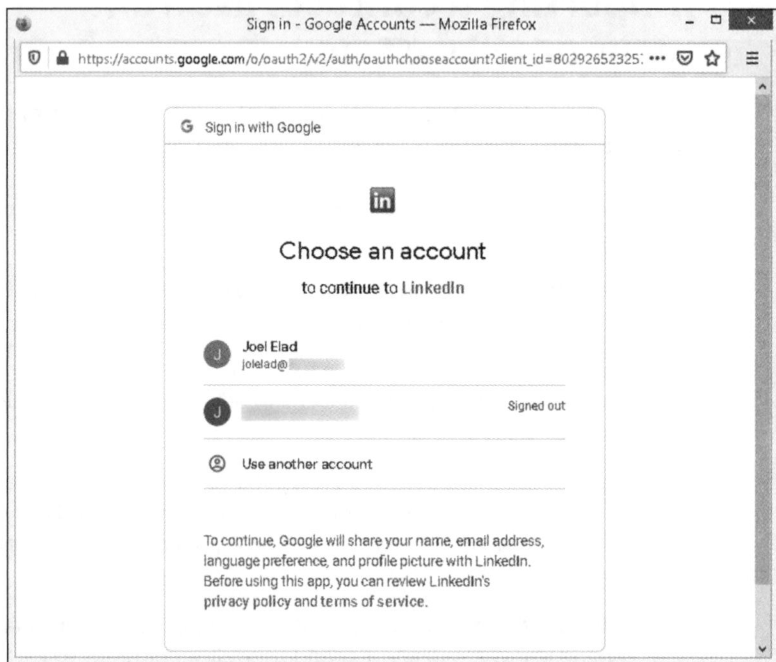

FIGURE 5-2: Select the email address account to sync.

5. **Click the Allow button.**

   LinkedIn spends some time accessing the account and checking to see whether any of your contacts are already on LinkedIn. Then the screen shown in Figure 5-4 appears, with a list of people from your email account who have LinkedIn accounts but are not currently connected to you.

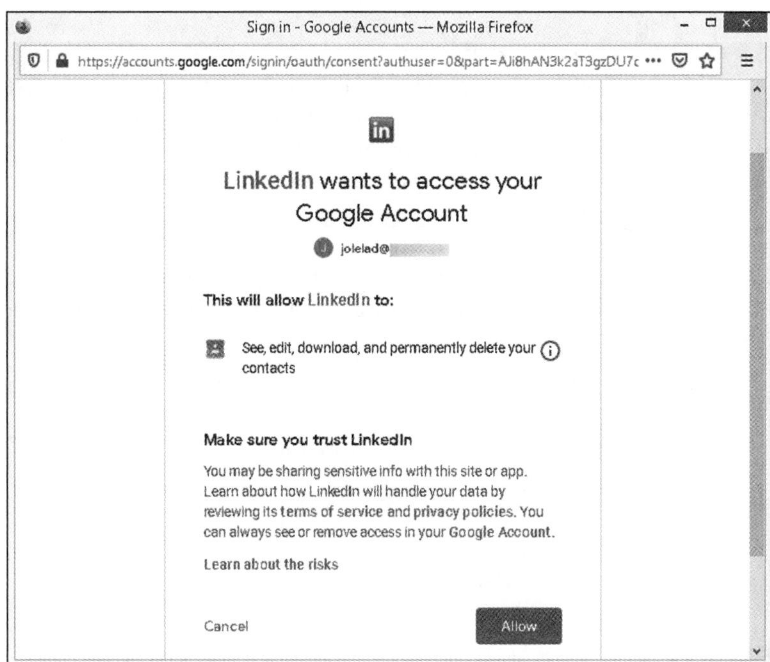

FIGURE 5-3: Let LinkedIn access your email account.

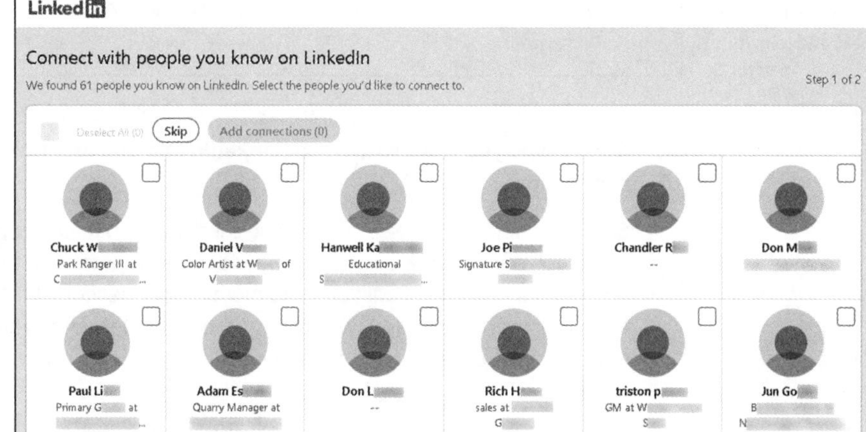

FIGURE 5-4: Choose which LinkedIn contacts from your email whom you want to invite to your network.

6. **Choose whom you want to invite to be your LinkedIn connections:**

   - *Add Connections:* Go through the list and select the connections you want to add. Then click the (now enabled) Add My Connections button. Each person will receive an automated invitation to connect with you. Because you can't tailor the messages to these people, this option isn't recommended. You must go to each person's profile page, and click Connect to send a customized invitation.

- *Deselect All:* If you've gone through and selected too many people, you can always start over by clicking the Deselect All link, which deselects every check box. Since you can't add customized invitation text to these connection requests, I recommend that you connect from each person's profile page to customize the invitation text, if you have the time to do so.
- *Skip:* Skip this screen and move on with the process.

A new screen appears, as shown in Figure 5-5, with the names of people imported from your email account who don't have a LinkedIn account.

Linked in

A LinkedIn connection means you'll never lose touch

Invite your contacts onto LinkedIn to keep up with their careers.
If someone you invite doesn't respond right away, we'll send up to two reminders.

Step 2 of 2

Deselect All (0) Skip Add to network (0)

masscarocci@ masscarocci@	kris m kris_ @
Kelley j k @	Paradise Co p @o .com
Jet pack cesradjr@	MICHAEL z misterzed@m
Fred a 1@hotmail.com	Rich H r s@
g ryan ryan@g	neil g himself@

FIGURE 5-5: Choose which email contacts you want to invite to use LinkedIn and join your network.

7. Decide who you want to invite to LinkedIn and add as a first-degree connection.

Similar to Step 6, you need to select the check boxes next to people you want to add to your network, and then click Add to Network to send those people an invitation to join LinkedIn and add them to your network. If you select too many check boxes and want to start over, click Deselect All and go back to manually choose people you want to invite to LinkedIn and add as a connection.

Finally, you can click the Skip button to move on. If you click Skip, LinkedIn will prompt you to either go back and review their suggestions or try another email account. You can click one of those links, or click the Done for Now link to exit the entire process and go back to your LinkedIn home page.

TIP

If you decide to skip Step 6 or 7, you'll be able to review LinkedIn's imported list of people at a later date by clicking the email system button, as you did in Step 3.

8. **To sync additional email accounts with LinkedIn, repeat Steps 2 to 7.**

   In this way, you can look for new contacts whom you can invite to your network. LinkedIn should be to interface with any email account that can be accessed over the Internet from your computer. Some work email systems may be inaccessible depending on security levels set by your employer.

Checking for members

When you fill out your LinkedIn profile, you create an opportunity to check for colleagues and classmates as well as import potential contacts and invite them to connect with you and stay in touch using LinkedIn. However, that search happens only after you define your profile (and when you update or add to your profile). After that, it's up to you to routinely check the LinkedIn network to look for new members on the site who might want to connect with you or with whom you might want to connect. Fortunately, LinkedIn provides a few tools that help you quickly scan the system to see whether a recently joined member is a past colleague or a classmate. In addition, it never hurts to use your friends to check for new members, as I discuss in a little bit.

Finding classmates

No matter how much time goes by since I graduated from college, I still remember my school years well. I met a lot of cool and interesting people, people I wanted to stay in contact with because of common goals, interests, or experiences. As time progressed and people moved on to new lives after graduation, it was all too easy to lose touch and not be able to reconnect.

Through LinkedIn, though, you can reconnect with former classmates and maintain that tie through your network, no matter where anyone moves on to. For you to find these people to begin with, of course, your former classmates have to properly list their dates of education. And, just as with the search for former colleagues, it's important to do an occasional search to see which classmates joined LinkedIn.

To search for classmates — and add them to your network, if you want — follow these steps:

1. **While logged in to your LinkedIn account,** click the Me icon, then select View Profile from the drop-down menu that appears.
2. **Scroll down to the Education section and click one of your educational** institutions to display the school's page.

3. **Click the Alumni link.**

   The Alumni window for your school appears, as shown in Figure 5-6.

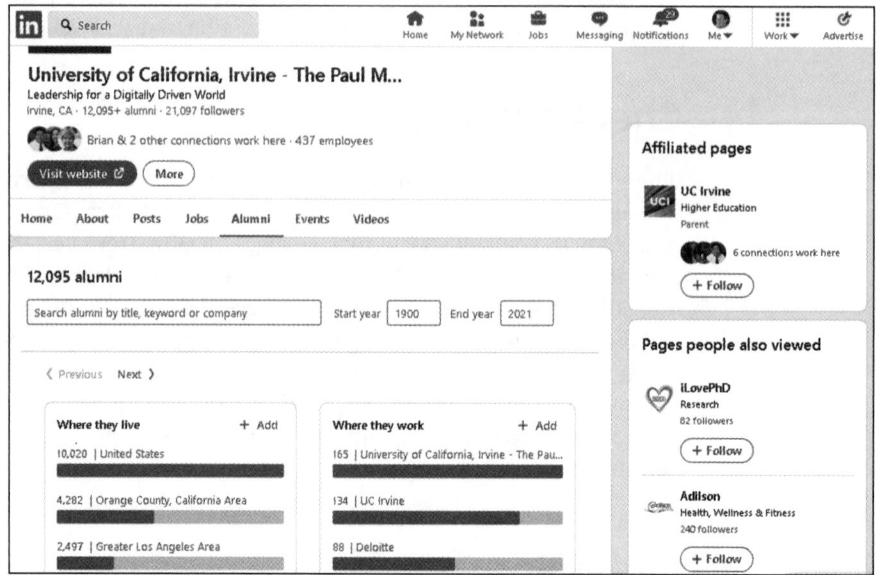

FIGURE 5-6: Visit your school's Alumni window to find past classmates.

4. **Filter the results for a better list.**

   Click any of the classifications, such as Where They Live or Where They Work, to add filters and get a more precise list. You can also change the years of attendance in the boxes provided to see a different set of candidates, and to search by a specific graduation date.

5. **Look over the list of potential classmates and connect with anyone you recognize.**

   You can always click the name of the classmate to see his or her profile first, or just click the Connect button below the name to send an invitation to connect. If you have any shared connections, you can hover your cursor over the connection symbol and number next to the person's picture to see what connections you have in common.

TIP

Before you invite people, click their name to read their profiles and see what they've been doing. Why ask them about their recent accomplishments or activities when you can read it for yourself? By doing your homework first, your invitation will sound more natural and be more likely to be accepted.

TIP

For more about sending invitations, see the "Sending Connection Requests" section, later in this chapter.

Using the People You May Know feature

One of the most common ways for you to increase your network is by using LinkedIn's suggestion system that it calls People You May Know. Given all the data that LinkedIn imports and the global network it maintains, it can use people's profile data, email imports, common experience, education, and LinkedIn activity or other commonalities to predict who may be in the same network with you. Currently, it goes even further to predict who you may know based on similar roles, similar LinkedIn group membership, and so on.

You can access the People You May Know feature in the middle section of your My Network page, as shown in Figure 5-7.

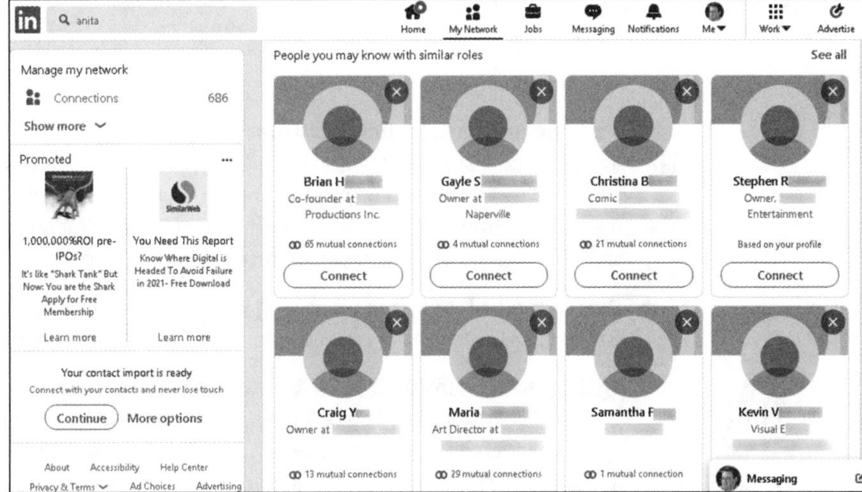

FIGURE 5-7: LinkedIn asks whether you know people to add to your network.

When you click Connect for someone, that spot is updated with a new potential connection for you to consider. As you scroll down, the page is updated with rows of people to whom you can send a connection request.

Here are some things to keep in mind as you review this section:

- **Study the connections you have in common.** A little symbol and a number at the bottom left corner of someone's picture indicates that you and this person have shared first-degree connections. You can click the link for your mutual shared connections to see a pop-up window of those connections, as shown in Figure 5-8. LinkedIn will automatically sort people with more shared connections to the top of the page, assuming that if you have a lot of shared connections, perhaps that person belongs in your network.

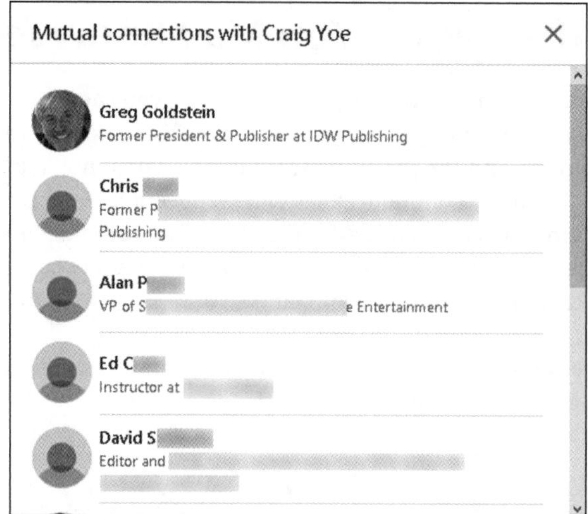

FIGURE 5-8: See the shared connections between you and a possible new connection.

- **Some people have an Invite button.** If you see an email address and the Invite button instead of the Connect button, the person is a contact that you imported to your LinkedIn account who isn't currently on LinkedIn. If you click the Invite button, LinkedIn will send that person an invitation to join LinkedIn, similar to the invitation you sent as an example in Chapter 2.
- **Don't spend a lot of time reviewing your connections.** Instead, visit this page every once in a while to see whom you may want to connect with.

REMEMBER

- **Visit a person's profile first before clicking Connect.** I can't stress this enough. When you click Connect from the People You May Know, LinkedIn sends that person a generic invitation. If you click the person's name instead and then click Connect, a screen appears, where you can write a customized message. (I cover this in detail in "Sending Connection Requests," later in this chapter.)

Browsing your connections' networks

Although it's helpful for LinkedIn to help you search the network, sometimes nothing gives as good results as good old-fashioned investigation. From time to time, I like to browse the network of a first-degree connection to see whether he or she has a contact who should be a part of my network. I don't recommend spending a lot of your time this way, but doing spot checks by choosing a few friends at random can yield nice results.

Why is this type of research effective? Lots of reasons, including these:

» **You travel in the same circles.** If someone is a part of your network, you know that person from a past experience, whether you worked together, learned together, spoke at a conference together, or lived next door to each other. Whatever the experience, you and this contact spent time with other people, so chances are you have shared connections — or, better yet, you'll find people in that person's network whom you want to be a part of your network.

» **You might find someone newly connected.** Say that you've already searched your undergraduate alumni contacts and added as many people as you could find. As time passes, someone new may connect to one of your friends.

TIP

One effective way to keep updated about the people that your connections have recently added is to review your notifications. LinkedIn may create a section of the news feed to show you this information.

» **You might recognize someone whose name you didn't fully remember.** Many of us have a contact whom we feel we know well, have fun talking to, and consider more than just an acquaintance, but we can't remember that person's last name. Then, when you search a common contact's network and see the temporarily forgotten name and job title, you suddenly remember. Now you can invite that person to join your network. Another common experience is seeing the name and job title of a contact whose last name changed after marriage.

» **You might see someone you've wanted to get to know better.** Have you ever watched a friend talking to someone whom you wanted to add to your network? Maybe your friend already introduced you, so the other person knows your name, but you consider this person a casual acquaintance at best. When you see that person's name listed in your friend's network, you can take the opportunity to deepen that connection. Having a friend in common who can recommend you can help smooth the way.

WARNING

Looking through your friend's contacts list can be a cumbersome process if he or she has hundreds of contacts, so allow some time if you choose this technique.

To browse the network of one of your connections, follow these steps:

1. **Click the My Network icon in the top navigation bar to bring up your network page.**
2. **Under the Manage My Network header, click the Connections link.**

3. **Click the name of a first-degree connection.**

   Alternatively, search for the name by using the Search box on the home page. Then, select the name in the search results list.

   When perusing the person's profile, look for a *X* Connections link in the middle left side, below the name and the person's LinkedIn headline. If you don't see this link, you can't proceed with this process because the person has chosen to make his or her connection list private. If that's the case, you need to select a different first-degree connection.

4. **Click the Connections link of the first-degree connection.**

   For the example in these steps, I chose a friend and associate, Kristie Spilios, from Simi Valley, California. Her connection list is shown in Figure 5-9.

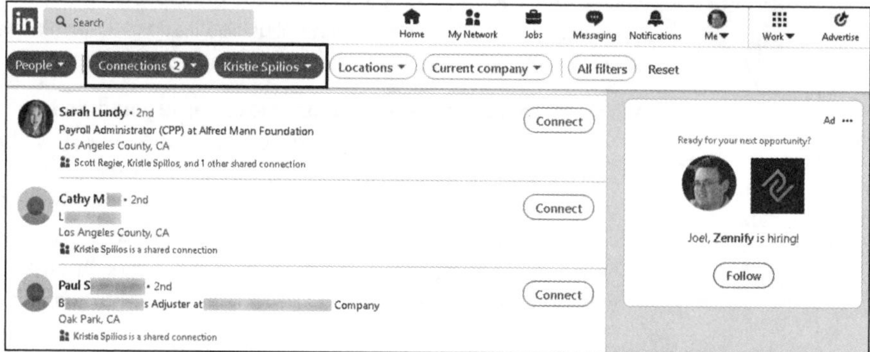

FIGURE 5-9: You can look through your friend's network.

5. **Look through the list and find someone to whom you'd like to send an invitation. Click the person's name to display his or her profile.**

   When I scan through Kristie's list, I see that someone I know, Sarah Lundy, is in her network. I click Sarah's name to display her profile, as shown in Figure 5-10.

6. **Click the blue Connect button.**

   LinkedIn prompts you with an option to customize the invitation by clicking the Add a Note button. When you do that, you see a new prompt window, as shown in Figure 5-11.

7. **To customize the invitation, click in the text box and write a message (up to 300 characters) to describe your connection to this person.**

   Remind the person you want to connect with exactly how you know him or her. Perhaps you simply have to indicate that you are a colleague, classmate, business partner, or friend, or have another association with this person.

8. **Click the blue Send button.**

   Presto! You're finished.

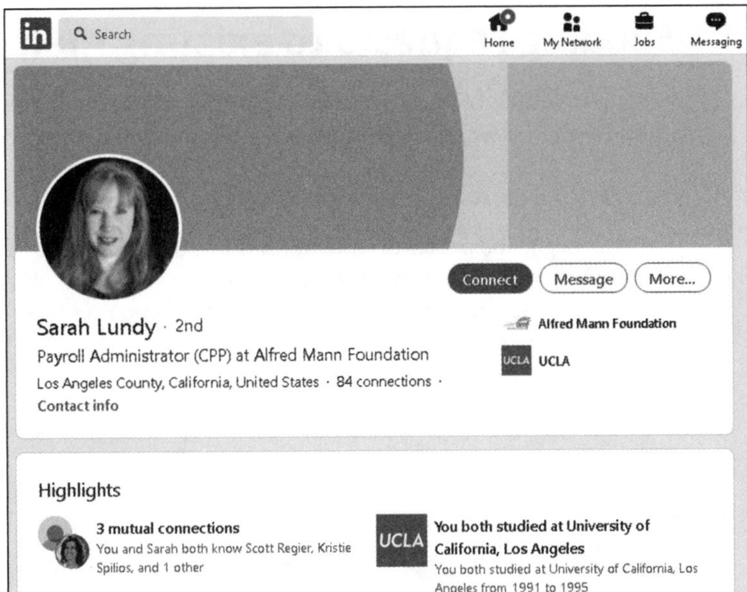

FIGURE 5-10: Pull up the person's profile to add the person to your network.

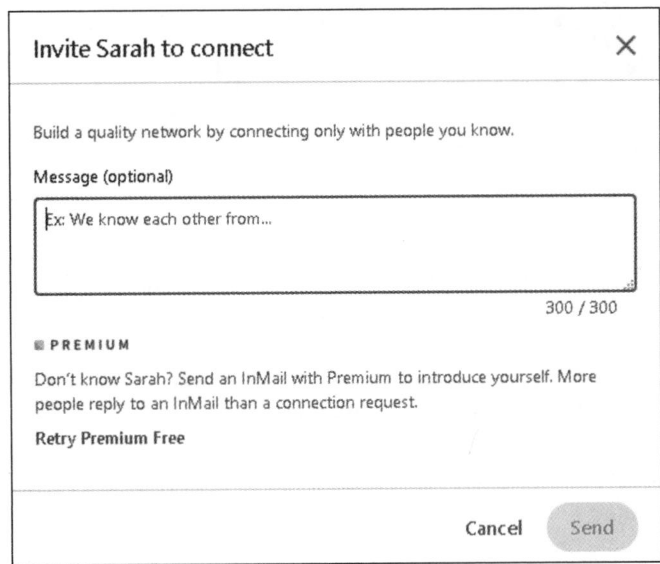

FIGURE 5-11: Send a custom invitation to your new contact.

Sending Connection Requests

You can check out previous sections of this chapter to find out how to search the entire user network and find people you want to invite to join your network. In this section, I focus on sending out the invitation, including how to go about inviting people who haven't yet joined LinkedIn.

Sending requests to existing members

When you're on a LinkedIn page and spot the name of a member who you want to invite to your network, follow these steps to send that person a connection request:

1. **Click the person's name to go to his or her profile page.**

   You might find people to invite by using one of the methods described in "Checking for members," earlier in this chapter. You might also find them while doing an advanced people search, which is covered in Chapter 4. Figure 5-12 shows a member's profile page.

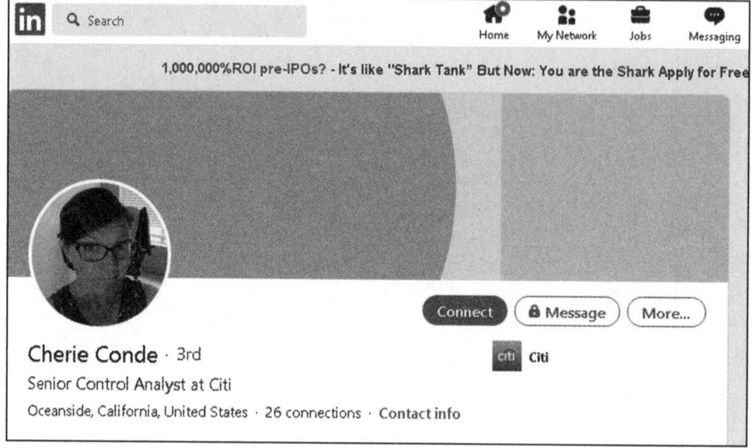

FIGURE 5-12: Add a person to your network from that person's profile page.

2. **Click the blue Connect button to start the connection request.**

   The Invitation page appears.

3. **If requested, provide the person's email address to help prove that you know the person (see Figure 5-13).**

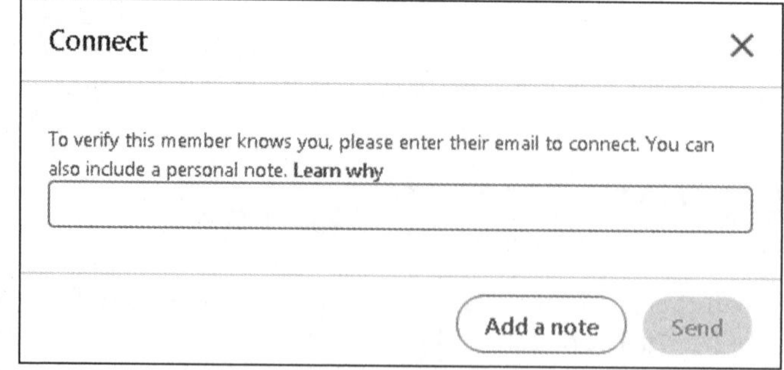

FIGURE 5-13: For some members, you must know their email address.

4. **(Optional but recommended) Click the Add a Note button and enter your invitation text in the Add a Note field.**

   I highly recommend that you compose a custom invitation rather than use the standard "I'd like to add you to my professional network on LinkedIn" text. In the example in Figure 5-14, I greet Cherie, acknowledge one of her recent achievements, and ask her to connect.

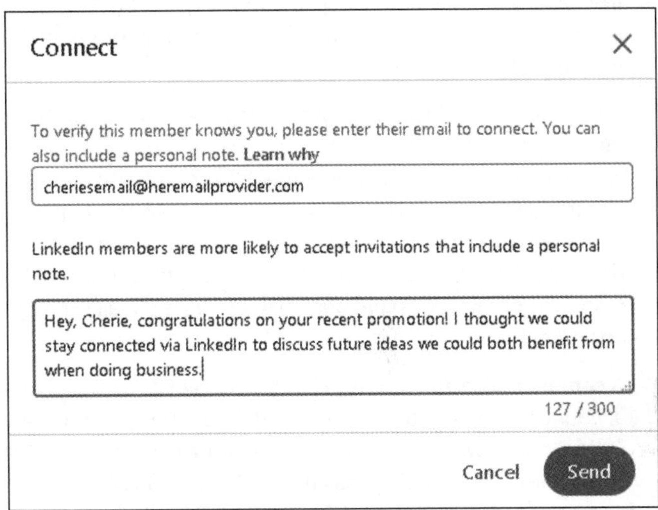

Connect
To verify this member knows you, please enter their email to connect. You can also include a personal note. Learn why
cheriesemail@heremailprovider.com
LinkedIn members are more likely to accept invitations that include a personal note.
Hey, Cherie, congratulations on your recent promotion! I thought we could stay connected via LinkedIn to discuss future ideas we could both benefit from when doing business.
127 / 300
Cancel
Send

FIGURE 5-14: Customize your invitation text.

5. **Click the blue Send button.**

   When the other party accepts your connection request, you're notified by email.

Understanding why you shouldn't use canned invitations

If you're having a rough or busy day, you might be tempted to send the canned invitation that LinkedIn displays when you go to the invitation request page. We all have things to do and goals to accomplish, so stopping to write a note for each invitation can grow tedious. However, it's important to replace that text with something that speaks to the recipient, for the following reasons:

- **The other person might not remember you.** Quite simply, your recipient can take one look at your name, see no additional information in the note that accompanied it, and think, "Who is this person?" A few might click your name to read your profile and try to figure it out, but most people are busy and won't take the time to investigate. They are likely to ignore your request. Not good.

- **The other person could report you as someone he doesn't know.** Having someone ignore your request isn't the worst possibility, though. Nope, the worst is being declined as unknown. Recipients of your invitation see an I Don't Know This Person button. If several people click this button from an invitation you sent, LinkedIn will eventually consider you a spammer and will suspend you — and possibly even remove your profile and account from the site!
- **You offer no motivation for a mutually beneficial relationship.** When people get an invitation request, they understand pretty clearly that you want something from them, whether it's access to them or to their network. If you've sent a canned invitation, they can't answer the question, "What's in it for me?" A canned invitation gives no motivation for or potential benefit of being connected to you. A custom note explaining that you'd like to swap resources or introduce that person to others is usually enough to encourage an acceptance.
- **A canned invitation implies that you don't care.** Some people will look at your canned invitation request and think, "This person doesn't have 30 to 60 seconds to write a quick note introducing herself? She must not think much of me." Worse, they may think, "This person just wants to increase her number of contacts to look more popular or to exploit my network." Either impression will quickly kill your chances of getting more connections.

Sending requests to nonmembers

Only members of LinkedIn can be part of anyone's network. Therefore, if you want to send a connection request to someone who hasn't yet joined LinkedIn, you must invite that person to create a LinkedIn account first. To do so, you can either send your invitee an email directly, asking him or her to join, or you can use a LinkedIn function that generates the email invitation that includes a link to join LinkedIn.

Either way, you need to have the nonmember's email address, and you'll probably have to provide your invitee with some incentive by offering reasons to take advantage of LinkedIn and create an account. (I give you some tips for doing that in the next section.)

When you're ready to send your request using LinkedIn, follow these steps:

1. **Click the My Network icon in the top navigation bar, and then scroll down and click the More Options link on the My Network page that appears.**

   The More Options link is below the Add Personal Contacts section. The Add Connections window appears.

2. **Click the Email Message icon (envelope) along the bottom middle of the page.**

   The envelope icon is to the right of the AOL button. The screen shown in Figure 5-15 appears.

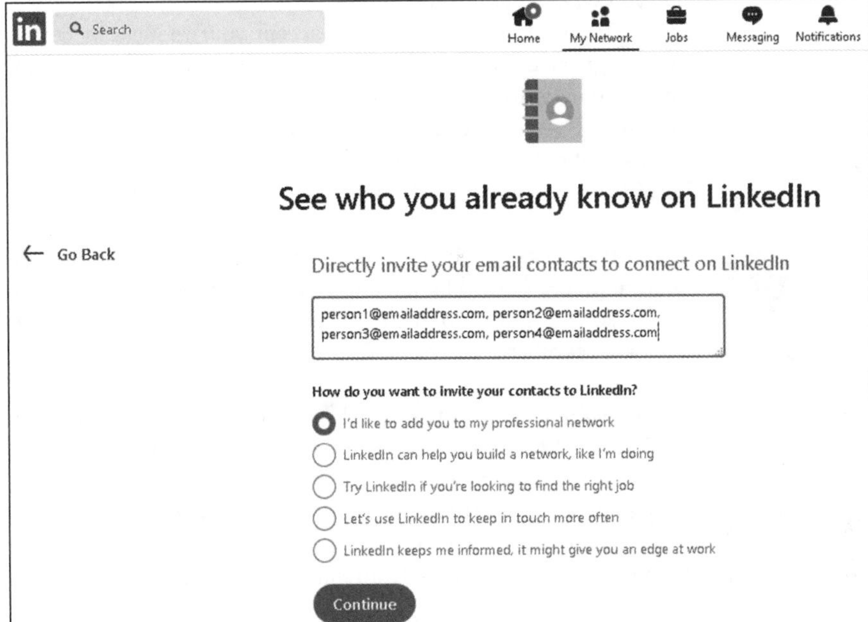

FIGURE 5-15: Fill in the email addresses of anyone you want to invite to join LinkedIn.

3. **In the box provided, fill in the email addresses of the people you want to invite to LinkedIn.**

4. **To personalize the invitation request to nonmembers a bit, select from a list of preprogrammed phrases or reasons to join LinkedIn, which will be included in the invitation.**

   Simply select the radio button next to the phrase you want included. As an extra step, you may want to contact those people via email or phone first to let them know that this request is coming and encourage them to consider joining LinkedIn.

5. **Click the blue Continue button.**

   A confirmation message pops up.

6. **To return to the Sync Contacts page, click the Go Back link on the left.**

   You can repeat the process at any time to invite additional people to join LinkedIn and be added to your network.

Communicating the value of joining LinkedIn

So you want to add some people to your network, but they haven't yet signed on to LinkedIn. If you want them to accept your request by setting up their account, you might need to tout the value of LinkedIn. After all, utilizing your existing and growing network is one of the most powerful sales tools, which is why all types of businesses — from e-commerce stores and retail businesses to service directories and social networking websites — use LinkedIn. Offering to help them build their profile or use LinkedIn effectively wouldn't hurt either.

REMEMBER

As of this writing, LinkedIn does not allow you to personalize your invitation to nonmembers (beyond choosing a canned phrase as detailed in the previous section), so you'll need to make this pitch either via email or directly with the person you are recruiting.

So, how do you make your pitch? If you send a thesis on the merits of LinkedIn, it'll most likely be ignored. Sending a simple "C'mon! You know you wanna . . ." request may or may not work. (You know your friends better than I.) You could buy them a copy of this book, but that could get expensive. (But I would be thrilled! C'mon! You know you wanna . . .) The simplest way is to mention some of the benefits they could enjoy from joining the site:

- **LinkedIn members always stay in touch with their connections.** If people you know move, change their email addresses, or change jobs, you still have a live link to them via LinkedIn. You'll always be able to see their new email addresses if you're connected (assuming that they provide it, of course).
- **LinkedIn members can tap into their friends' networks for jobs or opportunities, now or later.** Although someone might not need a job now, he or she may eventually need help, so why not access thousands or even millions of potential leads? LinkedIn has hundreds of millions of members in all sorts of industries, and people have obtained consulting leads, contract jobs, new careers, and even start-up venture capital or funding for a new film. After all, it's all about "who you know."

- **LinkedIn can help you build your own brand.** LinkedIn members get a free profile page to build their online presence, and can link to up to three of their own websites, such as a blog, personal website, social media page, or e-commerce store. The search engines love LinkedIn pages, which have high page rankings — and this can only boost your online identity.
- **LinkedIn can help you do all sorts of research.** You might need to know more about a company before an interview, or you're looking for a certain person to help your business, or you're curious what people's opinions would be regarding an idea you have. LinkedIn is a great resource in all these situations. You can use LinkedIn to get free advice and information, all from the comfort of your own computer.
- **Employers are using LinkedIn every day.** Many employers now use LinkedIn to do due diligence on a job seeker by reviewing his or her LinkedIn profile before an interview. If you're not on LinkedIn, an employer may see this as a red flag and it could affect your chances of getting the job.
- **A basic LinkedIn account is free, and joining LinkedIn is easy.** People have a lot of misconceptions about monthly fees or spending a lot of time updating their LinkedIn profiles. Simply remind people that joining is free, and that after they set up their profiles, LinkedIn is designed to take up little of their time keeping an active profile and benefitting from having an account.

Removing people from your network

The day might come when you feel you need to remove someone from your network. Perhaps you added the person in haste, or he repeatedly asks you for favors or introduction requests, or sends messages that you don't want to respond to. Not to worry — you're not doomed to suffer forever; simply remove the connection. When you do so, that person can no longer view your network or send you messages, unless he pays to send you an InMail message.

To remove a connection from your network, just follow these steps:

1. **While logged in to your LinkedIn account, click the My Network icon, on the top navigation bar.**
2. **Under the Manage My Network header, click Connections.**

   Your list of connections appears, as shown in Figure 5-16.
3. **Scroll through the list to find the connection to remove.**

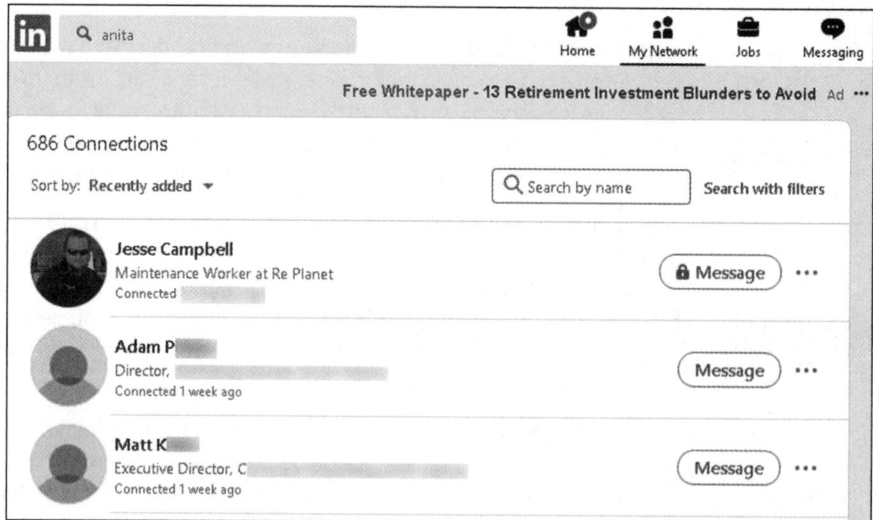

FIGURE 5-16: Find the connection you want to remove.

4. **To the far right of the person's name, click the three dots next to the Message button, and then select Remove Connection from the drop-down list that appears, as shown in Figure 5-17.**

   A pop-up box appears, warning you of what abilities you'll lose with this removal and asking you to confirm you want to remove the connection.

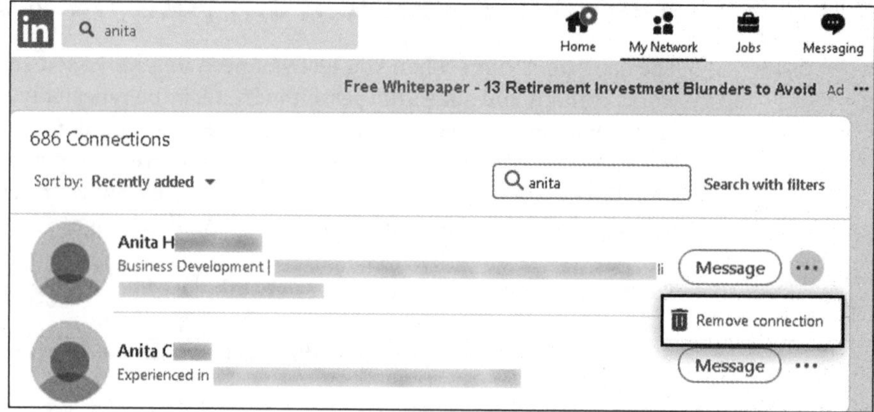

FIGURE 5-17: Remove your connection to this person.

5. **To remove the person from your network, click the Remove button, as shown in Figure 5-18.**

   Your removed connection won't be notified of the removal.

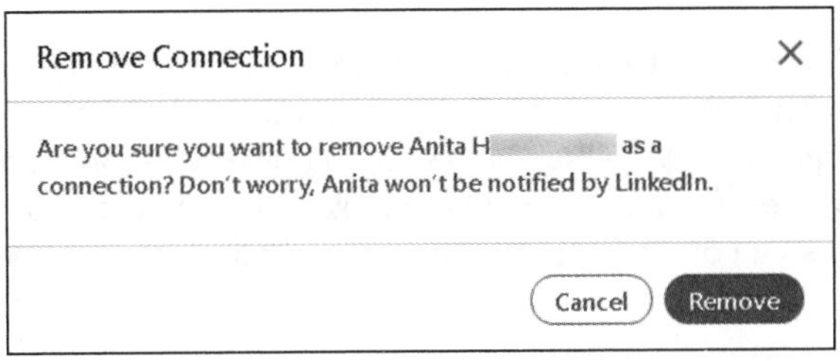

Remove Connection ×

Are you sure you want to remove Anita H[redacted] as a connection? Don't worry, Anita won't be notified by LinkedIn.

Cancel Remove

FIGURE 5-18: Make sure you understand what you'll lose by removing this connection.

Accepting (or Gracefully Declining) Invitations

In this chapter, I talk a lot about how and why you might send invitations and add people to your network, and even cover what to do when you need to remove someone from your network. But what about the flip side of that coin — that is, being the invitee? In this section, I offer some guidance on what to do when you have to decide whether to happily accept or gracefully decline an invitation.

When you receive an invitation to join someone's network of connections and you're not sure whether to accept or decline the invitation, ask yourself these questions:

- **How well do you know this person?** With any luck, the inviter has included a custom message clueing you in to who he or she is, in case you don't remember. You can, of course, click the name to read that person's profile, which usually helps trigger your memory. If you don't know or remember this person, you probably don't want to add him to your network just yet. If you do know the person, you need to consider whether he or she is worth adding to your network.
- **Does this person fit with the goals of your network?** As I mention early in this chapter, it's easier to put together a network when you've established a sense of the purpose you want it to serve. When you're looking at this invitation, simply ask yourself, "Does accepting this invitation help further my goals?"
- **Is this someone with whom you want to communicate and include in your network?** If you don't like someone or don't want to do business with him or her, you should certainly not feel obligated to accept the invitation. Keep in mind that these people will have access to your network and can hit you up with introduction messages and recommendation requests.

If you're thinking of declining an invitation, you can simply ignore the invitation message or click the X button on the screen to ignore the invitation. Optionally, you can respond to the person who sent you the invitation. Some people prefer to respond to be professional or polite, for example. If you decide to send a response message, instead of just ignoring the invite, here are some tips to help you do so gracefully:

- **Respond quickly.** If you wait to respond to the invitation and then decide to go ahead and decline the invite, the other person might be even more offended and confused. Respond quickly so that this issue isn't hanging over anyone's head.
- **If necessary, ask for more information.** If you feel uncomfortable because you don't know the person well but want to consider the invitation before you decline, respond with a request for more information, such as, "I appreciate your interest, but I am having trouble placing our previous meetings. What is your specific interest in connecting with me on LinkedIn? Please let me know how we know each other and what your goals are for LinkedIn. Thanks again."
- **Respond politely but with a firm no.** You can simply write something along the lines of, "Thank you for your interest; I appreciate your eagerness. Unfortunately, because I'm not familiar with you, I'm not interested in connecting with you on LinkedIn just yet." Then, if you want, you can spell out the terms in which you might be interested in connecting, such as if the opportunity ever arises to get to know the person better or if he or she is referred to you by a friend.

» Sending InMail

» Managing invitations and introduction requests

Chapter 6

Managing Messages and InMail

Two of the goals of using LinkedIn are to strengthen your existing personal network of friends and colleagues and to expand your network to include new people to see how they might fit into your network, goals, or ambitions. However, the system of contacting people requires some order and decorum (otherwise, nobody would feel comfortable signing up for the site in the first place). Therefore, LinkedIn offers a way to communicate with your existing network that is integrated with a way to meet and connect with people outside your immediate network: LinkedIn messages and InMail. Not so coincidentally, I cover those concepts in this chapter.

You use LinkedIn messages to contact a friend about anything, from a simple congratulations on a work anniversary to a request for a favor for you or a friend. InMail enables you to directly communicate with anyone in the LinkedIn network through a private LinkedIn message. I also cover what to do when you get a request from a connection on LinkedIn.

Using InMail versus Using LinkedIn Messages

Your first question is most likely, "What's the difference between sending a regular LinkedIn message and using InMail?" (Figure 6-1 shows a typical LinkedIn inbox, with the message marked *InMail* as an example of receiving InMail.) The answer comes down to how connected you are with the person you want to contact.

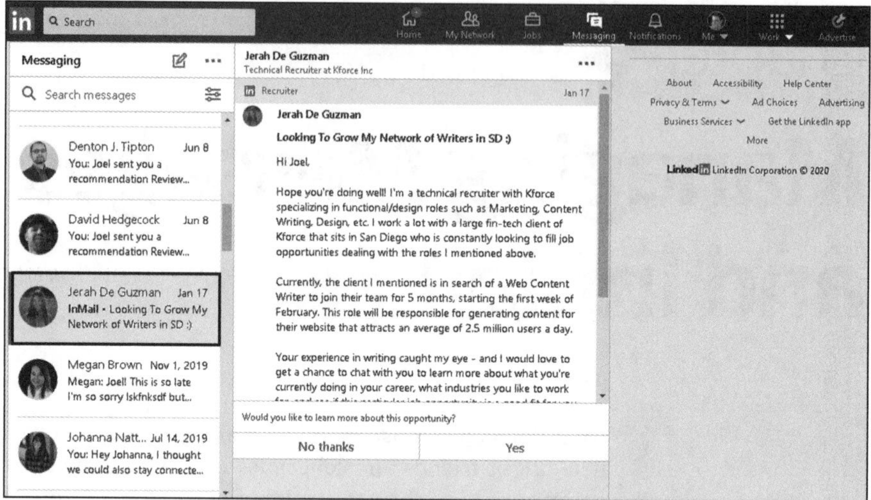

FIGURE 6-1: LinkedIn organizes your messages in the LinkedIn inbox.

WARNING

Every LinkedIn user decides on his own contact level, and a user can decline to allow any message or InMail to reach him, regardless of sender. If you don't want to receive any messages or InMail, simply deselect all the Contact Settings options. (See Chapter 11 for the section on checking your contact settings.)

If you don't mind your network sending you messages but don't want to have to deal with any InMail, just deselect the InMail option in the Communications part of the Settings & Privacy page, specifically the Messages from the Who Can Reach You section. Otherwise, leave the InMail option selected, because it's a valuable tool for sending and receiving communication with people who might become a valuable part of your network or help you with one of your professional goals.

Understanding LinkedIn messages

On LinkedIn, communication with your network (and the LinkedIn network at large) occurs for a variety of reasons. Whether the message is mundane or ultra-important, being able to communicate via LinkedIn makes your professional life a little easier because you don't have to dig up email addresses or past conversations, and you have the sender's LinkedIn profile information at your fingertips as you communicate. LinkedIn has created a centralized Messages system that accommodates all varieties of communication between you and other LinkedIn users.

Here are some benefits of the LinkedIn messaging system:

- **Threaded conversations:** In some email systems, every message you receive sits by itself in your inbox or a special folder, and every message you send is in the Sent folder. Therefore, to reconstruct a conversation, you may have to hunt through many messages. With LinkedIn, all your messages with a person are on one thread, so you can review the history of your conversation. You see the dates when each message was sent or received, as shown in Figure 6-2. You can exchange files as well as text, save time by using prebuilt replies, and most importantly, read a chronological thread of your discussion.

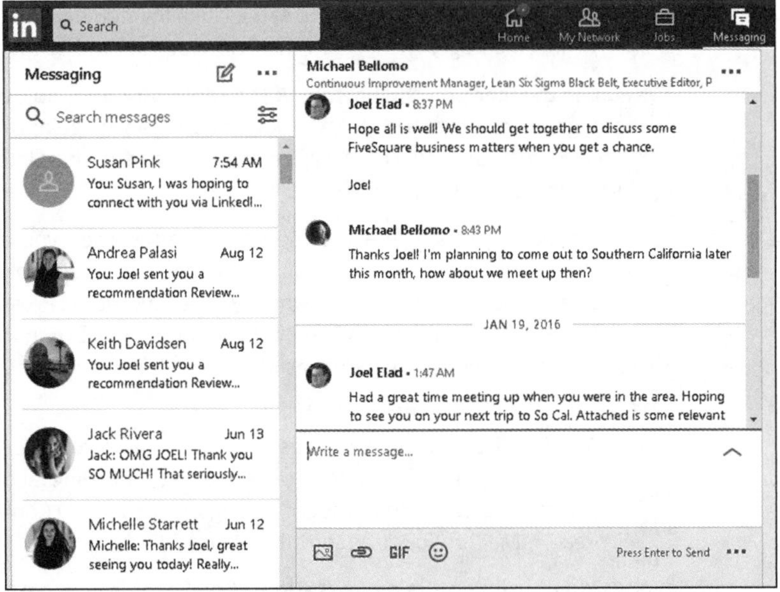

FIGURE 6-2: LinkedIn combines your sent and received messages as a thread.

- **Easy searches:** Type a name or keyword in the search messages box below the Messaging header, and LinkedIn will check all messages for those terms. Some systems allow you to search only the subject line quickly, but with a LinkedIn Messages search, you can search the subject line and message body quickly and the results pop up in the same screen.

- **Group messaging:** You can start one single thread but have multiple recipients to the message, so that everyone in the group can read and interact simultaneously. Even if you start a conversation with just one person, you can add more connections to the conversation as you communicate. You can also decide whether to include the conversation history so that newcomers to the conversation can see past discussions.

Understanding your inbox

Your communications hub is the LinkedIn inbox, which you access by clicking the Messaging icon in the top navigation bar. The list of messages in your inbox appears (refer to Figure 6-1).

Keep the following in mind when navigating your inbox:

- **Starting a new message:** To start a new conversation, click the pencil in a box icon. A message box appears in the middle of the screen. In the top line in the message box, type the name of the LinkedIn member to whom you want to send a message. Then, below that line, type your message.
- **Using the icons on the bottom of the reply window:** You can click the icons along the bottom of the reply window to attach an image or a file to the conversation or send a preprogrammed response (such as Interested, Maybe later, or No thanks in Figure 6-3).

  In addition, by clicking the three dots below the text box, you can choose between the Click Send option, where the message is sent only when you click the Send button (which appear where you see the words Press Enter to Send, in Figure 6-4), and the Press Enter to Send option, which mimics the functionality of a chat window, where pressing the Enter key sends your reply. See Figure 6-4.
- **Using the filters:** By default, you see all messages in your inbox. If you click the filter icon to the right of the Search Messages heading (above your first message), you can choose a specific category, such as My Connections, Unread, InMail, or Spam, as shown in Figure 6-5.
- **Taking action on the conversation:** Click the three dots next to the person's name in the main window to display action items for this conversation, as shown in Figure 6-6. You can add people to the existing conversation by creating a group chat, mute the conversation (which turns off your email notifications when new comments are made in this conversation), mark it as unread, delete it, or archive it.

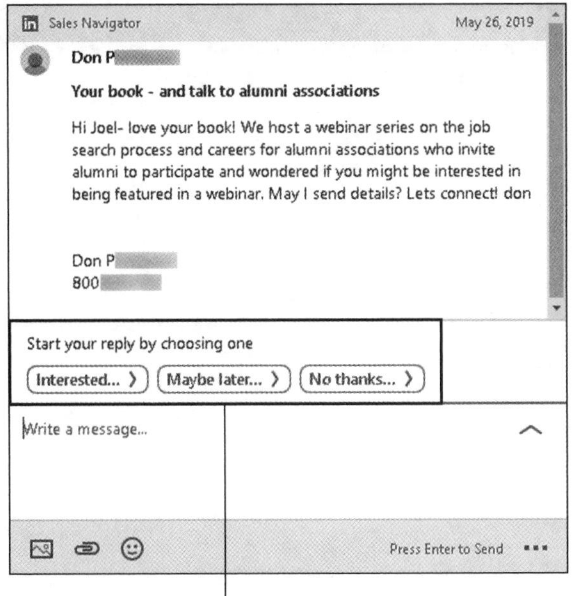

FIGURE 6-3: LinkedIn offers preprogrammed responses so you can reply quickly.

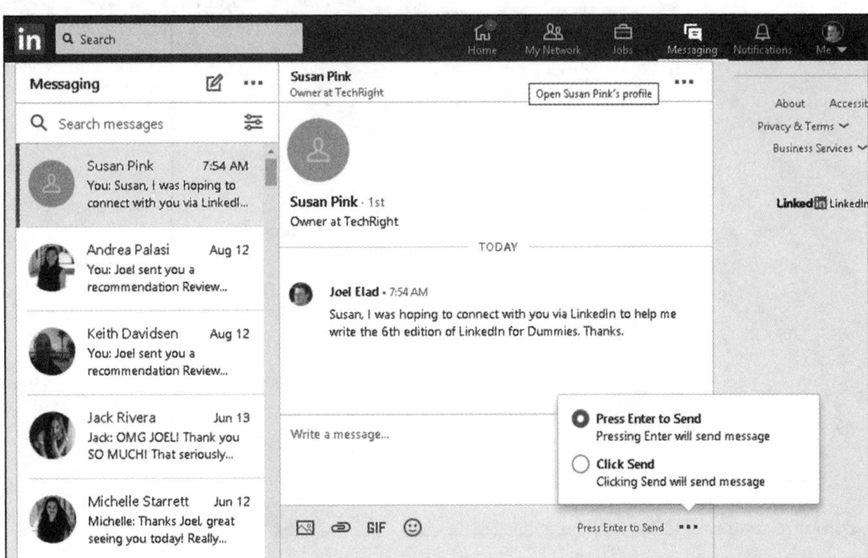

FIGURE 6-4: Use the Enter key or the Send button to send a reply.

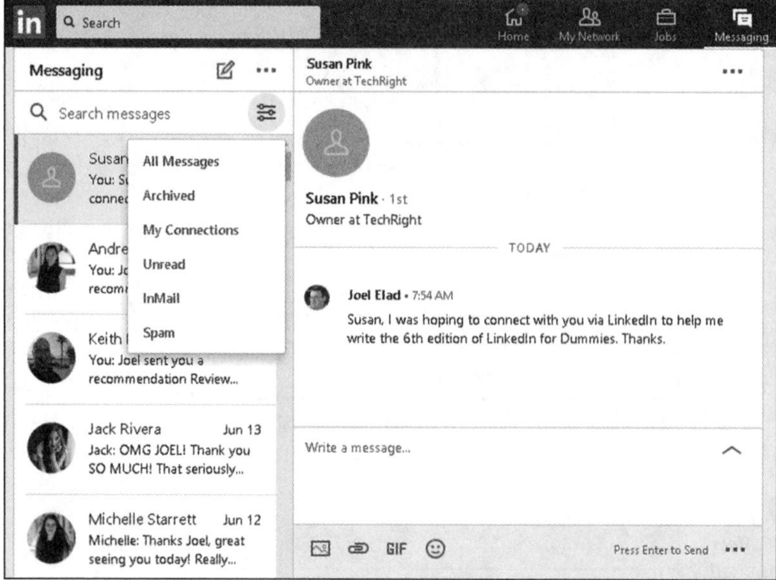

FIGURE 6-5: Use LinkedIn filters to isolate types of LinkedIn messages for easy viewing.

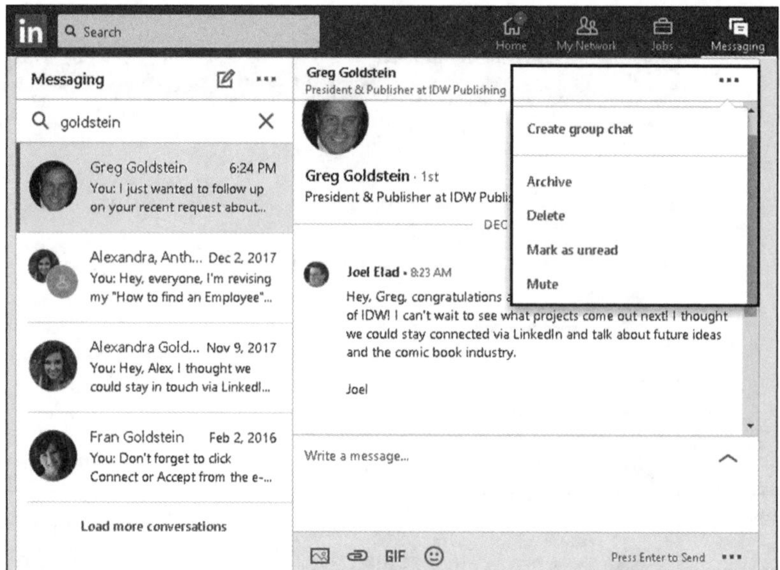

FIGURE 6-6: LinkedIn offers ways to expand your communication.

Getting to know InMail

Because everyone on LinkedIn has a profile and a secure message inbox, communicating with other people online is easy. LinkedIn allows you to send InMail directly to an intended party, regardless of whether she is directly or indirectly connected with you. The email is delivered immediately to the recipient's web-based inbox on the LinkedIn site (and, if the recipient has configured her settings to get emails of all her InMail, in the inbox at her email address). The sender never learns the recipient's address, so each party has some privacy. The recipient can then read your profile and decide whether to respond.

The cost of using InMail depends on your premium account level. If you have a Business Plus or Job Seeker account, you can purchase additional InMail credits (1 credit allows you to send one message) at a cost of $10 per InMail message. Premium accounts, such as the Job Seeker account for $29.99/month, come with a set number of InMail credits per month that roll over to the next month if unused. The Job Seeker account gets 5 credits per month, the Business Plus account gets 15 credits per month, the Sales Navigator Professional account gets 20 credits per month, and the Recruiter Lite account gets 30 credits per month.

Here are some benefits of using InMail:

- **Delivery is instant.** With InMail, you simply write your message or request and send it directly to the intended party. There's no delay as when you send a request through your network to reach that person, where that gets passed from person to person and waits for approval or forwarding.
- **You owe no favors.** Sometimes, you just want to reach somebody without asking your friends to vouch for you. InMail allows you to send a request to someone new without involving anyone else.
- **It's sure to be delivered.** With introductions, the party or parties involved in the middle could choose to deny your request and not pass along the message. With InMail, you know that the intended party will get a copy of your message in his or her email account and LinkedIn inbox.

Sending InMail

If you're looking to connect with someone right away and you don't have an immediate or secondary connection with someone, you can use the InMail feature to send a message directly to another LinkedIn member without anyone else getting involved.

REMEMBER

This feature is currently available to premium members of LinkedIn with available InMail credits. If you're using a free account, you have to upgrade your account or earn InMail credits through posting a job offer. Consult the LinkedIn Help Center for more information (`https://help.linkedin.com`).

InMail is basically a private email message that enables you to reach other members, but it protects those members' privacy and email address information. If your message is accepted, you'll receive a message in your LinkedIn inbox with the other party's name and link to her profile, and you can communicate further. In some cases, you see only the other person's professional headline first, and then you see the person's name after she accepts the InMail message.

When you're ready to send someone an InMail, follow these steps:

1. **While logged in to LinkedIn, search for the person you'd like to meet.**

   You can use the Search box at the top of any LinkedIn page, or you can click the My Network icon and search your friend's networks. (See Chapter 4 for details on searching LinkedIn.)

2. **From the list of search results, click the name of the person you want to contact.**

   The person's profile page appears. Suppose that I want to connect with Lynn Dralle, the Queen of Auctions, who can teach me how to sell on eBay. When I look at her profile, I see the Message button. When I click the Message button, I see the pop-up message to upgrade to Premium (see Figure 6-7), which means she is open to receiving InMail.

REMEMBER

   You need to upgrade to the Premium service to be able to purchase an InMail credit and send a message to this person before proceeding.

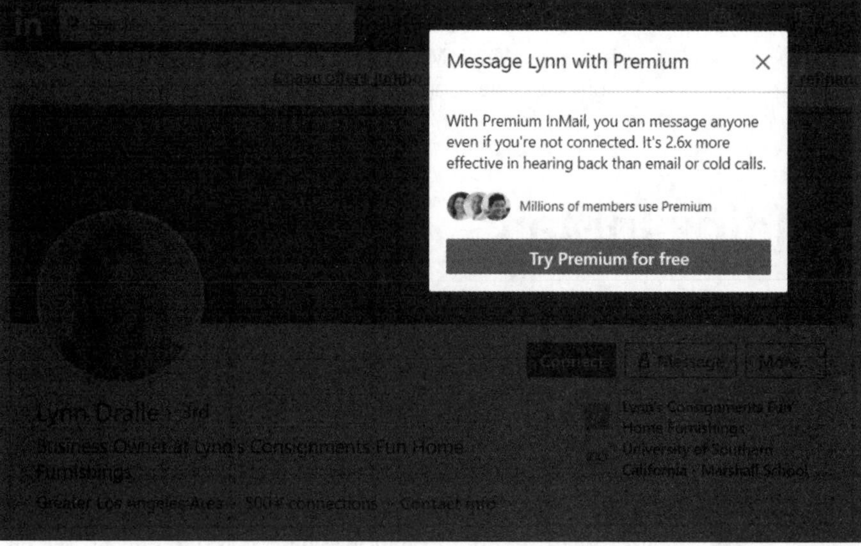

FIGURE 6-7: See whether the person you want to contact can receive InMail.

3. **Click the Send InMail link.**

   The New Message form appears. At the bottom of the form, you can see that message will use one credit.

4. **Type a subject, and then type your message in the text box.**

   Keep your message focused on why you would like to talk with this person and what information you hope to exchange. ("Planning your approach to each person," later in this chapter, has advice that applies to InMail messages as well.) At the bottom of your message, you will see how many InMail credits you have; remember that you need at least one credit to send the message.

TIP

   Be sure to proofread your message before sending it. If you send a message with typos, it won't help your case at all.

5. **Click the Send button.**

   Your recipient receives the InMail in her LinkedIn inbox and can decide whether to accept it. (If she has configured LinkedIn to get immediate emails of her InMail messages, she will receive the InMail in her email account inbox as well.) If your message is accepted, it's up to the recipient to contact you in return. Be patient. While you're waiting, I recommend a game of Connect Four or Internet Chess.

Managing Invitations

As you grow your network, you need to keep track of the invitations you send and receive. (For more on invitations, see Chapter 2.) This section describes way to manage your invitations on the LinkedIn website.

Tracking sent invitations

To avoid sending a repeat invitation by mistake, or to review your sent invitations to see whether someone has responded, you need to track your sent invitations.

Here's how to track your sent invitations:

1. **Click the My Network icon from the top navigation bar of any LinkedIn page.**
2. **Click the See All X link to the right of the Invitations header.**

   A screen appears with all pending invitations, as shown in Figure 6-8.

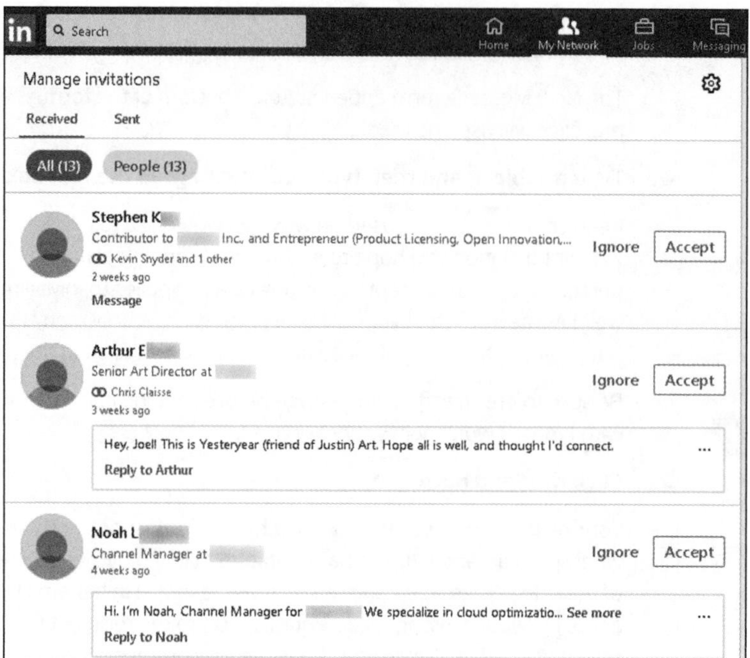

FIGURE 6-8: Track pending invitations.

3. **Click Sent, below the Manage Invitations header.**

   The Sent Invitations page shown in Figure 6-9 appears. The length of time since you sent the invitation is displayed below the person's name, along with the person's LinkedIn headline and profile photo.

To withdraw an invitation request, click the Withdraw link to the right of the person's name. LinkedIn automatically deletes the sent invitation and it drops off your list of sent invitations. When you withdraw the request, no message is sent to the other person. If you want, you can then send the person a new invitation request through either LinkedIn or, if you have the person's contact information, your own email account.

Tracking received invitations

When growing your LinkedIn network, you should be responsive to others who want to add you to their LinkedIn connections lists. To review your received invitations, follow these steps:

1. **Click the My Network icon from the top navigation bar.**
2. **Click the See All X link to the right of the Invitations header.**

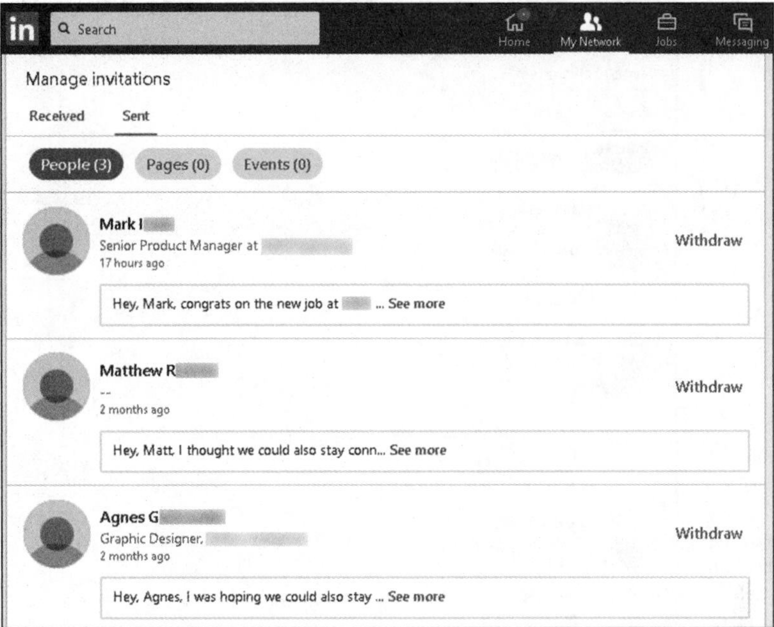

FIGURE 6-9: See your sent invitations and how long it's been since you sent the requests.

A list of invitations you've received appears. You can click a person's name or profile photo to see his or her profile. If you have mutual connections with the person requesting to connect with you, you can click the icon that looks like two conjoined rings below the person's headline to see which connections you have in common.

3. **To accept a pending invitation, click the Accept link. To ignore the invitation, click the Ignore link.**

   If you want to reply to the person without immediately accepting the invitation (say, to get clarification if you don't recognize the person), click the Message link below the person's name to generate a LinkedIn message where you can ask for clarification or let the person know that you plan not to accept the invitation, for example. In some cases, if the person wrote a note with his or her invitation, you'll see not the Message link but a special Reply to X link (see Figure 6-10), which you can use to communicate with the other person before acting on the invitation request.

   After you click the Accept or Ignore link, the invitation disappears from your view. If another invitation requires action, it appears in the list.

4. **Continue to act on each invitation in your list until there are no more pending invitations.**

FIGURE 6-10: Reply to an invitation before accepting or ignoring it.

Setting Up an Introduction

Say you're at a party with your friend Michael, and you say to him, "I'd like to meet someone who can help me with a few software tasks for my company." Michael looks around, sees his friend James, and introduces you to James by saying, "Hello, James. This is my entrepreneur friend from business school, [*your name here*]. [*Your name here*], this is my old buddy James. He and I studied computer science together in college." After that, Michael might provide additional background information about each person.

On LinkedIn, this example is called an *introduction*. Normally, you would start an introduction with a second-degree network member, who is a friend of a friend. When you want to bring two or more parties together, you usually need to think about the process, whether it's figuring out what both parties have in common, how you'll introduce party A to party B, or when and where to make the introduction.

The following sections give you tips and pointers for how to make the introduction process go smoothly.

Planning your approach to each person

When you want to ask someone in your first-degree network to introduce you to a second-degree network member, plan your request before sending it. Preparing a good-quality and proper introduction goes a long way toward keeping your network helpful and enthusiastic, and increases your chances of making a new and valuable connection.

You need to prepare two messages: one for your intended recipient and one for your connection. Each message has a specific objective. Start with the message to your connection, keeping the following tips in mind:

- **Be honest and upfront.** Say exactly what you want to achieve so there are no surprises. If you tell your friend that you're hoping her contact will be a new bowling buddy, but then ask the contact for funding for a new business plan, you're in trouble. Even if your eventual goal is something big, such as asking someone for a job, start with a reasonable goal, such as asking for information or advice. Let the other person know that you'd like to keep talking to see what possibilities might occur in the future.
- **Be polite and courteous.** Remember, you're asking your friend to vouch for you or back you up when your request goes to the intended party. So be polite when making your request and show your gratitude regardless of the outcome.
- **Be ready to give in order to get.** One of the best ways to go far with your network is to offer a reciprocal favor, such as introducing your friend to one of your other contacts.
- **Be patient.** Although you might be eager and under a deadline, your friends probably operate on a different schedule. Some people are online all the time and others log in to LinkedIn infrequently. And most people are disconnected at times, such as when they're on vacation or behind on a project. Asking your friend every day whether she forwarded your request is a surefire way of getting that request bounced back.

When writing your message to your intended recipient, keep these tips in mind:

- **Be honest and upfront.** Just like with your friend, when you have a specific goal or request, make it known in the message. If the recipient finds out that you have an ulterior motive, he will feel deceived, which is not the feeling to create when asking someone for help.
- **Be succinct.** You're asking someone for his time, resources, or advice, so don't beat around the bush. Introduce yourself in your first sentence or two. Then explain why you're contacting the recipient and how you hope he can help you.

» **Be original.** If you stick to LinkedIn's sample text, your message will have an air of "Hey, I want to talk to you, but I don't want to spend a few seconds of effort to tell you what I'm after." When you customize your message, you have a greater chance of capturing the other person's attention, especially if your intended recipient gets a lot of requests.

» **Be ready to give in order to get.** You're asking for help, so again, be ready to give something, whether it's gratitude, a reciprocal favor, or something more tangible. Most people are eager to help, especially when they understand the situation, but having something to offer in exchange doesn't hurt. Explain to your recipient how you might provide something useful in return.

Sending an introduction request message

When you've prepared your messages (one to your contact and one to the recipient) and you're ready to send an introduction request message, follow these steps:

1. **While logged in to LinkedIn, search for the person you'd like to meet.**

   Use the Search box at the top of any LinkedIn page, or click the My Network icon and search your friend's networks. (See Chapter 4 for the lowdown on searching LinkedIn.)

2. **In the list of search results, click the name of the person you want to contact.**

   The recipient's profile page appears.

3. **Scroll down the page to the Highlights section.**

   The Highlights section features the mutual connections you have with this person, if any, as well as other facts that you have in common. (If you don't have any mutual connections, you won't see the Highlights section.)

   Suppose I want to be introduced to Sarah Lundy, Payroll Supervisor at a charitable foundation. When I get to Sarah's profile page (shown in Figure 6-11), I see that I have a connection to her in the form of a business contact and friend of both Sarah and myself, Kristie Spilios.

4. **Click the Mutual Connections link.**

   A list of first connections appears, as shown in Figure 6-12.

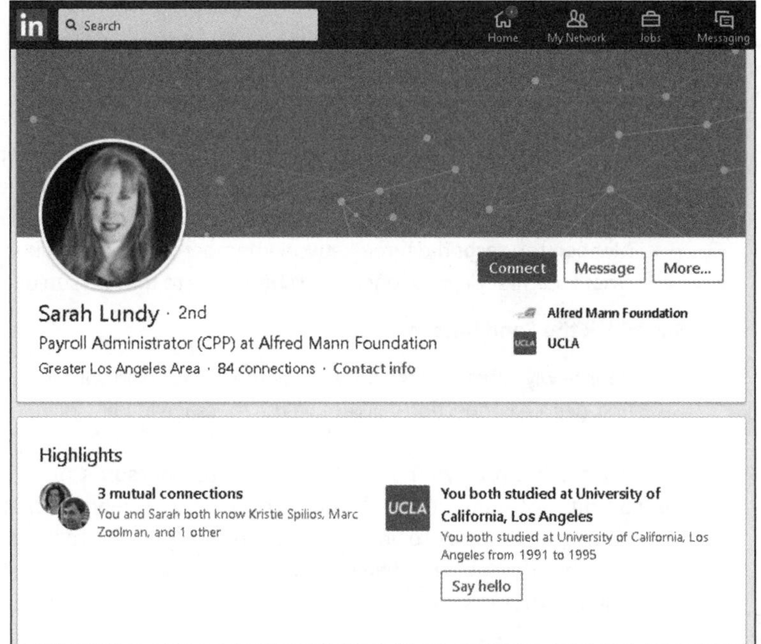

FIGURE 6-11: See how you're connected to your intended recipient via LinkedIn.

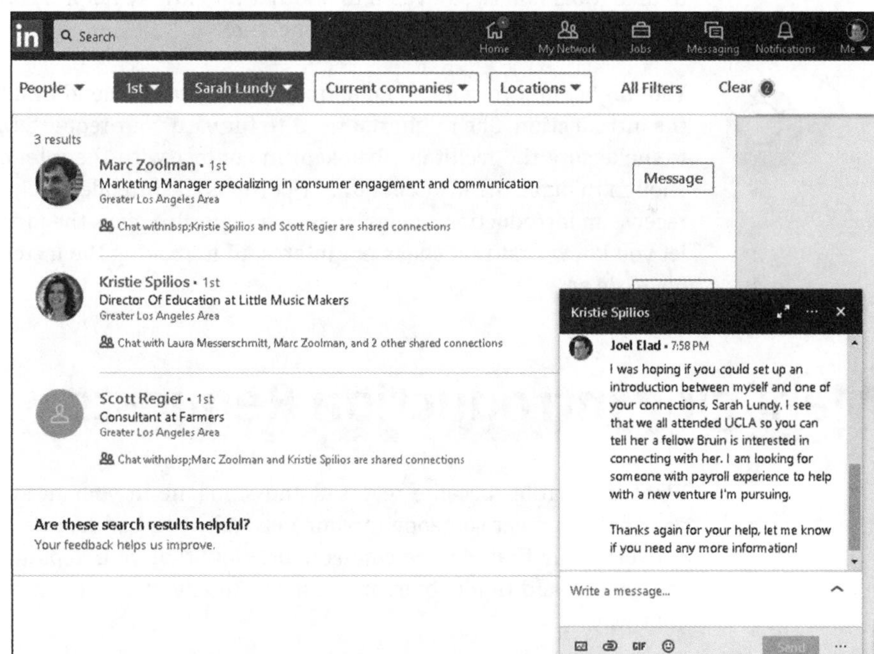

FIGURE 6-12: Message the person you are requesting to make your introduction.

5. **To start a LinkedIn message with your first-degree connection, click the Message button.**

   A new window appears at the bottom of the screen, with a new message window to your first-degree connection. If the window doesn't open, click the New Message icon and type the name of your first-degree connection, and send her a message that starts the introduction process, as shown in Figure 6-12. Mention the second-degree network member whom you'd like to meet, and what your first-degree connection should say to that person on your behalf.

6. **Click the Send button.**

   Your newly sent message appears as the top entry in your inbox screen. Your first-degree connection will receive the message in her LinkedIn inbox.

After that, it's up to your friend to share that person's profile with you so you can communicate directly with the second-degree network member. To add this second-degree member to your network, one of you has to invite the other person to your network. You can always view your introduction request message in your list of LinkedIn messages.

Keep in mind some LinkedIn members are inactive or may not respond, so try not to take it personally. Move on to another potentially helpful contact, especially if you have more than one mutual connection.

TIP

You might want to send an email to your facilitator friend first before requesting the introduction. She might not want to forward your request. Or you might want to make sure the facilitator has kept in contact with the intended recipient well enough to make the introduction. Or perhaps the intended recipient is too busy to receive an introduction request message. This also gives the facilitator a chance to let you know first that she is not interested in making the introduction or is unable to do so.

Managing Introduction Requests

What if the roles become reversed and someone in your network is looking for your help to meet someone in your network? You can facilitate the introduction between your first-degree connections. Now that your reputation is on the line too, you should think about and respond to any introduction requests that come your way.

You have only two options for handling an introduction request:

- Accept it by sending a message to both the person requesting the introduction and the party it's intended for, so they can communicate directly with each other.
- Politely decline it.

I cover these two options in more detail in the following sections. However you decide to handle the request, keep these tips in mind:

- **Act or reply quickly.** The reason why LinkedIn works so well is that people are active with their networks and build on their profile by answering questions, meeting new people, or joining groups. When you get a message requesting an introduction, act on it or respond to the person with the reason why you won't act on it. Ignoring the message isn't a productive use of the LinkedIn system and makes you look unprofessional.
- **Don't be afraid to ask for clarification.** Sometimes you need the person to remind you exactly how the two of you are connected. Check the note from the person for a reminder that helps you place her, as well as the information that LinkedIn keeps on both of you. If there's no information, don't be afraid to shoot back a message and ask for clarification or a gentle reminder.
- **Read your friend's request before forwarding.** Chances are good that the person to whom you forward this request might come back to you and ask, "Hey, why did I get this?" or "What do you really think about this person?" If you don't know the details of your friend's request, the intended party might think you're a rubber-stamper who sends requests without screening them, which lowers this person's impression of you. Knowing what your friend is requesting can help you decide how to promote and encourage the connection, perhaps by giving you an idea of how best to approach the intended party.

Accepting requests and forwarding the introduction

When you're ready to accept your friend's request and make the introduction, follow these steps:

1. **Click the Messaging icon in the top navigation bar.**
2. **In your inbox, display the message in which your friend is asking for the introduction.**

Your inbox of messages appears. On the left side of the screen, look for and click the message where the person asks for the introduction. The full message appears in the middle of the screen, as shown in Figure 6-13. In this example, I received a request from Jesse Campbell to be introduced to one of my contacts, Doug Tondro.

REMEMBER

Read the full text before acting on the request. Don't just skim it — you might miss an important detail.

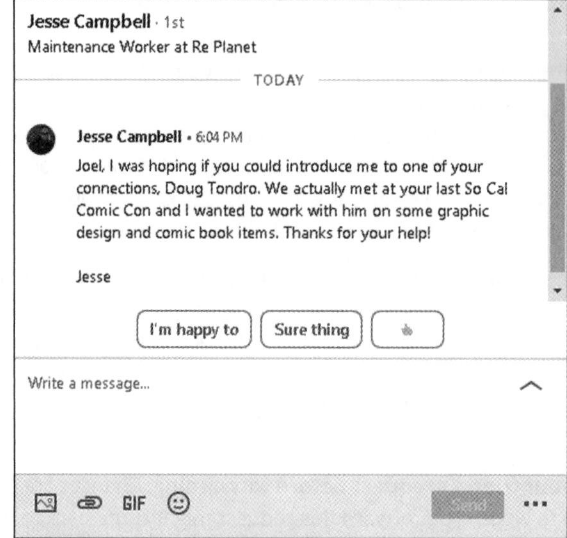

FIGURE 6-13: Look in your inbox for messages requesting an introduction.

3. **Search for the person he wants to meet.**
4. **Display the person's profile, click the More button, and then select Share Profile from the list to start the introduction.**

   A newly created message appears, as shown in Figure 6-14. You can see the link to Doug Tondro's profile in the text box.

5. **In the subject line of the message you just created, type the name of the person requesting the introduction and the name of the person you're introducing.**

   In this example, since Jesse asked to meet Doug Tondro, and I'm sharing Doug's profile, I enter Jesse's and Doug's names in the subject line so they each receive a copy of this message.

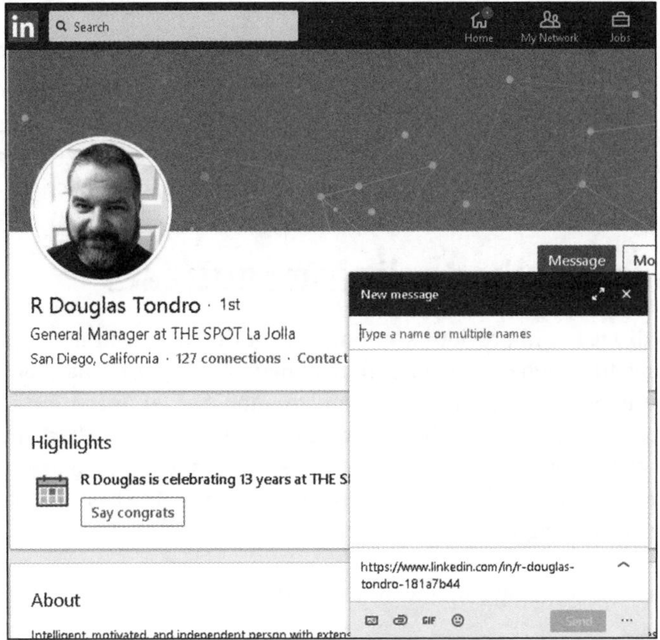

FIGURE 6-14: Share someone's profile to make the introduction.

6. **Click inside the message box to add text so the person receiving the introduction request understands why you're sending the message, as shown in Figure 6-15.**

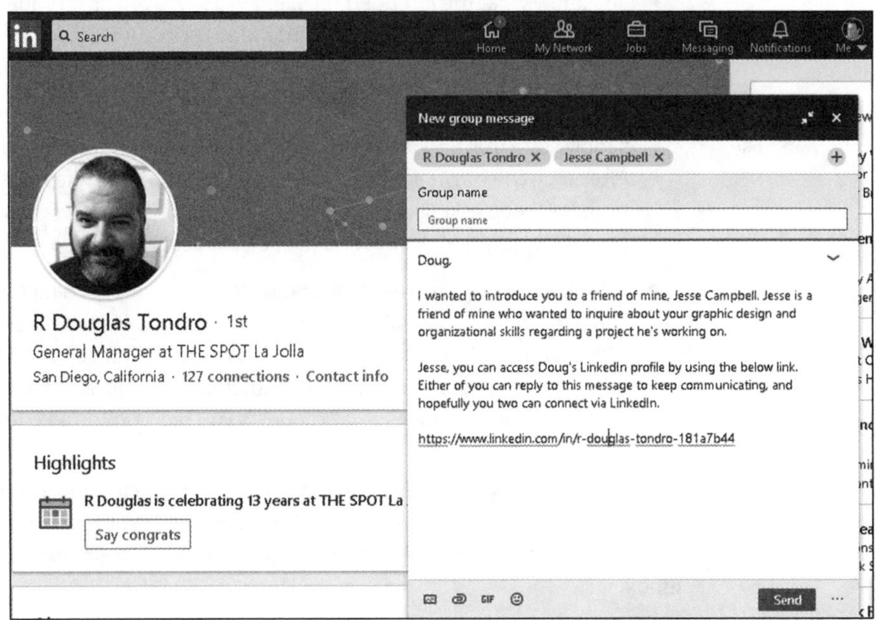

FIGURE 6-15: Write an introduction request on behalf of your contact.

7. **Click the Send button to send the request.**

   In this case, both Jesse Campbell and Doug Tondro will receive a LinkedIn message from me with the ability to see each other's profile. Jesse will not be able to send Doug a direct email, and Doug can decide whether to reach out to Jesse and form a connection by sending him an invitation.

Gracefully declining requests

As discussed in previous sections, one of the most common types of messages on LinkedIn is when someone in your network requests that you ask someone else you know for a favor. It's not uncommon to feel uncomfortable contacting the second person to get that favor for the first person. Perhaps you don't know enough about the person who made the request, or you're unclear about that person's true motivations. Whatever the reason, the best response is to gracefully decline the request.

Here are some tips on how to respond:

- **It's not you, it's me.** The most common way to decline is to simply inform the initial contact that you're not that deeply connected with the intended recipient, and you don't feel comfortable passing on a request to someone who isn't a strong contact.
- **The recipient doesn't respond well to this approach.** You can reply that you know what the intended recipient will say, from past requests or experiences. Because you feel that the intended recipient wouldn't be interested, you would rather not waste anyone's time in sending the request.
- **I just don't feel comfortable passing along the request.** Be honest and simply state that you don't feel right passing on the request you've received. After all, if the original contact doesn't understand your hesitation, he'll probably keep asking, and LinkedIn will want you to follow up on any unresolved introduction. Honesty is usually the best policy.
- **I think your request needs work.** Because you're vouching for this person, you don't want to pass along a shoddy or questionable request that could reflect badly on you. In this case, simply respond that you think the request needs to be reworded or clarified, and offer concrete suggestions on what should be said as well as what requests you feel comfortable forwarding.

When you're ready to decline the request, simply click Reply on the LinkedIn message and let the person requesting the favor know your reasons for not acting on his request. The person asking for the favor will see your response in his LinkedIn inbox.

contacts

» Understanding LinkedIn endorsements

» Endorsing your network connections

» Approving and displaying others' endorsements of you

Chapter 7

Interacting with and Endorsing Your Network

Let's look inward for a moment and think about the basic building block of your LinkedIn network — your relationship with each of your first-degree connections. Each of these relationships has a different identity, from the colleague you just met and added to your network, to a lifelong friend. LinkedIn wants to help you manage the qualities of that relationship, not just the fact that you know that person. This way, LinkedIn becomes more of your hub for managing your professional network and building your own brand or business or both.

In this chapter, I discuss two concepts that help you maintain a strong and vibrant network of connections on LinkedIn: interacting with your network and LinkedIn endorsements. I start by discussing how you can stay relevant to your LinkedIn network by using built-in functions, such as writing an update, to communicate appropriately with your network without being too overbearing. Then I shift gears and focus on LinkedIn endorsements, and how they differ from recommendations. You find out how to endorse your first-degree connections, review the endorsements they give you, and add those endorsements to your profile.

Interacting with Your Network

The goal of LinkedIn is to give users a smarter way to stay in touch. After you have a connection with someone on LinkedIn, you can always message him or her even if the person changes jobs, moves to a different city, or gets a new phone number.

REMEMBER

As you build your network, you should maintain your network so you're not desperately trying to connect only when you need something. When I say, "maintain your network," I am *not* saying that your network needs to know every meal you've eaten, what you did at the beach last weekend, or any other communication you might broadcast on another social networking site. Instead, focus on professional reasons to stay in contact, whether it's sharing a relevant and interesting article you found on the Internet, congratulating a connection on his or her work anniversary or new job title, or commenting on someone else's announcement. In the sections that follow, I talk about different way to interact with your network.

LinkedIn helps you manage your professional relationships, so use the tools that LinkedIn provides to reach out to your network en masse while still being personal. Here are some of the advantages of using this system:

- **Your network is more likely to help when needed.** It's easy to go months or years without direct or indirect communication with some of your network, especially fellow alumni or co-workers from past jobs. Normally, you're not going to know when you need to lean on your network until something bad happens, so reaching out in desperation to a cold contact isn't going to help. But when you communicate, even on an occasional basis, at least the contact is warmer and more receptive to respond and help when you need something big, such as a new job, a professional reference, or a connection to someone in the contact's network.
- **You can encourage new and ongoing communication.** Professionals use LinkedIn to record career accomplishments, from new jobs and promotions to receiving awards and certifications. LinkedIn notifies you when someone in your network has a career event (for example, a work anniversary) and encourages you to reach out and communicate, whether it's to write *Congrats* or connect with a common friend who just joined LinkedIn. By encouraging regular communication, LinkedIn helps reduce the awkwardness when you need to reach out to a contact.
- **LinkedIn Messaging is available at your fingertips 24/7.** No one good time exists to communicate with others on LinkedIn. Anytime during the week when you have a few minutes, reach out to one or a group of connections to stay in touch or make yourself relevant.

You don't need a laptop to stay connected; instead, use the LinkedIn mobile application. You can download and install the LinkedIn app for your Apple or Android OS system and have the same communication features found on the computer at your fingertips. The LinkedIn mobile app is covered in more detail in Chapter 10.

- **An active network can lead to unanticipated benefits.** As you communicate with your network, you might see more people wanting to connect with you, endorse your skills, or share your content on their networks. As more people view your profile and see what you contribute, the further your reach will extend, possibly resulting in immediate benefits as well as long-term success.

Creating a status update to stay connected

The good news is that you don't need to install anything or pay to use many of the features that will help you keep up regular communication with your network. You may have to adjust settings to get some automatic notifications.

One of the easiest ways to get started with good communication is to share an update, as follows:

1. **Pull up the home page and click in the update text box, in the middle of the screen, where the prompt reads *Start a Post.***

   A new window opens with full-featured post options, as shown in Figure 7-1.

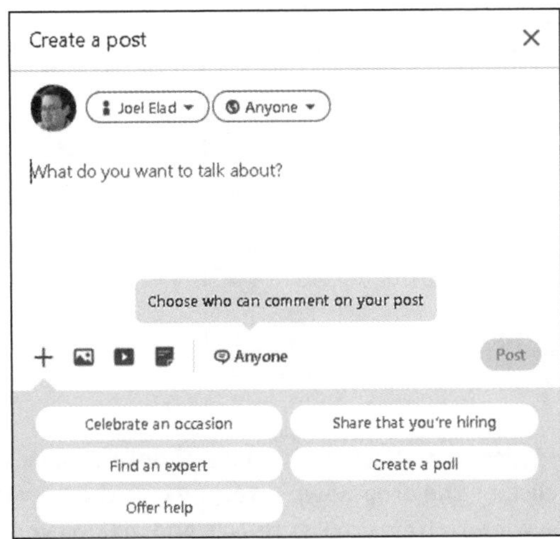

FIGURE 7-1: Post updates to stay in touch with your network.

2. **Click where it says *What do you want to talk about?* and start writing your update.**

   You can click the camera icon to add one or more pictures to your update, click the video icon (that appears to emulate the YouTube logo) to upload a video file to your update, or click the Page icon to share a document with your post. You can also click specialty buttons such as Celebrate an Occasion, Create a Poll, or Offer Help to enhance your post, if applicable.

3. **To link to someone while typing your update:**

   a. *Type the @ symbol and begin typing the person's name.*

      LinkedIn starts prompting you for potential matches, starting with first-degree connections, and then potential second- or third-degree network members, as seen in Figure 7-2.

   b. *Select the name you want to mention.*

      The name is highlighted and becomes part of your update. You can link to more than one person.

      When your update is posted, that person will receive a notification that he or she was mentioned in your post and will be able to go straight to the post to see what you wrote.

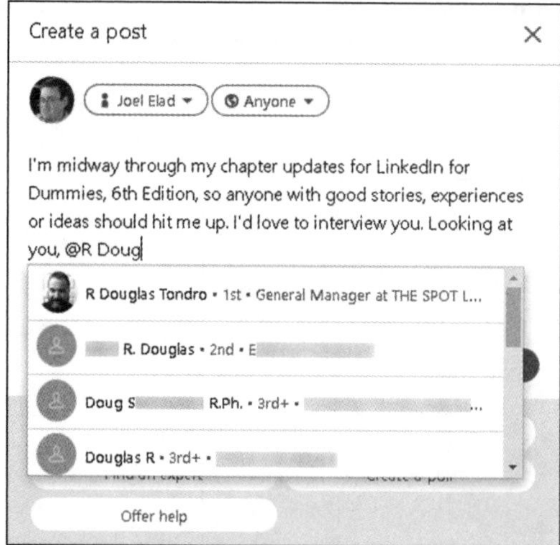

FIGURE 7-2: You can tag people in your status update by using the @ sign.

4. **When you've finished writing your update, choose privacy settings for this post by clicking the drop-down arrow next to the Anyone button, at the top of the window (refer to Figure 7-2), and making your selection.**

Your choices (see Figure 7-3) are as follows:

- *Anyone:* Anyone on LinkedIn and non-members of LinkedIn can see the post.
- *Anyone + Twitter:* Anyone on or off LinkedIn or Twitter can see the post.
- *Connections:* Only LinkedIn members who are connected to you will see this post on their news feed.
- *Group Members:* Anyone in a LinkedIn group that you select to see this post.

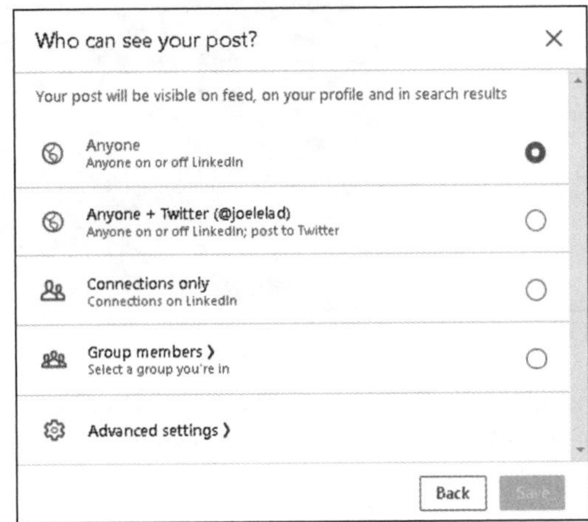

FIGURE 7-3: Determine the privacy level for your update post.

5. **If you want to disallow comments on your post:**

   a. *Click the Advanced Settings link.*

   b. *Deselect the Allow Comment on This Post option in the window that appears.* This option is set to Yes by default.

   c. *Click Save to record your change.*

REMEMBER

You can alter this setting later, after the post has been made, in case you forget to turn off (or on) the comments feature at this stage.

You return to the full-function post creation window that you generated after Step 1.

6. **To make your update live on LinkedIn, click the (now enabled) blue Post button near the bottom right of that window.**

   The post is added to the top of your news feed, as shown in Figure 7-4, and a message appears telling you that the post was successful. You might also see a notification pop-up in your notifications feed.

FIGURE 7-4: Your update post is live on LinkedIn!

Creating your own post is the first step. In the next section, I talk about interacting with your network's status updates to stay connected.

Interacting with status updates

Another way to stay connected is to look at updates from your connections and decide to contribute to the discussion, in a private message to the person or a public comment or reaction. Here are a few of the most common ways to stay in touch:

- **Interact with a news item.** Scroll down the home page, paying attention to the news feed items in the middle column, until you see a news item from a first-degree connection with whom you want to interact. Then select one or more of the following buttons:
  - *Like:* You can signal that you like the information the person is sharing by hovering your cursor over the Like icon and clicking Like, Celebrate, Support, Love, Insightful, or Curious.
  - *Comment:* Write a comment in the box provided, as shown in Figure 7-5. To tag one or more people in your comment, add the @ symbol.

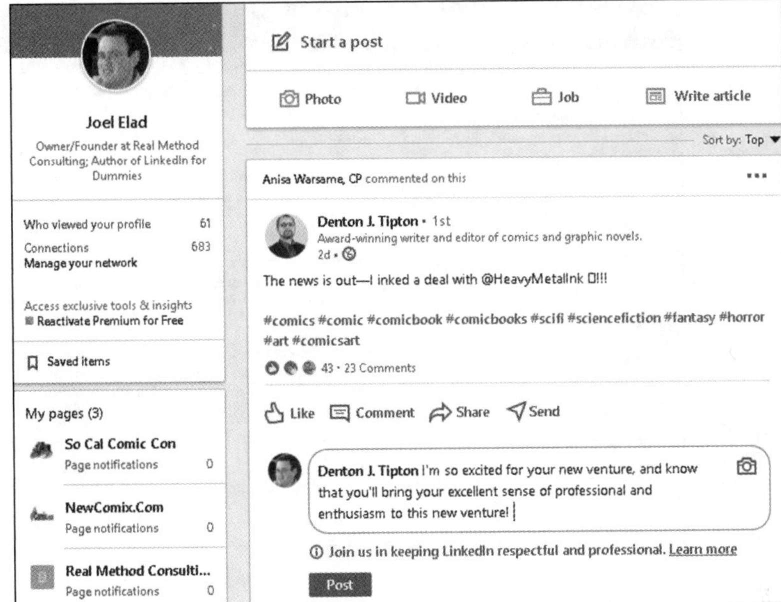

FIGURE 7-5: Comment on other people's updates.

- *Share:* Share this news item with your network while adding your comment at the top of the news item.
- *Send:* Create a LinkedIn message with this news item to send to someone in your LinkedIn network. You can add a comment at the top of the message; the link and overview of the news item will be in the body of the message.

» **See your most recent notifications.** Click Notifications (in the top navigation bar). Your notifications feed is a mix of notices regarding your activity, your network's activity, summaries of news items, and miscellaneous items of note.

Scroll through the list until you find a life event about someone in your network (such as a new job, a work anniversary, or a personal anniversary). Pay attention to items that start with *Congratulate* or *Wish* because this is LinkedIn's way of encouraging you to reach out to a first-degree connection.

For example, in Figure 7-6, Jack R. is celebrating a 5-year work anniversary, and LinkedIn offers the chance to say congrats. You can click the Say Congrats button to display the messaging window shown in Figure 7-7, write a message to Jack R., and click the Send button. (To attach a photo or document to the message, use the icons in the window.) You've just shown a first-degree connection that you're paying attention to her life events, which can open up a discussion that could benefit you in the short or long term.

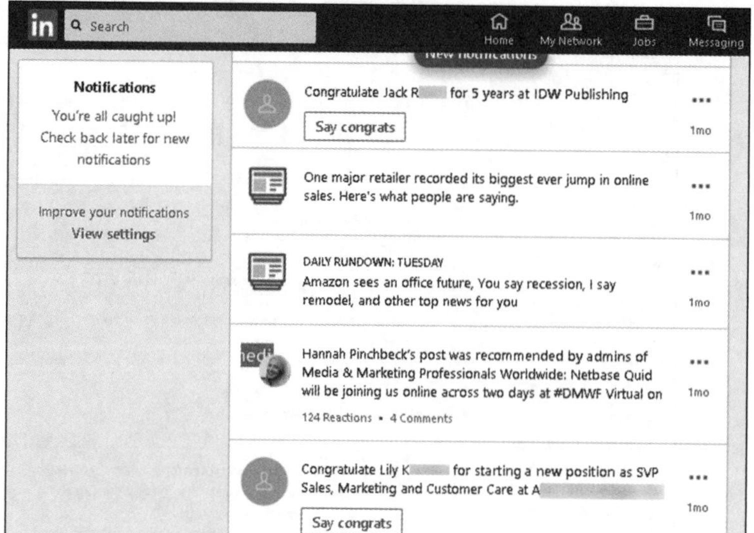

FIGURE 7-6: See who has a new job or work anniversary on LinkedIn.

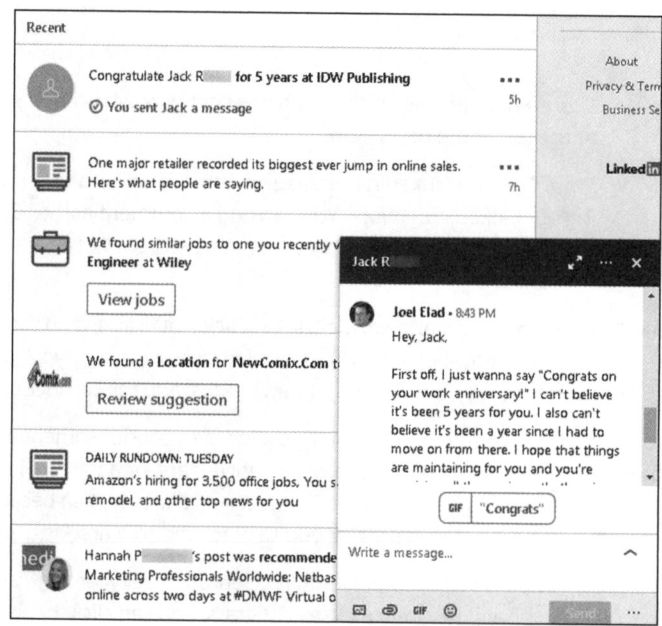

FIGURE 7-7: Send a message of congrats to your first-degree connection.

TIP

Keep track of your network without logging in to the LinkedIn site by receiving your notifications in an email. You enable this feature in the communication settings, which are described in detail in Chapter 11.

- **View a connection's activity.** If you have a connection with whom you're hoping to have an interaction, go to the person's profile and view the activity.

Use the search text box in the top navigation bar to search for the connection. When you see the connection's name in the results list, click it to display the person's profile. Scroll down to the Articles & Activity section, between the Highlights and Experience sections. (See Figure 7-8.) Click an article or post in the list, and then like, comment, or share the article or post.

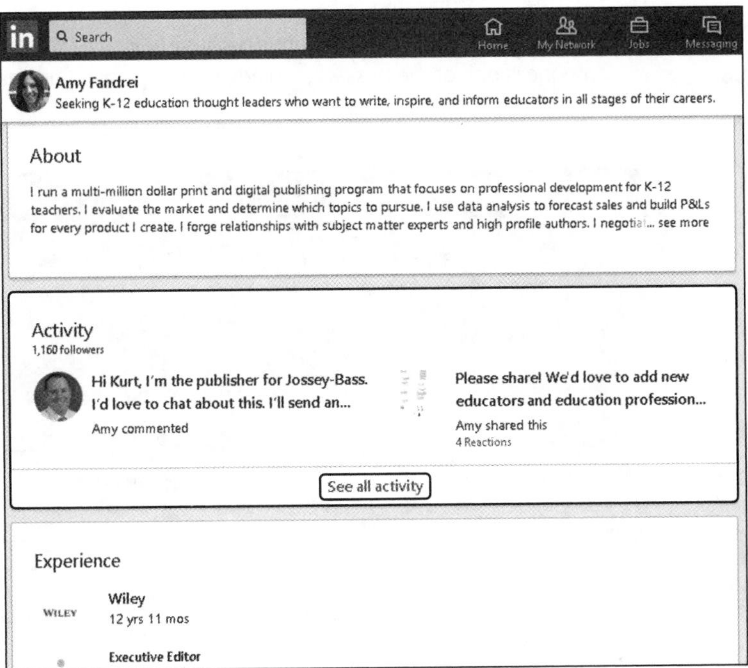

FIGURE 7-8: See what your connections are doing on LinkedIn.

- **View a connection's groups.** When studying someone's profile, scroll down to the Interests section of the profile and see what LinkedIn groups he or she belongs to. If the group is appropriate for you, join it and start participating in a few discussions in which your connection is already participating. Expanding your group affiliations raises your profile and allows you to meet new people as well.

REMEMBER

LinkedIn groups allow you to meet more people than just your first-degree connections. Learn more about groups and how to use them effectively in Chapter 16.

- **Follow your second- or third-degree connections.** If you have identified second- or third-degree network members that you want to add to your first-degree network, one way to strengthen the connection is to follow them. Then their status updates and articles appear in your news feed.

To follow someone, simply pull up the person's profile, click the More button, and select Follow in the drop-down list, as shown in Figure 7-9. (The menu item changes to Following.) To close the menu, click somewhere on the page that's not a link.

After you start following this person, watch your news feed and act on any item from this person in the hopes of learning more and creating a good reason to connect.

TIP

Pay attention to mutual connections because having a friend introduce you to someone is one of the best ways to add that person to your network.

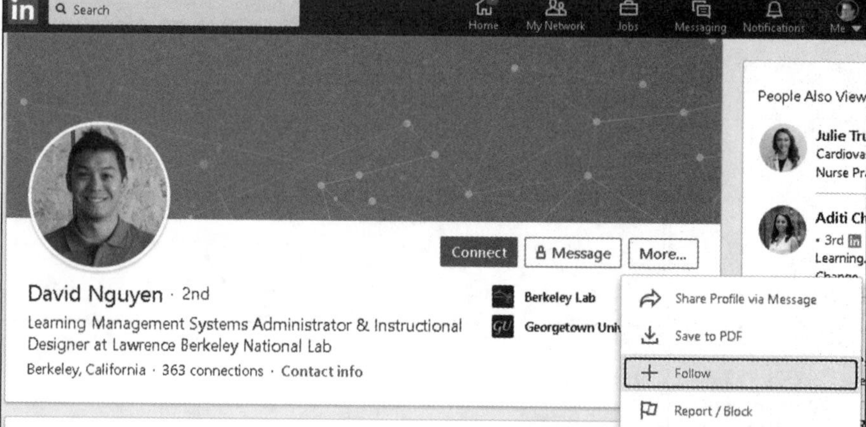

FIGURE 7-9: Follow someone's activity on LinkedIn to get to know the person better.

REMEMBER

New members join the site every day, so be sure to interact in these different ways on an ongoing basis.

Giving and Receiving Endorsements on LinkedIn

One of the main reasons why LinkedIn is so popular is that many people believe that "It's not what you know; it's who you know." However, recruiters, hiring managers, CEOs, investors, and more are interested in what you know. The people who know you best are the people in your network who have observed your work firsthand and can speak to the quality and degree of your skill set. LinkedIn endorsements are the way that users can identify the skills that they think their contacts have.

Initially, LinkedIn offered this ability through its recommendations feature (see Chapter 9). The endorsements function, which is less comprehensive, was created so that users could identify skills in their contacts more easily and quickly. Endorsements had been available only a short time when LinkedIn announced more than 2 billion endorsements had been given, signaling a widespread adoption of this new functionality.

So why are endorsements important to understand and use? Here are a few reasons:

- **Endorsements are an easier way to recognize someone's skill set.** Although a recommendation can be a thorough and positive review of someone's job, endorsing a particular skill can quickly show the community someone's skill set.
- **Endorsements are a great way for you to highlight important skills.** Having your key skill set as endorsements in your profile signals to recruiters and hiring managers not only that you have the skills to do the job but also that other people believe in your skills enough to endorse you. Just like with recommendations, people are more likely to believe other people's testimony about your skills than your own assertions.
- **Endorsements are independent of a specific position.** When you write a recommendation for someone on LinkedIn, it is tied to one position. When you endorse someone's skill, it's tied to that person's entire profile, not just to one job that was held any number of years ago.
- **Endorsements are faster and more specific than recommendations.** It's much easier and more precise for your contacts to endorse your specific skills than to write an entire recommendation. Many of your contacts can only speak to certain skills anyway, and with LinkedIn endorsements, they can "give kudos with just one click."

WARNING

The ease and speed of endorsing someone's skills, along with LinkedIn's prompts to endorse people's skills, create a trap you need to avoid: blindly endorsing skills that the person may not possess (and other people endorsing skills of yours that they can't verify you possess). It's important that your endorsements are authentic, so put some thought into giving and managing them.

You can have up to 50 skills endorsed by your network. The top endorsed skills appear in your profile page, under the Skills & Endorsements section, as shown in Figure 7-10. Although many skills come from what you entered as skills and experience in your profile, your contacts can add skills that you may not have identified yet. (For example, in Figure 7-10, I was endorsed for social media and entrepreneurship, which were skills I had not yet defined in my profile.)

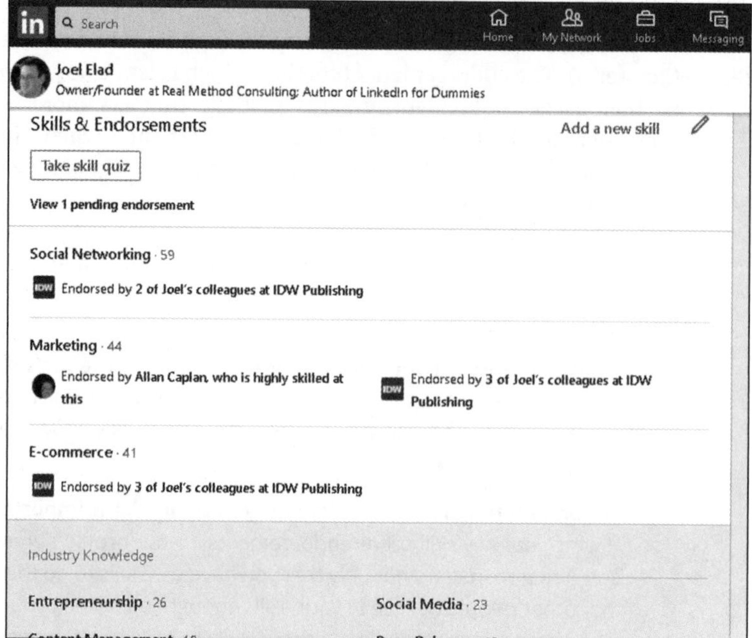

FIGURE 7-10: The Skills & Endorsements section shows your network's beliefs in your skill set.

Endorsing someone on LinkedIn

LinkedIn often prompts you to endorse your contacts for specific skills in their profile. This feature makes it easy and as automatic as possible to endorse your contacts.

When you're looking at a contact's profile, scroll down to the Skills & Endorsements section, as shown in Figure 7-11. In this section, you have several options:

- You can endorse a skill by clicking the + sign next to it. (The + sign changes to a check mark.)
- To withdraw an endorsement, click the check mark next to the skill. (The check mark returns to a + sign.)
- To expand the list, scroll down and click View *x* More Skills at the bottom of the section. You can endorse or withdraw your endorsement from the newly appeared skills that show up.
- When you're finished, scroll to a different part of your profile or perform another action. There's no Save button to save your work; each skill endorsement is recorded when you click the + sign.

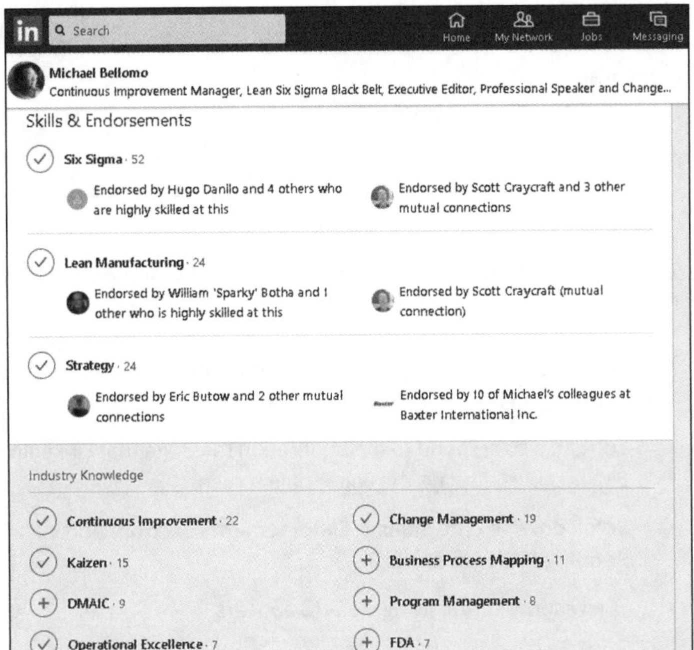

FIGURE 7-11: Endorse multiple skills for one contact.

At this point, the process is concluded for that contact. When you visit another contact's profile page, you can repeat the process for that contact.

TIP

Think carefully about which skills you can honestly endorse for another person. You should endorse only skills that you truly believe the other person has or have witnessed in action. You may also want to consider what skills the other person wants highlighted in his or her profile, which can be evident from the person's most endorsed skills. Don't feel compelled to endorse someone's skill just because LinkedIn prompts you.

REMEMBER

You can add skill endorsements at any time, even after you initially endorse someone's skills.

Accepting endorsements on LinkedIn

LinkedIn does not automatically add incoming endorsements to your profile; you must accept those endorsements first. When you receive an endorsement, it appears in your notifications list at the top-right corner of the screen, as shown in Figure 7-12. In addition, if you signed up to receive notifications (see Chapter 11), you'll receive an email letting you know who endorsed you and for what skills.

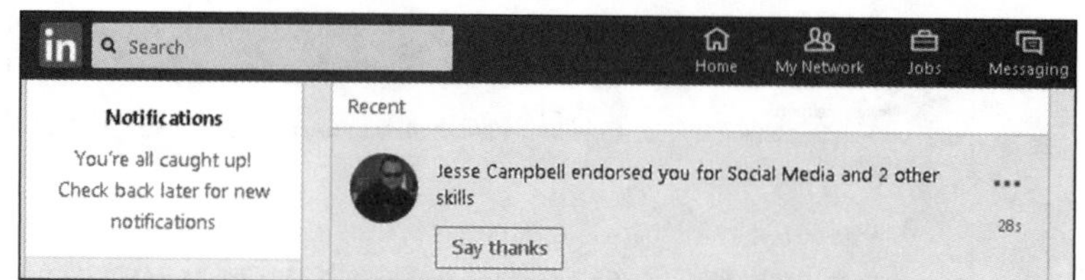

FIGURE 7-12: LinkedIn notifies you when someone endorses your skills!

The easiest way to accept (or reject) these endorsements is to view and edit your LinkedIn profile:

1. **Click the Me icon, in the top navigation bar, and then select View Profile from the drop-down list that appears.**

   You can also respond to the notification message that LinkedIn sends you. Either choice displays the Edit Profile screen.

2. **Scroll down to the Skills & Endorsements section, and click View Your Pending Endorsements.**

   The window shown in Figure 7-13 appears.

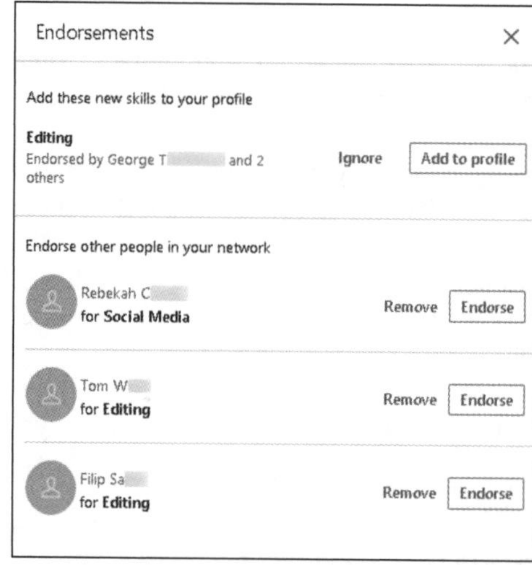

FIGURE 7-13: LinkedIn asks you whether to add new endorsements to your profile.

3. **Decide whether or not to add these endorsements to your profile:**

   - To add the incoming endorsement to your profile, click the Add to Profile button. (You can manage your endorsements later, which I discuss in the next section.)
   - To ignore this endorsement and deal with it later, click the Ignore button.

While you're deciding whether to add these endorsements to your profile, LinkedIn offers you the chance to give endorsements to people in your network (refer to Figure 7-13).

TIP

4. **(Optional) After you've accepted the endorsements, contact the person or people who endorsed you with a quick note to say thanks.**

   By doing so, you have a valid reason to stay in touch and you cultivate the relationship. You can also visit the person's profile page and decide to reciprocate by endorsing some of his or her skills. Either way, staying in contact is a great networking chance that shouldn't be missed.

Managing your skills and endorsements

Now that you've added endorsements to your profile, you should decide whether you want to keep in your profile the endorsements that you've received and add new skills that can be endorsed by your connections. When you're ready to manage your skills and endorsements, follow these steps:

1. **Click the Me icon in the top navigation bar and select View Profile from the list that appears.**
2. **Scroll down to the Skills & Endorsements header, and click Add a New Skill, which is next to the header.**

   The window shown in Figure 7-14 appears.

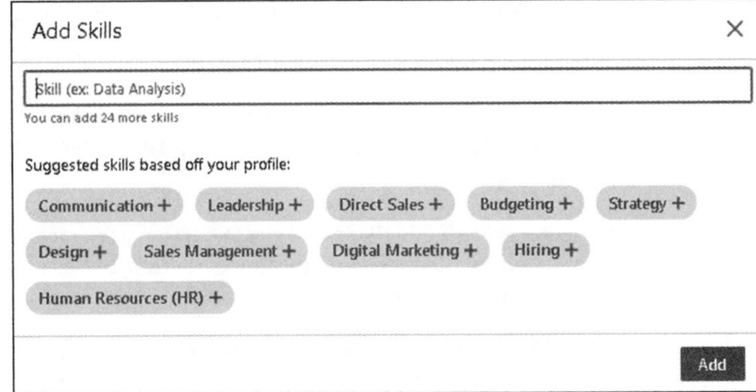

FIGURE 7-14: Click Add a New Skill to display this window.

3. **Enter the name of the new skill you want to add:**

   a. *Start typing the skill name.* As you type, a list of skill names appears, based on other users' profiles, as shown in Figure 7-15.

b. Select the skill in the list that best matches what you want, or finish typing your own skill name.

TIP

You don't have to accept what LinkedIn prompts you for, especially if you are trying to ensure the right keywords come up for your skills.

c. Click the Add button to add the skill to your list. You return to the Skills & Endorsements section of your profile.

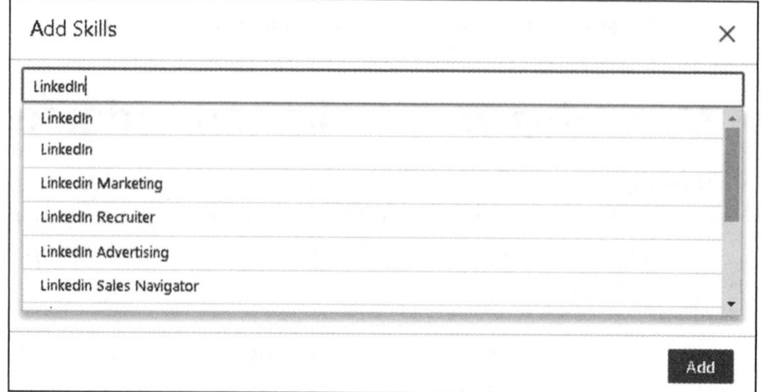

FIGURE 7-15: Add a skill to be endorsed later.

4. **To add more skills to your list, repeat Steps 2 and 3.**
5. **At the Skills & Endorsements header, click the pencil icon next to Add a New Skill.**

   The Reorder Skills & Endorsements window appears, as shown in Figure 7-16.

6. **(Optional) Review your endorsement settings:**

   a. Scroll down and click the Adjust Endorsement Settings link. The window shown in Figure 7-17 appears, where you can change a few settings related to endorsements.

   b. Review your settings and make sure you can receive endorsements and leave endorsements for other people. To change a setting to Yes or No, click the slider next to the option.

   c. When you're finished, click the X in the top-right corner to close the window. You return to the Skills & Endorsements section of your profile.

   d. Click the pencil icon next to the Add a Skill link to display the Reorder Skills & Endorsements window.

7. **To delete a skill from your profile, click the trash can icon next to the skill.**

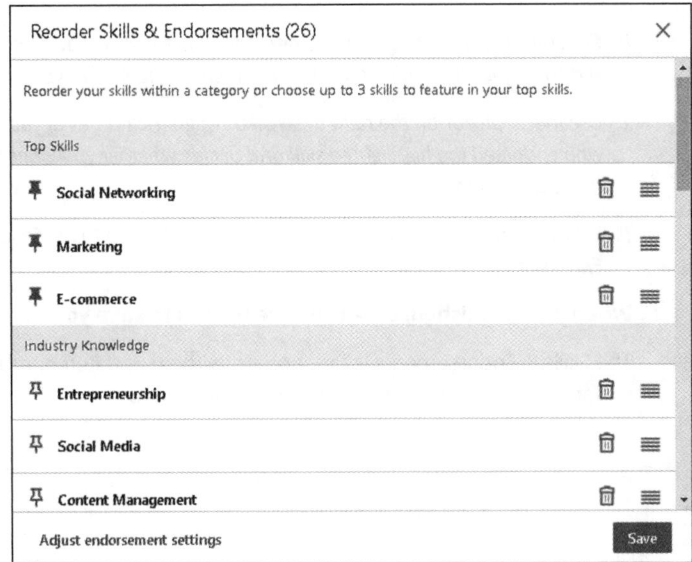

FIGURE 7-16: Manage and reorder the skills that show up in your profile.

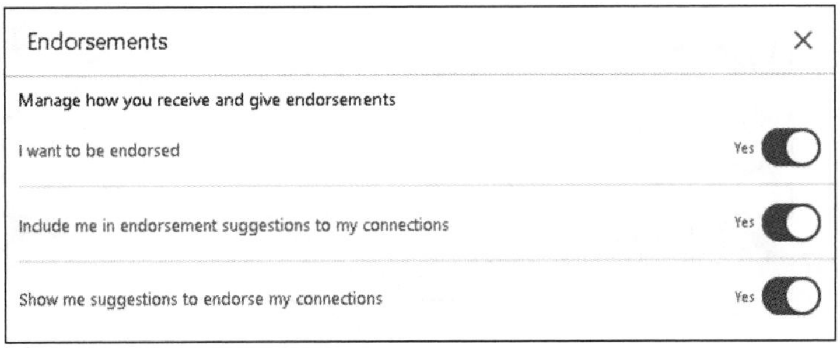

Endorsements

Manage how you receive and give endorsements

I want to be endorsed — Yes

Include me in endorsement suggestions to my connections — Yes

Show me suggestions to endorse my connections — Yes

FIGURE 7-17: Change your endorsement settings.

8. **To designate a skill as one of your top three skills, click the pushpin icon to the left of the skill name.**

   These three skills will appear at the top of your endorsements section. To deselect one of your three current top skills, click its pushpin icon again.

9. **To reorder a skill, hover your cursor over the four-line icon to the right of the skill; when you see an X, click and drag the skill to its new position in your skill list.**

   When you release the mouse button, the skill will fall into place.

10. **To hide an endorsement:**

    a. *Click the skill name or the number next to the skill.* The window shown in Figure 7-18 appears, displaying which of your connections endorsed you for that skill.

b. *Click the slider to the right of the person's name to make that endorsement Hidden, effectively hiding that person's endorsement from your profile.*

c. *Use the scroll bar on the right to scroll through the names of your connections who endorsed the highlighted skill and decide whether you want to hide any of those endorsements.*

d. *When you're done, click the X at the top right to return to the Skills & Endorsements window.*

11. **When you're finished, click the Save button to save your changes.**

    The Skills & Endorsements list reappears, with an updated number of endorsements for your skills based on your changes.

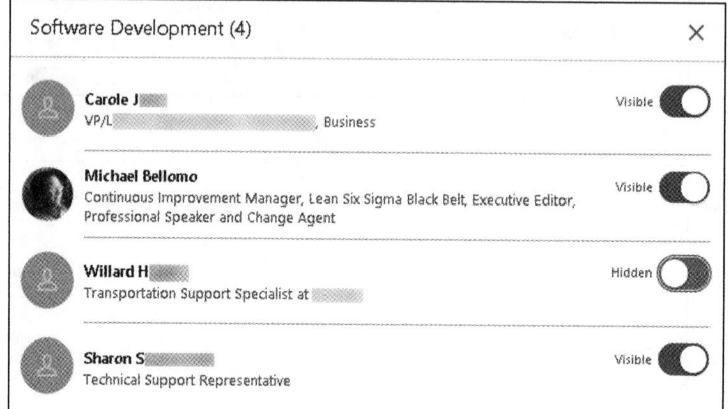

FIGURE 7-18: You can hide someone's skill endorsement from appearing in your profile.

3 Growing and Managing Your Network

IN THIS PART . . .

Use the LinkedIn news feed function for personalized news.

Learn the ins and outs of the Recommendations feature, which can help you earn trust and even find a new job.

Install and use the LinkedIn mobile application.

Configure your LinkedIn settings to improve your LinkedIn experience.

Integrate your LinkedIn activities with other Internet activities.

» Reading the news feed when you're on the go

» Setting up digest notifications

» Managing interactions after you publish a post

Chapter 8
Understanding Your News Feed

As far back as 1597, Sir Francis Bacon said that "Knowledge is power." Today's information age only emphasizes how true that point still is. We are constantly using the tools at our disposal to stay better informed and become better at what we do, for our career and our lives in general. LinkedIn strives to support that goal for its members, beyond the core tools of networking and advertising your skills with your profile.

Enter the LinkedIn news feed. Years ago, LinkedIn purchased the popular Pulse news feed application for $90 million and began to integrate the app into the overall LinkedIn website. Simply put, the news feed pulls together traditional and user-based news for its members to browse, share, and discuss. The goal is to create a news feed that's tailored to each member, increasing the likelihood that news is shared among this networked community.

In this chapter, I discuss how the LinkedIn news feed works and how you can access it, either on a web browser (by going to `www.linkedin.com`) or on your mobile device with the LinkedIn app. You find out how to customize your news feed to get the most use out of it, create long-form posts that can be shared on LinkedIn to your connections or your overall network, and interact with any LinkedIn post.

Understanding the News Feed

Imagine if you read a newspaper that showed you only articles that mattered to you. (For that matter, for many of you, imagine the days you might have read a newspaper.) Customized news is ubiquitous on the Internet nowadays, and on LinkedIn, it's called your LinkedIn news feed.

Your news feed is already part of the LinkedIn experience, taking up the center column of your home screen, below the box where you share an update, photo, or post. When you bring up LinkedIn in your web browser, you see news articles and updates, as shown in Figure 8-1.

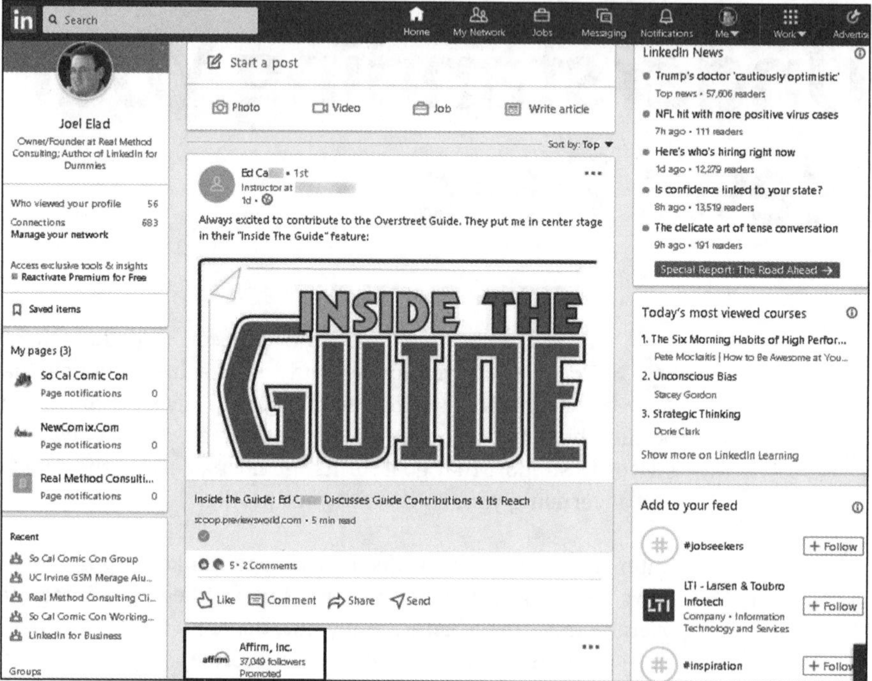

FIGURE 8-1: The LinkedIn news feed shows you various articles.

First off, let's talk about the different elements that make up your news feed. You can expect to see these types of elements:

» **Network updates:** Your activity on LinkedIn and the events of your LinkedIn network are considered to be news. On occasion LinkedIn will give you updates on what's occurred in your network, or give you updates when LinkedIn members are celebrating work anniversaries, have changed jobs, or have recorded events on their LinkedIn page.

- **Posts from your network:** When someone in your immediate network posts something, such as an article, a photo, or a status update (for example, the article my friend Ed C. shared in Figure 8-1), that post is added to your feed, similar to how other social networks build your feed based on your interactions.
- **Mentions of your network:** When someone in your network is mentioned in a news article, that article is added to your news feed, with the top line stating *So-and-so was mentioned in the news.*
- **News articles:** The primary type of element on your news feed are articles posted from either your first-degree connection, or influencers, companies, or topics that you're following. (Later on in the chapter, you find out how to configure whom and what you are following, which will affect the content in your news feed.) In some cases, you'll see trending articles in a category or topic you're following, and posts or articles from influencers you're following.
- **News articles that received a response from your network:** If an article is important to a first-degree connection of yours, LinkedIn assumes that you might be interested in that article as well. Therefore, LinkedIn inserts different articles in your news feed that your first-degree connections have liked, commented on, or shared. A statement at the top of the article block reads *So-and-so liked this* or *So-and-so commented on this,* or even *So-and-so replied to another-so-and-so's comment on this.*
- **Promoted articles:** Like many other websites, LinkedIn offers advertising in your news feed, such as sponsored content from companies you're following or promoted posts, which are paid advertising from new companies trying to catch your interest. You can always tell a promoted or sponsored post because *Promoted* or *Sponsored,* respectively, appears below the company name, as shown in Figure 8-1 with Affirm, Inc.

TIP

If you want to change the sort order of elements in your news feed, click the drop-down arrow next to Sort By at the top of your feed, and choose Top (top choices decided by LinkedIn) or Recent (the most recent additions to your feed).

Now that you know which items will appear in your news feed, it's time to find out about the basic structure of each item:

- **Person or company who sent the post:** Above every article's graphic is the name and LinkedIn headline of the person or company that made the post on LinkedIn, not necessarily the author of the article. If you click the name or profile photo, you are taken to the profile page for that person or company. Below the headline, you see how long ago the post was made, in minutes, hours, days, or weeks (for example, 30m, 7h, 2d, or 1w, respectively).

- **Article headline:** The article's headline and shortened URL appear below the article, in the middle of the news feed block. Clicking the headline displays the article in a new browser window. When you close the window, you return to your news feed.
- **Follow button:** In some cases, if you receive a news article in your feed from a source you're not following (such as when Jesse Campbell shared the article in Figure 8-2, left), a Follow button appears to the right of the author's name. To add that person's articles to your sources of news for your news feed, click Follow.

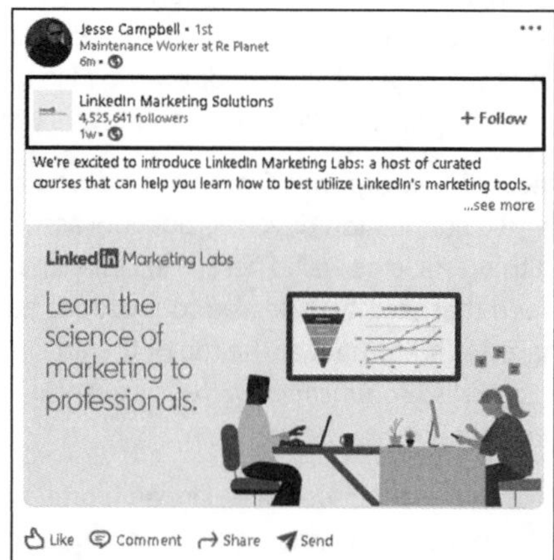

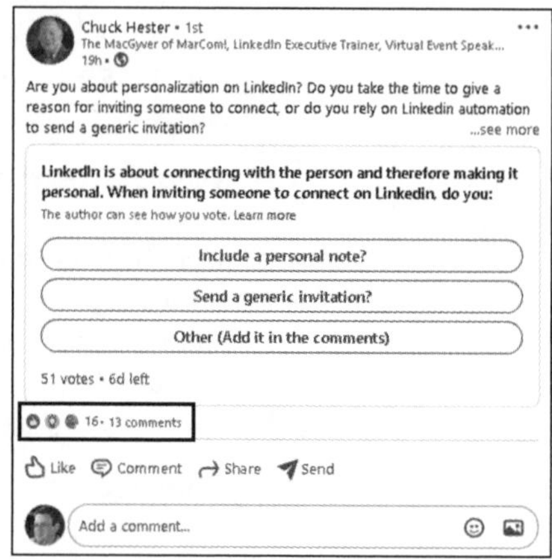

FIGURE 8-2: Understand the basic structure of a news feed post.

- **Like, Comment, and Share buttons:** To add your opinion to the post and interact with the author and other readers, click the Like button to signal your approval of the post, the Comment button so you can add a comment to the discussion, or the Share button to distribute the post to the news feeds of your network. (If you don't see a comment box, clicking Comment will display one.) As shown in Figure 8-2 (right) with Chuck Hester's post, the existing number of likes and comments appears above the buttons.
- **Additional options:** At the top-right corner of the news feed article is a three-dot icon. Click this icon to display the menu shown in Figure 8-3, with options that let you get more out of the post, identify articles or sources that are not of interest to you, and more.

LinkedIn provides a nearly limitless source of news and information, as you can see as you scroll down the news feed page. When you've scrolled enough, you may see a blue New Posts button. Click it to refresh and return to the top of the feed.

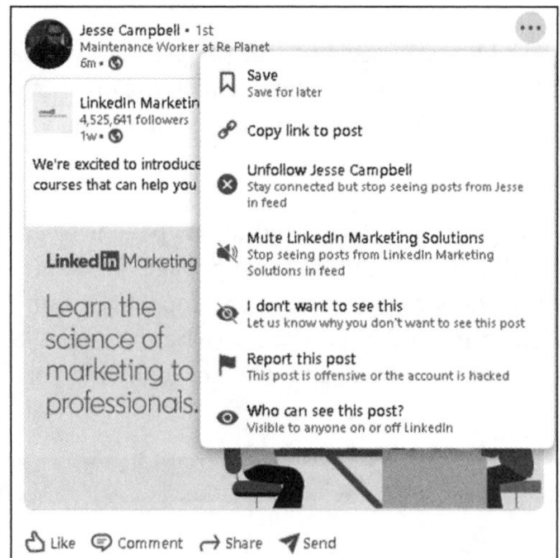

FIGURE 8-3: Tell LinkedIn how you react to particular news feed item.

Configuring Your News Feed

You may wonder how LinkedIn pulls together relevant articles and news sources. LinkedIn uses an undisclosed algorithm and additional variables to decide what articles are included in your news feed. In addition, your first-degree connections plus the following three sources help determine the content of each person's news feed:

- **Influencers:** Years ago, LinkedIn reached out to 500 prominent people around the world — from CEOs such as Jack Welch and Richard Branson, to authors such as Deepak Chopra, Guy Kawasaki, and Tony Robbins, and to popular entrepreneurs such as Mark Cuban — to share their wisdom and experience and generate discussions in the business community. The content of these thought leaders was published on LinkedIn and given prominent placement. Because of the high number of members viewing, liking, and commenting on these influencers' posts, LinkedIn adds more influencers every year.
- **Channels:** The articles in your feed can be categorized by topic, such as career aspects (leadership and management or marketing and advertising), large industries (such as banking and finance, big data, or social media), and specialized niches (such as green business or customer experience).
- **Publishers:** When you need to catalog and present lots of publishable information, it helps to go directly to the source. LinkedIn identifies publishers of all shapes and sizes, including traditional news outlets such as *The New York Times, The Wall Street Journal,* and *Time Magazine,* services such as Reuters and Yahoo! News, and even niche audiences such as National Geographic, Entrepreneur Media, Harvard Business Review, and the TED Talks series.

When you set up your LinkedIn account (see Chapter 2), you may have been asked to choose some of these elements to follow, which means they will appear in your news feed. However, you can customize which sources you want to follow at any time.

The easiest way to display your News Feed follow page is to go to `www.linkedin.com/feed/follow`. The news feed following page is displayed, as shown in Figure 8-4. Three headers appear below the top navigation bar: Follow Fresh Perspectives, *X* Following, and *Y* Followers (where *X* and *Y* are the number of people and topics you are following and who are following you, respectively).

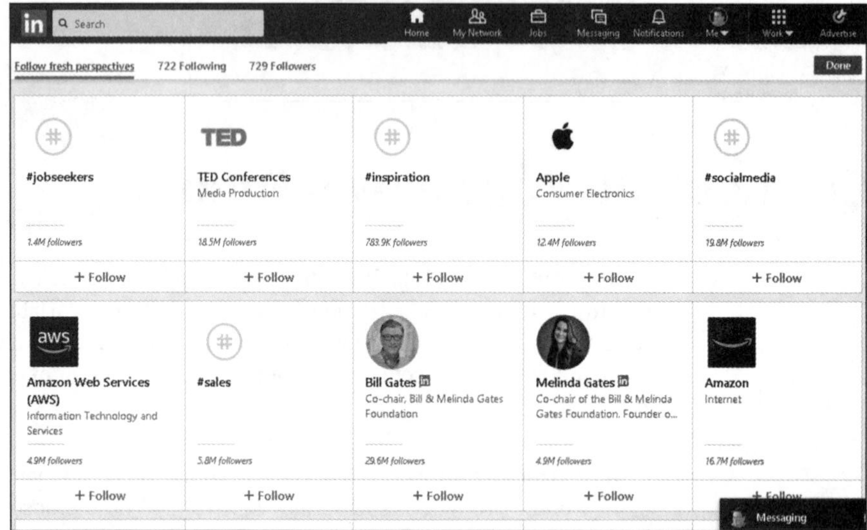

FIGURE 8-4: See whom LinkedIn recommends you can follow.

Click the Follow Fresh Perspectives header, if necessary, to display influencers, channels, people, topics, and publishers you might want to follow, based on your profile and how interactions. Each tile contains an icon or placeholder, a name, a title, the number of followers, and a Follow button.

Click tiles to see their LinkedIn page and read their most recent set of articles. If you want to follow a source, click the Follow button at the bottom of the tile; the button changes to Following. If you change your mind at any time, just click the Following button to unfollow that source.

REMEMBER

As you decide which influencers, channels, or publishers to follow, keep in mind that if you simply click inside the tiles, you will be taken to their LinkedIn pages. You're not changing your subscription to those sources.

When you want to curate the sources you're following, click Following (next to the Follow Fresh Perspectives header) to see all your sources. By default, every first-degree connection is a source, along with the influencers, companies, and topics you've chosen. When you don't want a person or source in your news feed, simply click Following to unfollow (which will then change to Follow).

To speed up the process, click the filter icon near the top right of the screen to display the filter menu shown in Figure 8-5. You can display only your first-degree connections (the Connections option), people you're following whom you're not connected to (Out-of-Network), and more.

When you've finished following and unfollowing news sources, click the blue Done button in the top-right corner to return to your home page.

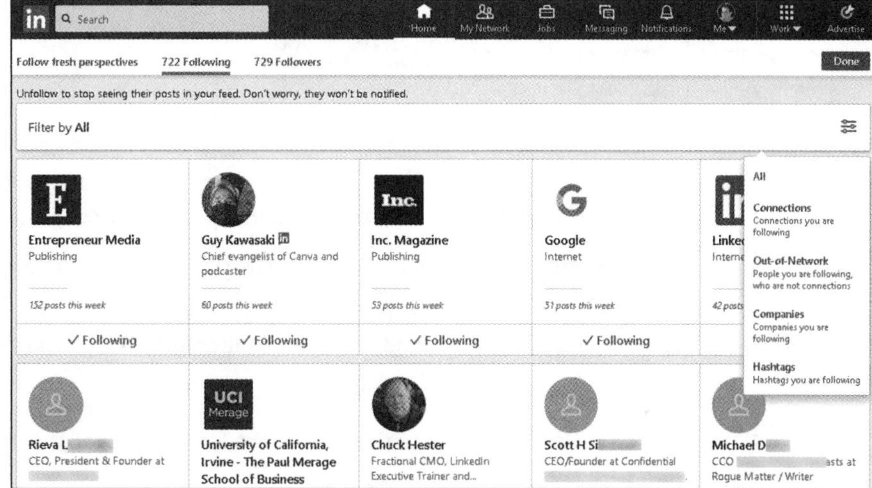

FIGURE 8-5: Review your news sources to decide whom you still want to follow in your news feed.

Setting Up Digest Notifications

One way to help ensure that you are always up to date on breaking news is to have the news delivered to you. Instead of the paperboy dropping off your customized newspaper on your doorstep, LinkedIn can send you a digest of your top news articles to your email address.

When you're ready to set up this digest, follow these steps:

1. **Click the Me icon at the top of any LinkedIn page, and select the Settings & Privacy option under the Account header.**

   The Settings & Privacy main menu appears.

2. **Click the Communications link, on the left side of the page, to display the Communications screen as shown in Figure 8-6.**

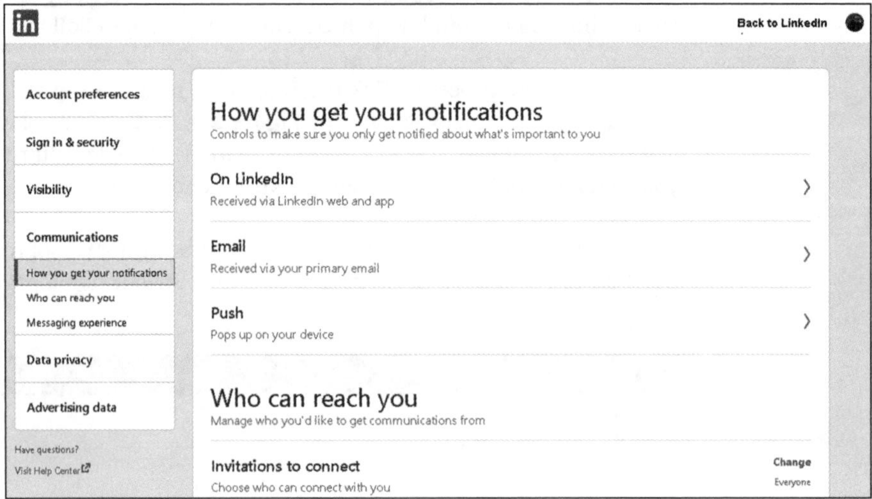

FIGURE 8-6: Configure your settings from this page.

3. **In the How You Get Your Notifications section, click the Email header.**

   The Email screen appears, so you can determine when and how frequently LinkedIn notifies you of actions related to your account.

4. **Scroll down and expand the News header by clicking the word News.**

   The News options screen appears.

5. **Click the pencil icon to the right of the LinkedIn Highlights header.**

   The options in Figure 8-7 appear.

6. **Click the arrow in the drop-down list below the LinkedIn Highlights header, and then select, Weekly Digest, Daily Digest Individually, or Recommended.**

   The Recommended feature will send you news that is "relevant to you, just when it counts," which means you'll get updates based on what appears in your LinkedIn news feed and your preferences in LinkedIn that match the news article. If you select Individually, you'll get an email for every news feed item in your news feed. You can also select the Off option to turn off LinkedIn Highlights, in which case you will not receive emails regarding news updates.

7. **Review the other settings or exit the process by scrolling to the top of the page and clicking the Back to Email link.**

   Your selections are saved automatically.

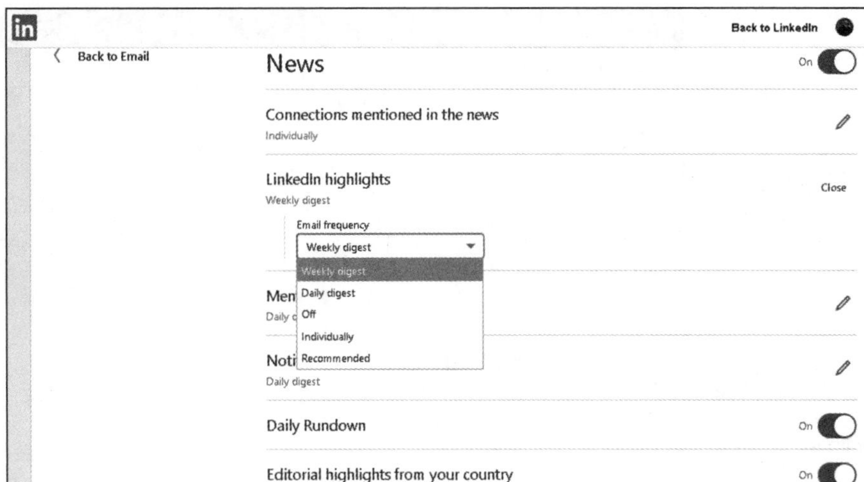

FIGURE 8-7: Choose the frequency with which you want to receive a digest of news stories.

You're done! The email you receive will provide the top headlines and a link to each post or article mentioned, so you can read more of what's happening in your world.

Writing an Article on LinkedIn

All members, whether they have a free or premium account, may publish a *long-form post* (or *article* for short), which can reach your entire network. Guidelines prevent someone from spamming the network with purely promotional information or information without value. All help pages for articles, including guidelines, are here: `www.linkedin.com/help/linkedin/answer/47538`.

The easiest way to publish an article (or long-form post) follows:

1. **Go to your LinkedIn home page and click the Write Article icon.**

   The icon is below the Start a Post prompt near the top of the screen and next to the Photo, Video, and Event icons.

   The screen shown in Figure 8-8, appears, with the word *Headline*.

2. **(Optional but highly recommended) Add an image to be associated with your article by clicking the image icons with the + sign.**

   LinkedIn recommends using a 2000-by-600-pixel image for optimal viewing (see `www.linkedin.com/help/linkedin/answer/86781` for details). When you click the image icons, LinkedIn opens a window so you can find and upload the image file on your computer. If you change your mind, click the X in the top-right corner.

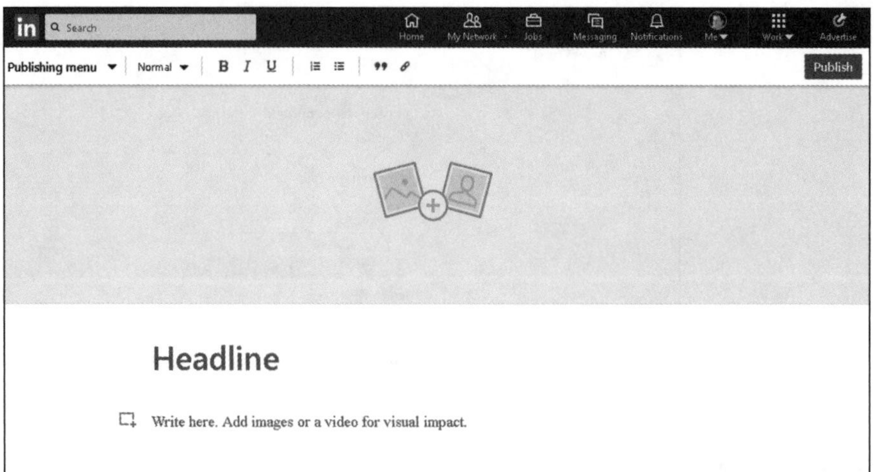

FIGURE 8-8: Your starting point for writing a post.

3. **Click Headline and type your post's headline.**

   Think of a headline that will capture the essence of your post and encourage your target audience to read it.

TIP

   Use some appropriate keywords that will be picked up by search engines and the human eye. But save some of your keywords for the body of your post, which you write next. I talk about keyword choice for your LinkedIn profile in Chapter 3.

4. **Write your post in the space provided.**

   Click the *Write here* prompt, and start writing or copy and paste your text. Above the text area, note the series of icons, as shown in Figure 8-9. You can use the formatting buttons (B, I, and U) to format the text.

   You can also add images, videos, presentations, tweets, podcasts, and other kinds of rich media to your post by clicking the Add Multimedia icon, which appears at the bottom of Figure 8-9 (and in this book's margin.)

   Posts can be any length, but if you want your post to be read, don't make it too long. LinkedIn Editor-in-Chief Daniel Roth wrote a great article for LinkedIn containing seven tips for writing a killer post. Regarding length, he stated that "800–2,000 words was the sweet spot," but he also added that the demands of your content should dictate the length of your post, not what statistical data shows. (See more of his tips at `www.linkedin.com/pulse/20120906170105-29092-the-7-secrets-to-writing-killer-content-on-linkedin`.)

   At the bottom of your post, be sure to write a one- or two-sentence biography, describing who you are, what you are doing, and how you can help other people. The biography can include links to your website, your blog, or even a call-to-action to gather leads.

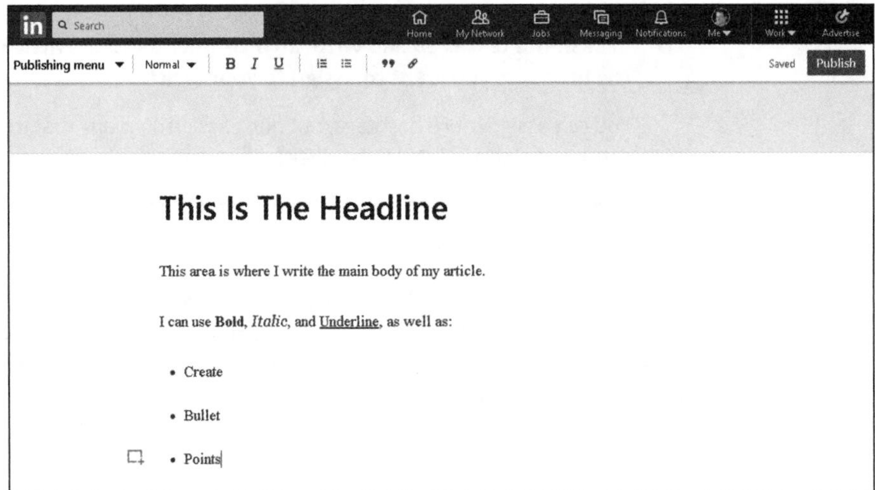

FIGURE 8-9: Write your post in the space provided.

TIP

LinkedIn created an informative slide presentation of tips on publishing a post at `www.slideshare.net/linkedin/everything-you-need-to-know-about-publishing-on-linkedin`.

5. **When you have finished the article, click the blue Publish button.**

   Even though you've clicked Publish, LinkedIn has a few more tasks for you to complete. The window shown in Figure 8-10 appears. The final step is creating hashtags to assign topics to your post so others can easily find your post and so that LinkedIn knows where to display it.

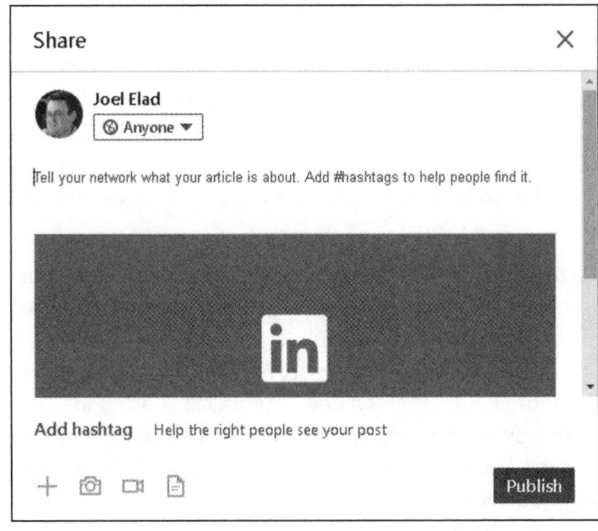

FIGURE 8-10: Create tags for your post to identify relevant topics.

6. **Click in the text area and write an introduction to the article, as well as the hashtags you want to assign to your article.**

   You can assign more hashtags, but don't assign so many that they lose any sense of being a valuable identifier for your post.

7. **When you're ready to publish your post, click the blue Publish button in the window.**

That's it! LinkedIn publishes your post. The Posts section of your profile catalogs and displays your posts. Based on LinkedIn's algorithms, this post could appear in other people's LinkedIn news feeds, and your first-degree connections will see the post in their home page feed and receive a notification that you've published a post.

REMEMBER

If you can't complete your post in one sitting, don't worry. LinkedIn saves your work as you type so you can come back to it at a later time. (You'll occasionally see a Saved message in the top-right corner of the screen.) Simply click the Publishing button, below the LinkedIn search box, to view options to open existing articles (My Articles) and drafts (My Drafts).

Managing Post Interactions

After you click Publish, you may think your job is done, but it has only begun. As people read your post, they can interact with it and with you as the author. Remember the following after you publish a post:

- **Monitor the statistics.** When you look at your post, you'll see three key numbers associated with views, likes, and comments. These represent how many people viewed your post, how many people clicked Like for your post, and how many comments were left for your post. As you publish more posts, you can start to judge their effectiveness by seeing which topics generated the most interest.
- **Go further with article analytics.** When you click the Me button on the top navigation bar of the home page, and then click the Posts & Activity link (under the Manage header), you see a list of the articles you've published. Below each article is an Analytics icon. Select that icon and LinkedIn will display more information on how your article affected the community. For example, you see how many views and likes came from you (and others) sharing the article, and the number of reshares. More valuable can be the viewing audience demographics, where you can see data such as the companies, job titles, and locations of your readers.

- **Read and respond to comments.** As people read your post, they may be inspired to write a comment. You should check the Comments section of your posts regularly to see whether anyone is asking you a question. Also feel free to respond publicly in the Comments section. You can also click the link for that user and respond privately, depending on the nature of the comment.
- **Follow up with your own comments.** As the post gets more visibility, you can leave your own comments. Perhaps you want to share an effect your post had or a follow-up you did that might be relevant to the readers of your post.
- **Share your post on other platforms.** Your LinkedIn posts aren't exclusive to LinkedIn. You can share your post on other social media networks, and on your own publishing platforms, such as a blog or a website. And if your company has a LinkedIn Company page, you can share it there too (see Chapter 15).

» Writing a good recommendation

» Requesting a recommendation

» Declining a recommendation or a request for one

» Managing your recommendations

Chapter 9

Exploring the Power of Recommendations

Endorsements and testimonials have long been a mainstay of traditional marketing. But really, how much value is there in reading testimonials on someone's own website, like the following:

Maria is a great real estate attorney — I'd definitely use her again.
ELIZABETH T. LONDON

or

Jack is a fine lobbyist — a man of impeccable character.
EMANUEL R. SEATTLE

Without knowing who these people are, anyone reading the testimonials tends to be highly skeptical about them. At the very least, the reader wants to know that they're real people who have some degree of accountability for those endorsements.

The reader is looking for something called *social validation.* Basically, that's just a fancy-shmancy term meaning that people feel better about their decision to conduct business with someone if other people in their extended network are pleased with that person's work. The reader knows that people are putting their own reputations at stake, even if just to a small degree, by making a public recommendation of another person. You don't have to look much further than Yelp, HomeAdvisor, or Amazon reviews to understand this point.

As this chapter shows you, the LinkedIn recommendations feature offers you a powerful tool for finding out more about the people you're considering doing business with, as well as a means to publicly build your own reputation. I walk you through all the steps needed to create a recommendation for someone else, request a recommendation for your profile, and manage your existing recommendations.

Understanding Recommendations

The LinkedIn recommendation process starts in one of three ways:

- **Unsolicited:** When viewing the profile of any first-degree connection, click the More button below the person's profile picture to display the menu shown in Figure 9-1. To give an unsolicited recommendation, select the Recommend option.
- **Requested:** To request a recommendation from a first-degree connection, select Request a Recommendation in the drop-down menu shown in Figure 9-1. You might ask for a recommendation at the end of a successful project, for example, or before your transition to a new job.
- **Reciprocated:** Whenever you accept a recommendation from someone, you have the option of recommending that person in return. Some people do this as a thank you for receiving the recommendation, others reciprocate only because they mistakenly think they can't leave a recommendation until someone leaves them one, and still others don't feel comfortable reciprocating unless they truly believe the person deserves one. You should decide in each circumstance whether to reciprocate. (Sometimes the situation might be awkward, such as if you get a recommendation from a supervisor or boss.)

REMEMBER

After the recommendation is written, it's not posted immediately. Instead, it goes to the recipient for review, and he or she has the option to accept it, reject it, or request a revision. So even though the majority of recommendations you see on LinkedIn are genuine, they're also almost entirely positive because they have to be accepted by the recipient.

LinkedIn shows all recommendations you've received as well as links to the profiles of the people who recommended you, as shown in Figure 9-2. Allowing people to see who is endorsing you provides social validation.

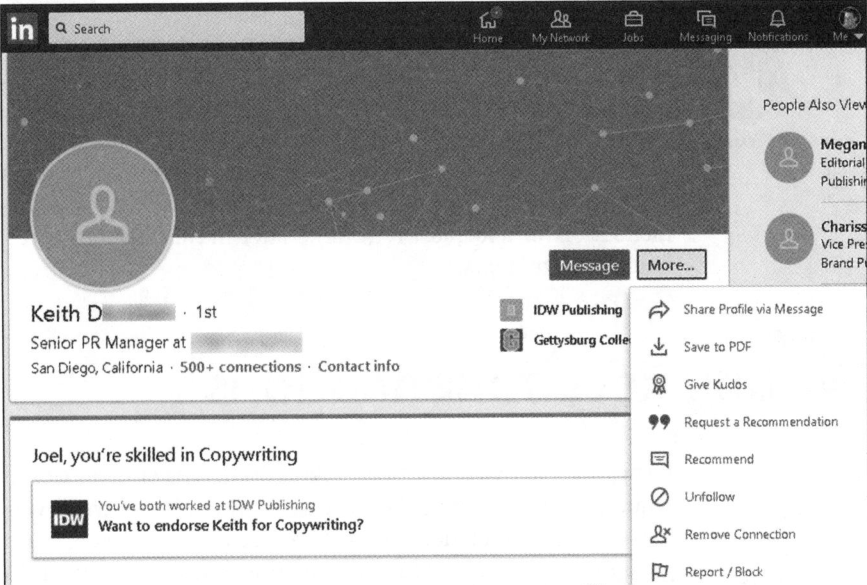

FIGURE 9-1: You can start a recommendation with any first-degree connection.

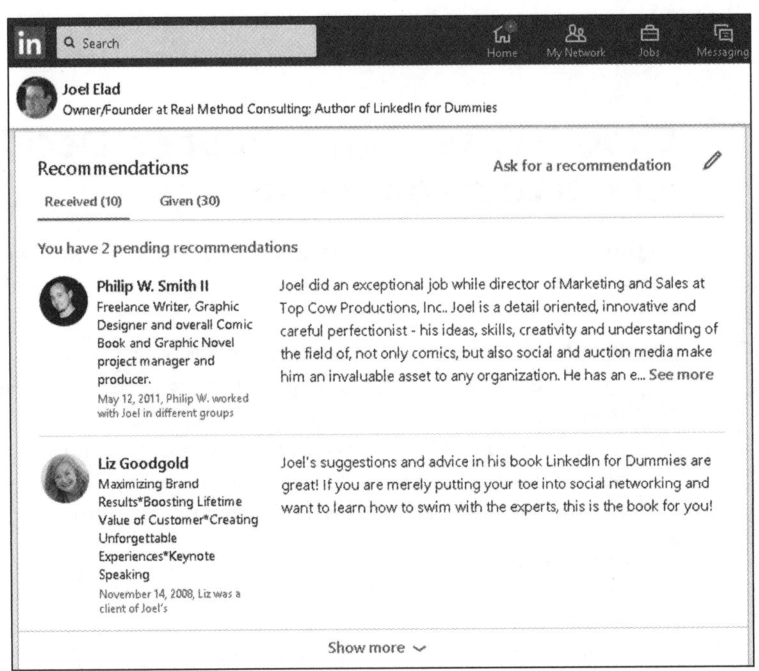

FIGURE 9-2: Recommendations on a profile page.

REMEMBER

The quality and source of recommendations matter. A handful of specific recommendations from actual clients talking about how you helped them solve a problem are worth more than 50 general recommendations from business acquaintances saying, "I like Sally — she's cool," or "Hector is a great networker." And any recommendations that heartily endorse the number of cocktails you had at the last formal event probably need revision. Check out "Gracefully Declining a Recommendation (or a Request for One)," later in this chapter, if you're receiving those kinds of statements.

Writing Recommendations

I suggest that you practice making some recommendations before you start requesting them. Here's the method to my madness: When you know how to write a good recommendation yourself, you're in a better position to help others write good recommendations for you. And the easiest way to get recommendations is to give them. Every time you make a recommendation and the recipient accepts it, he or she is prompted to give you a recommendation. Thanks to the basic desire to be fair that most exhibit dealing with their network, many people will go ahead and endorse you in return.

Choose wisely, grasshopper: Deciding whom to recommend

Go through your contacts and make a list of the people you want to recommend. As you build your list, consider recommending the following types of contacts:

- **People with whom you've worked:** I'm not going to say that personal references are worthless, but they tend to ring hollow next to specific recommendations from colleagues and clients. Business recommendations are much stronger in the LinkedIn context. Your recommendation is rooted in actual side-by-side experiences with the other party, you can be specific regarding the behavior and accomplishments of the other party.
- **People you know well:** You may choose to connect with casual acquaintances or even strangers, but reserve your personal recommendations for people with whom you have an established relationship (friends and family). Remember, you're putting your reputation on the line with that recommendation. Are you comfortable risking your rep on them?

WARNING

Recommend only those people whose performance you're happy with. I can't say it enough: Your reputation is on the line. Here's a great question to ask yourself when deciding whether to recommend someone: Would you feel comfortable recommending this person to a best friend or a family member? If not, you have your answer.

When you complete your list, you're probably not going to write all the recommendations at once, so I suggest copying and pasting the names in a word processing document or a spreadsheet so that you can keep track as you complete them.

Look right here: Making your recommendation stand out

Keep the following in mind when trying to make your recommendation stand out from the rest of the crowd:

- **Be specific.** Don't just write that the person you're recommending is great. Instead, mention his specific strengths and skills. If you need help, ask him whether he can think of any helpful elements you could highlight in your recommendation.
- **Talk about results.** Adjectives and descriptions are fluff. Clichés are also useless. Tell what the person actually did and the effect it had on you and your business. It's one thing to say, "She has a great eye," and another to say, "The logo she designed for us has been instrumental in building our brand and received numerous positive comments from customers." Detailed results make a great impression, from the scope of difficulty of a project to the degree of challenge the person faced.
- **State how you know the person.** LinkedIn provides only two basic overall categories to represent your relationship to the person you're recommending: professional and education. If you've known this person for 10 years, say so. If she's your cousin, say so. If you've never met her in person, say so. Save it for the end, though. Open with the positive results this person provided, or the positive qualities the person exhibited in your interaction; then qualify the type of interaction.
- **Reinforce the requestor's major skills or goals.** Look at her profile. How is she trying to position herself now? What can you say in your recommendation that will support that? The recipient will appreciate this approach. For example, if you read her profile and see that she's focusing on her project management skills as opposed to her earlier software development skills, your recommendation should reinforce the message she's trying to convey in her profile.

» **Don't gush.** By all means, if you think someone is fantastic, exceptional, extraordinary, or the best at what she does, say so. Just don't go on and on about it, and watch the clichéd adjectives.

» **Be concise.** Although LinkedIn has a 3,000-character limit on the length of recommendations, you shouldn't reach that limit. Make your recommendation as long as it needs to be to say what you have to say, but no longer.

TIP

Don't be afraid to contact the requestor and ask for feedback on what you should highlight in your recommendation of that person. He knows his own brand better than anyone, so go right to the source!

Creating a recommendation

Now you're ready to write your first recommendation. To create a recommendation, first you need to pull up the person's profile:

1. **Click the My Network icon in the top navigation bar of any page.**
2. **When your network page appears, click the Connections link under the Manage My Network header on the left side of the screen.**

   Your list of connections appears.
3. **Select the person you're recommending.**

   REMEMBER

   Your recommendation goes directly to that person, not to prospective employers. Any prospective employer who wants a specific reference can request it by contacting that person directly on LinkedIn.
4. **Visit the profile of the person you want to recommend.**

Before you write up your recommendation, review the person's experience, summary, professional headline, and other elements of his profile. This helps you get a sense of what skills, attributes, or results should be reflected in your recommendation. After all, if the person you want to recommend is trying to build a career as a finance executive, your recommendation will serve him better if you focus on finance instead of his event planning or writing skills.

After you inform yourself a bit more about the person and have thought about what you are going to say, you can get your recommending groove on. Follow these steps:

1. **Click the More button to the right of the person's profile picture and headline, and then click Recommend in the drop-down list that appears.**

   The Write X a Recommendation page appears, as shown in Figure 9-3.

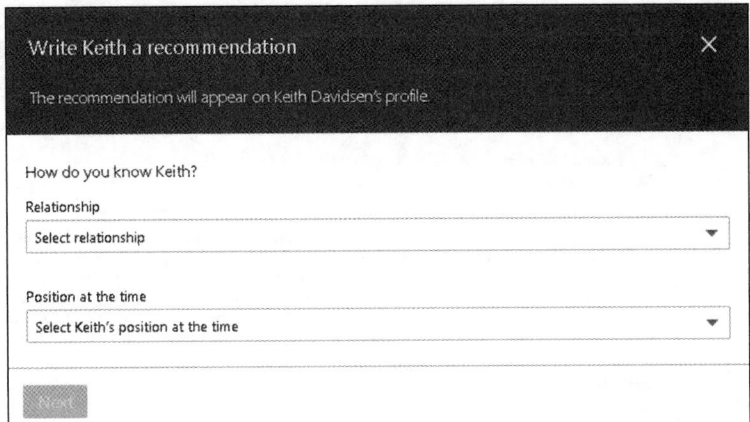

FIGURE 9-3: Tell LinkedIn how you know the person you are recommending.

2. **Define your relationship:**

   a. *Under Relationship, define the basis of the recommendation. You have several options, including whether you were a colleague, client, or supervisor.*

   b. *Define the other person's position at the time.* Select at least one position that the other party held. You can enter only one recommendation per position, but you can recommend the other party for multiple positions.

   c. *Click Next.*

3. **In the text box shown in Figure 9-4, enter the text for your recommendation.**

   Throughout this chapter, I stress staying specific, concise, and professional while focusing on a person's results and skills.

   REMEMBER

   The recommendations you write that are accepted by the other party appear also in your profile on the Recommendations tab. Believe it or not, people judge you by the comments you make about others, so read your recommendation before you post it and look for spelling or grammatical errors.

4. **Click Send.**

   The recommendation is sent to the recipient.

After you send your recommendation, the other person must accept it before it's posted. Don't take it personally if she doesn't post it, or at least not right away. After all, it's a gift, freely given. The primary value to *you* is in the gesture to the recipient, not the public visibility of your recommendation. And if she comes back with requested changes to the recommendation, by all means accommodate her as long as it's all true and you feel comfortable with it. It's a service to her, not you.

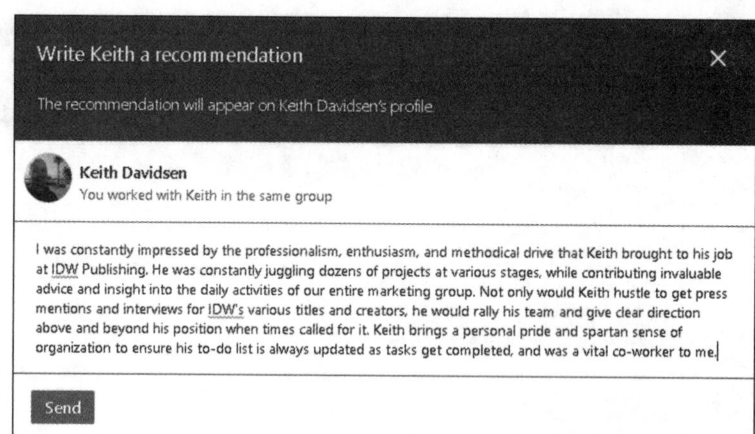

FIGURE 9-4: Write the recommendation here.

Requesting Recommendations

In an ideal world, you'd never request a recommendation. Everyone who's had a positive experience working with you would just automatically post a raving recommendation on LinkedIn. But the reality is that most likely only your raving fans and very heavy LinkedIn users are going to make unsolicited recommendations. Your mildly happy customers, former bosses whose jokes you laughed at consistently, and co-workers who you haven't seen in five years could all stand a little prompting.

Be prepared, though: Some people feel that recommendations should only be given freely, and they may be taken aback by receiving a recommendation request. So it's imperative that you frame your request with a personal message, not just a generic message from LinkedIn.

TIP

Don't be afraid to consider off-line methods of requesting a recommendation, such as a phone call or a face-to-face meeting, to make the request more personal and more likely for the person to say yes.

Choosing whom to ask

Request recommendations from the same people you might write them for: colleagues, business partners, and educational contacts. The only difference is that you're looking at it from his point of view.

Relationships aren't all symmetrical. For example, if someone hears me speak at a conference and buys this book, that person is my customer. My customers know my skills and expertise fairly well — perhaps not on the same level as a consulting client, but still well enough to make a recommendation. I, on the other hand, might not know a customer at all. I'm open to getting to know him, and I'm willing to connect, but I can't write a recommendation for him yet.

Creating a polite recommendation request

When you identify a person whom you want to write your recommendation, you're ready to create a recommendation request. To get started on authoring your request, follow these steps:

1. **Click the Me icon, on the top navigation bar, and then click View Profile.**
2. **Scroll down to the Recommendations header, and click the Ask for a Recommendation link (to the right of the header).**

   The Ask for Recommendations box appears.
3. **Enter the name of the first-degree connection:**

   a. *Below the Who Do You Want to Ask? header, start typing the name of the first-degree connection, as shown in Figure 9-5.*

   b. *When the name appears in the list, click it.*

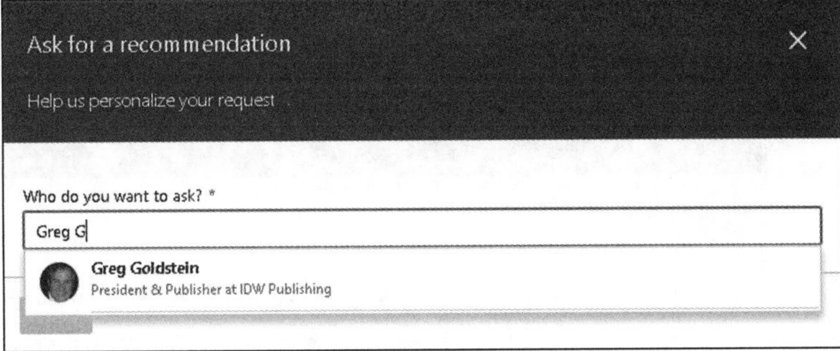

FIGURE 9-5: Select the position to be associated with your requested recommendation.

4. **Define your relationship with the person in the drop-down boxes provided, as shown in Figure 9-6, and then click Next.**

   Similar to the process of writing a recommendation, LinkedIn asks you to define the basis of your relationship with this person (Professional or Educational) and your position during the time when the other person is basing his or her recommendation of you.

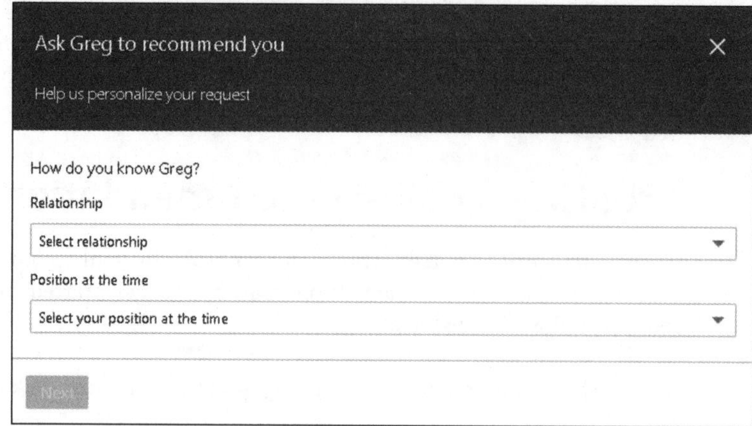

FIGURE 9-6: Confirm the person from whom you're requesting a recommendation.

5. **Type your message in the field provided.**

   The same etiquette is recommended here as in other requests: Don't just accept the boilerplate text that LinkedIn fills in, but rather customize it to create a personal note, as shown in Figure 9-7. You can customize only the body of your message.

TIP

   Don't forget to thank the person for the time and the effort in leaving you a recommendation!

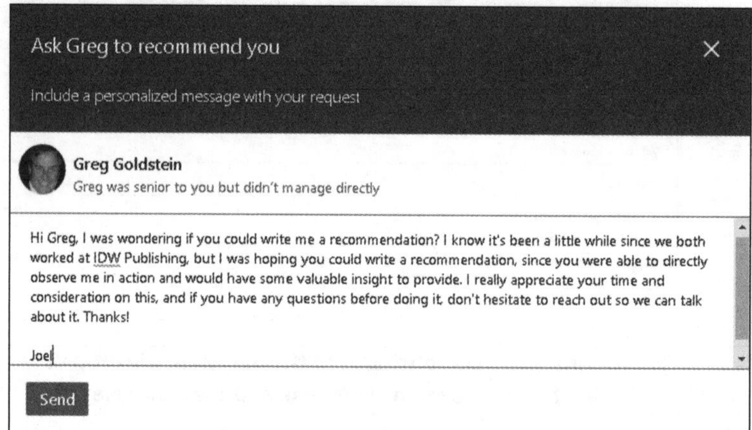

FIGURE 9-7: A customized recommendation request.

6. **Check your spelling and grammar.**

   You can write your message first using a program such as Microsoft Word, run the spelling and grammar check, and then cut and paste your message into the space provided, if you like.

7. **Click Send.**

   The recommendation request is sent to the intended recipient.

REMEMBER

Giving people some context as to why you're making the request helps motivate them, especially if they're nervous about or don't know how to use LinkedIn. Let them know you're available for any technical or follow-up help. Also, even though you should be asking only people who would be comfortable recommending you (you are, aren't you?), you still want to give them a gracious way to decline. After all, you're asking a favor. The person you're contacting is in no way obligated. Don't expect anything, and you won't be disappointed.

TIP

There's no such thing as too many recommendations as long as the quality is good. However, if you start accepting mediocre recommendations (on the assumption that "something is better than nothing"), people will start to think that a lot of them are fluff. LinkedIn doesn't give you control over the display order, either, so you have all the more reason to make sure that the recommendations displayed are good quality.

Gracefully Declining a Recommendation (or a Request for One)

Unfortunately, not everyone writes good recommendations — and not all your LinkedIn connections have read this book — so eventually, someone will write a recommendation that you don't want in your profile.

No problem. Just politely request a replacement when you receive it. Thank him for thinking of you, and give him the context of what you're trying to accomplish:

> Wei:
>
> Thank you so much for your gracious recommendation. I'd like to ask a small favor, though. I'm trying to position myself more as a public speaker in the widget industry, rather than as a gadget trainer. Because you've heard me speak on the topic, if you could gear your recommendation more toward that, I'd greatly appreciate it.
>
> Thanks,
>
> Alexa

If he's sincerely trying to be of service to you, he should have no problem changing it. Just make sure you ask him for something based on your experience with him.

WARNING

You may receive a request for a recommendation from someone you don't feel comfortable recommending. If it's because she gave you poor service or was less than competent, you have to consider whether you should even be connected to her at all because, after all, LinkedIn is a business referral system. I discuss how to remove a connection in Chapter 5.

Perhaps you don't have sufficient experience with her services to provide her a recommendation. If that's the case, just reply to her request with an explanation:

> Alexa:
>
> I received your request for a recommendation. Although I am happy to be connected to you on LinkedIn and look forward to getting to know you better or even work together in the future, at this time I just don't feel as though I have enough basis to give you a substantive recommendation.
>
> After we've worked together on something successfully, I'll be more than happy to provide a recommendation.
>
> Thanks,
>
> Wei

Managing Recommendations

Relationships change over time. Some get better, others they get worse, and still others just change. As you get more recommendations, you might decide that you don't want to display them all or you would like some of them updated to support your current branding or initiatives.

Fortunately, neither the recommendation you give nor those you receive are etched in stone (or computer chips, as the case may be). You can edit or remove recommendations you've written at any time, and you can hide or request revisions to those you receive.

Editing or removing recommendations you've made

To edit or remove a recommendation you've made, follow these steps:

1. **Click the Me icon, on the top navigation bar, and then click View Profile from the drop-down list that appears.**
2. **Scroll down to the Recommendations header, and click the pencil icon (edit) to the far right of the header.**

   A Manage Recommendations window appears, containing all the recommendations you've received or given as well as pending requests.
3. **Click the Given link.**

   All the recommendations you've made are listed in reverse chronological order (see Figure 9-8).

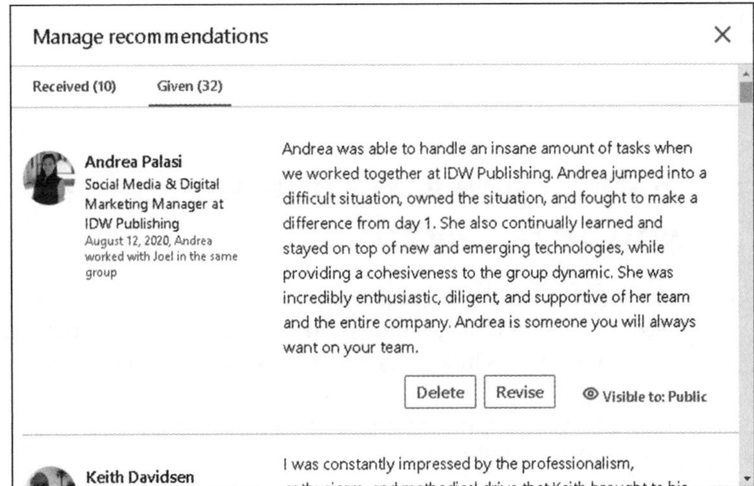

FIGURE 9-8: Delete or change the visibility of a recommendation.

4. **To change the visibility of a recommendation:**

   a. *Click the Visible to X link.* The screen updates and displays three options you can assign for the recommendation's visibility, as shown in Figure 9-9.

   b. *Make your selection.* You can choose Only You, Your Connections, or Public. If you change to Only You or Your Connections, you'll be limiting who can view the recommendation.
5. **To delete a recommendation, click the Delete button.**

   LinkedIn will display a message box asking you to click Yes to confirm the recommendation removal.
6. **When you're finished, scroll down to the bottom of the Manage Recommendations window and click the Save button to save your changes.**

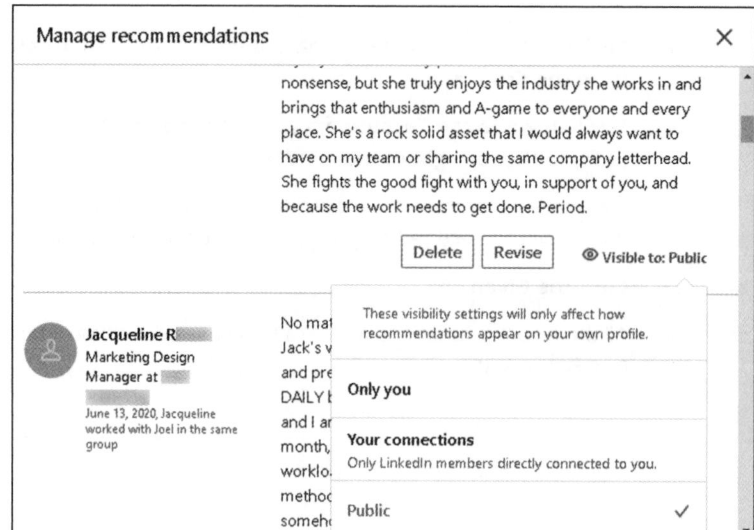

FIGURE 9-9: Change the visibility of your recommendation.

Handling new recommendations you've received

When you receive a recommendation from someone, you see it on your Recommendations page, under the Received tab, with the You Have *X* Pending Recommendations link. Click that link to read the full text, as shown in Figure 9-10.

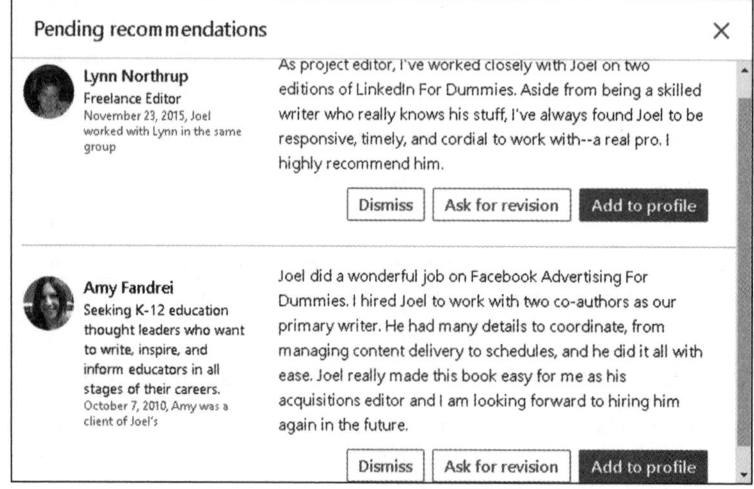

FIGURE 9-10: Here is where you can accept an incoming recommendation.

When you receive a recommendation, you have these options:

- **Add it to your profile.** Click the Add to Profile button to add this recommendation, as stated, to your profile.
- **Ask for a revision.** Click the Ask for Revision button to request that the person make changes to his or her recommendation of you. Detail what revisions you would like the person to make, such as adding specific details, including or removing a certain project, or highlighting previously unmentioned skills you now need to help make a career change.
- **Get rid of it.** If you aren't happy with the person's recommendation or aren't interested in having the recommendation in your profile, click the Dismiss button. If you want, you can send the person a brief note explaining why you're not adding the recommendation to your profile or requesting changes.
- **Ignore it.** Until you take action, the recommendation is pending and will not appear in your profile. Perhaps you don't want the recommendation to become visible until a certain event happens, such as applying for a different job. You can return to this screen at any time to add the recommendation or ask for changes.

Removing or requesting to revise a recommendation

To remove a recommendation you've received or to request a revision, do the following:

1. **Click the Me icon, in the top navigation bar, and then click View profile in the drop-down list that appears.**
2. **Scroll down to the Recommendations header, and click the pencil icon (edit) to the far right of the header.**

   The Recommendations page appears.
3. **If necessary, click the Received tab.**

   Doing so takes you to the Recommendations You've Received page.
4. **Scroll down the page to find the recommendation in question.**
5. **To remove a recommendation, change the slider (on the right of the recommendation) from Show to Hide, as in Figure 9-11.**

   Your recommendation will be hidden after you complete this process. At any time, you can come back to this window and change the slider from Hide to Show, to return the recommendation to your profile.

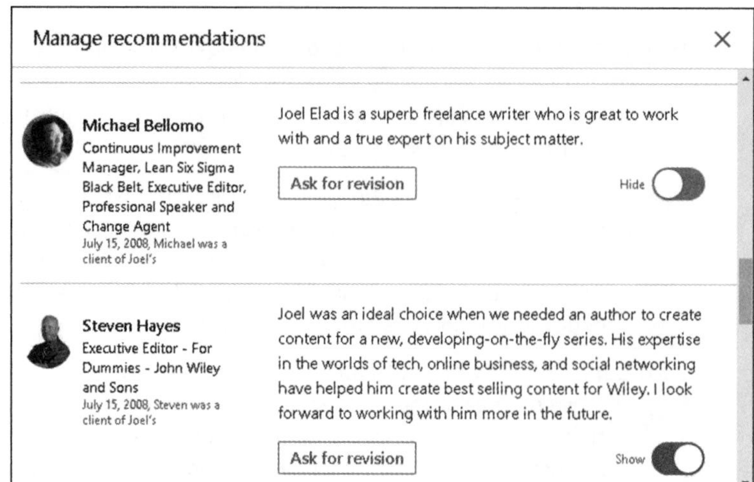

FIGURE 9-11: Remove a recommendation by changing its visibility to Hide.

6. **When you want changes made to your recommendation:**

   a. *Click the Ask for Revision button (just below the recommendation you want to revise).* A message to the other party appears, as shown in Figure 9-12.

   b. *Write your message.* Detail what revisions you would like the person to make, such as adding specific details, including or removing a certain project, or highlighting previously unmentioned skills you now need to help make a career change.

   c. *Click the Send button to send the message.*

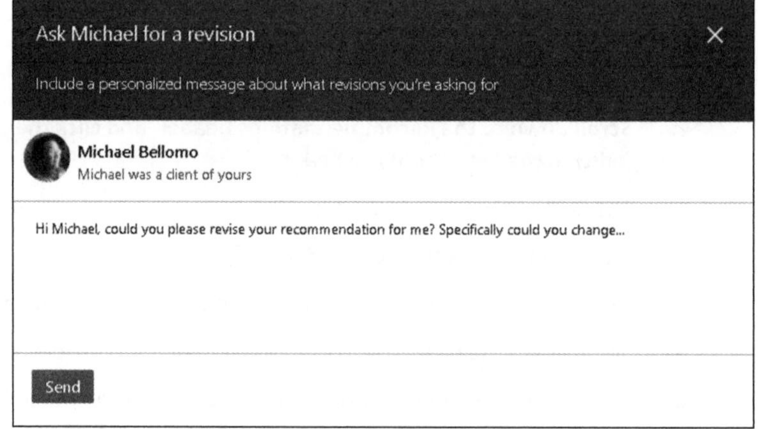

FIGURE 9-12: Ask your friend to revise his or her recommendation of you.

7. **To save your choice, scroll down to the bottom of the Manage Recommendations window and click the Save button.**

Negotiating the social graces concerning recommendations might feel awkward at first, but with practice you'll quickly become comfortable. By both giving and receiving good recommendations, you'll build your public reputation, increase your social capital with your connections, and have a good excuse for renewing relationships with people you haven't contacted recently.

» Installing a LinkedIn mobile app

» Breaking down the sections of the main LinkedIn mobile app

» Understanding how mobile app usage affects your LinkedIn experience

Chapter 10
Accessing LinkedIn with a Mobile Device

Mobile devices are everywhere these days. Smartphones, tablet devices, wearable devices such as the Apple Watch, and whatever portable devices are being invented as I type this sentence are having increased usage, especially as more people use their mobile device as their main (or only) gateway to Internet content. Because of this shift, companies of all sizes have been paying more and more attention to developing mobile applications, or apps for short, that give their user base an easier way to interface with the company than opening a web browser for their device and surfing to the company's website.

LinkedIn is no exception, and its mobile strategy has been evolving for years. Assisted by some outside purchases, LinkedIn provides its user base with a robust mobile app that caters to general and specific uses of the LinkedIn website and its functions, while maintaining a suite of targeted apps for specific functions. LinkedIn launched a major redesign of its flagship mobile app to simplify the experience and encourage users to access LinkedIn through the app when they're on the go, perhaps on the way to a client meeting or expanding their personal network at a conference.

In this chapter, I detail LinkedIn's presence in the mobile app space. I discuss the different apps available as of this writing, and then talk about installing an app on your mobile device. I then analyze the main LinkedIn app and detail the functionality currently available in that app. Finally, I talk about how your activity on the app affects your use of LinkedIn on the desktop or laptop.

Surveying the LinkedIn Mobile App

As more and more people use their mobile devices to access the Internet and do their daily tasks, companies such as LinkedIn have been aggressively ramping up their mobile app development to meet the needs of their device-toting user base. The look and design of the apps have evolved to give LinkedIn users data in an easy-to-read format.

In addition, the number of LinkedIn apps has decreased over time to keep the user experience simple and effective. As of this writing, rather than having you use multiple apps to accomplish core tasks, LinkedIn redesigned and streamlined their main mobile app so that it focuses on most user's basic needs. That said, premium and specialized apps are still available and can be used separately or with LinkedIn's main mobile app. To check out LinkedIn's different mobile offerings, visit the mobile page at `https://mobile.linkedin.com` (see Figure 10-1).

FIGURE 10-1: Learn about the different LinkedIn mobile apps.

As of this writing, LinkedIn offers apps in the following areas:

- **LinkedIn mobile app:** The main LinkedIn app allows you to interact with LinkedIn as you would when using your desktop or laptop computer. You can view your news feed of friends' stories, update your profile, talk to your connections, search and apply for jobs, add people to your network, and search for more information.
- **LinkedIn SlideShare:** This app gives you mobile access to over 18 million slide presentations, information graphics, and videos that have been

uploaded by LinkedIn members around the world. Learn about various topics from your network and leading industry professionals, all from the ease of your mobile device.

» **LinkedIn Learning and Lynda.com:** In April 2015, LinkedIn acquired Lynda.com, a subscription-based online learning website. While Lynda.com maintains its own app, LinkedIn and Lynda.com developed a new LinkedIn Learning mobile app, which is available to LinkedIn Learning subscribers and allows users to access a vast library of educational presentations to learn about thousands of different skills. Learn from the experts while on the go and advance your skills and career with a LinkedIn Learning monthly subscription and this app. You can also download this content to your mobile device for future viewing.

In the iTunes App Store and Google Play Store, you can find apps owned by LinkedIn by searching for apps where the developer is LinkedIn Corporation.

You can see from Figure 10-2, the variety of apps available for different devices for Apple iOS devices, for example.

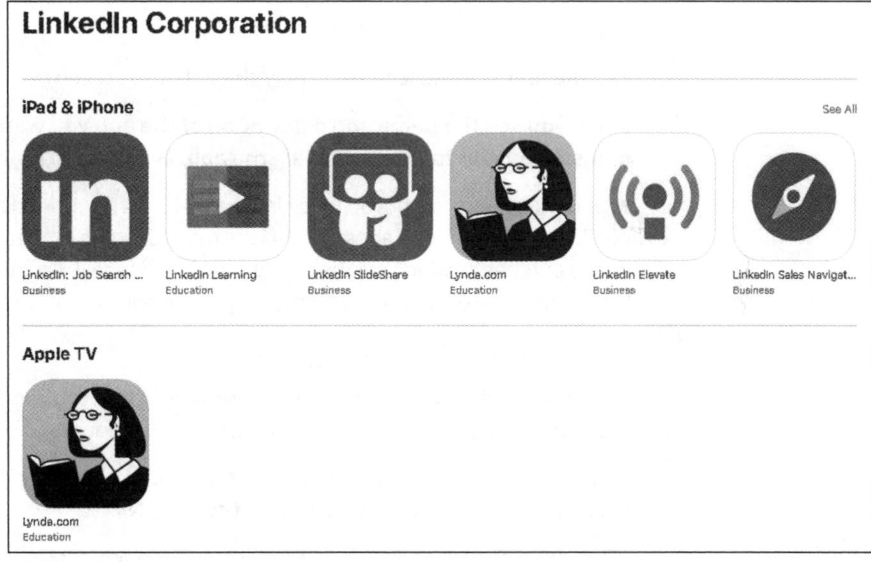

FIGURE 10-2: Download different LinkedIn apps to your iOS device.

REMEMBER

Other apps are available to premium users, targeting specific users such as recruiters and sales professionals. Consult the app store for your device for more information about these apps.

Installing Any LinkedIn Mobile App

WARNING

As of this writing, LinkedIn apps are only available for mobile devices running the Apple iOS operating system or the Android operating system, and not every app will work on every device. (Refer to Figure 10-2, which shows six apps for an iPhone or iPad, and only one of those six for AppleTV.) Consult the app store for your device to see what you can install.

When you're ready to install an app, follow these steps from your mobile device. (In the following steps, I used an iPhone to install the main LinkedIn app.)

1. **Pull up your main source for installing mobile apps.**

   If you have an Apple device, go to the App Store; if you have an Android device, go to the Google Play Store. You can also go to LinkedIn's mobile page at `https://mobile.linkedin.com`, and then tap either the App Store or Google Play Store button, depending on your device.

2. **On the search screen, type the word LinkedIn (and any additional words, if you want one of the specialized LinkedIn mobile apps, such as LinkedIn Slideshare or LinkedIn Learning).**

   A results screen of apps appears (refer to Figure 10-2).

3. **Tap the appropriate icon to display the app info screen.**
4. **When you see the name and description of the app you want, tap the Get or Install button to start installing the app, as shown in Figure 10-3.**

   Your device may prompt you to log into your iTunes or Android account at this point. In addition, some apps, such as the main LinkedIn mobile app, offer in-app purchases, which means that Apple or Google will want to verify your billing method in case you buy something in the app.

5. **After the app is fully installed, tap its icon.**

   A login screen appears, as shown in Figure 10-4, where you can sign in with your LinkedIn account or join LinkedIn with a new account.

6. **From the login screen, tap Sign In, type your LinkedIn user ID and password in the boxes provided, and then tap Next.**

   After you've signed into your LinkedIn account, the box shown in Figure 10-5 appears, asking whether you want to enable notifications, so the app can send a message to your device's screen when certain actions occur.

7. **Tap Allow to turn on notifications, or tap Don't Allow to keep notifications turned off.**

   At any time, you can go into the app's settings to change this setting.

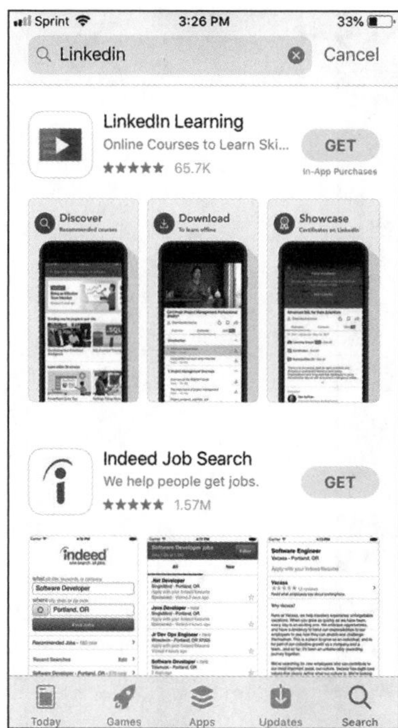

FIGURE 10-3: Tap the Get or Install button to start the installation process.

FIGURE 10-4: Sign in to your LinkedIn account from the app.

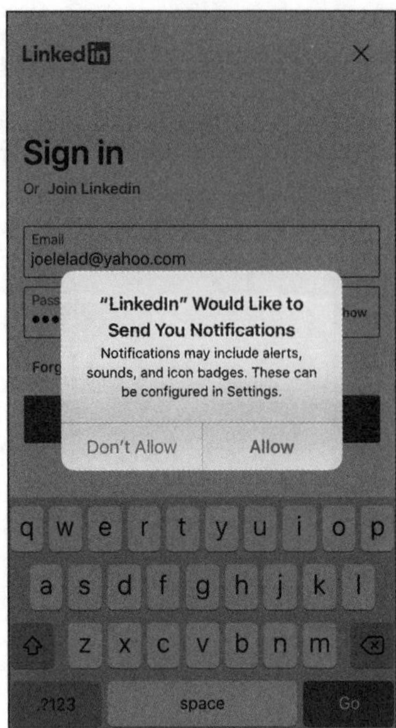

FIGURE 10-5: Decide whether you want the mobile app to send notifications to your device.

Congratulations, you've installed the app! Repeat this process with any other app you want to install on your device.

Breaking Down the Sections of the LinkedIn Mobile App

After you install the main LinkedIn mobile app and sign in to your LinkedIn account from the app, you'll be ready to start using the app. Before you do, though, it's important to understand the capabilities now at your fingertips.

You can swipe right (or click the Profile photo in the top-left corner) to display a different navigation menu (see Figure 10-6), similar to what you see on the left side of your LinkedIn desktop screen. From this menu, you can view (and edit) your profile, access your LinkedIn settings, or go to any LinkedIn page for which you're an administrator. Scroll down the menu to access your groups, events, and followed hashtags and to discover more content.

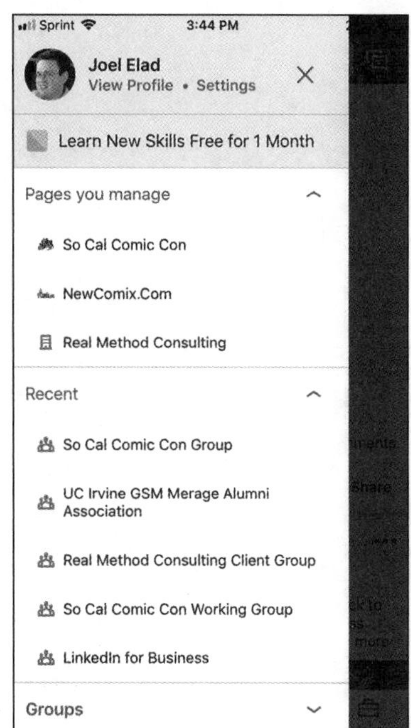

FIGURE 10-6: Bring up some core navigation with a right swipe.

When you use the LinkedIn mobile app, note the series of buttons along the bottom of the screen. These buttons enable you to easily reach the five core sections of the LinkedIn app:

- **Home:** This section (see Figure 10-7) mirrors your home page news feed, integrating elements from your first-degree connections and the news sources you follow on LinkedIn, news items and blog posts that LinkedIn thinks you may like, and job recommendations. Because you're on the go with your mobile device, when you see any post you want to read later, tap the three dots to the right of the post header, and then tap Save from the menu that appears. You can then revisit that post later using your mobile or desktop device. From this menu, you can also share the post and send it as a message to someone else.
- **My Network:** This section works in a similar way as the My Network icon on the LinkedIn website home page. You can see a list of your connections, add contacts to your account, view and respond to incoming invitations to join your network, and see people you may know whom you can add to your network. Figure 10-8 shows the Manage My Network and Invitations sections (tap the check mark to accept or the X to ignore invitations). Scroll down to find the People You May Know section, where you can review the list of people and tap the icon to invite them to your network.

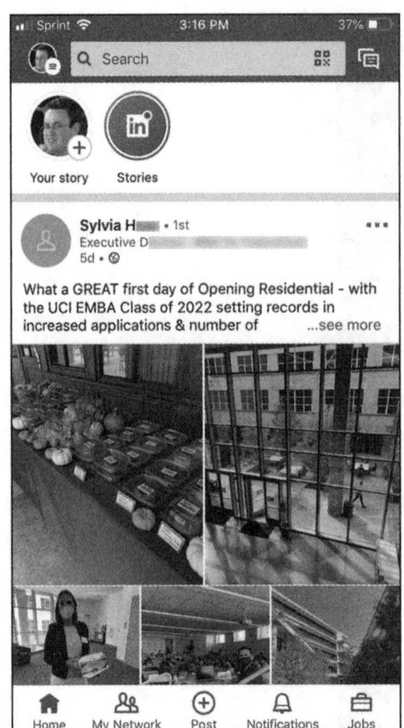

FIGURE 10-7: See your feed elements from LinkedIn on the home screen.

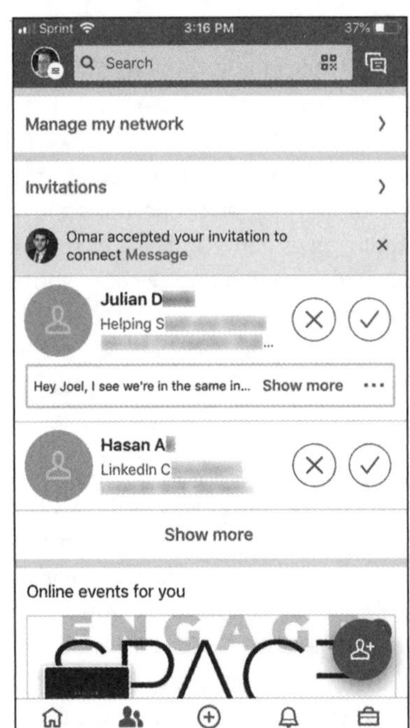

FIGURE 10-8: See what invitations you've received and whom you may know on LinkedIn.

» **Post:** This section enables you to create a post for your LinkedIn feed. You can enter text, add a photo, capture a video, attach a document, celebrate an occasion, share a LinkedIn story, create a poll, or do a find an expert post, asking specific people to help you fill a need. As with the desktop version, you can set your privacy level for each post, and decide whether you're posting as yourself or on behalf of a Company page for which you are the administrator.

» **Notifications:** This section (see Figure 10-9), which is the same as the Notifications list that LinkedIn provides on the website, shows you when and where you're being mentioned and who is reading your profile or your posts. LinkedIn may recommend influencers you can follow and give you a daily rundown of news that might interest you.

To update your notification settings, swipe right, tap Settings (to the right of your name and profile picture), tap Communications, and then tap Push below the How You Get Your Notifications header. These notification settings are important to mobile users because they can set up push notifications from this screen, allowing them to see pop-up notifications on their device, such as an incoming text message, job posting, or news feed item, so they don't miss a new item of interest.

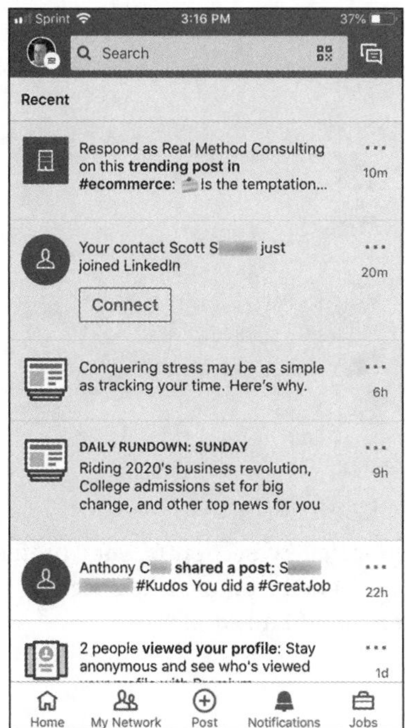

FIGURE 10-9: Review your notifications through the mobile app.

» **Jobs:** This section is the same as the general LinkedIn jobs screen. You can search for jobs, apply to jobs, and see jobs that you may be interested in. When you type keywords in the search bar at the top, job search results appear based on those keywords.

In addition to the five main icons along the bottom of the LinkedIn mobile app screen, you can also easily update your profile by tapping your profile photo, in the top left of any mobile app screen and to the left of the Search box, and then clicking View Profile from the links that appear. Your LinkedIn profile page appears, as shown in Figure 10-10. You can tap the blue + button, at the bottom right, to add information to your profile so your professional brand can stay strong or get refreshed.

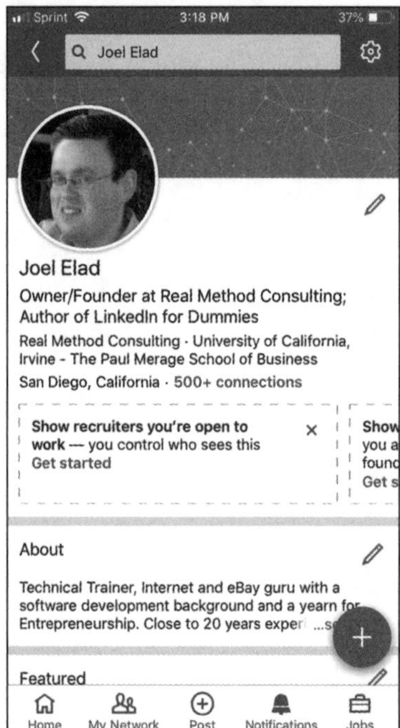

FIGURE 10-10: Use the LinkedIn app to update your profile page.

WARNING

As of this writing, you can't edit every section of your profile in the LinkedIn mobile app. If you don't see the pencil icon next to a section, you'll have to edit that section on the desktop version of LinkedIn.

The Messaging icon has been moved from the bottom navigation bar to the top-right corner of the screen. Clicking the icon (or swiping left from any LinkedIn Mobile app screen) mirrors your LinkedIn inbox, enabling you to message or chat with your LinkedIn connections. You can initiate a conversation or follow up on existing communications while you're away from your desk. You can change your notifications for a conversation or delete a conversation from the screen.

Finally, a Search box appears along the top of all LinkedIn app screens. When you search for people, LinkedIn tries to guess what you're looking for by studying variations of what you've typed, coupled with your network of connections and the list of companies where you have been employed. You can also type a collection of keywords (someone's name and employer, job skills, or alma mater, for example) to help find the person on LinkedIn.

Connecting Your App Usage with Website Usage

After you have installed one or more of LinkedIn mobile apps, and start using the apps interchangeably with your desktop or laptop, you should notice a synergy in which all your actions are captured and available regardless of platform. Many of your actions are replicated or transmitted to your main LinkedIn account and will be reflected when you log into the LinkedIn website with your desktop computer:

- Communications will show up in LinkedIn Messages, and you will see the same order of conversations on both the app and the website, where the most recent conversation is at the top of the screen.
- Any profile updates you made with the app will be stored in the profile you see through the website and vice versa. Depending on your profile settings, your network will be notified of any profile changes you make on either the app or the website.
- Any interactions you have with LinkedIn members, whether you like or comment on someone's update, participate in a group discussion, or accept or reject an invitation, will be the same whether you did it through the app or the website.

Similar to the settings available from the LinkedIn website, a number of settings through the LinkedIn app can be updated by tapping the Profile Photo button and then clicking the Settings link at the top of the screen. Any settings updated with your mobile device are reflected when you next log into the desktop version of LinkedIn. As of this writing, only some settings are accessible through the app, and they are divided into six categories:

- **Account Preferences:** Update your profile details, customize your site preferences, sync your contacts and calendar, set up your connection between LinkedIn and Twitter, close your account, upgrade to LinkedIn Premium, and review the active sessions you have where you're logged into LinkedIn from your various devices.
- **Sign In and Security:** Update your list of email addresses, add a phone number, change your password, see your active sessions, and manage the list of devices that have stored your LinkedIn account and password information. Decide whether to turn on two-step verification to access your account, and for phones with Touch ID, enable an app lock through your device's Touch ID system.
- **Visibility:** You can choose whether your network is notified when you make profile changes, and who can follow you. Change the setting where you are visible or private when viewing someone else's profile and manage your active status visibility and the list of whom you're blocking. Manage who can find your profile by typing your email address or phone number.
- **Communication:** Decide which, if any, mobile push notifications you receive from LinkedIn. In addition, you can set the types of messages you want to receive from members and partners, whether you want read receipts and typing indicators, and whether you want smart replies when you respond to a message.
- **Data Privacy:** Manage the data you've created and download a copy of your LinkedIn activity and data. Set your personal demographic information and decide whether to clear your search history. Set up your job search specifications and decide who can see your profile when you apply for a job. Decide whether public data can be used to improve your profile, and whether work experience from your profile can be accessed by Resume Assistant, a feature in Microsoft Word.
- **Advertising Data:** Decide what profile data, if any, can be used for ad personalization. Define your interest in specific categories, and decide per category what can be profiled to customize your ad content, and whether ads you see beyond LinkedIn can be affected by your LinkedIn account data.

» Privacy page

» Developing your own Privacy preferences

» Setting communication preferences to make life easier

Chapter 11

Configuring Settings Like a Pro

I talk a lot about the different functions available on LinkedIn, and I hope you've started to set aside some time on a regular basis to keep track of various tasks as you build up your profile and network. To manage this new set of tasks most effectively, look around LinkedIn and its growing number of functions.

In this chapter, I shift gears a little and talk about the underpinning of the entire site — your LinkedIn settings. As LinkedIn grows in terms of functionality, you get to decide how you want to interact with LinkedIn and communication, privacy, and site usage features you want to automate. I discuss the majority of options on the Settings & Privacy page, including how you can use them to improve your usage of LinkedIn and your professional life in general. I also describe many of the options for several core components, namely Account Preferences, Sign In & Security, Visibility, Communications, and Data Privacy. Further, I detail how some settings offer more than a few choices and how to set them up regardless of complexity.

Using the Settings & Privacy Page as a Command Console

The LinkedIn Settings & Privacy page is, by default, full of information about how you interact with the site. Think of the Settings & Privacy page as your command console for working with LinkedIn. You can get to the page at any time by clicking the Me icon, on the top navigation bar, and then clicking Settings & Privacy under Account. Your Settings & Privacy page will look similar to most other users of LinkedIn, so it will probably look similar to mine (shown in Figure 11-1), except the name, headline, number of connections, and date you joined LinkedIn will reflect your own account.

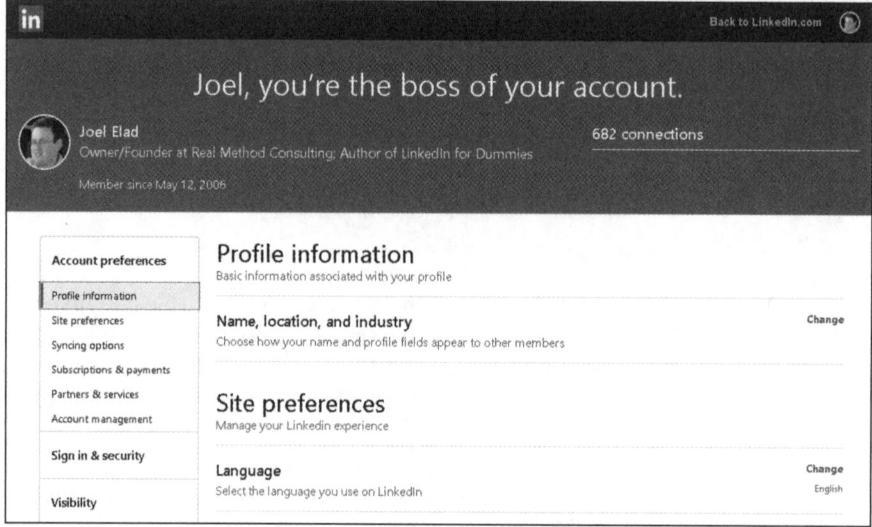

FIGURE 11-1: Coordinate all your settings here.

REMEMBER

When you load the Settings & Privacy page, LinkedIn defaults to showing Account Preferences, a specific section of the Settings & Privacy page.

On the left side of the screen is a navigation menu. When you first pull up the settings page, you'll need to scroll down to see the full navigation menu, as shown in Figure 11-2. From this page, you can click any section name in the left menu to jump to that part of the selected settings page. For example, the Account Preferences page has six sections: Profile Information, Site Preferences, Syncing Options, Subscriptions & Payments, Partners & Services, and Account Management. The Profile Information section is selected in Figure 11-2. As you scroll down through a section of the Account Preferences page, the section menu item is highlighted.

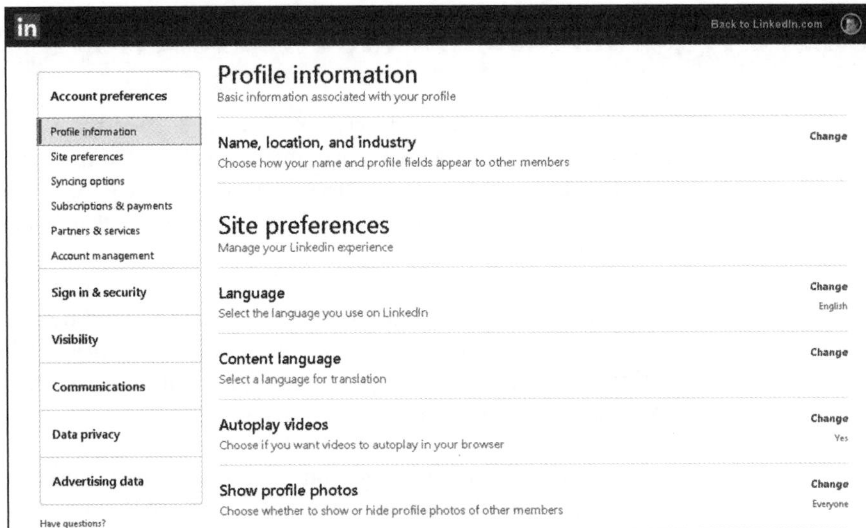

FIGURE 11-2: The sections for the selected page (Account) appear on the left.

Note the Change link to the right of each setting. When you want to change a setting, start by clicking Change. The area below the setting expands so you can make changes on the same page. For example, in Figure 11-3, I clicked Change next to the Language setting so that I could change the language setting for my account. The section expanded, displaying a description of the setting and a drop-down menu to make my selection. Always click the Close link (where the Change link used to be) to save your changes, close the section, and move on.

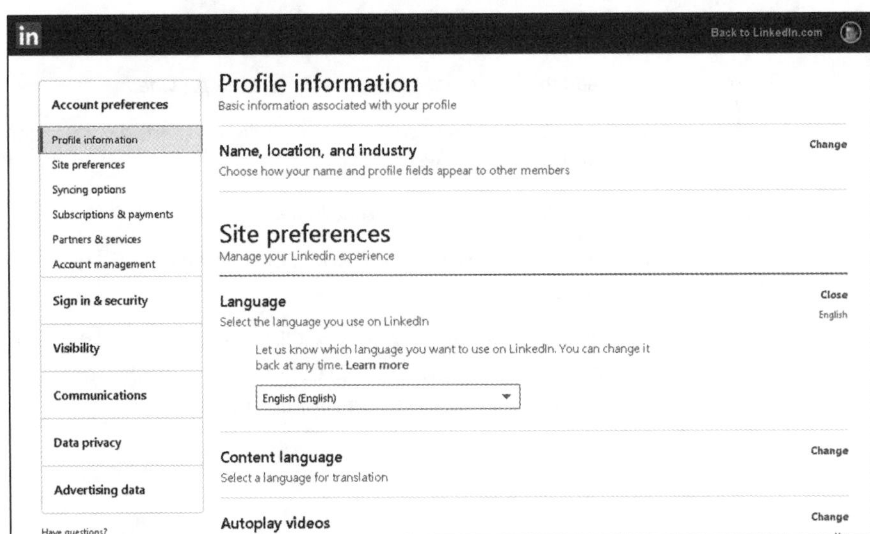

FIGURE 11-3: Language setting expanded on the settings page.

Starting with Basic Account Changes

Let's dive into the second section, Sign In & Security. On this settings page, Account Access, the only subhead, enables you to see the basics of your account (email addresses, phone numbers, password, active sessions, and so on) and which sessions are active with your account. You can also add extra verification to access your account.

To review the settings, begin by clicking the Me icon on the top navigation bar of any LinkedIn page. Then under the Account header, click Settings & Privacy. The Settings & Privacy screen appears (refer to Figure 11-1). Click Sign In & Security, which brings up the Account Access screen.

Following are the basic settings you can update, either one at a time or all at once, depending on whether you're in the initial setup phase or refining your account as time goes by. Here's how to update the basic Account settings:

- **To add another email address to your account:**
  a. *Click the Change link to the right of the E-Mail Addresses header.* The screen shown in Figure 11-4 appears. When you started your LinkedIn account, you had to provide a valid email address. But if you use multiple email addresses, or have a past email account that previous colleagues or friends used with you, you probably want to add them to your account so that more people can find you. Don't worry; the email addresses are not publicly viewable unless you give the okay.
  b. *Click the Add E-Mail Address link.*
  c. *Add the new email address in the text box provided.*
  d. *Click the Send Verification button.* LinkedIn sends a verification email to the address you've provided.
  e. *Click the link in the verification email.*
- **To choose a new primary email:** Click Make Primary next to the email address.
- **To get rid of an email address:** Click Remove next to the address. This feature is useful if an email account becomes inactive or is hacked, or you don't want it associated with your account.

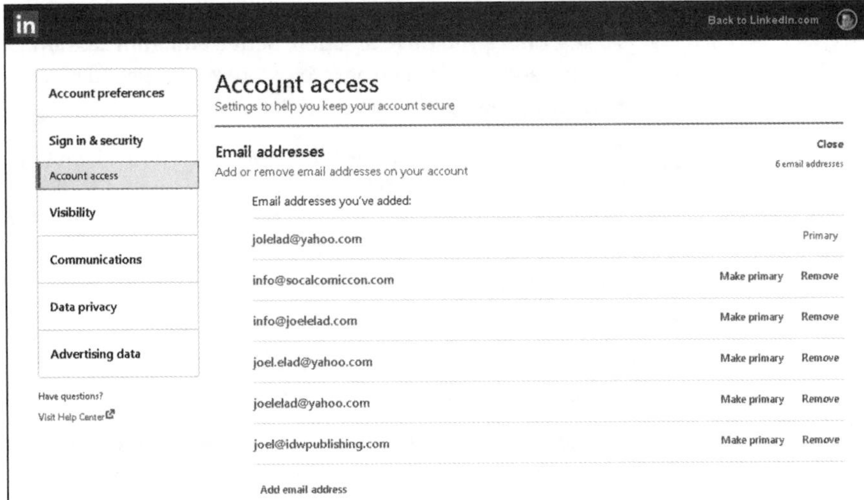

FIGURE 11-4: Track the email addresses associated with your account.

» **To associate a phone number with your account:**

   a. *Click Close to the right of Email Addresses. Then click Change next to Phone Numbers.*

   b. *Click the Add Phone Number link and then choose the Country from the newly displayed drop-down list. Add the phone number in the New Phone Number box.*

   c. *Click the Send Code button to send the number to LinkedIn.*

   d. *When you receive a text message from LinkedIn with a 6-digit verification code, add that code in the appropriate text.*

TIP

You might want to associate a phone number with your account so that LinkedIn can call or text your phone to verify your identity if you forget your password. Just select the Use for Password Reset check box next to your phone number.

» **To change your password:**

   a. *Click Close next to Phone numbers. Then click Change next to the Change Password setting.* Below the Change link is a date for the last time you changed your password.

   b. *Type your current password. Next, type your new password twice, and then verify that you're not a computer or robot.*

   c. *Click the Save button.* LinkedIn updates your account with your new password.

» **To see where you have an open, active LinkedIn session:** Scroll down a little bit, and click Change next to Where You're Signed In. When you've finished reviewing this section, click Close.

Every time you bring up LinkedIn on your computer, tablet, smartphone, or other Internet-capable device, you create a new session tied to your account. When you expand this option, you see not only your current session, as shown in Figure 11-5, but also any additional sessions and the length of time those sessions have been open.

To close any sessions that you're no longer using, click Sign Out of All These Sessions or click Sign Out for an individual session. In this way, someone else with access to your device won't also have access to your account.

» **To add two-step authentication to LinkedIn for enhanced account security:** Click Change next to Two-Step Verification. When you add a phone number and turn on two-step verification, LinkedIn will use that phone number to send verification codes anytime a change is attempted from your LinkedIn account. No change can occur until you enter the verification code. Two-step verification can be cumbersome if you are making a lot of changes or updates, but it also makes it much harder for a stranger to damage your LinkedIn account.

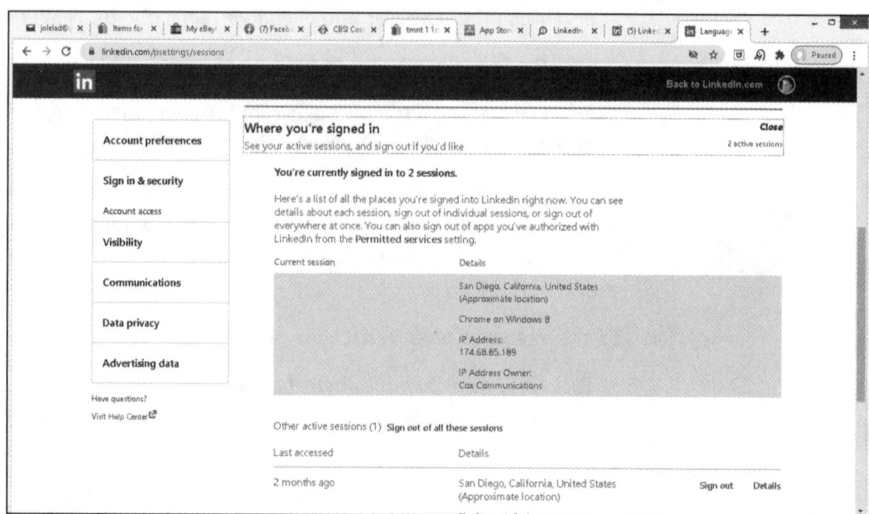

FIGURE 11-5: The list of current open LinkedIn sessions.

To complete changing the basic settings, click the Account Preferences header in the left navigation menu, and go through the various subheaders. Here's how to finish updating the basic Account settings:

- **To change your name, location and industry:** Click Change next to Name, Location and Industry. The Edit Intro window appears, and you can change lots of basic information for your account, such as your name headline, assigned location, industry, and other profile fields. I cover a lot of these fields in Chapter 3, where you complete your profile.

  If you get married and your name changes, you may want to update your name here. And of course, if you move, you'll want to change your Location setting. (Adding a new job and its location does not change your Location setting.) If a new job means you are now working in a different industry, change your Industry setting so people see the appropriate setting on your LinkedIn page.
- **To make videos on your LinkedIn screen play automatically:** Click Change next to Autoplay Videos, and make sure the setting is set to Yes.
- **To hide the profile photos of people you see on LinkedIn:** Click Change next to Show Profile Photos. Change the Select Whose Photos You'd Like to See setting to No One. (You can also set it to Your Connections, Your Network, or All LinkedIn Members.) These settings can be helpful if you have a slow Internet connection and want to optimize how much data is coming through when you use LinkedIn. If you prevent videos from playing and pictures from displaying, your LinkedIn web pages should load faster if you have a slow connection.
- **To upgrade your account to a paid Premium account:** Scroll down or click the Subscriptions & Payments header in the left sidebar. Click Change next to Try Premium for Free. The different types of Premium accounts are described in Chapter 1. You can also click Change next to View Purchase History to see a list of everything you've bought from LinkedIn (such as subscriptions, ads, and job postings).
- **To manage which Microsoft services you've authorized to share data with LinkedIn:** Click the Partners & Services link in the left sidebar. Then click Change next to Microsoft. When you open your list of permitted services, you'll see a list of processes that can interface with your LinkedIn account, as shown in Figure 11-6. (Several are LinkedIn functions, such as Business and Developer.) To delete a function that you don't want interfacing with your account, click the function's Remove link.

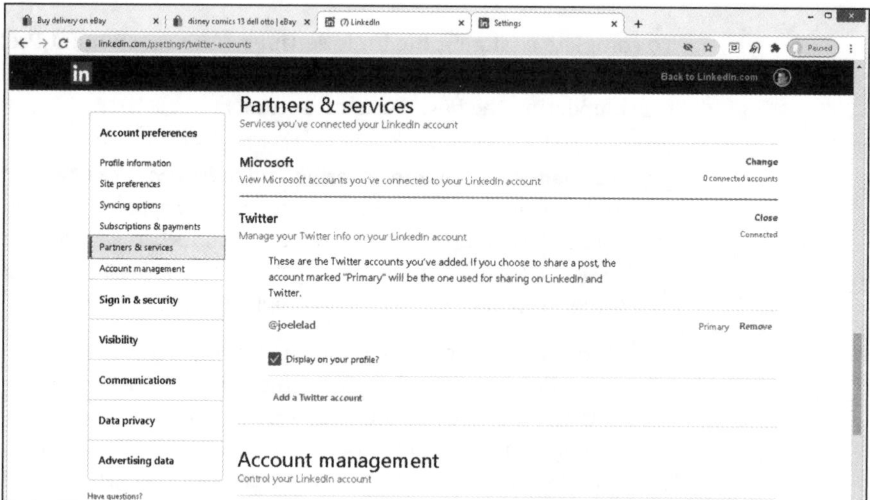

FIGURE 11-6: Manage the Twitter account that can interface with your LinkedIn account.

- **To connect your Twitter account to your LinkedIn account:** Click Change next to Twitter Settings to display the Twitter Options screen (refer to Figure 11-6). You can add one or more Twitter accounts to your LinkedIn account, and set whether you want to display your Twitter account in your LinkedIn profile.

  One of the primary benefits of linking the two accounts is if you want to share LinkedIn updates, long-form posts, or articles with your Twitter followers. Be warned that sharing every post on Twitter, as well as LinkedIn, could be seen as off-putting to your Twitter followers, so share when appropriate.

- **To close your LinkedIn account for good:** Click Change next to Close Account. Naturally, the point of this book is to encourage you to use your LinkedIn account to the fullest, so I rarely advocate closing your account. The main reason to use this setting is if you have more than one LinkedIn account, which is addressed next.

- **To merge two LinkedIn accounts:** Click the Change link next to Merge Accounts. Provide the login information for your duplicate account, and then click Submit.

  Perhaps you joined LinkedIn years ago and did a little business, but then forgot your login information and created a new account a few years later. When you have multiple accounts, people will find it confusing and wonder which account to connect with or send messages to. Therefore, LinkedIn enables you to merge accounts, without losing any connections on the old account.

When you click Change, you see the account you're currently logged into, as shown in Figure 11-7. In the boxes, enter the email address and password for your second account. After you click Submit, LinkedIn transfers your connections from the second account to the first account, and allows you to review and confirm the transfer. After you do that, LinkedIn closes the second account.

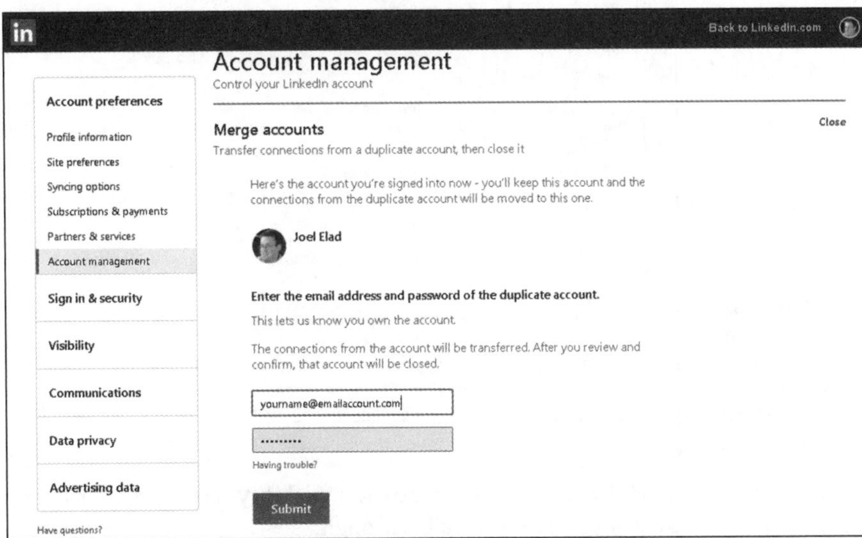

FIGURE 11-7: Merge two accounts into one.

Controlling Visibility and Privacy Settings

Now it's time to tackle another popular area of concern for LinkedIn members, namely Visibility and Data Privacy settings. On these settings pages, you see everything from protecting the information in your profile and how often you use LinkedIn, to allowing people to follow or contact you on LinkedIn or access your network.

You start with the Visibility Settings section, where you decide how your public profile looks; whether you want your connections to know when you edit your profile, use LinkedIn, or make the news; and even whether you display your last name. Then you move to the Blocking and Hiding section, where you control lists of who can follow you, who is blocked from interfacing with you, and whom you've unfollowed. Next is Job Seeking, which has valuable job hunting settings that can help your efforts. You finish with Data Privacy, where you control where your profile appears on and off LinkedIn.

To begin, click the Me icon on the top navigation bar of any LinkedIn page. Then under the Account header, click Settings & Privacy, and then click the Visibility header. The Visibility screen shown in Figure 11-8 appears.

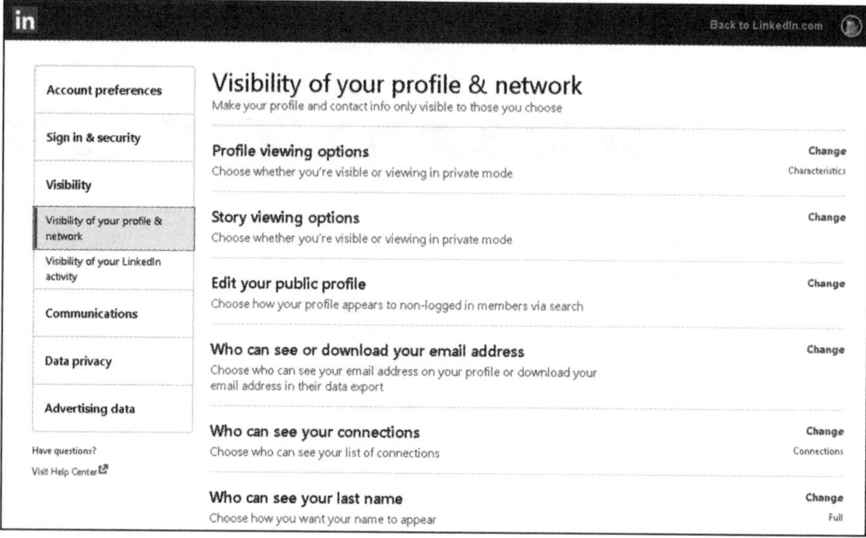

FIGURE 11-8: Access your LinkedIn visibility settings from this screen.

Read through the headers on the Visibility screen, and decide which ones you want to change. Here's a walk-through:

- **If you don't want other LinkedIn members to know that you're viewing their profile or story:** Click the Change link next to either Profile Viewing Options or Story Viewing Options and choose a private option. LinkedIn offers its members the ability to see who has viewed their profile or story, but each user can decide on the particular visibility of those lists. You can decide whether you want your full name and details, limited details, or no details displayed when you view someone's profile. When you click either Change link, you're presented with three options, as shown in Figure 11-9: Your Name and Headline, Private Profile Characteristics (for example, mine displays Business Owner in the Retail Industry from San Diego County), and Private Mode.

  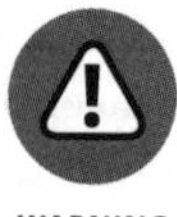
  WARNING

  If you change the Profile Viewing option to a private mode option, you lose the ability to see who's viewed your profile, unless you upgrade to a Premium account. In either case, if someone else chooses a private mode, you'll never see his or her name on the list of people who have viewed your own profile anyway.

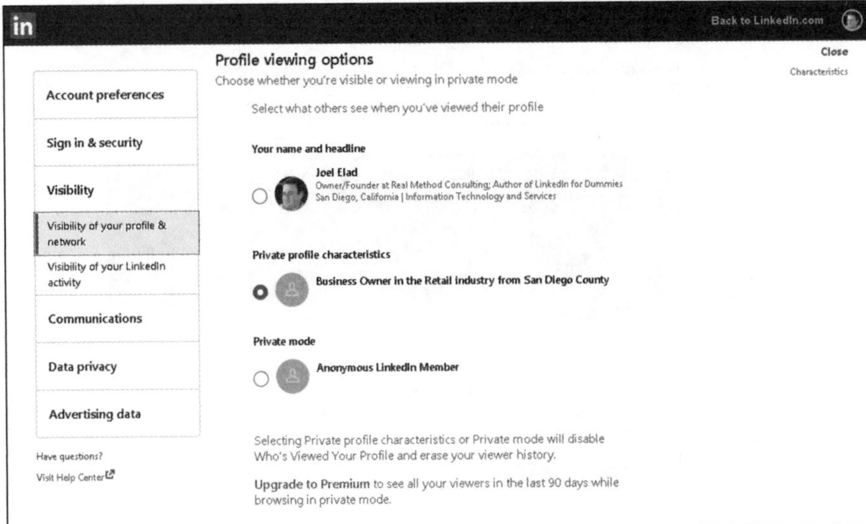

FIGURE 11-9: Decide how you want to be described when viewing someone else's profile.

- **To set your LinkedIn URL and decide which sections of your LinkedIn profile are visible to anyone on the Internet:**

  a. *Click Change next to Edit Your Public Profile.* A screen appears where you can customize your randomly assigned URL as well as your profile visibility.

  b. *Under Edit Your Custom URL, click the pencil next to your stored LinkedIn URL.*

  c. *In the text box that appears, enter a new URL (after* `www.linkedin.com/in/`*), as shown in Figure 11-10.* You can use 5-30 characters, but you can't use spaces, symbols, or special characters. The URL must be unique to LinkedIn, because two people can't have the same URL for their profiles.

  d. *Click the Save button.*

  e. *Scroll down to review your settings for customizing your public profile.* You can control what is accessible to search engines and permitted services such as external email accounts (for example, Microsoft Outlook) that can read publicly available information.

  f. *Select your profile visibility and then click Save.* If you're in the beginning phase of setting up your account and you don't want anyone to see your profile, select the Off option for Your Profile's Public Visibility. Just remember to go back and change this setting after your profile is defined and you're ready to network!

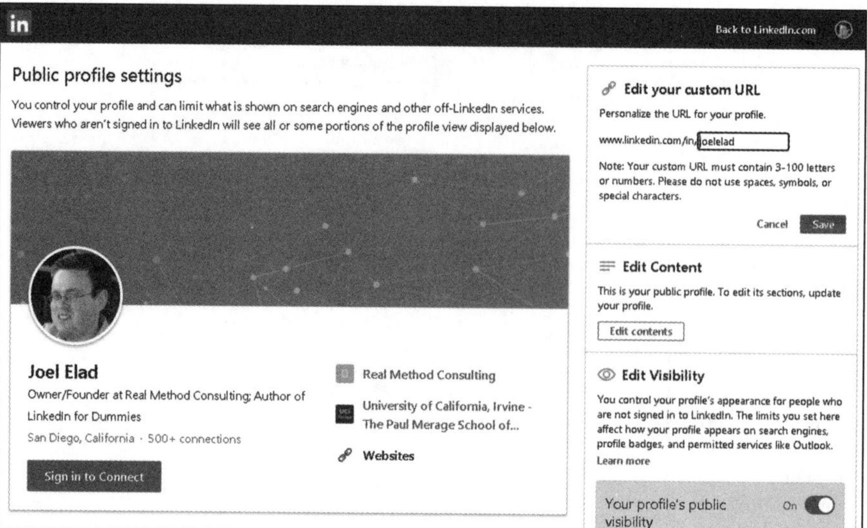

FIGURE 11-10: Assign a LinkedIn public profile URL that's readable and meaningful.

Most people will turn on the Your Profile's Public Visibility setting. If you select this setting, a laundry list of the sections in your profile appears, as shown in Figure 11-11. Simply select the radio button or click the slider to Show for the sections that you want visible; click the slider to Hide for the sections that you don't want visible. There's no universal answer regarding which sections to display and which to hide, but you usually want to display as much information as possible so that recruiters, colleagues, and classmates can find you and potential network members can learn about you.

g. *Click the Back button on your browser to return to the settings page.*

- **To determine who can see or download your email address:** Click the Change link next to Who can see or download your e-mail address. You can tell LinkedIn to only show your email on your profile to either your first-degree connections, your first- or second-degree connections, or anyone on LinkedIn. (You can also block anyone from seeing your email address.) You can also assign a setting for allowing your connections to download your email address to Yes or No.
- **To change the privacy level of your connections list:** Click Change next to Who Can See Your Connections. You can make your first-degree connections list visible to just you or to your connections. When set to Your Connections, your connections can see everyone else with whom you're connected. At times, this setting is useful, but if you're unsure whether you want everyone in your network able to communicate with someone else in your network, you may want to change the setting to Only You.

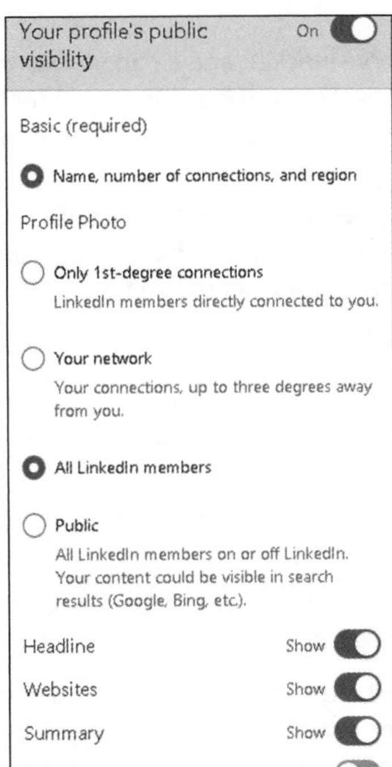

FIGURE 11-11: Manage the publicly available sections of your LinkedIn profile.

- **To add some privacy to your overall LinkedIn profile:** Click Change next to Who Can See Your Last Name, and select the option that displays only your last initial. Your LinkedIn connections will always be able to see your full name. After all, they're part of your network. But if you don't want to display your full name in your profile, you can use this setting to hide your name from non-connections.
- **If you're okay with partners of LinkedIn (such as Microsoft Outlook) displaying your public LinkedIn information in their program or app:** Click Change next to Profile Visibility Off LinkedIn, and assign the setting to Yes.
- **If you want potential contacts to find your profile by using your email address or phone number:** Click Change next to Manage Who Can Discover Your Profile from Your E-Mail Address. If you want those contacts to find you with a phone number search, click Change next to Manage Who Can Discover Your Profile from Your Phone Number.

  When you're trying to grow your network or build a following, choose Everyone for the settings for who can discover your profile. If you're trying to keep a lower profile, set these to 2nd Degree Connections so that only first-degree connections and friends of those connections (that is, second-degree connections) can find you. If you want a very low profile, select Nobody from both lists.

» **To see the list of people you've blocked and decide whether you want to unblock them:** Click Change next to Blocking. If you see someone's name that you want to unblock, simply click the Unblock link next to the name.

At this point, you've reached the second part of the Visibility settings page, specifically the visibility of your LinkedIn activity. This section contains settings that determine which of your LinkedIn activities are visible to either your network or the public:

» **To determine when the public knows that you're using LinkedIn:** Click the Change link next to Manage Active Status. LinkedIn can show your connections when you're active (logged into LinkedIn from a computer or a mobile device). You can assign the Display Your Active Status setting to Yes or No.

TIP

You can also hide your active status from particular people by typing their names in the appropriate text box. This feature is useful if you want to hide your status from, say, your boss but not your friends or recruiters.

» **To decide when your LinkedIn network learns that you updated your LinkedIn profile:** Click Change next to Sharing Job Changes, Education Changes, and Work Anniversaries from Profile. When this feature is set to Yes, your network gets an update every time you update your profile or have a work anniversary. If you're self-employed or want to increase your follower base, you probably want to change the setting to Yes, so that LinkedIn helps advertise you to your network for free.

WARNING

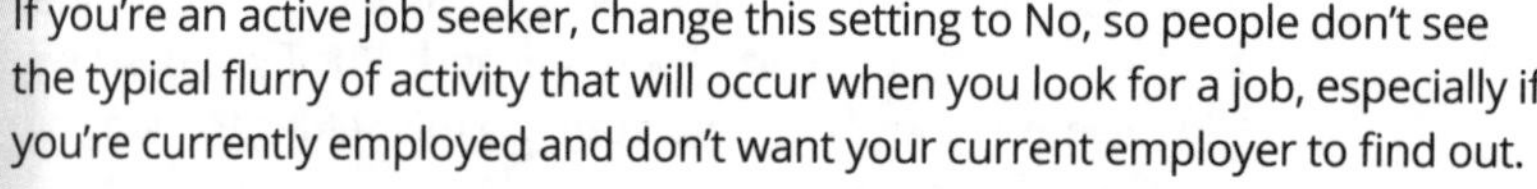

If you're an active job seeker, change this setting to No, so people don't see the typical flurry of activity that will occur when you look for a job, especially if you're currently employed and don't want your current employer to find out.

» **If you want your first-degree connections to know when you're mentioned in the news:** Click Change next to Notify Connections When You're in the News, and make sure the setting is set to Yes. This setting is helpful if you're trying to stay "top of mind" with your connections because LinkedIn automatically advertises any article mentions to your network, both in their news feed and, if the members elect to receive email, in an email announcing which of their connections are in the news. However, if you are trying to keep a low profile or you appear in articles that feature bad news or something you don't want your connections to learn, change this setting to No.

» **To enable people to mention or tag you when they use LinkedIn:** Click Change next to Mentioned by Others. You can click the slider to Yes to make sure that other LinkedIn members can mention or tag you when they post on LinkedIn or make a comment on someone's post, which can lead LinkedIn members to check out your profile.

- **To decide whether anyone can follow your updates:** Click Change next to Followers. You can choose everyone on LinkedIn or only your connections. When you're building a following, whether you're a small business owner, an entrepreneur, or someone who posts a lot of articles or information, choose the Everyone on LinkedIn option. If you're trying to keep a low profile and don't want just anyone to track your updates, change the setting to Your Connections so others can't automatically follow you. You can also set the Make Follow Primary slider to Yes, if you want LinkedIn to offer Follow as the primary action when a LinkedIn member views your profile.

Next, click the Data Privacy header from the left navigation menu. Following are some of the key settings that you should be aware of when customizing your account settings:

- **To download your LinkedIn data from the server:** Click Change next to Get a Copy of Your Data. A number of options are available for data you can retrieve from LinkedIn's server; see Chapter 12 for details.
- **To see the salary information you provided to LinkedIn:** Click Change next to Salary Data on LinkedIn. If you want to delete this information from your account, click the Delete link next to the salary data you want deleted. Note that this data is never visible to anyone else, is not part of your public profile, and is never shared with companies or recruiters.
- **To clear your search history on LinkedIn:** Click Change next to Search History to clear any record of your search history on LinkedIn. This search history is visible only to you, but LinkedIn does use it to tailor future search results.
- **If you frequently use LinkedIn to apply for jobs:** Click Change next to Job Application Settings. Set to Yes the filter that allows LinkedIn to save the resume you submitted and your answers in your job application. Now when you apply to jobs on LinkedIn, you'll be able to store certain answers so you can reuse them on future applications. In addition, you'll be able to use the Stored Job Applicant Accounts setting to manage which account info (from external job sites) you want saved as part of your LinkedIn account.
- **To appear available in recruiter searches matching your career interests:** Click Change next to Let Recruiters Know You're Open to Opportunities, and then click Yes for the setting that shares your name and allows your name to appear when recruiters search for interested job seekers.

WARNING

Although LinkedIn will let only recruiters know whether you've selected Yes for this setting, there's a slight chance that an employer could learn that you're open to opportunities. Proceed cautiously, especially if your current employer uses a recruiter to fill current job openings using LinkedIn.

- **To decide whether a job poster can view your full profile when you apply for a job that requires that you use the employer's website to file the application:** Click Job Seeking from the left sidebar, and then click Change next to Sharing Your Profile When You Click Apply.
- **To review which LinkedIn associated software can access your LinkedIn account:** Click Change next to Permitted Services, and then review the list of services. If you don't want to be automatically associated with a service, click Remove next to that service.
- **If you are okay with Microsoft Word possibly showing your work experience summary to users who use Resume Assistant in Word:** Click the Change link next to Microsoft Word, and assign the setting to Yes. As of this writing, only Office 365 users who are part of the Office Insider program can use this feature.

Finalizing Your LinkedIn Communications Settings

Last but definitely not least, you should review the Communications settings. On this settings page, you see every major facet of communications involving LinkedIn, starting with Basics: what kind of notifications should LinkedIn alert you to, what kinds of messages you want to receive from members, who can invite you, how often LinkedIn can email you, and what options you want when using LinkedIn messaging. You also look at group settings, such as whether you are open to receiving invitations to join a LinkedIn group or whether you want your network to know when you join a group. Finally, you check out the Messages section, where you can decide whether you want to receive invitations for LinkedIn research efforts.

To begin reviewing the Communications settings, click the Me icon on the top navigation bar of any LinkedIn page. Below the Account heading, click Settings & Privacy, and then click the Communications header from the left navigation menu. The Communications screen shown in Figure 11-12 appears.

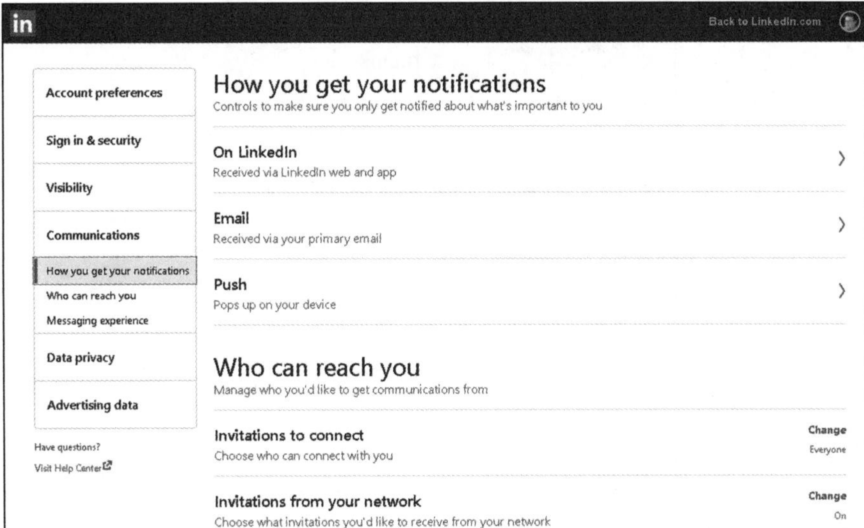

FIGURE 11-12: Review the LinkedIn communication settings here.

You can make the following changes to your communications settings:

- **To decide which actions on LinkedIn will appear on your LinkedIn Notifications screen:** Click Change next to Notifications on LinkedIn. The screen shown in Figure 11-13 appears, displaying the major categories of events that can create notifications.

  Click a category in the Notifications screen. (The Conversations category is shown in Figure 11-14.) You see a list of events in that category that could trigger a notification. Each option has a slider button that you can set to On or Off. If you want to be notified when the event occurs, set it to On; otherwise, set it to Off.

- **To determine how often LinkedIn emails you and for what reasons:**

  a. *Click the Change link next to E-Mail.* The Email page appears, as shown in Figure 11-15. Each section, such as Conversations, Jobs, and News, has universal On and Off settings.

  b. *Click each section link to see the subcategories for each section, as shown in Figure 11-16 for Conversations.*

  c. *For each subcategory, click the pencil edit link to review the list of options from the drop-down box that appears and decide in each circumstance how you want to receive your emails.* The available choices follow:

     - *Recommended:* Based on the category, LinkedIn will send you a summary of messages if you have a lot of incoming messages or notify you only of items you may have missed when using the site.

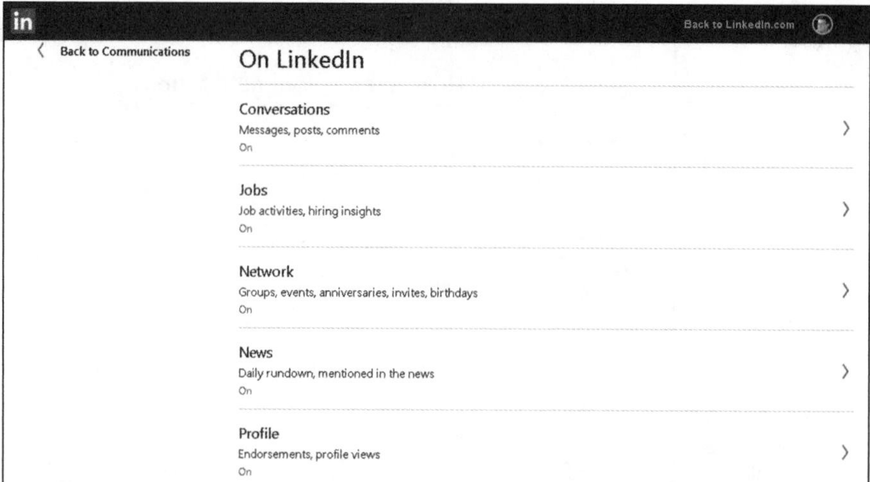

FIGURE 11-13: See the categories of events that could result in LinkedIn notifications.

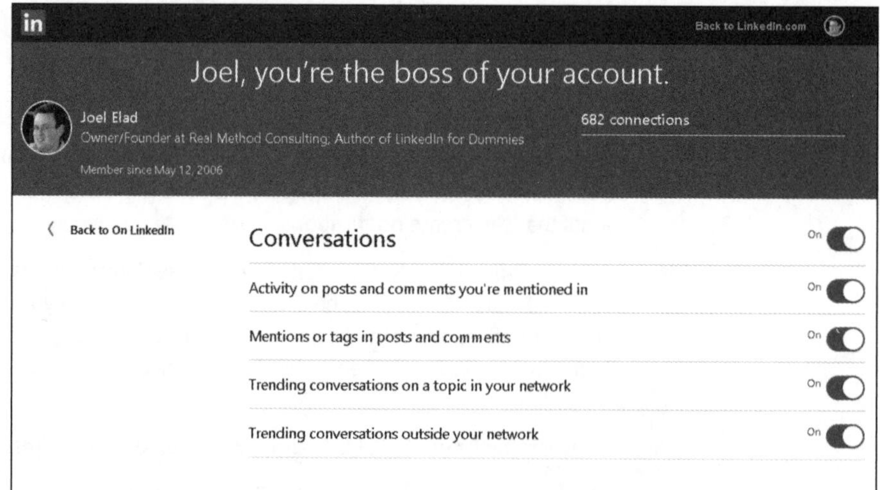

FIGURE 11-14: Decide when you want LinkedIn to notify you when certain events occur.

- *Individual Email:* As soon as something occurs in a given category, such as an introduction, an invitation, or a job notification, LinkedIn sends you an email with that one item in the email.
- *Weekly Digest Email or Daily Digest Email:* Instead of individual emails, LinkedIn groups activities in a given category and sends you one email in a digest format, with a summary at the top and the detailed activities below. Note that daily digests are for group updates, and weekly digests are for general and group updates. Not every category has a digest option.

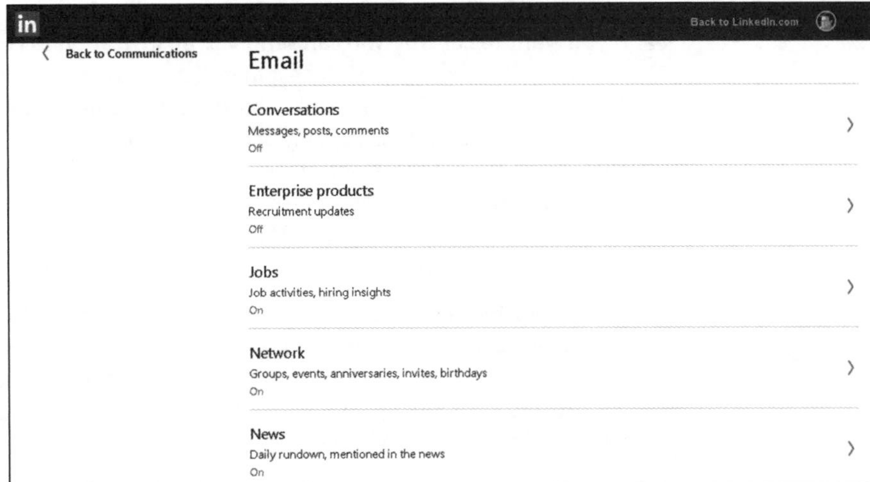

FIGURE 11-15: Decide when you want LinkedIn to email you based on event category.

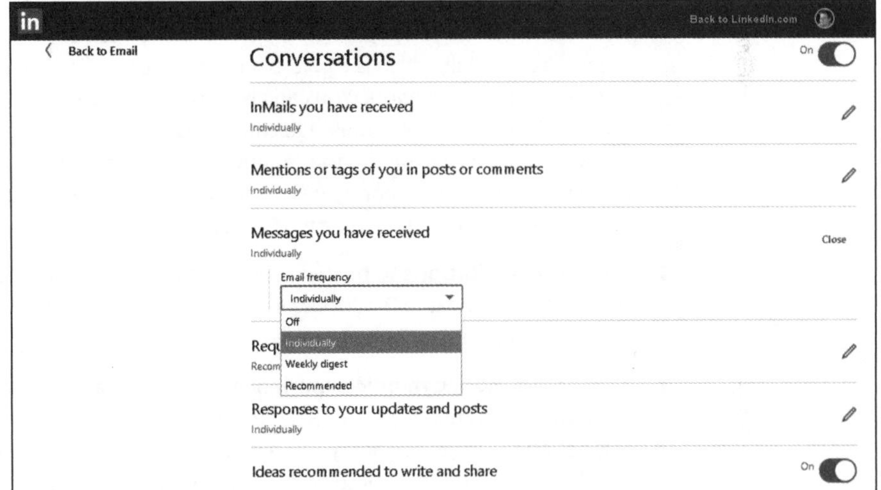

FIGURE 11-16: Decide what messages you want emailed and their email frequency.

TIP

If you don't want to receive any emails for a given circumstance, set the condition to Off. However, you can still read the message when you're logged into the LinkedIn site.

d. *Repeat these steps for each category in the list of Which Emails Do You Want to Receive.* Spending time to visit each category and make wise decisions on what needs an immediate email, what can be summarized in a digest, and what isn't needed can save you lots of time. Click the Back to Email link at the top of the screen when you're finished with each subcategory.

e. *When you've finished with all Email subcategory settings, click the Back to Communications link (at the top of the screen).*

- **If you want to control who can send you an invitation to connect on LinkedIn:** Click the Change link next to Invitations to Connect. You can choose everyone on LinkedIn; only people who know your email address or appear in your imported contacts list; or only people who appear on your imported contacts list. If you choose one of the last two options, a new potential contact must either know your email or be someone whom you have imported from your email program, for example. This setting is especially helpful if you need to control who is in your network.
- **To decide whether you are open to receiving invitations to follow companies and attend events:** Click Change next to Invitations from Your Network and change the setting to Yes if you want to receive invitations to follow companies and organizations. Change the setting to Yes if you want to receive invitations to attend events.
- **To control unsolicited messages from other LinkedIn members or third parties:** Click Change next to Messages. Three questions regarding potential incoming communications appear. You can say Yes or No to enable getting notifications when you get a message request. You can say Yes or No to receiving an InMail, which is a paid email from a LinkedIn member who is not a member of your network. You can also say Yes or No to receiving sponsored InMail, which is typically a message containing a marketing or promotional message from a LinkedIn partner or advertiser. Your name and email address are not disclosed by responding Yes; you are simply receiving the message and can decide on your own whether to respond.
- **To receive invitations to participate in LinkedIn's research efforts:** Click the Change link next to Participate in Research. Or click LinkedIn Messages from the left sidebar. Change the setting to Yes.
- **To create a more dynamic experience when messaging someone on LinkedIn:** Click Change next to Read Receipts and Typing Indicators. If you set this option to On, as you are typing a message on LinkedIn, the recipient will see the typing indicator (three dots). (And you will see the typing indicator when the other person is typing.) In addition, both of you will see a read receipt, which is confirmation that the other party has seen your reply. This feature is similar to that on other social media networks and makes LinkedIn a little more familiar to use when messaging.
- **To get preprogrammed replies you can click when sending a message:** Click Change next to Reply Suggestions. This feature appears only on certain messages where LinkedIn can automatically provide a potentially helpful reply to an incoming message.

This completes the most important options in Communications settings. Remember, you can always go back and revisit your settings at any time.

» Exporting your LinkedIn profile to a PDF file

» Creating a LinkedIn public profile badge

Chapter 12

Using LinkedIn with Your Internet Activities

This chapter delves in to how you can use LinkedIn as part of your overall presence on the Internet, especially when it comes to communication. Specifically, I focus on two aspects of your Internet experience: your email account and your non-LinkedIn Internet activities.

LinkedIn makes exchanging some information between your email program and your LinkedIn profile convenient by enabling you to export your LinkedIn contacts list to a variety of programs, including Office 365 and Gmail. You can also enhance your web browsing experience with specialized LinkedIn functions. You can add a colorful link, called a public profile badge, from other websites back to your LinkedIn profile, and you can capture your profile information into a PDF file for easy offline or online distribution. In this chapter, you see how to use each of these tools effectively.

Exporting LinkedIn Connections to Your Email Application

As you build up your network, you might end up with more contacts on file in your LinkedIn network than stored away in your email program. However, you may want to keep a record outside LinkedIn of your first-degree connections. Adding these people one by one to any contact management system could take a while. Thankfully, LinkedIn has a function to make this task easier.

Your list of LinkedIn connections is similar to a list of names in any contact program's address book. And just as you can import people's contact information from an email program into LinkedIn, you can export your LinkedIn connections to your contact management system. Exporting is a simple process:

1. You export your LinkedIn connections into a contacts file.
2. You import the contacts file into your main contact management program.

You can choose which contacts to export. Your contact management program should be able to detect any duplicates — if you try to import a name that already exists, you should get a warning message. I walk you through the process of exporting your LinkedIn contacts in this section.

Creating your contacts export file in LinkedIn

First, you need to generate an exported file of contacts from LinkedIn. To do so, follow these steps:

1. **On any LinkedIn page, click the My Network icon in the top navigation bar.**
2. **In the Manage My Network section, in the top left, click the Connections link.**

   The Connections page appears, as shown in Figure 12-1.
3. **Click the Manage Synced and Imported Contacts link, in the top-right corner of the screen.**

   The screen shown in Figure 12-2 appears, so you can review any names you've brought into LinkedIn from various sources.

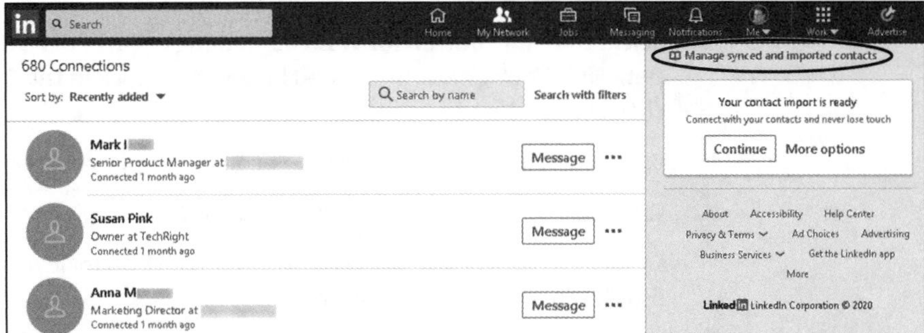

FIGURE 12-1: Your connections list on LinkedIn.

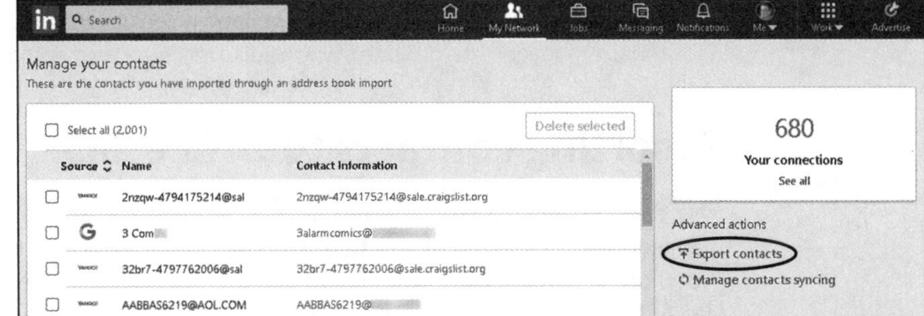

FIGURE 12-2: Manage your LinkedIn contacts here.

4. **On the right side of the screen, under the Advanced Actions header, click the Export Contacts link.**

   The How LinkedIn Uses Your Data section of the Data Privacy page (in Settings) appears, as shown in Figure 12-3, specifically the Get a Copy of Your Data option. From here, you can download all sorts of data, not just your connections list.

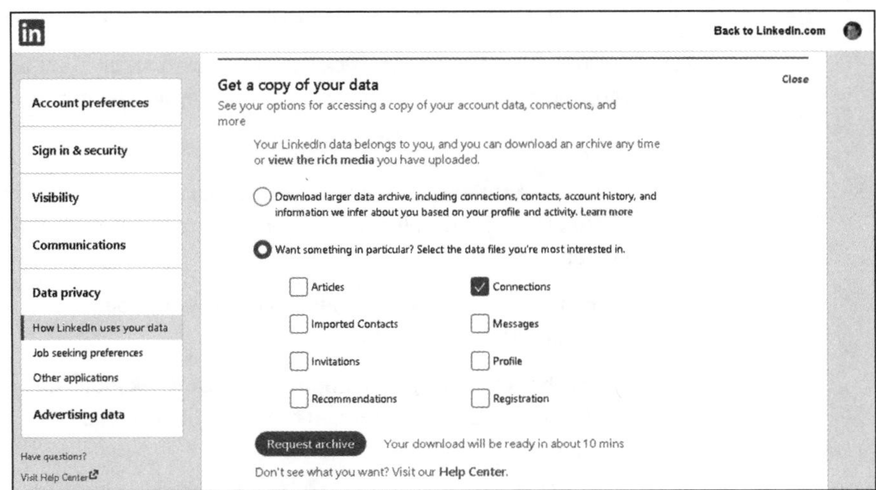

FIGURE 12-3: Download your exported file of LinkedIn contacts.

5. **Select the radio button for Want Something in Particular? Select the Data Files You're Most Interested In, and then click in the Connections check box.**
6. **Click the Request Archive button to generate your contacts file.**
7. **When asked, enter your LinkedIn password to complete the request.**

   LinkedIn sends you an email with instructions on how to download the file, usually within 10 minutes of your request.
8. **Follow the instructions in the email to save the file on your computer.**

TIP

   Give the file a custom name, if you like, but remember the filename and location because you'll need that information when you load the file into your contact management program, which I discuss in the next sections.

Exporting contacts to Office 365

Now that you've created your contacts file, it's time to import it to your contact management program. For the first example, I use Microsoft Office 365, but the procedure is similar with other email clients. (The next few sections give you an idea of how to handle other email clients.)

After you create your LinkedIn export file and are ready to export your LinkedIn contacts to Microsoft Office 365, follow these steps:

1. **Log into outlook.live.com or your Office 365 account or both. Select Outlook from the Apps screen.**

   The main window appears.
2. **Select the Contacts or People tab from the left side navigation bar.**
3. **From the Contacts page, click the drop-down arrow next to the Manage tab, and then select the Import Contacts option from the list.**

   The program asks you for the file to import.
4. **Enter the path and filename of your exported file, or click the Browse button to find and select the file on your computer. Click the Import button.**
5. **When Outlook asks you to select a destination folder, click the Contacts folder and then click Next.**
6. **Check that the text you're importing to Outlook looks okay and then click the Looks Ok, Continue button to finish the process.**

Exporting contacts to Outlook (non-Office-Suite version)

If you prefer Outlook to the full Office 365 suite, you're in luck: Your LinkedIn contacts can go live there just as easily as they can elsewhere. After you create your export file (as described in "Creating your contacts export file in LinkedIn," earlier in this chapter), you can export your connections to Outlook by following these steps:

1. **On your main Outlook screen, choose File ➪ Open & Export ➪ Import/Export.**

   The Import and Export Wizard window appears.

2. **Select the Import from Another Program or File option, and then click Next.**

   Outlook asks you to select a file type to import from.

3. **Select the Comma Separated Values option and then click Next.**

   Outlook Express asks you for the file to import.

4. **Enter the path and filename of your exported file, or click the Browse button and find and select the file on your computer. Click Next.**
5. **When Outlook asks you to Select a Destination Folder, click the Contacts folder. Click Next.**
6. **Select the Map Custom Fields option.**
7. **Verify the fields that you're importing to Outlook, and then click Finish to start the process.**

Exporting contacts to Gmail

If you're using a web-based mail program, such as Google's Gmail, you can use the following basic procedure to take your exported LinkedIn contacts and import them into the Contacts function of your webmail program. After you create an export file (as described in "Creating your contacts export file in LinkedIn," earlier in this chapter), you can import those connections to Gmail by following these steps:

1. **Using your web browser, log in to Gmail. Click the nine-dot grid next to your icon at the top right of the screen, and then click Contacts, as shown in Figure 12-4.**

   The Google Contacts page appears.

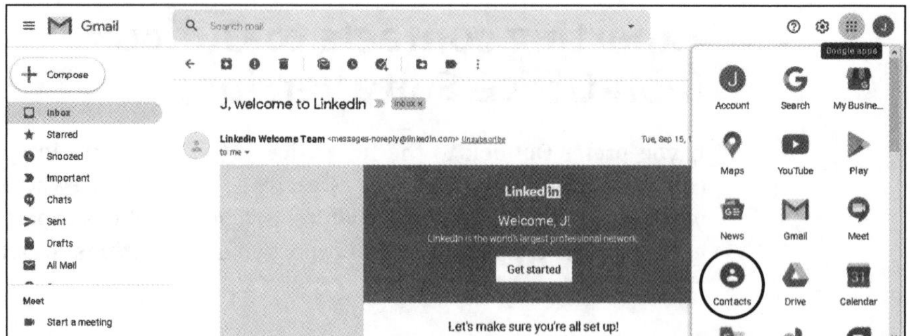

FIGURE 12-4: Start at your Google Gmail page.

2. **Click the Import link in the left navigation menu, as shown in Figure 12-5.**

   A new window pops up, as shown in Figure 12-6.

3. **Click the Select File button and search your computer for the export file. Click Open to designate that file.**

4. **Click the newly activated Import button to start the process.**

   Google Contacts process the exports file; you'll see a progress box as the connections are imported. You will be redirected to your Google Contacts screen when the process is complete.

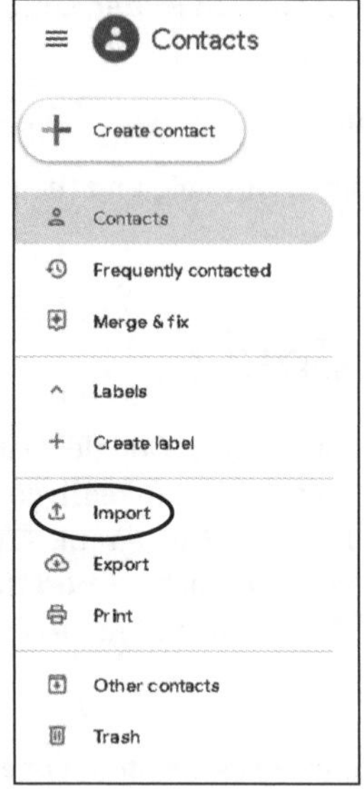

FIGURE 12-5: Google Contacts gives you the option to import contacts.

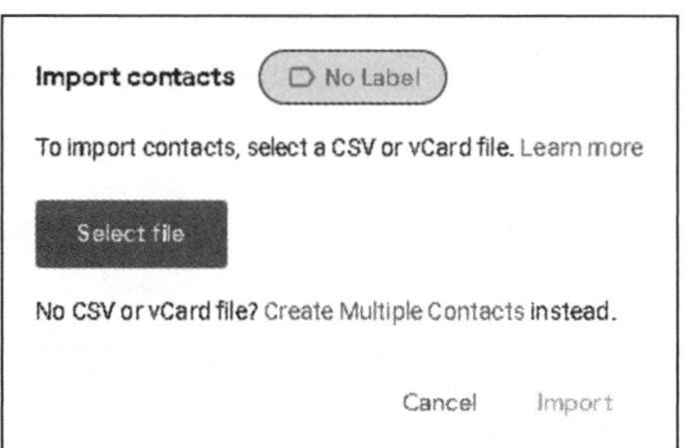

FIGURE 12-6: Find your exported file to import your contacts.

You can see the newly imported names on your Google Contacts page. You also see a Custom tag on the left side navigation menu of Google Contacts, with the name Imported on *MM/DD,* indicating when these contacts were added. Anytime you want to see the imported names, click the Custom tag.

Exporting Your Profile and Badge

I've spent a lot of time talking about how you should fill out your LinkedIn profile so that it contains the most up-to-date information, documenting your experience, skills, recommendations, network of connections, and professional identity. All that information is collected in your LinkedIn profile, which is easily accessible, but you have to be on LinkedIn to get access to it. Thankfully, you can distribute this information, offline and online, in several ways, whenever needed. This section provides just a few examples of accessing your LinkedIn information when you're not on LinkedIn.

Exporting your profile to a PDF file

Sometimes, you might have to send a file that documents your experience instead of pointing people to your LinkedIn account. Suppose that your resume or CV is out of date, but your LinkedIn account is current. The easiest solution is to quickly take a snapshot of your LinkedIn profile and save it in a file that can be easily shared. PDF (Portable Document Format) is one of the most popular file formats for distributing information that is locked.

This section shows you how to export your LinkedIn profile to a PDF file. To do so, follow these steps:

1. **Click the Me icon, and then click View Profile from the drop-down list that appears.**
2. **On your profile page, click the More button to the right of your profile photo.**

   The drop-down list shown in Figure 12-7 appears.

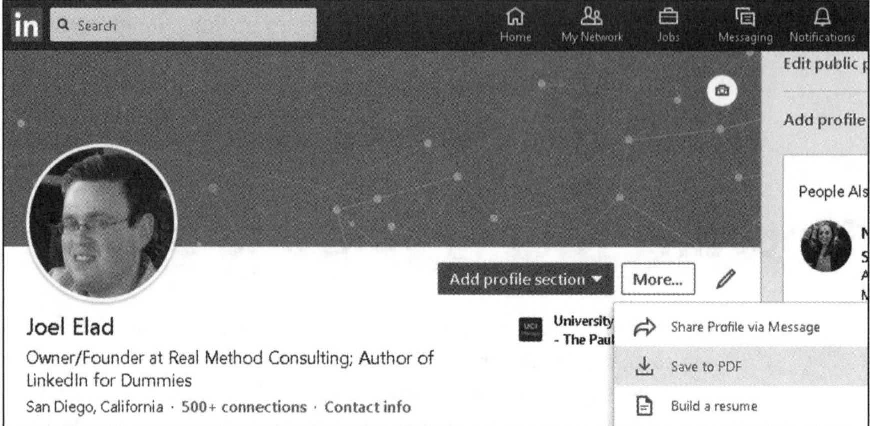

FIGURE 12-7: Start the PDF process from your profile page.

3. **Click Save to PDF.**

   LinkedIn prepares your PDF file and, depending on your web browser and the download settings for that browser, will issue a prompt for you to save the PDF file on your computer or open the program on your computer using a program, as shown in Figure 12-8.

4. **Click OK.**

   The PDF file is saved to your computer.

In Step 3, if you chose instead to open the PDF file on your computer, using a program such as Adobe Acrobat Reader, you'd see your profile, as shown in Figure 12-9. Your name, LinkedIn headline, location, and Contact settings are at the top of the file, with your Summary, Experience, and Education sections organized neatly below, similar to a resume.

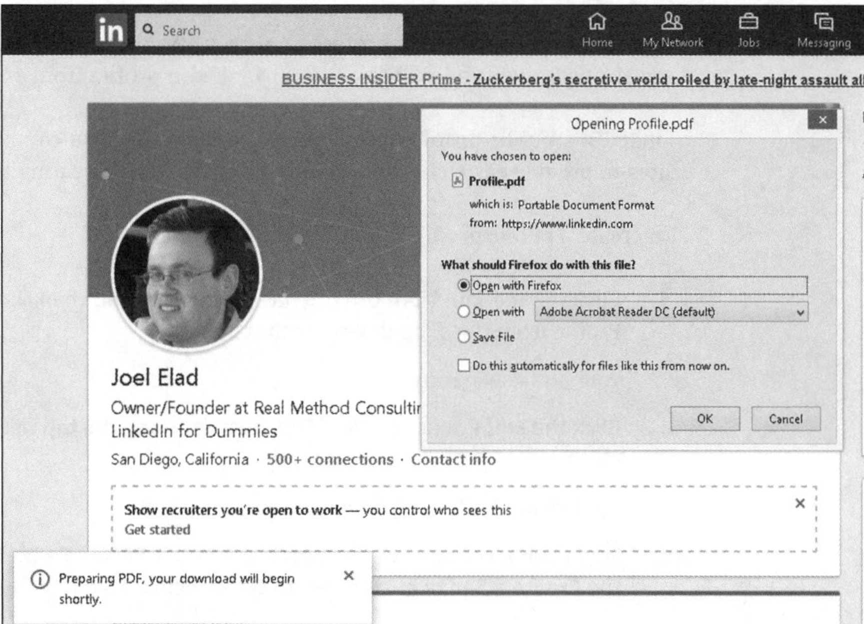

FIGURE 12-8: LinkedIn prompts you to save or open your PDF file.

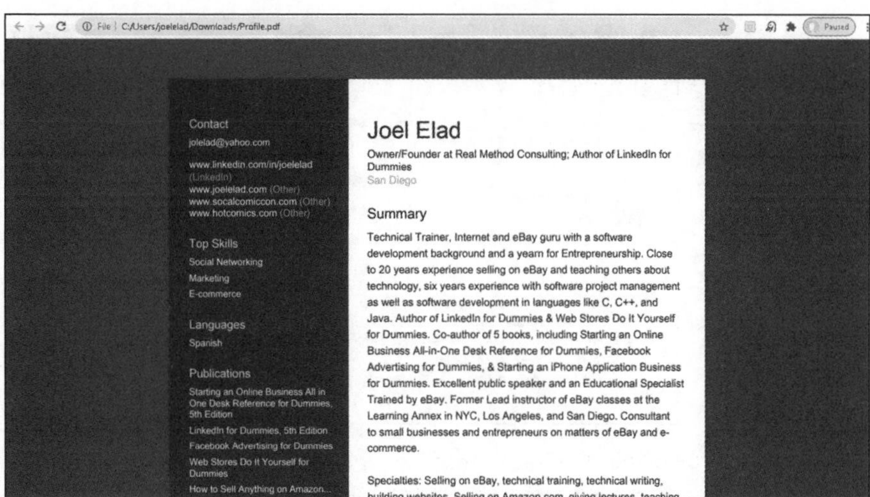

FIGURE 12-9: Your LinkedIn profile as a PDF file.

Creating a public profile badge for other websites

Many people have more than one website that communicates what they do, both professionally and personally, on the Internet, such as a variety of social media accounts, a website, a blog, or a company website. Why should you repeat yourself, in terms of your professional identity, across all these sites, when you can simply provide a link back to your LinkedIn profile from any other web page!

LinkedIn's public profile badge creates an icon that you can add to other online sites to provide easy, clickable access to your profile. Creating this badge is easy.

To create a public profile badge, follow these steps:

1. **Click the Me icon from the top navigation bar, and then click on View Profile from the drop-down list that displays.**

   Your profile page appears.

2. **Click the Edit Public Profile & URL button, along the top right of the screen.**

   The Edit My Public Profile window appears.

3. **Scroll down the page until you see the Public Profile Badge header. Click the Create a Badge button, as shown in Figure 12-10.**

   The Public Profile Badge Builder page appears.

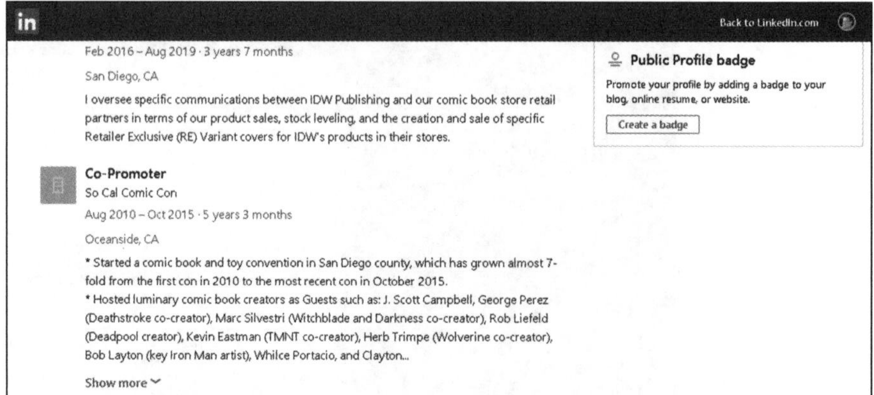

FIGURE 12-10: Scroll down the Edit My Public Profile page.

4. **For Step 1 (shown in Figure 12-11):**

   a. *Click the Copy the Code button.* This copies the line of code starting with <script> and ending with </script>.

   b. *Go to the website where you want to add your LinkedIn badge, and paste this line of code in the header part of the HTML file.* Paste the line of code between the <head> and </head> commands in your HTML file.

   This line of code basically allows the other web page to load instructions and information from LinkedIn to display the badge. You have to copy this line of code only once to the new page.

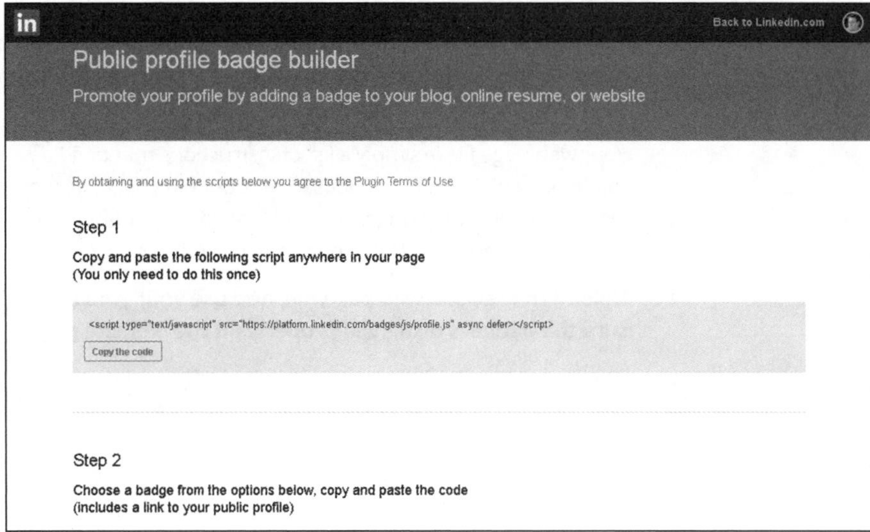

FIGURE 12-11: Start building your LinkedIn public profile badge here.

5. **For Step 2:**

   a. *Scroll down so you can see examples of each badge type.* Badge type 1 is shown in Figure 12-12.

   b. *Choose a format and color scheme, and then click the Copy the Code button below that design.*

   LinkedIn offers badges that fit inside the main part of a website page (featured in Figure 12-12) and in the sidebar of a page (scroll down the page to see them). You can change the width of the badge by selecting another option from the Size list.

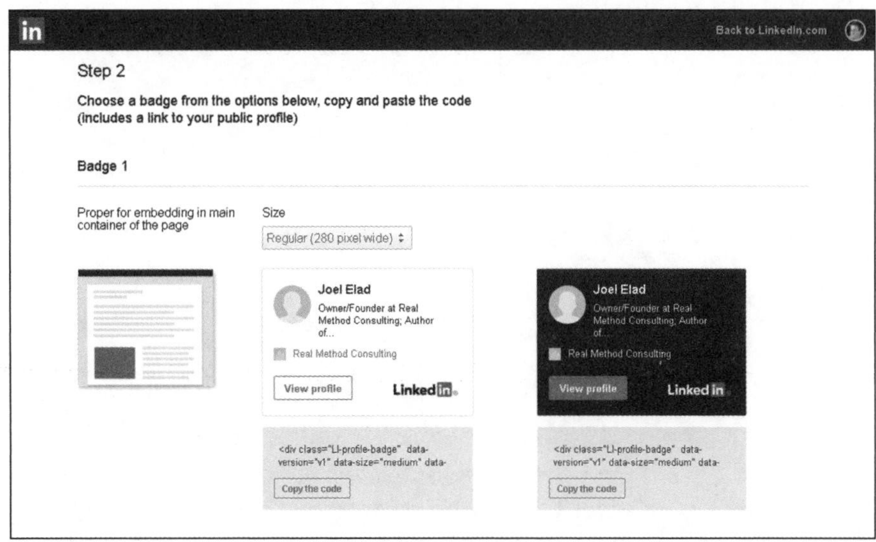

FIGURE 12-12: Find the badge style you want for your website.

6. **Go back to your website files, and paste the code that you just copied into the precise spot in your HTML or web page file where you want the badge to appear. Save your file with the new code.**

   Your web page file is simply a list of instructions that build a web page, from top to bottom. Therefore, choose the spot on the website where you want to insert your LinkedIn badge, and find that corresponding spot in the web page file. That's where you should paste the LinkedIn code.

7. **Upload the revised web page file, and use your web browser to make sure the badge is displayed properly on the website page.**

4

Finding Employees, Jobs, and Companies

IN THIS PART . . .

Use LinkedIn to post a job listing and hire employees.

Apply for jobs on LinkedIn as an active or passive job seeker.

Search Company pages and see how you're connected to companies through your own network.

» Screening any potential applicants using LinkedIn

» Finding active or passive job seekers

Chapter 13
Finding Employees

When you have a handle on the key elements of improving your LinkedIn profile and experience, it's time to look outward toward the LinkedIn network and talk about some of the benefits you can reap from a professional network of tens of millions of people.

Whether you're an entrepreneur looking for your first employee, a growing start-up needing to add a knowledgeable staffer, or a part of a Fortune 500 company filling a recent opening, LinkedIn can provide a rich and powerful pool of potential applicants and job candidates, including the perfectly skilled person who isn't even looking for a job!

When it comes to looking for an employee, one of the benefits of LinkedIn is that you aren't limited to an applicant's one- or two-page resume and cover letter. Instead, you get the full picture of the applicant's professional history, coupled with recommendations, skill assessments, and his or her knowledge and willingness to share information. Even if you find your candidate outside LinkedIn, you can use the site to perform reference checks and get more information about the person. This information can augment what you learn from the candidate during the hiring process and from the references he or she provides. LinkedIn cannot replace your hiring process, but it can help you along the way.

In this chapter, I cover the basics of using LinkedIn to find an employee for your company or start-up. I begin with the basics of how you can post your job listing on LinkedIn and review applicants. I then move on to using LinkedIn to screen potential candidates, and I finish the chapter with search strategies you should employ to find the right person.

Managing Your Job Listings

LinkedIn offers a Talent Solutions page for companies to manage their job listings. Click the Work icon on the top navigation bar on the home page, and select LinkedIn Talent Solutions from the drop-down list that appears. The Talent Solutions home page appears, as shown in Figure 13-1. This is where you can start the process of creating a job listing, reviewing the applicants you get, and paying LinkedIn to post the listing. You can also post a job without using Talent Solutions, but if you're managing a company account that will need more than the occasional job posting, you may want to investigate Talent Solutions further.

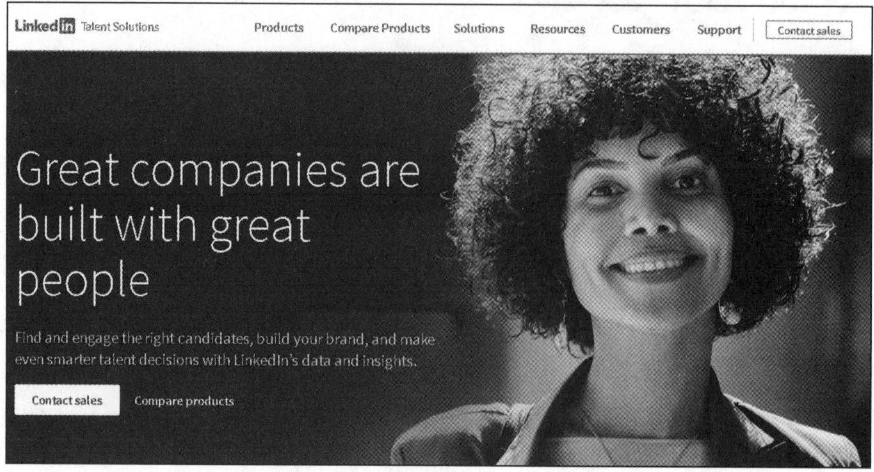

FIGURE 13-1: LinkedIn offers a Talent Solutions page for managing your job listings.

You set the cost for each job listing with a daily budget, and are charged only when potential job candidates click your job listing. You can cancel the job listing at any time, so you don't have to run the listing for a long time if you get enough candidates quickly. You can pay for your job listing with PayPal or a major credit card such as Visa, MasterCard, American Express, or Discover.

TIP

If you know you're going to need multiple or ongoing job postings on LinkedIn, consider LinkedIn Recruiter to get discounts on job postings and InMail. You can get more information by completing a request for a demo at `https://business.linkedin.com/talent-solutions/recruiter`.

You can choose to renew your listing at the end of the 30-day window. Your *date posted* (the date you set up the job listing) is updated with the renewal date instead of the original posting date, so the listing appears at the top of search results. Renewing a job listing costs the same as the initial job posting.

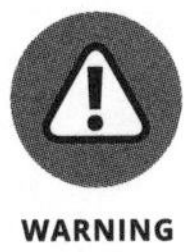

WARNING

You can advertise only one open position per job listing. If you solicit applications for more than one position in a single job listing, LinkedIn will remove your listing.

Posting a job listing

To post your job opening, follow these steps:

1. **Click the Work icon on the top navigation bar, and select Post a Job from the drop-down list that appears.**

   The screen shown in Figure 13-2 appears, asking you to set the job title, company, location, and employment type first before tackling the other details.

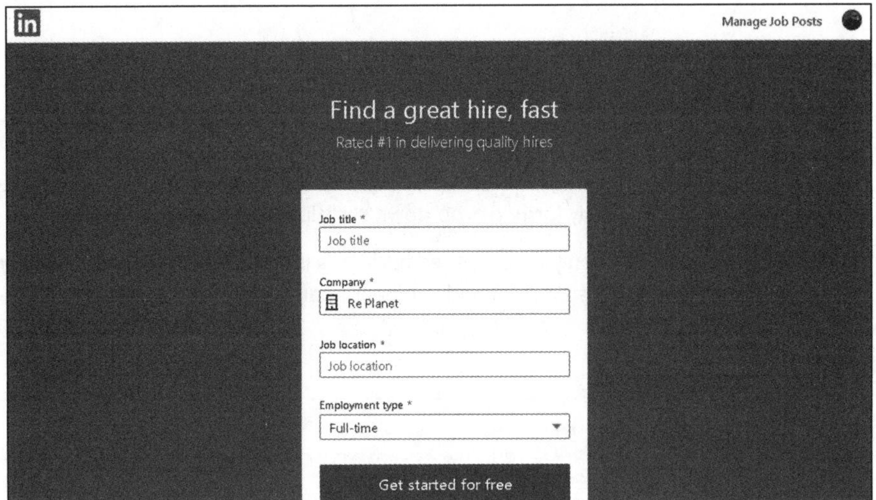

FIGURE 13-2: Start composing your job posting details here.

2. **Enter the required information about your company and the job you're offering, and then click the Get Started for Free button to continue.**

   LinkedIn asks for your job title, job location, and employment type, and also defaults the company name to your most current position.

3. **Enter the required information about your company and the job you're offering.**

   In Step 1 of 2, Job Details, compose your job description in the Add a Job Description text box provided (refer to Figure 13-3) or copy the description from another source and paste it into the box. If you paste the text, make sure the formatting (spacing, bullet points, font size, and so on) is correct. You can use the icons to add bold, italics, underlining, bullets, and numbered list formatting to your description text.

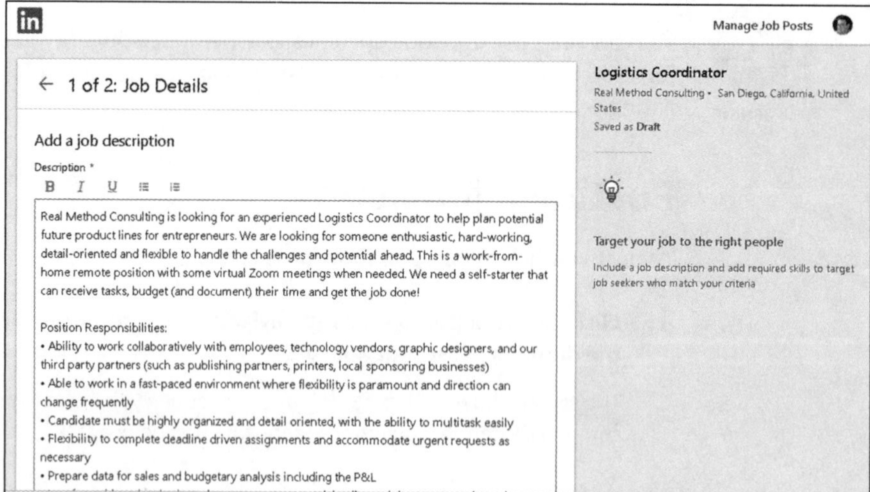

FIGURE 13-3: Enter your job description here.

4. **Scroll down and complete the Add Skills section (see Figure 13-4). Then click Continue.**

   LinkedIn will choose at least one skill based on the keywords it has detected so far. Click the Add Skill button and start typing to choose skills from LinkedIn's newly formed drop-down skills list.

   When you've finished adding skills, click the drop-down arrow under the question "How did you hear about us?" to select how you learned of this job posting application.

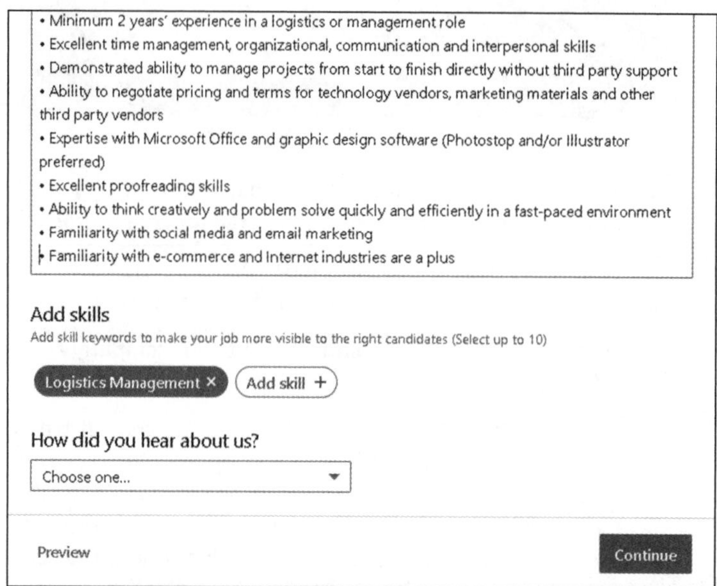

FIGURE 13-4: Enter necessary job skills for your applicant here.

5. **Complete Step 2, Applicant Options.**

   In the How Would You Like to Receive Your Applicants section (see Figure 13-5), decide whether to receive applications by email or an external website. If you choose email, you can choose one of the email addresses listed in your profile or another email address. If you choose external website, supply a direct URL for applicants to use that will send their application to your own system.

   LinkedIn generates several screening questions to help you narrow the pool of applicants to find the best qualified candidates for your needs. Review these questions, editing the listed skill if necessary. Determine the ideal numerical answer for that skill (on a 10-point scale), and whether the skill level is required or preferred. If you don't want to include a particular question in your listing, click the big X to the right of the question to remove it from your listing. You can scroll down and add additional screening questions based on other skills you think you may need from your job applicant.

TIP

   After you complete the screening questions, scroll down and click the Preview link to review the job posting before you post it.

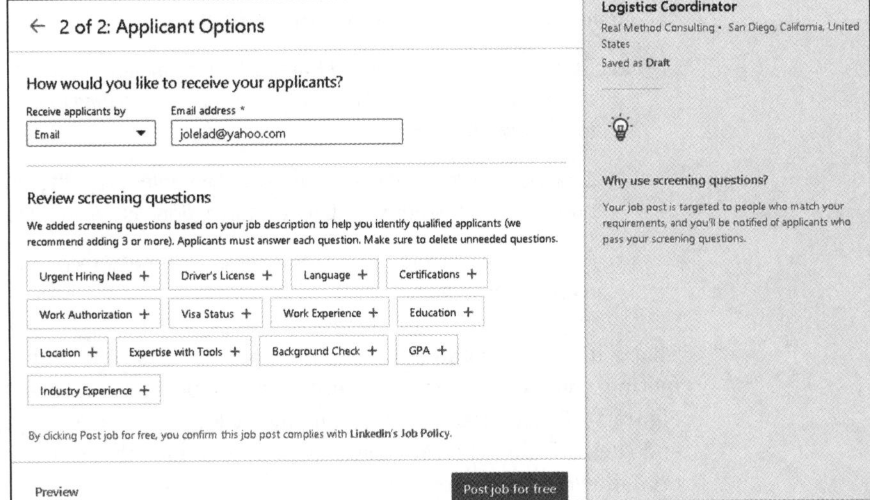

FIGURE 13-5: Enter candidate routing information here.

6. **Scroll down and click the blue Post Job for Free button to proceed to the budget phase.**

   A confirmation message telling you that the job posting is active appears at the top of the next screen, as shown in Figure 13-6. LinkedIn analyzes your job listing and provides a suggested daily budget you could spend to promote your listing, and predicts the number of applications you'll receive in 30 days based on its suggested budget.

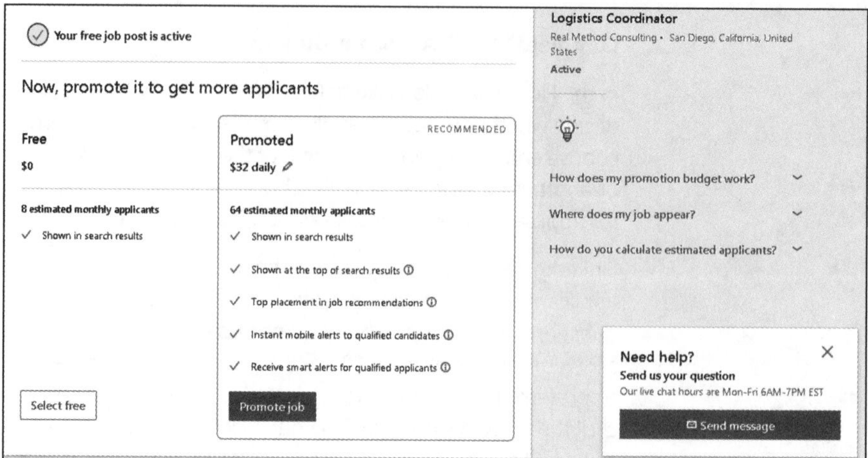

FIGURE 13-6: Decide the daily PPC budget you want to set.

7. **If you want to keep your listing as-is without a promotion budget, click the Select Free button.**

   You're finished and can skip to the end of this numbered list.

8. **If you want to pay to promote your job listing:**

   a. *Decide whether you to spend LinkedIn's recommended amount. If not, click the blue pencil icon next to the amount to change the setting to a daily budget or a total budget amount.*

   b. *Click the blue Promote Job button.* After LinkedIn has gathered your daily budget limit, it needs your billing information, as shown in Figure 13-7.

   c. *Provide payment information, review your order, and then click the blue Promote Job button.*

That's it! You've completed the all-important first two steps: posting and promoting your job listing. You receive a job posting confirmation, as shown in Figure 13-8. The listing is available by clicking the Me icon (your profile photo), and then clicking the My Posted Jobs link (under the Manage header) from the drop-down list that appears.

You have several options for improving your job posting right after creating the post. You can decide whether you want your profile summary to appear with the job listing by leaving the appropriate check box selected (refer to Figure 13-8). You can also suggest that applicants take LinkedIn skills assessments by leaving the appropriate check box selected, clicking the Add Skill Assessment button, and then adding the particular skills assessments you want your applicants to complete. Scroll down and decide if you want to print a help wanted sign, add compensation information, and select provided benefits to be listed in your job description. Scroll down again and click the blue View Applicants button to complete your choices.

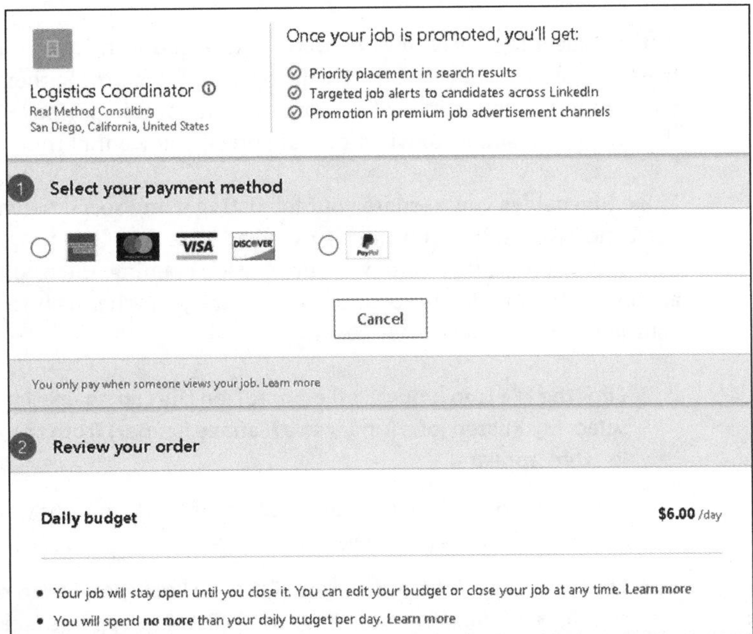

FIGURE 13-7: Confirm the details for your job listing.

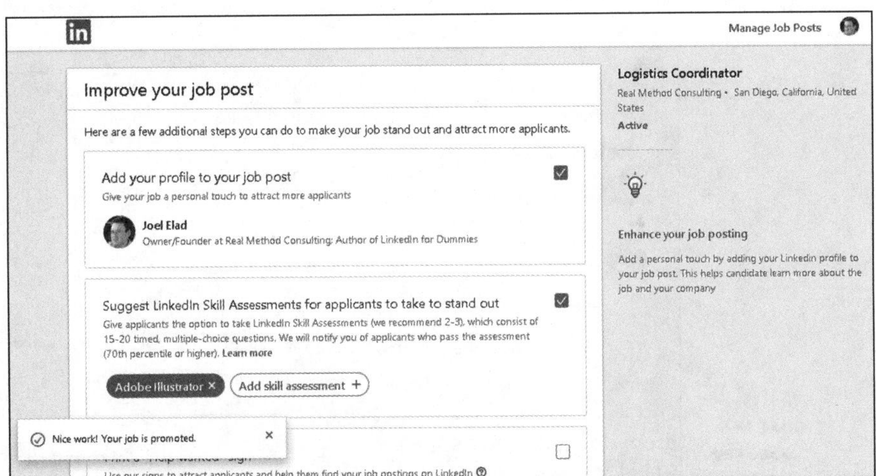

FIGURE 13-8: Make some final touches on your LinkedIn job listing.

Advertising your job listing to your network

Traditionally, when someone posted a job opening on the Internet using one of those ubiquitous job search sites, that person would hope the extensive pool of job seekers would find the posting and the appropriate parties would submit resumes and cover letters. When you use LinkedIn to fill a job, however, you still benefit from the pool of job seekers who search LinkedIn's Jobs page, but you have a distinct advantage: *your own network*. You're connected to people you know and trust, people you have worked with before so you know their capabilities, and most importantly, people who know you and (you hope) have a better idea than the average person as to what kind of person you would hire.

LinkedIn enables you to share your job listing using social networking sites Facebook and Twitter, and you can also send all or some of the people in your network a message, letting them know about your job opening and asking them if they, or anyone they know, might be interested in the job. When you're ready to advertise your job listing, follow these steps:

1. **Click the Me icon (your profile photo), on the top navigation bar, and select My Posted Jobs (under the Manage header) from the drop-down list that appears.**

   After you've posted your job, the position is listed in the Jobs window, which automatically loads any active job postings.

2. **Click the three dots to the right of the job listing, and then click one of the share options from the drop-down list that appears (see Figure 13-9).**

   Next, you'll select one or more networks in turn for sharing the job listing.

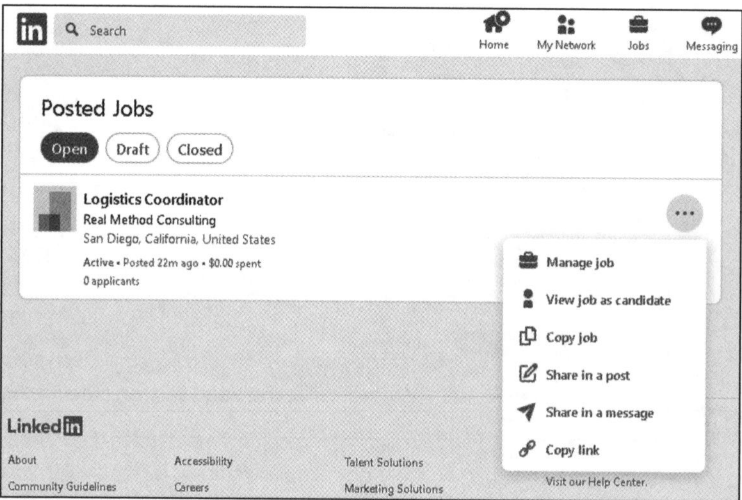

FIGURE 13-9: See key information about your new job listing.

3. **Share the job listing on LinkedIn:**

   a. *Click the Share in a Post option.* A Create a Post box appears that you can send to your LinkedIn network (see Figure 13-10).

   b. *Write an introduction in the What Do You Want to Talk About text area to encourage people in your network to view and share your job listing.*

c. *To change the privacy settings for this update, select whom you want to share with by using the appropriate drop-down box to select an audience. Click the blue Post button to create the post on your LinkedIn news feed.*

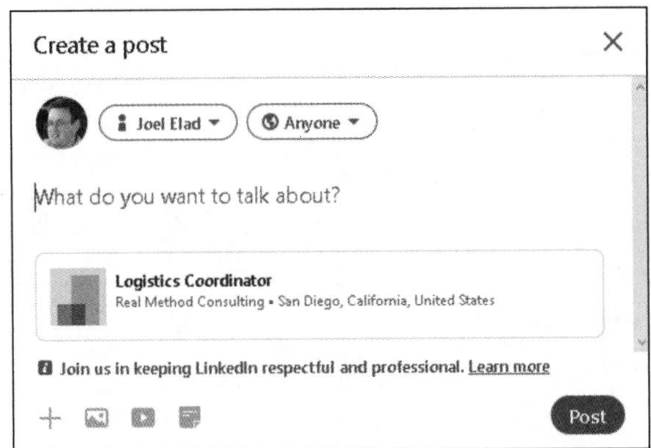

FIGURE 13-10: LinkedIn lets you ask your network for help.

4. **Click the Share in a Message link to send the listing to individual connections:**

   a. *Start typing name of a first-degree connection in the Type a Name or Multiple Names box.*

   b. *When the name you want appears in the box, click the name, which then moves that name to the To box.*

   c. *Continue to type additional names, up to a recommended maximum of ten people.*

   When you're sending the listing to individual connections, feel free to edit the text in the message box to make it sound as if it's coming from you, or leave the default message in place.

5. **Look over the text in the window again, making sure you have the right people selected, and then click the Send button (see Figure 13-11).**

   Your LinkedIn connections will receive a message in their LinkedIn inboxes and, depending on their notification settings, an email with this message as well. They can click a link from the message to see the job listing and either apply themselves or forward it to their contacts for consideration.

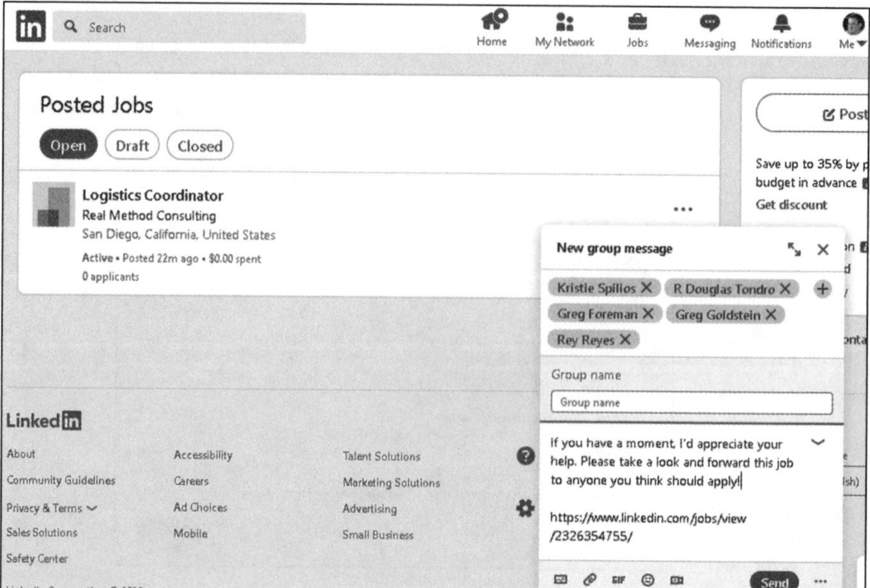

FIGURE 13-11: Proofread your message and then send it!

Reviewing applicants

After you've posted your job listing on LinkedIn, you should expect to get some applicants for the position. Every time someone applies for that job, you receive an email from LinkedIn notifying you of the application. In addition, LinkedIn records the application in the Applicants number of the Active Jobs window. (Refer to Figure 13-9.)

When you're ready to review the applicants for your job, follow these steps:

1. **Click the Me icon, and then select Manage Posted Jobs (under the Manage header) from the drop-down list that appears.**

   You see the Posted Jobs screen (refer to Figure 13-9). Click the job title of the job listing you want to review, which brings you to the Overview screen, as shown in Figure 13-12.

2. **Click an applicant's name to see his LinkedIn profile and read up on his experience.**

   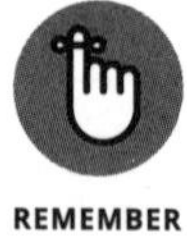

   REMEMBER

   You should review all the potential applicants first, labeling them Good Fit, Maybe, or Not a Fit (see the next step), before moving onto the next phase, where you start contacting and interviewing potential matches.

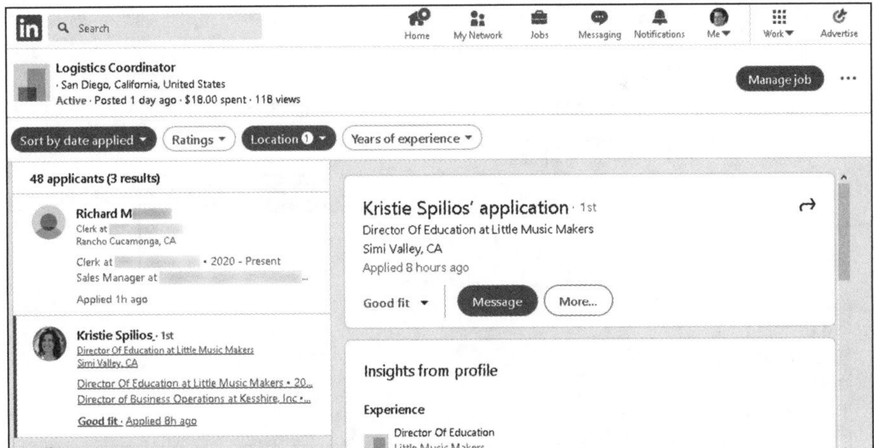

FIGURE 13-12: Review your open job listings to see who has applied.

3. **As you're reviewing each applicant's profile, you can use the different icons and links to take one or more of the following actions:**

   - *Rate their fit:* Click the blue Rate As button (see Figure 13-13), and you can label the person as Good Fit, Maybe, or Not a Fit. You can then sort applicant results by ratings to view only people you see as a Good Fit, when doing further analysis, which I cover in Step 6.

     WARNING

     The first time you rate a candidate as Not a Fit, LinkedIn will offer to send the potential candidate a rejection notice automatically that you can customize. You will be given the option at this point to have the message go out automatically, at a later date, or not at all.

   - *Message:* Send the applicant a message. Clicking the Message button will create a new LinkedIn message with a preprogrammed letter letting the applicant know that you'd like to speak further about interviewing him or her for the position.
   - *Share Profile:* Click the right arrow to the right of the person's name to share the person's application with other people, such as other members of a hiring committee. A new LinkedIn message will be created with a prefilled note asking them to review this candidate and a link to the applicant's LinkedIn profile.
   - *More:* See the applicant's full profile, email address on file, or phone number on file.

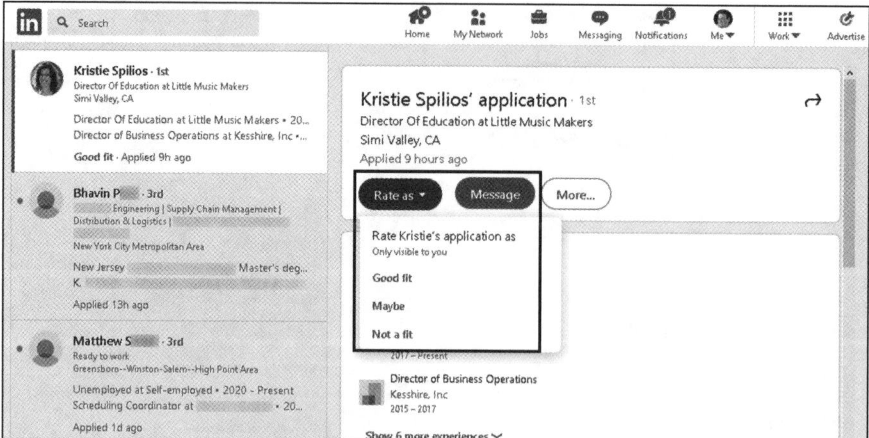

FIGURE 13-13: Go through the applicants to decide on good fits for your company.

4. **Scroll down to reveal Insights that LinkedIn has pulled from the applicant's profile.**

   This section usually contains highlights such as education entries that the applicant has listed.

5. **Scroll down past the Insights from Profile section to review the applicant's resume, if one was included, as shown in Figure 13-14.**

   You can use the Download link to download the resume to your computer for later review.

WARNING

Be aware that LinkedIn will automatically notify the applicant when his or her resume is downloaded, as well as when you review their job request.

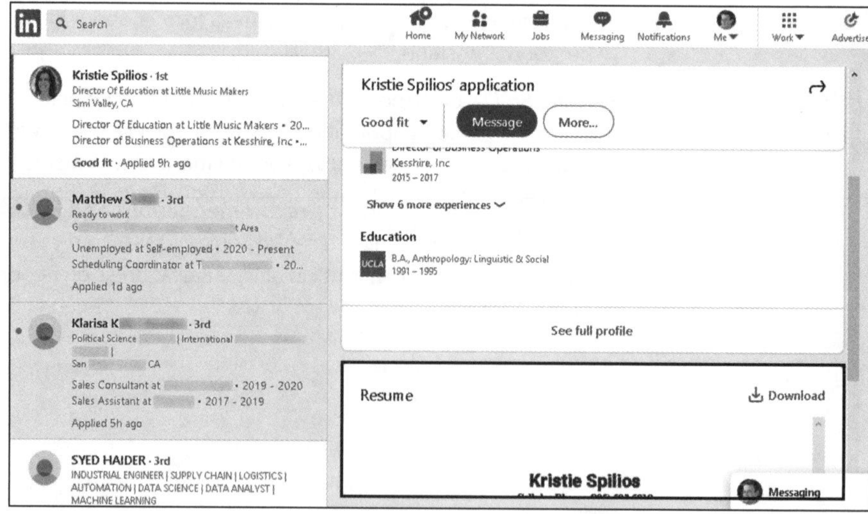

FIGURE 13-14: Review an attached resume if the applicant included one.

6. **After you've reviewed the potential applicants, scroll back to the top of the screen and click the Ratings button again. Now you can narrow your list of potential applicants.**

   Four options appear for the applicants to display on your screen: Unrated (not reviewed yet), Good Fit, Maybe, and Not a Fit. If you only leave the check box next to Good Fit selected, you will see only the list of Good Fit applicants for you to further review and perhaps interview for the job. You can always go back and select the box next to Maybe to add more names to your consideration. You can also have only the Unrated box selected to get a list of who you haven't reviewed yet.

7. **If you think the applicant is worth pursuing, contact the person to set up the next part of your application process.**

   You can contact the person by clicking the Message button on his or her profile page, or by clicking the Message button on the person's application page (refer to Step 3).

Screening Candidates with LinkedIn

After you use LinkedIn to post a job request, you can continue to use LinkedIn to assist you in the screening part of your hiring process. In addition to asking for references from the applicant or possibly ordering a background check from an independent background check agency, you can use LinkedIn to verify information in your applicant's resume and application at any stage of the process, without paying a dime!

Here are some strategies to keep in mind:

- **Start by thoroughly reviewing the applicant's profile.** When you review an applicant's profile, compare it with her resume, cover letter, and application. Is she consistent in how she presents her experience?
- **Read through the applicant's recommendations and follow up.** If your candidate has received recommendations, go through them, noting the date the recommendation was written, and see whether any are applicable toward your open position. Pay particular attention to recommendations from former bosses or co-workers. If necessary, ask your candidate whether you can contact the recommender through InMail and use that person as a reference.
- **See whether you're connected to your candidate.** When you pull up your candidate's profile, you see whether she is a second- or third-degree network member, which would mean one or two people connect you with the

candidate. If so, contact that person (or ask for an introduction to reach the correct party) and ask for more information about the candidate. Chances are good that you'll get a more honest assessment from someone you know rather than the recommendations provided by the candidate. Understand, however, that although the two people may be connected, they may not know each other that well, or their connection may be outside the professional expertise you're looking to learn about from this job candidate.

- **Evaluate the candidate's total picture.** If your candidate mentions any websites, blogs, or other online presence in her profile, look at the listed interests and group affiliations and see whether they add to (or detract from) your picture of the job candidate.

  Because most LinkedIn users have already defined each position they've held, the companies where they've worked, and the years of employment, you can get a sense of their abilities, what they've handled in the past, and depending on the completeness of their profile, examples of their past accomplishments.

TIP

As helpful as LinkedIn can be when reviewing a candidate, don't be afraid to use other Internet websites and searches to gain a well-rounded view of the candidate in question.

Using Strategies to Find Active or Passive Job Seekers

One of the powers of LinkedIn is its ability to find not only the active job seeker but also the passive job seeker or someone who doesn't even realize he or she wants a new job! You can tap an extensive network of professionals who have already identified their past experiences, skill sets, interests, educational backgrounds, and group affiliations.

The best piece of advice, in my opinion, for this type of search comes from Harvey Mackay and the book he wrote back in 1999, *Dig Your Well Before You're Thirsty* (Currency Books): You should be building a healthy network and keeping your eye on potential candidates before you have a job opening to fill. The earlier you start, and the more consistent you are with the time you spend weekly or monthly expanding your network, the easier it is to identify and then recruit a potential candidate to fill your opening.

You should take specific steps to make your strategy a reality. Whether you start this process in advance or just need to fill a position as soon as possible, here are some tactics to consider:

- **Perform detailed advanced searches.** If you want the perfect candidate, search for that candidate. Put multiple keywords in the Advanced Search form, look for a big skill set, narrow your search to a specific industry, and maybe even limit your range to people who already live close to you. If you come up with zero results, remove the least necessary keyword and repeat the search. Keep doing that until you come up with potential candidates.
- **Focus on your industry.** If you know that you're probably going to need software developers, start getting to know potential candidates on the LinkedIn site and stay in touch with them. Look for people to connect with, whether or not they share a group affiliation with you, and actively network with these people. Even if they say no to a future job opportunity, chances are good that someone in their networks will be more responsive than the average connection.
- **Start some conversations in the Groups section.** After you've found some LinkedIn groups full of like -minded or interesting professionals, start exchanging information! Pose a question or start a group discussion that you would ask in an interview to potential candidates, and see who responds. Better yet, you'll see *how* the people respond and be able to decide from their answers whom to focus on for a follow-up. You can then review their public profiles and send them a message.

- » **Improving your visibility and attractiveness on LinkedIn**
- » **Optimizing your LinkedIn profile for job search success**
- » **Devising LinkedIn job search strategies**
- » **Leveraging your connections**

Chapter 14
Finding a Job

One of the most important ways that LinkedIn has benefitted people is how it improves their job search experience. Before LinkedIn, a job search involved making lots of phone calls and visits (and sending some emails) to people you know, asking them whether they knew anybody who was hiring, somebody at Company X who might talk to you, or something else related to your search. LinkedIn has improved this tedious and inefficient process.

However, LinkedIn hasn't replaced the entire process. You still need to hold some face-to-face meetings and to make phone calls, but LinkedIn can help you find the right person before you pick up the phone. One of the most potent aspects of LinkedIn and a job search is the speed with which you can connect with people and find opportunities.

In this chapter, I discuss some of the ways that you can use LinkedIn to help find a job, whether you're an active job seeker (I need a job right now!) or a passive job seeker (I don't mind where I'm working, but if the right opportunity comes along, I'm listening). I start by talking about LinkedIn's job board and how you can search for openings. Then I move into more strategic options such as improving your profile, devising specific strategies, searching your network for specific people, and targeting specific companies when you search.

Searching for an Open Position

LinkedIn offers a few different ways that can help you look for a job. The most direct way is to search for open positions on the LinkedIn job board. After all, someone is getting hired when a company runs a job listing, so why can't that candidate be you? When you search for a job on LinkedIn, you can see what skills seem attractive to companies these days and then keep those skills in mind as you refine your job search and LinkedIn profile.

When you're ready to search for a job opening, follow these steps:

1. **Click the Jobs icon in the top navigation bar.**

   The Jobs home page appears, as shown in Figure 14-1.

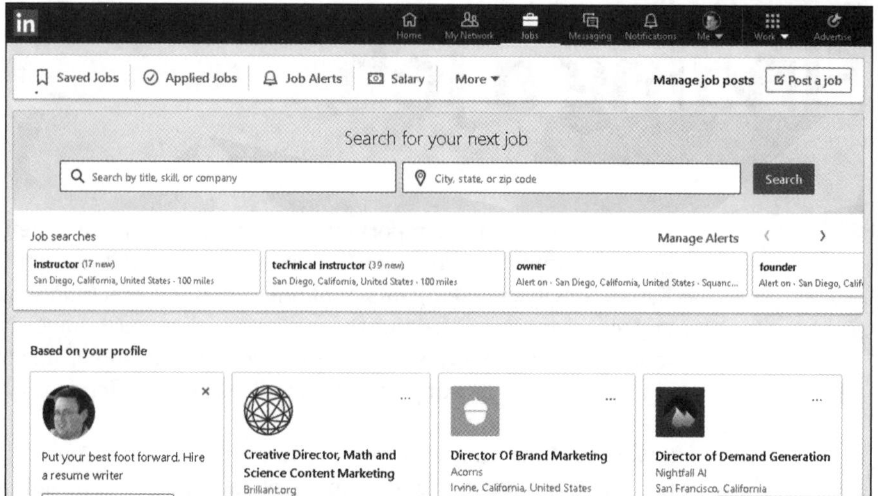

FIGURE 14-1: Look for a job on LinkedIn.

2. **In the left search box below the Search for Your Next Job header, enter keywords describing the job you want.**

   The Search box contains *Search by title, skill, or company.*

3. **To limit your search to a particular location, fill in the second text box.**

   Indicate the city, state, and postal code or country where you want the job to be located.

4. **Click the Search button.**

   The jobs results screen shown in Figure 14-2 appears.

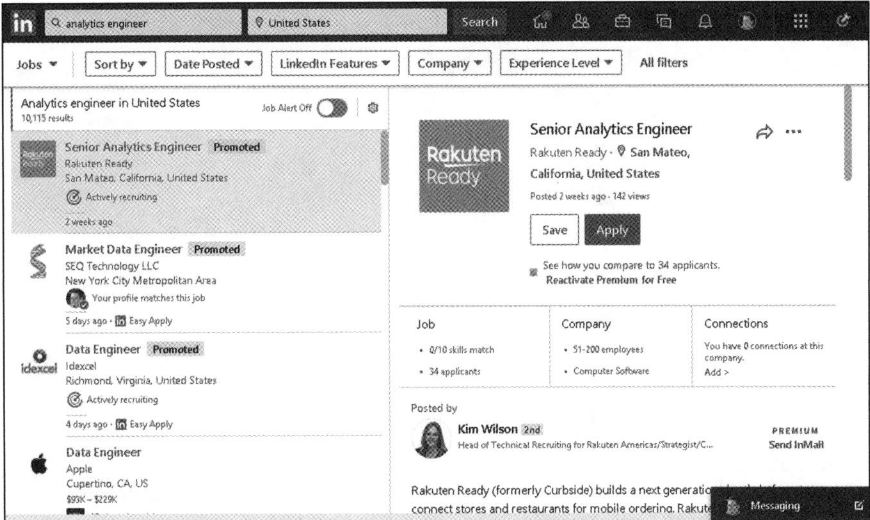

FIGURE 14-2: Check out your job search results.

5. **If you want to refine your job results, enter additional keywords in the Search box or use the filters just below the box.**

   You can sort your results by most relevant or most recent and refine results by using the following filters: Date Posted, LinkedIn Features, Company, and Experience Level. Or click All Filters and refine your results from the screen that appears.

6. **Click a job title to see the details of the posting.**

   A detailed write-up appears in the right pane of the window, where you can find out more about the job (and in some cases, the job poster) before deciding whether to apply. In the example in Figure 14-3, you can see that you have 11 first-degree connections who work for the company, so you could reach out to them to see whether they can help you find the job poster (if the person isn't listed) and give you advice about applying for the job.

   As you scroll down the listing, LinkedIn shows you how many others have applied, which of your skills are most relevant for the job posting, the responsibilities and benefits that come with the job, and even a maps feature to gauge your commute. Finally, you see an excerpt of the LinkedIn Company page for this posting, and a list of similar jobs on LinkedIn's job board.

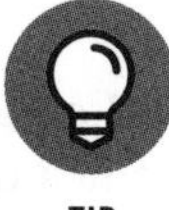

TIP

If the job poster is in your extended network and you have the time, approach that person first with a LinkedIn message or InMail to get more information about the job posting before you apply. (I discuss messaging and InMail at length in Chapter 6.)

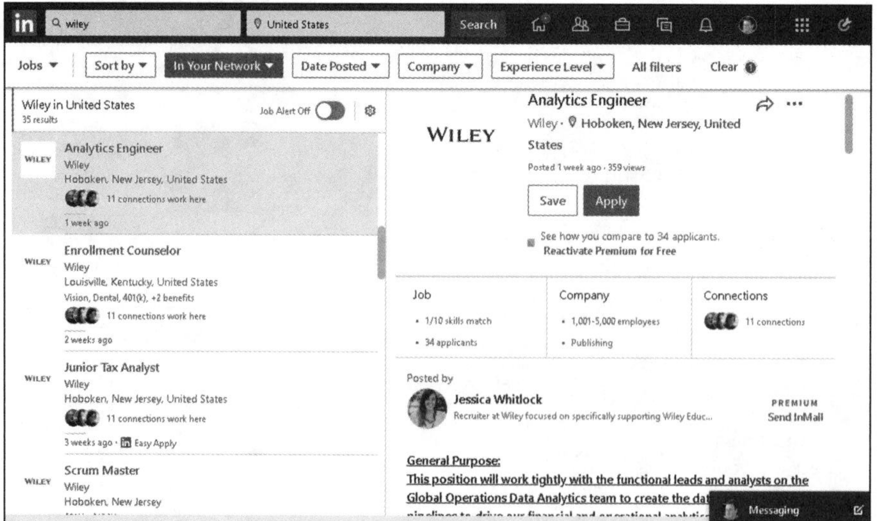

FIGURE 14-3: Find out more about a specific job listing.

7. **When you see a job you want to apply for, click the Apply button (or the Easy Apply button, depending on the employer) and then do the following:**

   - *If you clicked Apply:* A window appears, asking if it's okay to share your profile with the job poster. If you've previously turned on the Privacy setting called Sharing Your Profile When You Apply, LinkedIn will do two things when you click Continue from this new window. It shares your profile with the job poster and takes you to the employer's website, where you should follow the instructions displayed to apply for that job.
   - *If you clicked Easy Apply:* A window appears like the one in Figure 14-4, where your profile information is used to populate some of the fields. After you verify this information and click Next, you see an option to upload a resume. While LinkedIn will attach your most recent resume, you can update an existing resume to highlight the needs of this particular job and use that updated resume instead. Verify the resume you want, and then click Next to answer any additional questions the job poster may have. Then click Submit Your Application to finish your application process.

8. **Click the Submit Application button.**

   Off your application goes!

TIP

When you see a job posting that you like, scroll down to the Similar Jobs section, shown in Figure 14-5. LinkedIn shows you jobs from other companies that are similar to the one you're viewing so you can compare positions.

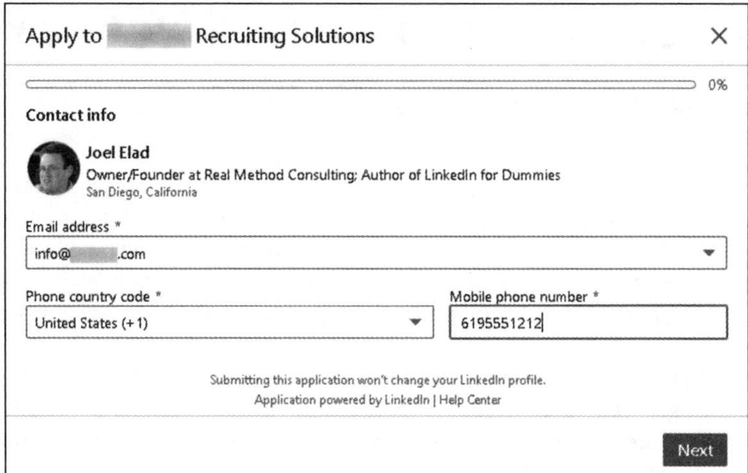

FIGURE 14-4: Start applying for a job on LinkedIn.

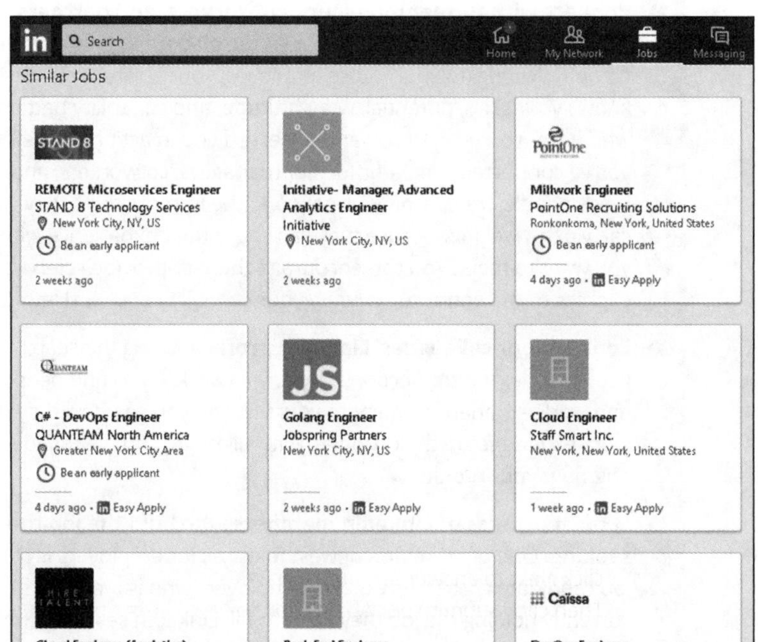

FIGURE 14-5: See similar job postings to the one you're reviewing.

Tuning Up Your Profile and Network to Make a Good Impression

When you're looking for a job, manually scanning job listings and sending resumes are only part of the process. You also have to prepare your job-seeking strategies. The most obvious examples of these are your resume (or CV) and your cover letter. When you include LinkedIn in your job search, you need to prepare your total LinkedIn profile and network to get the optimal job search experience.

Although no strategy can guarantee the job of your dreams, the following strategies can improve your odds of getting the attention of the right contact person, an interview, or extra consideration for your job application that's in a stack of potential candidates:

- **Connect with former managers, co-workers, and partners.** This might seem like an obvious strategy, but let me elaborate. Part of getting the job is communicating (to your future employer) your ability to do the job. Nobody knows your skills, potential, work attitude, and capability better than people who have worked with you and observed you in action. Therefore, make sure you've connected with your former managers, co-workers, and so on. When these people are part of your network, the introductions they can facilitate will carry extra weight because they can share their experience with the person you want to meet. You can encourage them to provide referrals so you can express to the entire community your capability and work ethic.
- **Look at your colleagues' LinkedIn profiles.** Using the search functions or your first-degree connections in your network, try to find people with goals and work experience similar to yours. When you see how they describe their work experience in their profiles, you might get some good ideas on how to augment your profile.
- **Look at profiles of LinkedIn members who hold the job title you are seeking.** One of LinkedIn's newest features for employers is the ability to find job candidates based on an ideal employee, who is typically the person currently holding the job they want to fill. LinkedIn searches for candidates based on the profile an employer selects as the model. Therefore, study the profiles of people doing similar work to see what keywords, skills, and other elements they put in their profile that may be applicable to yours.
- **Contact people when they change jobs.** LinkedIn lets you know when someone in your immediate network has changed positions. This is an excellent opportunity for you to connect and congratulate that person. As she begins her new job, it's likely she may bring other contacts with her, or will

know of advertised or unadvertised opportunities at this new company. Start with a short congratulatory email to help remind the person of your past work together, and then follow up occasionally.

- **Get referrals from past bosses and co-workers.** After you add past bosses and co-workers to your network, keep in contact with them, letting them know your current job search goals and asking for an appropriate referral or introduction. They can use their knowledge of your work history and their expanded networks to make more powerful introductions or requests than just a friend asking another friend, "Hey, can you hire my friend, Joel?"

  Don't be afraid to provide extra information to your past bosses or co-workers to help them make an effective referral. Before the Internet, when job seekers asked a past boss or co-worker to write a letter of recommendation, it was acceptable to include some bullet points you hoped they would cover in their letters. The same is true in the LinkedIn world. Guide your contact to emphasize a work quality or an anecdote that would be effective in the referral or introduction.

- **Collect your recommendations.** Nothing communicates a vote of confidence from your network quite like a recommendation. When anyone reads your LinkedIn profile, he can see exactly what other people have said about you. Because he knows that you can't alter a recommendation, he's more likely to trust the content and believe you're the right person for the job. (See Chapter 9 for more information on how to get more recommendations.)

Preparing Your Profile and Account Settings for Job Searches

Part of the success of finding a job is to have an appealing LinkedIn identity so hiring managers can find you and want to contact you with an opening. According to *Forbes* magazine, 90 percent of employers are using social media sites to recruit employees, with LinkedIn the most used of those sites. After all, the best search is when someone comes to you with an opportunity without you sweating the details.

TIP

If you want to focus on optimizing your profile, don't forget to check out *LinkedIn Profile Optimization For Dummies,* by Donna Serdula.

Checking your profile's visibility

If you're currently employed but decide to quietly start looking for a new position, consider what you're broadcasting to your LinkedIn network before getting ready to make a change. You don't want your current employer or co-workers to see a flurry of activity that's typically a sign of moving on to greener pastures!

To check your visibility settings, click the Me icon, at the top of any LinkedIn page, and then click Settings & Privacy under the Account header. On your Settings page, click the Visibility link in the left navigation menu (see Figure 14-6), and pay careful attention to the following three options:

- **Under Visibility of Your Profile & Network, look at the Who Can See Your Connections option:** Typically, this option is set to Your Connections so first-degree connections can see your other connections. You can change this option to Only You so that your boss or co-workers can't see when you, for example, add a bunch of recruiters or competitors to your network.
- **Under Visibility of Your LinkedIn Activity, check out the Share Job Changes, Education Changes and Work Anniversaries from Profile option:** Click the Change link for this option, and make sure the slider is set to No for the Choose Whether Your Network Is Notified about changes to your profile. That way, your boss or co-workers won't see a flurry of activity if you update your profile.
- **Under Visibility of Your LinkedIn Activity, see the Followers option:** Again, typically, this option is set to Your Connections so first-degree connections can see all your public activity on LinkedIn. If you change this option to Everyone, people outside your network, such as recruiters and potential hiring managers, can get an idea of the information you regularly share on LinkedIn.

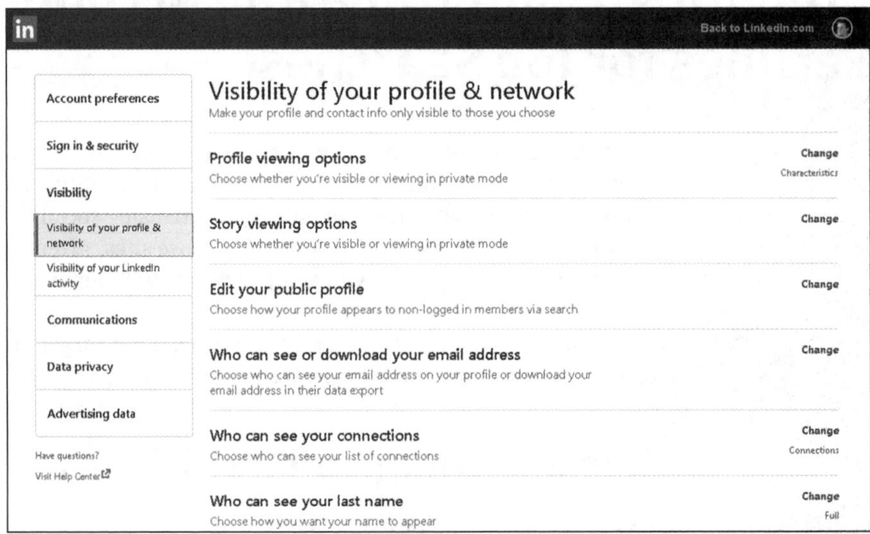

FIGURE 14-6: Manage your profile visibility.

Optimizing your profile

The core of your LinkedIn presence is your profile, which is included with every job application you make on LinkedIn. Odds are good that prospective employers are going to check your LinkedIn profile when evaluating you for a job, so you want to make sure your profile is optimized to make you as appealing as possible.

Now that you've checked your settings, here are some things to keep in mind when bulking up your profile for a job search:

- **Complete all the sections in your profile with as much accurate information as possible.** It's easy to put up a skeleton of your employment history and never get around to fully completing your profile. Unlike a resume (where you could feel confined in terms of page length), you can be as expansive as you want with your LinkedIn profile. You never know what part of your profile will get you included in someone's search result, but the more information you provide, the better the chances that someone will find you.

  TIP

  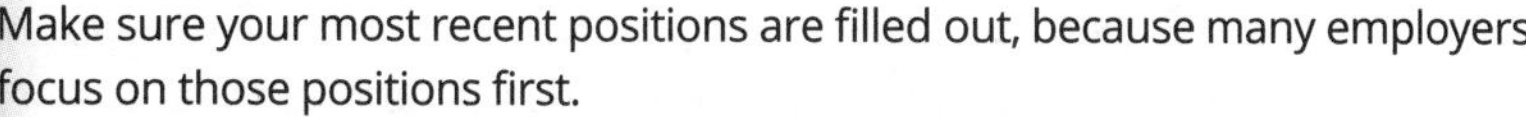

  Make sure your most recent positions are filled out, because many employers focus on those positions first.

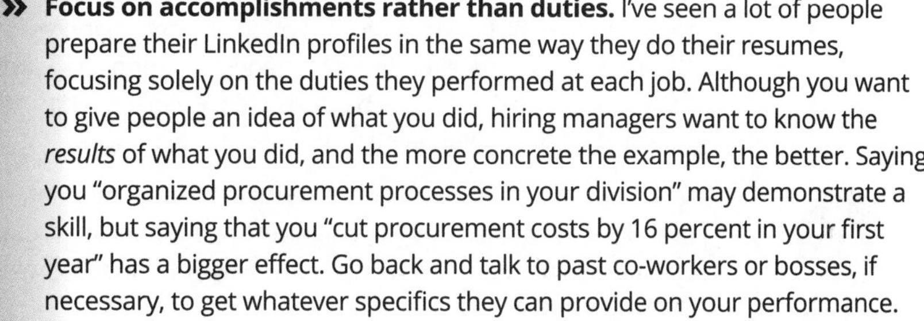

- **Focus on accomplishments rather than duties.** I've seen a lot of people prepare their LinkedIn profiles in the same way they do their resumes, focusing solely on the duties they performed at each job. Although you want to give people an idea of what you did, hiring managers want to know the *results* of what you did, and the more concrete the example, the better. Saying you "organized procurement processes in your division" may demonstrate a skill, but saying that you "cut procurement costs by 16 percent in your first year" has a bigger effect. Go back and talk to past co-workers or bosses, if necessary, to get whatever specifics they can provide on your performance.

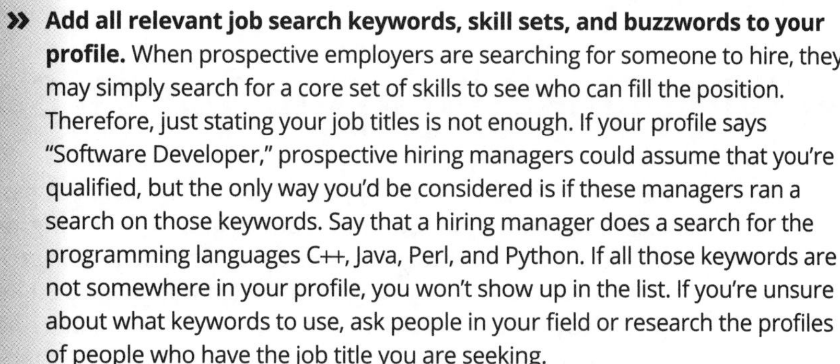

- **Add all relevant job search keywords, skill sets, and buzzwords to your profile.** When prospective employers are searching for someone to hire, they may simply search for a core set of skills to see who can fill the position. Therefore, just stating your job titles is not enough. If your profile says "Software Developer," prospective hiring managers could assume that you're qualified, but the only way you'd be considered is if these managers ran a search on those keywords. Say that a hiring manager does a search for the programming languages C++, Java, Perl, and Python. If all those keywords are not somewhere in your profile, you won't show up in the list. If you're unsure about what keywords to use, ask people in your field or research the profiles of people who have the job title you are seeking.

» **Use an appropriate and professional profile photo.** It has been said before but is worth repeating: LinkedIn is designed so you can network like a professional, and your profile photo is an important part of that process. Ditch the party photo best suited for Facebook. LinkedIn provides tips for choosing a profile picture on its talent blog at `https://business.linkedin.com/talent-solutions/blog/2014/12/5-tips-for-picking-the-right-linkedin-profile-picture`.

TIP

Use a photo of yourself rather than the generic icon supplied by LinkedIn. According to research done by LinkedIn Talent Solutions, profiles with a profile photo are 14 times more likely to be viewed by other members.

» **See how other people position themselves.** Imagine if you could get a book of thousands of resumes from current employees and use them as models to position yourself. Do a search for people with a job, education, or skill set similar to yours and see how they've worded their profiles or how they put their experiences in context. Use that insight to adapt your profile to make it clearer to others.

» **List all your job experiences in your profile, not just full-time positions.** Did you do any short-term or contract jobs? Were you an advisor to another company? Perhaps you're a board member for a local nonprofit group or religious organization. Your LinkedIn profile is designed to reflect all your job experiences, which is *not* limited to a full-time job that provided a W-2 slip. Document any work experience that adds to your overall profile, whether or not you were paid for that job or experience. LinkedIn has sections in which you can highlight volunteer and nonprofit experience.

WARNING

Make sure that every experience you list in your profile contributes to your overall career goals. After all, employers might not care that you were a pastry chef one summer — and will question why you thought it was so important that you listed it in your profile.

Involving LinkedIn in Job Search Strategies

When you're looking for a job, you can include LinkedIn as part of your overall job search in many ways, beyond the direct task of searching the jobs listings and emailing a job request to your immediate network. In this section, I discuss various job search strategies you can implement that involve LinkedIn to some degree and can help add information, contacts, interviews, and (I hope) some offers to your job search. Choose the methods you feel most comfortable implementing.

REMEMBER

Anytime you look for a job, the job search itself should be considered a time commitment, even with the power of LinkedIn. Some of these strategies apply to working or unemployed people and might not instantly result in multiple offers.

Leveraging connections

One of the biggest benefits of LinkedIn is being able to answer the question, "Who do my contacts know?" LinkedIn is not only the sum of your first-degree connections. It's also an extended network of second- and third-degree members, who your first-degree connections can help connect you with for information, referrals, and a new career.

Keep these second- and third-degree network members in mind so you can best leverage your connections to achieve progress. Consider these points when you're working on your job search using LinkedIn:

- **Look for connections to the job poster.** When searching for a job, pay attention to job listings where the job poster is a second- or third-degree network member, such as the listing in Figure 14-7. You can click the link of the job poster to see who in your extended network can refer you directly to the employee who posted that job.
- **Ask for referrals whenever possible.** Exchange information first and then work your way up to a referral request.
- **Get your friends involved.** Let your immediate network know about your goals so they can recommend the right people for you to talk to — and generate the right introductions for you as well.

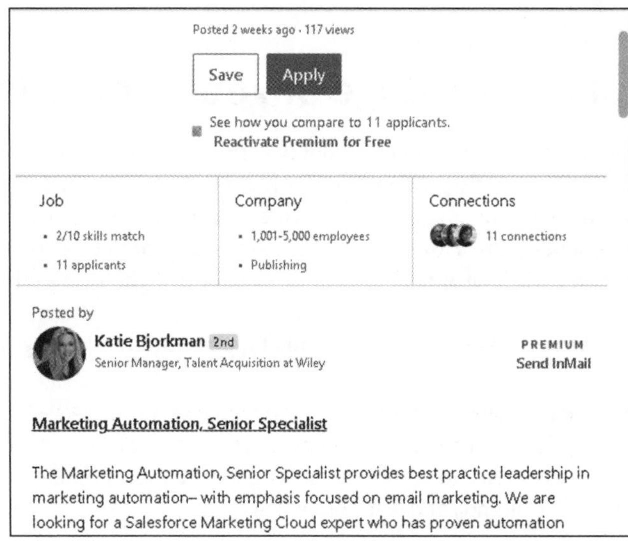

FIGURE 14-7: See whether you have a connection who can refer you to the job poster.

Finding people with the same or similar job

If you're looking for a specific job, remember that the people doing a similar job know the most about the job you're interested in. Although these people might not have hiring authority, they can help give you the right perspective, share the right insider tips about what the job truly entails, and let you know what skills or background the hiring manager considered when they were hired.

Because these people are already employed and not your direct competition, they're more likely to offer help and advice. They have practical knowledge of what it takes to do the job and what qualities will best help someone succeed in that position. When you're ready to implement this strategy, keep these points in mind:

- **Perform an advanced search for people with a similar job title as the one you're applying for.** Put the job title in either the keywords section or the title section.
- **Narrow and clarify your search by industry.** For example, Project Manager of Software Development is different than Project Manager for the Construction industry. Choose multiple industries if they are similar enough.
- **When you find someone who has a job title you'd like to have, see whether she's interested in meeting.** Ask for an informational interview or, if she is outside your geographic area, a phone conversation. Asking outright for a job lead will most likely not result in anything positive.

Taking advantage of your alma mater

Typically, people who a share school in common have an ongoing affinity, whether the school is an undergraduate or graduate college or even a high school. You can rapidly increase the chance of someone considering your request if you and that person attended the same school. Take advantage of your alumni status and try to connect and work with people who went to one of the same schools as you.

Here are some tips to help further this type of search by using LinkedIn:

- **Start with your Alumni page.** Go to the university page(s) in LinkedIn for your defined educational outlet by searching for your school on LinkedIn. From here, you can search the alumni, see the most popular companies that hire these alumni, and learn other key facts.

- **Search for alumni association groups of any school you attended.** From the top navigation bar, type your alma mater in the Search box, and when the drop-down list appears, click All Results. From that results screen, click the Groups button below the Search box. When the refined search results appear, search and join any alumni LinkedIn groups for schools you attended. These LinkedIn groups give you access to their member list, so you can see other alumni, regardless of graduation year, and communicate with them.
- **Connect as a former classmate and ask for information first and a referral second.** Your shared alumni status helps open the door, but don't expect a handout right away. Be ready to offer one of your contacts in exchange for a former classmate's help or consideration.
- **Check the connection list of any of your contacts who attended school with you.** This is a good safety check to look for any classmates on your contacts' lists whom you might not have initially considered. (I discuss connection lists in Chapter 5.)
- **Conduct an advanced people search with the school name as a keyword.** If necessary, try different variations of the school name. For example, try the school name with and without acronyms. When I look for classmates from the University of California, Irvine, I search for *UCI* as well as *University California Irvine.* (I talk more about advanced searches in Chapter 4.)
- **If your school has changed or updated its name, conduct an advanced people search for both the old and new names as keywords.** For example, because my school's department name at UCI had changed from the Graduate School of Management, or GSM, to the Paul Merage School of Business, I search for the old and new search terms because my classmates may have defined their educational listings differently.

Finding target company referrals

Sometimes your job search involves a specific company and not necessarily a job title. Suppose you know you want to work at one of the top computer database software companies. Now you can use LinkedIn to help you find the right people at those companies who can help you. Here are some points to consider:

- **Make a list of the ten companies you'd like to work for and do an advanced people search for each company to find potential contacts.** Type the company name in the Search box at the top of the home page and then click the Search button. The results page displays a list of people on the results page who are in your extended network and who have the company name in their titles.

For larger companies, you need to search for a specific department or an industry area to find the right contact. Ask the people you've identified for referrals to someone in your target organization, such as a hiring manager. You can refine your search by relationship by searching for any combination of first-degree connections, second- or third-degree network members, or LinkedIn Group members.

- **Follow the companies themselves.** LinkedIn allows you to follow companies through their Company page. When you know what companies you want to follow, simply enter their name in the text box in the top navigation bar, press Enter, and then click Companies. When you find the company in the results list, click the Follow button next to the company listing. After you are following all your target companies, review each Company page weekly for news, information, job openings, and useful contacts.
- **If you can't find someone who currently works at your target company, look for people who used to work there.** Conduct an advanced people search, and set the option under Company to Past. Many times, past employees maintain contacts at their old company and can attest to the work environment and corporate culture.
- **Consider getting a Job Seeker premium account on LinkedIn.** When you upgrade to a Job Seeker premium account, you get extra tools to help you find that next job. Any job application that you submit through LinkedIn will show you with Featured Applicant Status, so your name will sit above nonpremium members who applied to the same job. You will have full view of who looked at your LinkedIn profile in the last 90 days and how they arrived at your profile page, which can come in handy when you reach out to communicate with them. (After all, they showed interest in looking for you by searching and looking at your profile page.) You also get credit towards InMail messaging, so you can reach out to LinkedIn members who aren't connected to you. There are other features as well, so check it out!

» Creating a Company page

» Sharing company updates with the community

Chapter 15
Following Companies

Two of the main reasons why people search the LinkedIn network are to find a job and to find a new employee. In both cases, LinkedIn users are trying to learn more about the company, not just the job seeker or hiring manager. Millions of self-employed people who use LinkedIn to promote not only themselves but also their services are always looking for a way to expand their brand and look for new business opportunities. LinkedIn organizes all these efforts under its Company pages.

LinkedIn maintains a directory of Company pages that allow people to learn about each company's products, services, and job opportunities. Each Company page has at least one administrator who can add his company to the directory, edit the information, connect his employees to the Company page, and provide company updates to the LinkedIn community. LinkedIn members can follow their favorite companies to get company and industry updates, and see how each member's network is connected to the employees of each company they follow.

In this chapter, I cover how you can search Company pages, follow different companies, and, if you're an employee or owner of your own company, create and update your own Company page.

Searching for Companies

When you need to learn more about your current industry or find a potential business partner for a big deal, your first step is to do some research. Company pages allow users to explore companies of interest, whether it's a for-profit or nonprofit company, and receive company updates and industry news, as well as research each company's products and services — and, of course, learn about job opportunities the company has to offer.

You can follow multiple companies; their news, updates, and posts will appear as part of your news feed and help populate the news feed items you see.

To search for a Company page, follow these steps:

1. **In the Search box at the top of any LinkedIn page, start typing the keywords for your company search.**

   As you're typing, a drop-down list appears, as shown in Figure 15-1.

2. **If the company you're searching for is listed:**

   a. *Click its entry.* You're taken to the company page.

   b. *Review the information on this page to make sure this is the company you were hoping to find.*

   c. *To add this company to the list of companies you're following, click Follow.*

   You've completed your company search at this point!

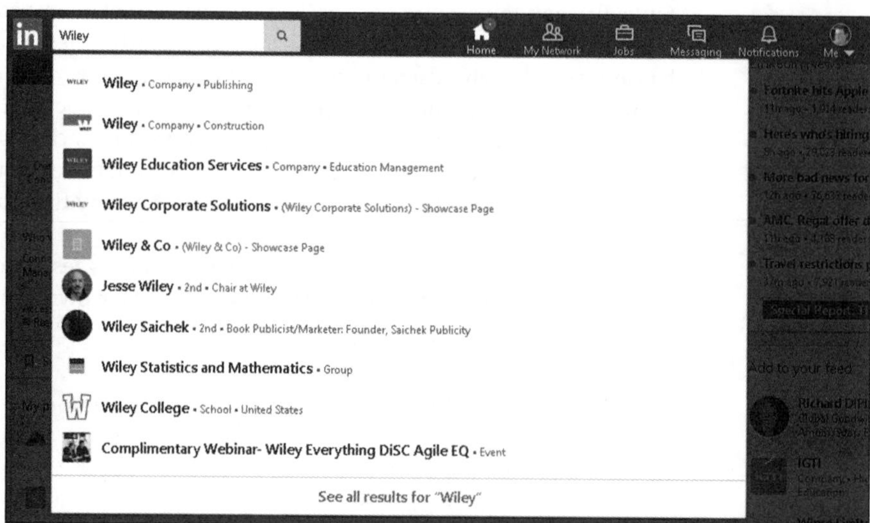

FIGURE 15-1: Start a simple company search here.

3. **If the company isn't in the list, finish typing and press Enter.**

   The search results page appears.

4. **Click the Companies button, below the Search box, to focus the search on Companies.**

   The Companies search results page appears, as shown in Figure 15-2. (In this example, I simply typed *Internet* as the keyword.)

5. **Click the name of the company in the list to go to their Company page.**

   You can also click the Follow button next to the company's entry, so any updates or mentions of that company will appear in your news feed. If you want to look into the company first, simply go to the Company page. If you like what you see, click the Follow button on the Company page.

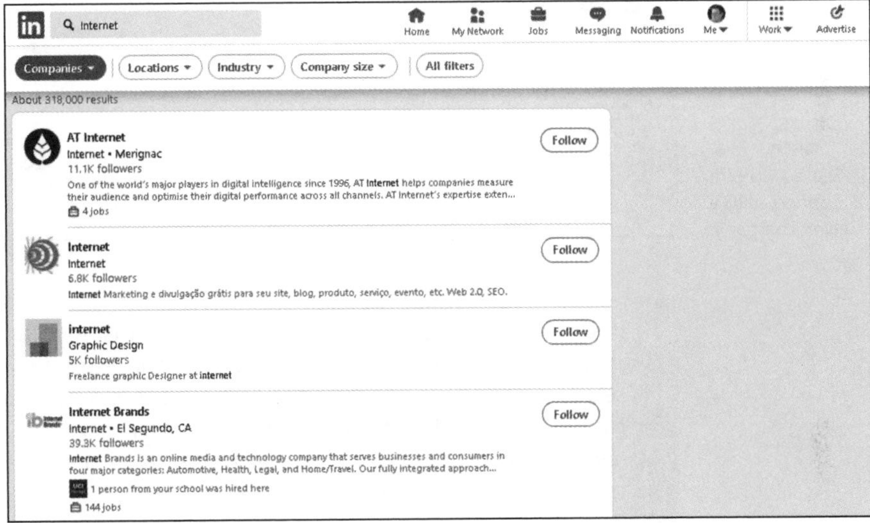

FIGURE 15-2: See companies that match your search results.

After you reach a page loaded with potential companies, use the following tricks to find the one that's just right for you:

- **Click the Follow button to keep track of the company.** As mentioned, when you click the Follow button next to any company listing, you'll see all the company's updates in the Companies section of your LinkedIn page.
- **View the Company page and study your connections.** To see the Company page, click the name of the company. Study the information on that page before deciding whether to follow the company. You can also view how you're connected to people inside the company.

For example, Figure 15-3 is the Company page for Wiley, which publishes this book. On the left side of the page, under the Wiley logo, I can see how many people in my immediate network, or first-degree connections, are associated with that company.

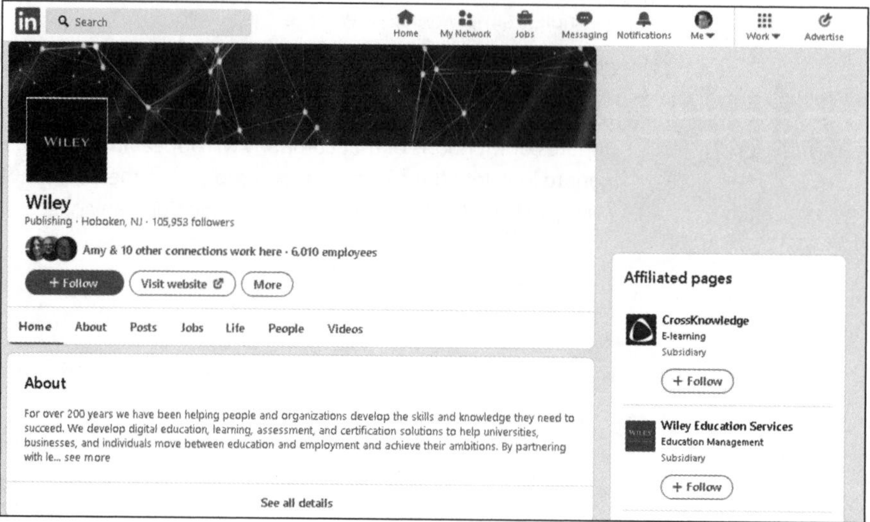

FIGURE 15-3: See how you're connected to a given company.

If I click *X* & *Y* other Connections Work Here, I get a list showing how I'm connected to people in that company, as shown in Figure 15-4. This page is a search results screen, so I can add more keywords or filters, if I want, to get a custom list of how I relate to any given company. For example, I could click 1st (above the search results) and add second-degree connections to see second-degree network members.

- **Explore the Company page to learn new information.** As you scroll down the Company page, you'll see a section of current job openings, as well as a news feed featuring the company's recent and past posts to LinkedIn, including videos, images, documents, and articles. On the left side of the Company page is a navigation menu that can take you to pages providing information on company life, jobs, and people, as well as video, and ads. On the right side of the Company page, you can click affiliated company pages and even similar company pages to the one you're studying here.
- **Decide whom to follow by studying the number of followers.** If you have a lot of potential companies to follow and want the best chance of finding a connection inside a company, check out the number of followers to decide

whether a particular company is worth your continued attention. The number of followers appears on the search results screen for Companies as well as below the name of the company on their Company page.

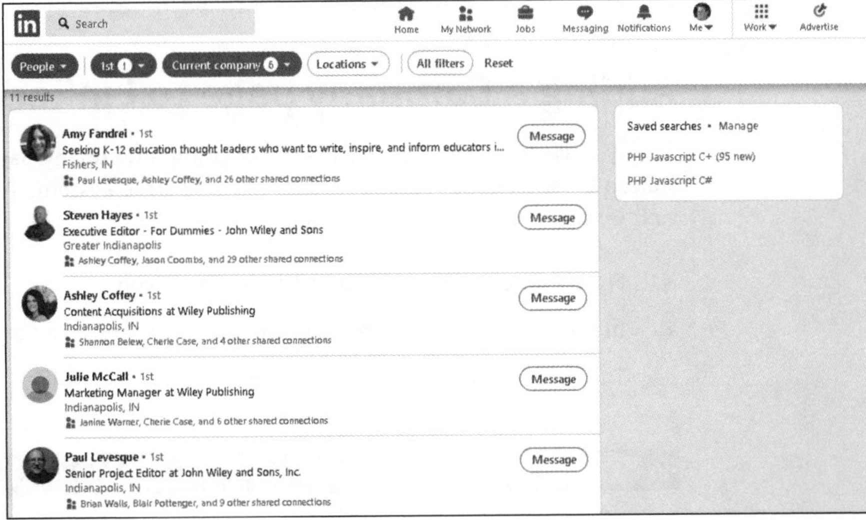

FIGURE 15-4: See a full list of connections to search further.

TIP

Most Company pages have a Jobs section. Click the link in that section to see a list of active job listings for that company. You can then apply directly through LinkedIn's job board and get an idea of who may be involved in the job hiring.

Putting Your Company on LinkedIn

The flip side of LinkedIn Company pages is that company leaders and employees should use them on behalf of the company itself. Companies are always looking for ways to tell their story and engage interested members who want to follow their activities in a way that encourages word of mouth, highlights their products and services, and advertises career opportunities. Company pages enable companies to do all this as well as enable their customers to offer recommendations, which are spotlighted on the Company page.

As of this writing, LinkedIn has more than 13 million Company pages. The millions of users who follow these companies are current and potential customers, interested job applicants, business partners, or curious industry watchers who want to hear the latest news, see the latest products and services, and reach out and interact with company leaders, managers, and employees. LinkedIn bills its Company pages as a central hub where millions of LinkedIn users can stay in the loop of company news and activities.

TIP

You can read more about the benefits of Company pages at `https://business.linkedin.com/marketing-solutions/linkedin-pages`.

Adding a Company page to LinkedIn

After you've met the requirements for creating a Company page, it's time to get started by adding the Company page to LinkedIn's system. To create or update your Company page, follow these steps:

1. **From the top navigation bar, click the Work icon.**
2. **In the list that appears, scroll down and select Create a Company page.**

   The page shown in Figure 15-5 appears.

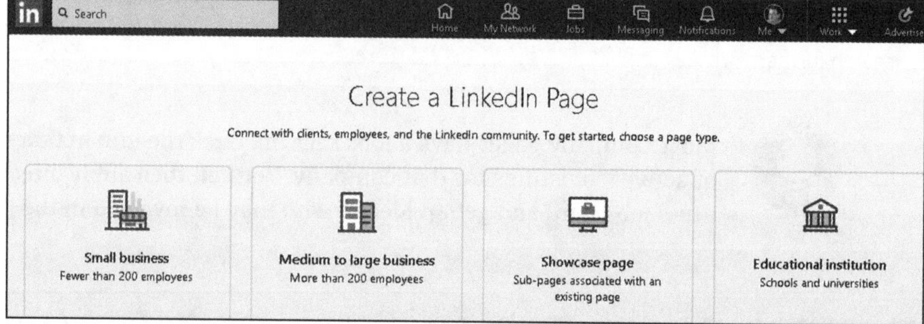

FIGURE 15-5: Choose the type of Company page you need on LinkedIn.

3. **Click the selection for the type of Company page you want to create.**

   Choose whether you're creating a Company page for a small business, a medium to large business, or an educational institution, or a showcase page to augment an existing page. The screen shown in Figure 15-6 appears. (For this example, I clicked Small Business.)

4. **Fill in the information in the fields provided:**

   a. *Enter the company name.*

   b. *Enter a name in the text box for the LinkedIn public URL so the URL will be unique as well as easy to remember and promote.*

   c. *(Optional) Edit the website URL in the Website box so your LinkedIn company page can link to your external website.*

d. Complete the drop-down boxes offered to select the Industry, Company Size, and Company Type for your company, so LinkedIn can classify your company.

e. (Optional) Upload a logo for your company and write a tagline in the box provided. The logo and tagline will appear when someone searches for a company and your company is part of the search results.

f. Select the check box verifying that you are an authorized representative of your company.

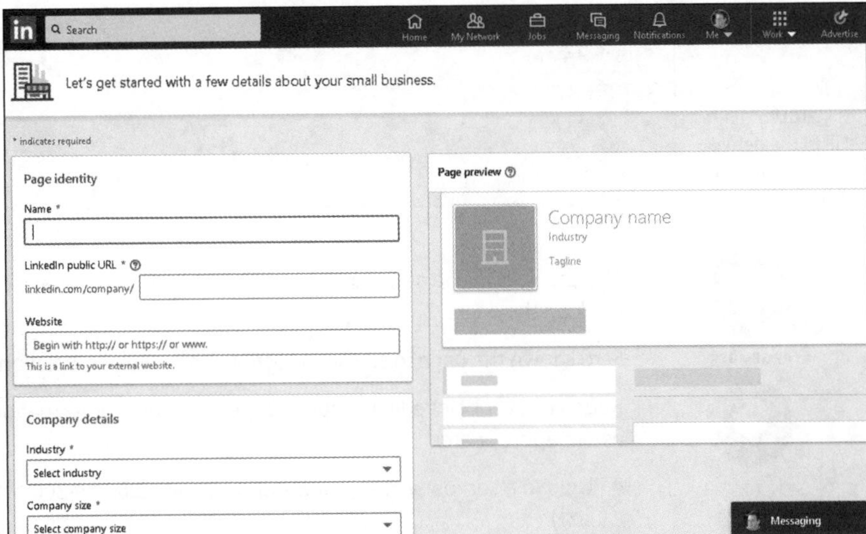

FIGURE 15-6: Define your Company page on LinkedIn.

5. **Click the Create Page button.**

   The screen changes to Admin mode, as shown in Figure 15-7.

6. **Use the Build Your Page tool to provide more information for your page.**

   For example, complete the Location action as follows to assign at least one office location to your Company page:

   a. Click the blue Add button under Location.

   b. Complete the text fields presented. Remember that any text field with an asterisk is required.

   c. When you have completed the information, click the blue Add button.

   You return to the Build Your Page tool element at the top of your Company page.

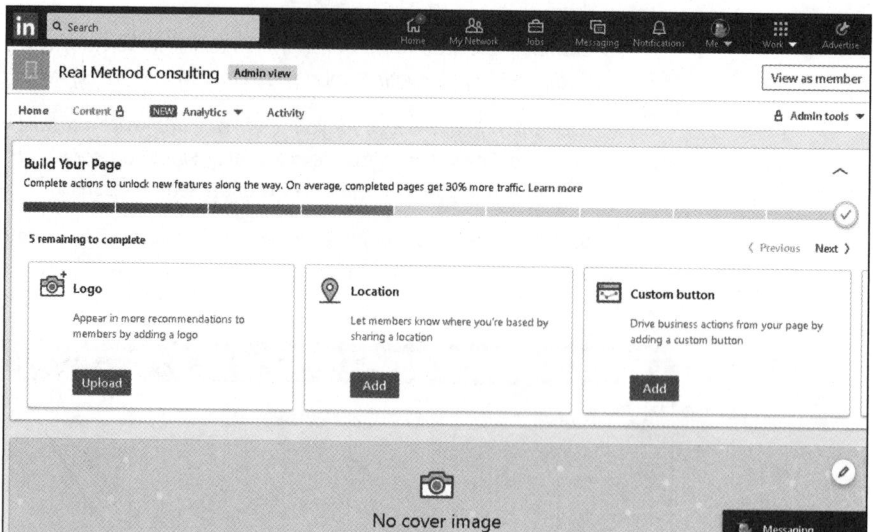

FIGURE 15-7: Fill in the details for your Company page.

REMEMBER

The changes will be automatically published to your Company page as you work on the page.

Scroll down the page to see all the actions that need completion.

TIP

Round out your LinkedIn Company page by entering information and pictures where appropriate:

- Upload a company image or a standard logo (300-by-300 pixels image size).
- Upload a cover image that's a minimum of 1,192-by-220 pixels and a maximum of 1,536-by-768 pixels.
- List any company specialties and LinkedIn groups that are relevant to your company in the fields provided.

7. **To see how your Company page will appear to the members, click View as Member.**

A screen similar to Figure 15-8 appears.

Now you can start to provide company updates, add products or services, or edit your page.

REMEMBER

After your page is created, you should click the Follow button so your company has at least one follower. Doing this is also a good check to see how company updates are appearing on a LinkedIn member's page (in this case, your page).

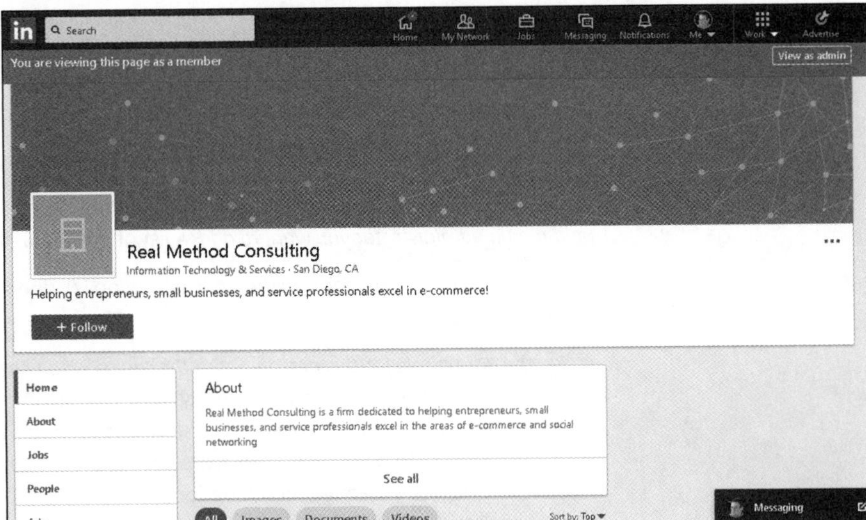

FIGURE 15-8: See how your Company page looks to the public!

You can add additional administrators to your Company page, and you can also add direct sponsored content posters — LinkedIn members who are allowed to create sponsored content for your Company page. Just do the following:

1. **Make sure you're in admin view.**

   You should see Admin View to the right of the Company name along the left side and the Admin Tools link at the top right.

   Click the View as Admin button if you're looking at member view.

2. **Click the Admin Tools link, and select Manage Admins under the Settings header.**

   The Manage Admins window opens.

3. **To add an administrator:**

   a. *Click the blue Add Admin button on the right side of the page.*

   b. *In the text box that appears in the pop-up window, start typing the name of the new administrator.* A list of first-degree connections appears.

   REMEMBER

   The person you name as a page administrator must be a first-degree connection.

   c. *Click the desired person's name in the list.*

   d. *Assign the admin role for this person.* Select the radio button next to the level of administration duties you want to give this person. You can pick between Super admin (ability to manage all elements and administrators), Content admin (manage contents, comments, and access analytics), or Analyst (ability to view and export logistics).

   e. *Click the blue Save button at the bottom right of your window to save your choice.*

4. **To add a Paid Media administrator:**

   a. *Below the Admin Roles header, click the Paid Media Admins link.*

   b. *Click the blue Add Paid Media Admin button on the right side of the page.*

   c. *In the text box that appears in the pop-up window, start typing the name of the paid media administrator you want to add.* A list of potential names appears.

   d. *Click the desired person's name in the list.* The person is added as a paid media administrator.

   e. *Assign the admin role for this person. Select the radio button next to the level of administration duties you want to give this person.* You can choose Sponsored Content Poster (can create sponsored content ads for your page), Lead Gen Forms Manager (can download leads from your LinkedIn ad account), or Pipeline Builder (can manage recruiting-focused stand-alone pipeline builder pages; applies to people paying for LinkedIn Talent Solutions).

   f. *Click the blue Save button at the bottom right of your window to save your choice.*

Now that you've created your Company page, think about incorporating your page management duties into your normal LinkedIn activity schedule. On an ongoing basis, you should make sure that you're properly communicating with and responding to your followers and the community in large.

Here are some tips on how to proceed with administering your Company page:

- **Follow your competitors.** You will not only gain insight into what your competitors are doing but also see how they're using their Company page, which may give you ideas on how to position your Company page and what updates to share with your followers.
- **Add Showcase pages.** Providing your basic company information is the first step. Next is defining the aspects of your business that deserve their own page, called a Showcase page, so prospective customers can receive targeted messages and focused content about the parts of your business relevant to them. Think about highlighting the right keywords and features that your customers want to see when defining your Showcase pages.

TIP

You are limited to 10 Showcase pages per parent Company page. However, you can contact LinkedIn and request additional pages.

- **Consider writing sponsored updates for your company.** Similar to sponsoring a status update on Facebook with an ad budget, you can sponsor a company update on LinkedIn, which will allow that update to be shown on people's LinkedIn news feeds, whether or not they're following your company. Sponsored updates allow you to expand the reach of your company's message and help your company gain more followers on LinkedIn.
- **Refine the message your company is projecting by testing your sponsored content.** You can use direct sponsored content also to test the responsiveness of your message, because this content doesn't appear on the original company's news feed. By studying the click rates of different sponsored content you pay for at the same time, you can discover which message is most effective at reaching your target audience.
- **Gain insight into the LinkedIn social actions regarding your company.** When you click the Activity tab (located near the top of your Company page), you can see some overall sets of information, such as the amount of likes, comments, shares, and mentions regarding your company, as well as company posts or updates, for the current day, week, and month. You'll also see a list of notifications of people trying to reach your company through LinkedIn.
- **Review suggestions to improve your content.** When you click the Content tab (near the top of your Company page), you see LinkedIn's recommendations for improving the content on your Company page, based on information you provided, including industry, company size, your website URL, company description, logo, and location.
- **Keep an eye on the analytics.** LinkedIn provides a lot of information about how its members are viewing and interacting with Company pages. Click the Analytics tab (located near the top of your Company page) to see how your followers are viewing and responding to your updates, how many people you're reaching through your Company page, and how engaged they are with your Company page.

5 Using LinkedIn for Everyday Business

IN THIS PART . . .

Use LinkedIn groups to meet like-minded people, expand your network, and grow your knowledge base.

Get tips on marketing your own business or start-up through LinkedIn.

Understand how LinkedIn can help increase sales.

Learn how to create an ad on LinkedIn and measure the ad's effectiveness.

Discover some creative ways people have used LinkedIn to achieve their professional goals.

» Starting and participating in group discussions

» Searching a group's membership list

» Creating a group

» Managing a group

Chapter 16

Getting Connected with Groups

There's more to a professional's life than colleagues and classmates. People have always been drawn to groups based on common interests, backgrounds, or goals. This natural tendency to join can be seen in sports teams to Boy Scouts and Girl Scouts, social action organizations, and nonprofit charity groups. Naturally, LinkedIn also offers a way for people to connect with each other as a group — LinkedIn groups.

In this chapter, I discuss the value in LinkedIn groups, from gaining information and exposure to growing your network, and cover the overall idea and structure of groups and what you can expect to find. You then learn how to search for existing groups and how to join a group. Finally, you discover how to start your own group and invite others to join.

Reaping the Benefits of Groups

When people who are familiar with other social networking tools are first exposed to LinkedIn groups, they see some similarities. The group interactions in LinkedIn groups — discussion threads, job postings, and so on — feel like discussions or groups on most other social networking sites. And yet, being a member of a LinkedIn group has benefits that groups on other networking sites don't have:

- **Connections:** Group members share a special sort of connection. Although you don't have access to their extended networks, you're considered connected to them in that you can see their profile and send them a message through LinkedIn, and they can appear in your search results even if you aren't within three degrees of everyone in the group. Your search results can include fellow group members as well as your first-degree connections and second-degree network members.

  WARNING

  LinkedIn imposes a monthly limit of 15 messages you can send to group members outside your network, so use this feature sparingly. Otherwise, your LinkedIn account may be suspended or cancelled.

- **Visibility:** By participating in groups — particularly large, open ones — and sharing your knowledge and expertise with people who are not yet in your network, you can increase your visibility in the LinkedIn network without adding thousands of contacts.
- **Knowledge:** LinkedIn groups share information and expertise among their members through the Discussions page of the group, which you can benefit from as a group member. Because there are thousands of groups for most industries and fields, LinkedIn groups can be a valuable source of knowledge.
- **Recognition:** Employers like to see that you're connected with professional groups because it shows a desire to expand your knowledge base, stay current in your industry or field, and be open and eager to network with like-minded people.
- **Group logos:** The logos of the groups you're in are available in your profile under Interests, and you can see all the group logos for a user when someone clicks See All under Interests, and then clicks the Groups tab from the Following window that opens. This visual branding reinforces your association with those groups. For example, Figure 16-1 shows the profile for a LinkedIn member who belongs to several groups.

Some LinkedIn groups are extensions of existing organizations, and others are created on LinkedIn by an individual or business as a way to identify and network with people who share a common interest. In either case, groups are useful tools for growing your network and leveraging your existing affiliations.

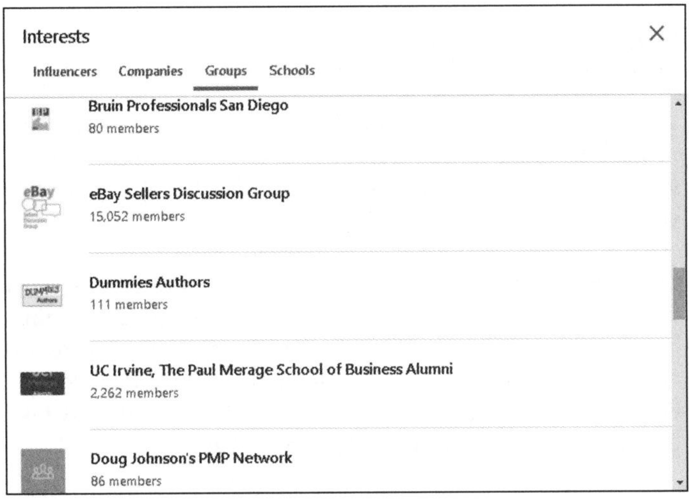

FIGURE 16-1: Group logos displayed in a profile.

Understanding the Two Types of Groups

Over the years, LinkedIn groups have evolved to provide a quality place for interactions and content while fighting attempts to flood groups with spam or promotional content. Therefore, LinkedIn groups are now private, members-only groups, which means that you can't join a group without approval or an invitation, and the conversations in a group are not visible to the outside world (including search engines). In this way, only members of the group can see and contribute to conversations.

Following are the two types of LinkedIn groups:

- **Listed:** These groups are the most common form of LinkedIn groups, and they show up in search results. Membership in this group is displayed on each member's profile page under the Interests header; and to see all of a person's groups, you click See All below the Interests header. The group's summary page appears in search engine results, but the conversations in the group do not.
- **Unlisted:** Because these groups are not discoverable by LinkedIn members by searching groups, they have become invitation-only groups; the only way you can join is to be invited by the group owner or manager. These groups do not appear in a LinkedIn search or any search engine, and non-group members can't see the group logo in a member's profile page. Examples of unlisted groups include employee-only groups for a company, customer-only groups to handle customer service or new product ideas, and focus groups to share and collaborate on new ideas or discuss potential upcoming products for a company.

Joining a Group

When you look at the LinkedIn groups available, one of the most important things to keep in mind is that you should join only those groups that are relevant. Although you might think it's fun to join another alumni association group besides your alma mater, it won't help you in the long run.

That said, if you're self-employed or in sales, for example, you may consider joining groups that appeal to your customers or prospects, to gain a better perspective on what they need, or to share your expertise with a market that could appreciate and use the knowledge you've gained. On an individual level, though, groups are best for networking with colleagues or like-minded individuals to share knowledge and grow from each other's experience.

Keep in mind that some professional groups have special requirements and you may not be eligible to join due to your particular educational or professional experience.

To seek out a group to join, follow these steps:

1. **In the top navigation bar, click the Work icon and then click the Groups icon in the drop-down list that appears.**

   Your Groups page appears, as shown in Figure 16-2.

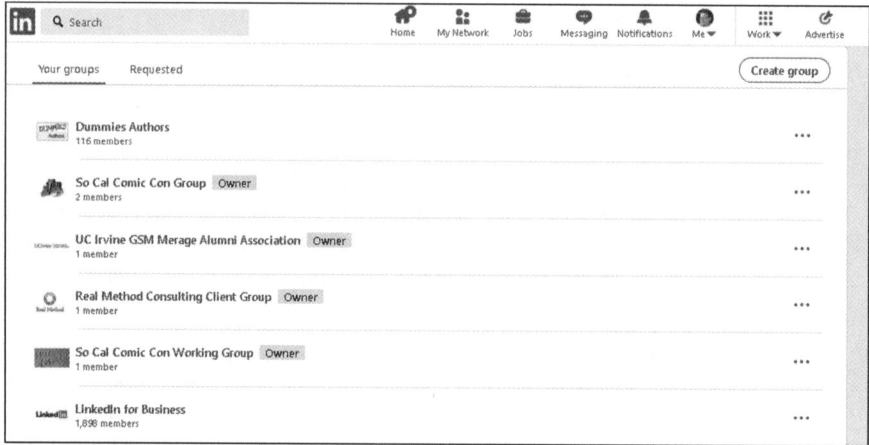

FIGURE 16-2: See the activity of your groups here.

2. **Click the Search link at the bottom of the page to see potential groups you can join.**

   The search results page appears, as shown in Figure 16-3, filled with groups that may appeal to you.

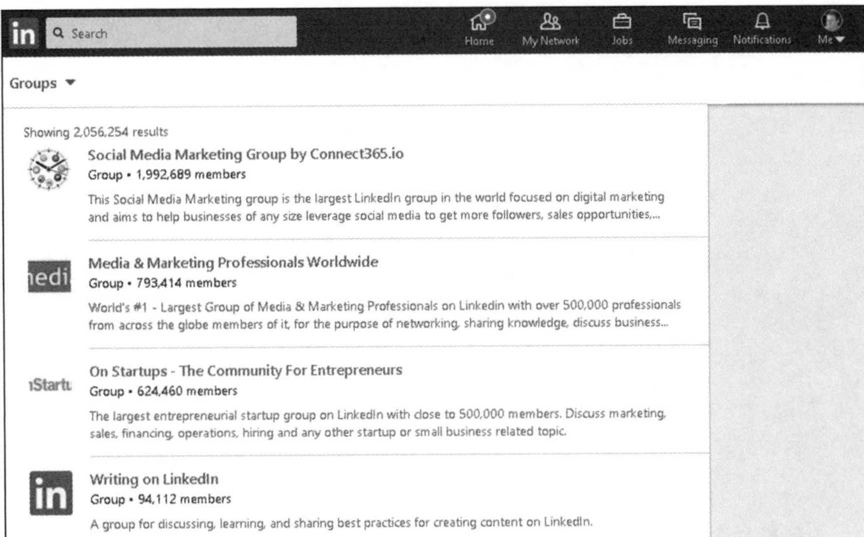

FIGURE 16-3: LinkedIn helps you discover groups to join.

3. **To find more specific groups to join, conduct a search:**

   a. *Enter keywords in the text box at the top of the page.* Use keywords that describe the group that interests you. If you're looking to join a group that deals with social media management, for example, type *social media management* in the text box.

   b. *Press Enter.* The search results list appears, with Groups already selected, as shown in Figure 16-4.

   c. *Click a group in the list, and read the group's description on the summary page that appears.* You can also click the group administrator name to see that person's profile and send a message requesting a few details about the group.

   d. *Click the Request to Join button to join the group.* That's it! Your request is sent to the group manager for approval. A Successfully Sent the Request message appears in the bottom-left corner of your screen, and the button changes to Withdraw Request, as shown in Figure 16-5. As mentioned, your request may not be approved depending on the criteria for that group.

TIP

Another way to look for a new group to join is to click the Group logo in the profile of one of your first-degree connections. Then click the Request to Join button on the page that appears, and you've completed your part of the process.

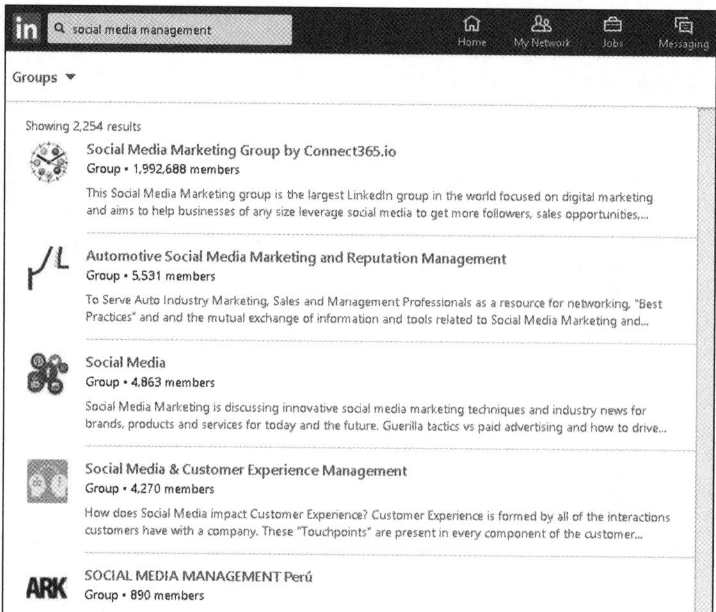

FIGURE 16-4: Review a list of potential groups to join.

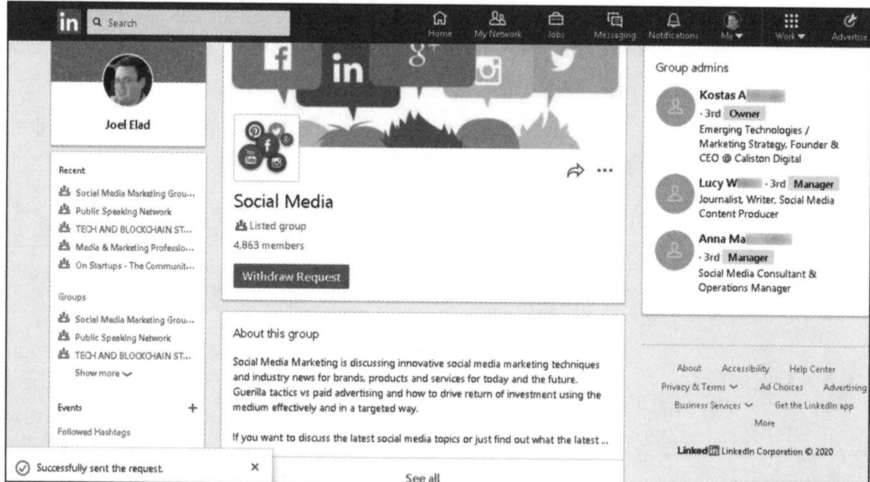

FIGURE 16-5: Your request to join this group is now pending.

Starting and participating in group discussions

The core of LinkedIn groups is to start and maintain conversations among group members that aid in sharing content and job postings, making business or professional connections, finding answers, and establishing industry experts.

As you look at a typical LinkedIn groups conversation, as shown in Figure 16-6, you can choose to interact with each entry in a way similar to what you can do on other social media sites:

- **Like the conversation.** By clicking the Like link, you signal that you found the post useful. Some group members may assess whether to participate in any given discussion based on the amount of likes that the discussion has received.

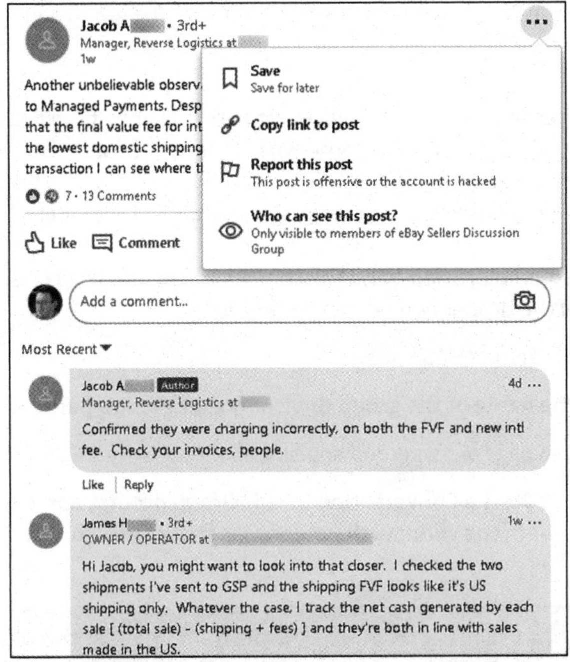

FIGURE 16-6: Interact by liking or commenting on the conversation.

- **Comment on the conversation.** By clicking the Comment link and adding a comment to the discussion thread, you unlock the true power of group conversations by adding your viewpoint, replying to the original point, or replying to another comment. To truly expand the conversation, you can also provide links to other articles or resources in your comment.
- **Reply privately to the group member.** When you read a conversation or another comment from a fellow group member, you can click the name of the author and send the person a message through LinkedIn. In this way, you can communicate with the group member directly, without the rest of the group viewing your communication. Perhaps you want to offer individualized help or generate a lead.

» **Act on the conversation.** Click the three dots at the top right of the conversation to display options for interacting with the conversation. Then click the Save link to save this conversation to review later when you're on LinkedIn. You can also click Copy Link to Post, which copies the direct URL of the group conversation to your clipboard. This way, if you create a post or comment on some other conversation, you can paste the link to bring others into this conversation.

» **Report a post or a comment.** If you're interested in keeping the group as spam-free as possible, you can click the three dots at the top of the conversation post or below any individual comment, and then click the Report link to report the post or comment as inappropriate. The group administrator will be notified and can review the item for further action.

After you join a group, start by participating in existing discussions and then decide how you can best contribute with your own posts.

When you are ready to start a conversation, follow these steps:

1. **In the top navigation bar, click the Work icon and then click the Groups icon in the drop-down list that appears.**

   Your Groups page appears.

2. **Click the name of the group to display that group's page.**

   The main page of that group appears, as shown in Figure 16-7.

3. **Click the Start a Conversation in This Group prompt and begin writing your post in the window that opens, as shown in Figure 16-8.**

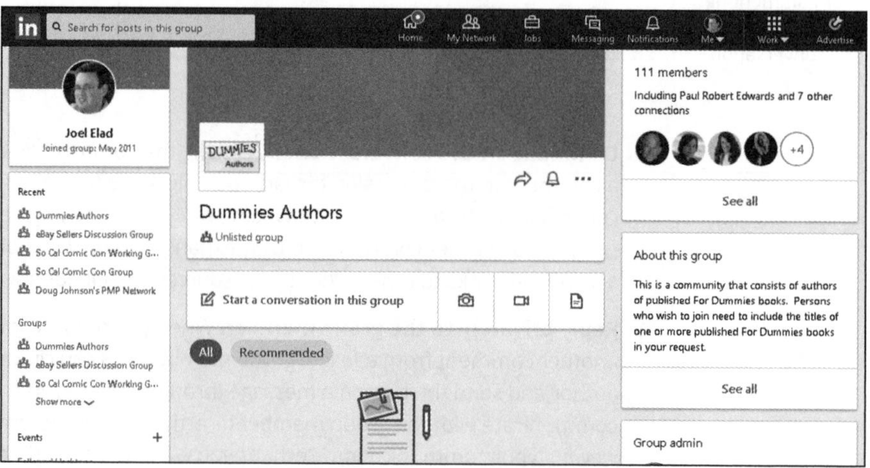

FIGURE 16-7: Start a conversation in your group.

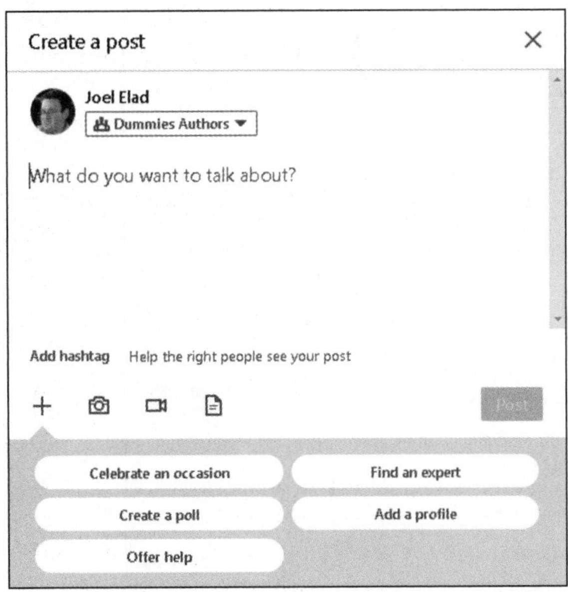

FIGURE 16-8: Create a conversation in your group.

4. **Click "What Do You Want To Talk About?" and write the content of your post.**

TIP

Start by asking an open-ended question to generate discussion, instead of something generic, such as *Here's a great article I discovered.*

5. **If you want to pull someone into the conversation:**

   a. *Type the @ symbol and begin typing the person's name.* A list of first-degree connections appears, as shown in Figure 16-9.

   b. *Select the person's name.* He or she will be flagged, regardless of whether the person is already in the group, and will see this conversation and be able to contribute.

6. **To link an article or post to your discussion, enter the URL for that item.**

   LinkedIn automatically formats the conversation so people will see a summary of that item in the conversation, and can click that summary to see the rest of the article or post.

7. **To add one or more hashtags to your post, click the Add Hashtag link (below the main section of the window) and enter one or more relevant hashtags for your post.**

   By adding hashtags, you'll help people find your post based on their interest.

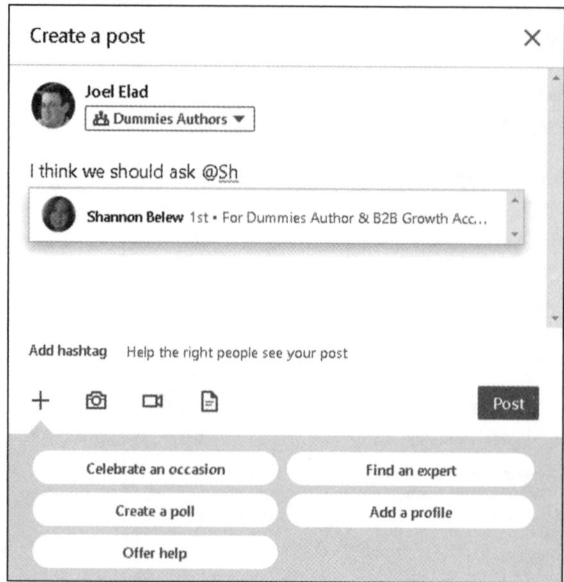

FIGURE 16-9: Tag people to include them in the discussion.

8. **To insert a photo, video, or document, click the icon representing that graphic (in the middle of the window) and select the file from your computer.**

REMEMBER

Upload graphics, videos, or documents only if they will add to the discussion or be useful visual content for the conversation.

9. **Enhance your post.**

Click one or more of the themed buttons to celebrate an occasion, create a poll, offer help, find an expert, or add a profile. Then follow the prompts. These options can be helpful for entrepreneurs who want to offer help by advertising their capabilities to a larger audience or people who want to gather opinions so they create a poll.

10. **Click the blue Post button to start the conversation in the group.**

Your newly created post will appear at the top of the Conversations feed for the group. Other group members can then click the Like button below the conversation or click the Comment link and participate in the discussion, similar to other social media sites.

WARNING

Although all conversations are automatically posted, group administrators retain the power to remove any post they consider spam, offensive, or counterproductive to the purpose of the group. Additionally, if a group member reports a post, it is temporarily hidden while the group administrator reviews the report to see whether that post should be removed.

Viewing a group's membership list

After you join a group, you'll probably want to see who's in the group and find out whether or how the group members are connected to you. After all, the point of these groups is to stay in touch with like-minded individuals and perhaps invite them to become part of your network.

To view a group's membership, go to the group's home page and click the See All link below the count of the number of members in the group. (The link is on the top-right side of the screen.) The Members screen shown in Figure 16-10 appears. Then click an individual member's name to go to his or her profile page and find out whether you share any connections.

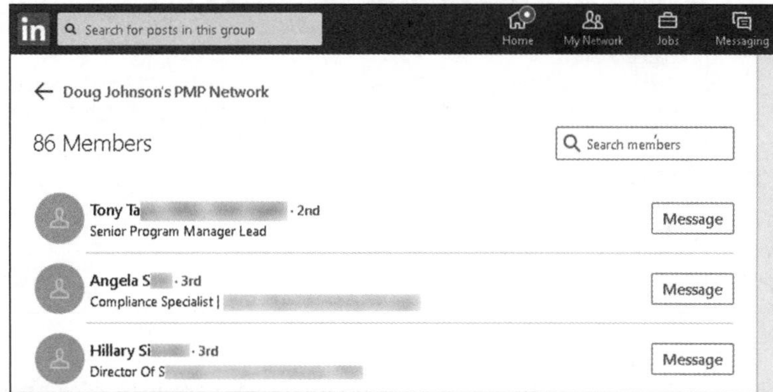

FIGURE 16-10: See your group membership list in one place.

TIP

Member aren't automatically sorted by last name or degrees of connection, so use the Search box to the right of the member count to find particular people in the list.

Click the Message button to the right of a member's name to send a LinkedIn message directly to that group member. As mentioned, LinkedIn doesn't want its members to abuse this feature, so you're limited to 15 of these messages per month for all the groups where you're either a member or an administrator.

Creating a Group

When you're ready to create your own group, follow these steps:

1. **In the top navigation bar, click the Work icon and then click the Groups icon in the drop-down list that appears.**

   Your Groups page appear.

2. **On the right side, click the Create Group button.**

   The group creation window pops up, as shown in Figure 16-11. This is where you input the information about your newly requested group.

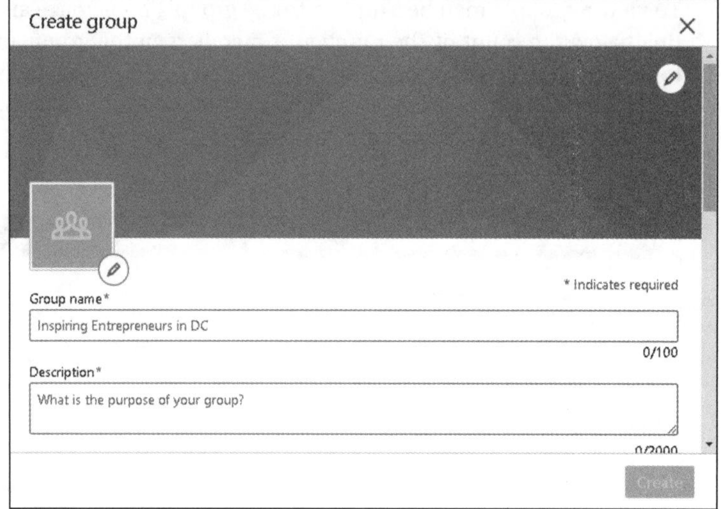

FIGURE 16-11: Enter your new group information here.

3. **(Optional) Upload a cover photo for your group by clicking the Edit icon (pencil) in the top right of the window, locating the photo on your computer, and clicking Open.**

   Many social media sites encourage the use of a larger cover photo above the group logo.

4. **Upload the logo for your group by clicking the Edit icon (pencil) next to the logo box, locating the file on your computer, and clicking Open.**

   LinkedIn requires a logo. The file format must be PNG, JPEG, or GIF, and the logo can't exceed 100K.

TIP

"But where do I get a logo?" you might ask. Well, you can design your own logo at sites such as `www.logoworks.com`. If a logo already exists, such as one for an alumni association, ask one of the administrators for a high-resolution copy of the logo, or save a copy of the logo from the group's personal website — as long as you know you have the rights to use that image, of course. If you're not sure whether you have the right to use the image, check with the group's administrator.

5. **Provide your group information and settings.**

   The group name and description are required, so input those values in their respective text boxes. You have 100 characters for the group name and 2,000 characters for the group description, so choose your words wisely.

   Scroll down the window and assign the visibility of the group to either Listed or Unlisted. You can also assign lots of other optional fields, such as Industry, Location, and group rules for members to follow, as shown in Figure 16-12 and described in the next section.

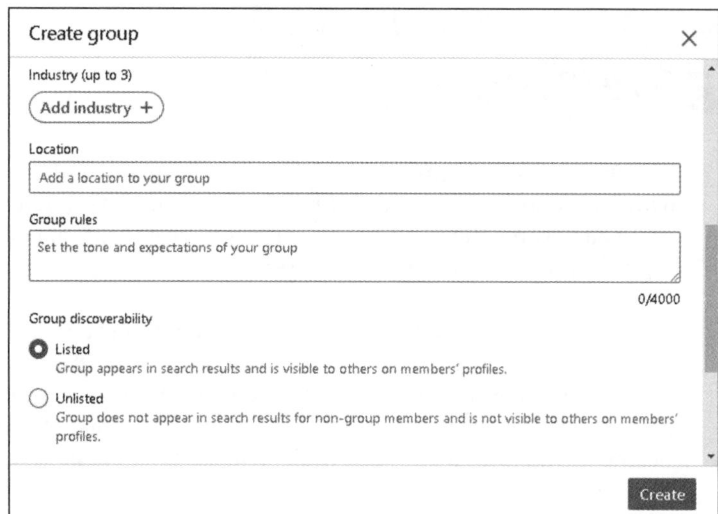

FIGURE 16-12: Your group request is ready to be submitted.

6. **Click the Create button to create your group on LinkedIn.**

   The newly created home page for your group appears, as shown in Figure 16-13. Your new group is ready for members!

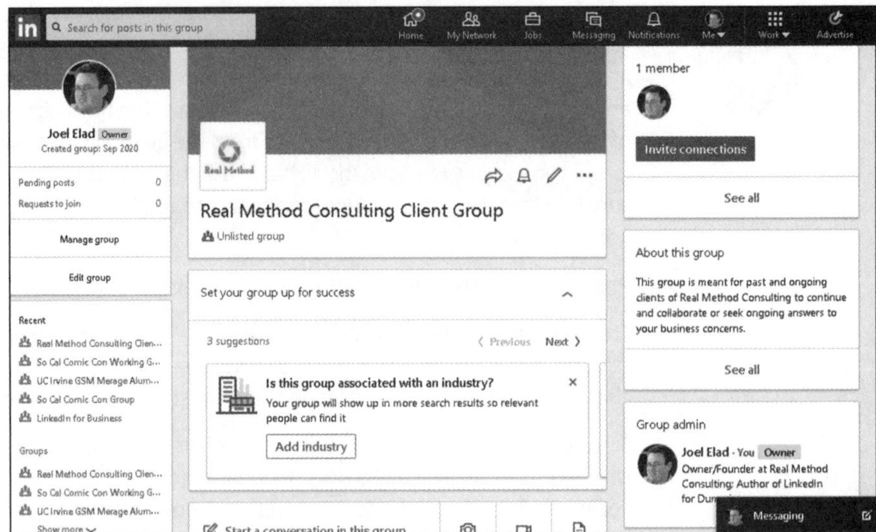

FIGURE 16-13: Your group has been created.

Setting Up the Group and Inviting Members

After you create your group, your next step is to set up the group properly and invite members to be a part of this group. In some cases, LinkedIn may prompt you to add people the moment you click the Create button, but you can take this step at any point after the group is created.

First, review the group details and consider defining rules and automated messages to help run your group more smoothly. You should do this before you send out any invitations or before members start using the group regularly basis. You can configure your group by going to the left menu on your Groups screen and clicking the Edit Group link below the Manage Group link:

- **Group name, logo, and description:** Update the group name, logo, and description, information you provided when you created your group.
- **Group industry and location:** Update the industry (or industries) best associated with your group, as well as the physical location of your group.

* **Group rules:** Every LinkedIn Group is allowed to write its own rules, which can be recommended rules for conduct, or any specific instructions or guidelines you want to offer your group members (what is acceptable and not acceptable in terms of content, how you will handle abuse or inappropriate comments, and so on).
* **Group discoverability:** Change your group from Listed (the group shows up in group searches) to Unlisted (the group is hidden from all public views) or vice versa.
* **Group permissions:** Decide whether members are allowed to invite their connections to the group (admins still retain the right to approve all requests to join the group) and whether new posts need to be reviewed by group admins before they can be displayed on the Group discussions page.

Building and managing your member list

When you're ready to build your list of members, just follow these steps:

1. **In the top navigation bar, click the Work icon and then click Groups in the drop-down list that appears.**

   A list of groups you belong to appears.

2. **When you see the name and logo of the group you're maintaining, click that group name.**
3. **To send automated invitations to your group:**

   a. *Click the Invite Connections button in the top-right corner.*

   b. *In the Invite Connections box, start typing the name of a first-degree connection.*

   c. *In the list that LinkedIn provides, click the check box next to a name to select it.* You can select multiple names, as shown in Figure 16-14.

   d. *Click the blue Invite* x *button at the bottom right of the window to complete this process.*

4. **To display your manage group page, click the Manage group link on the top left of the screen, under the Group owner photo and statistics.**

   A screen similar to the one in Figure 16-15 appears. The manage group page is your hub for group management duties.

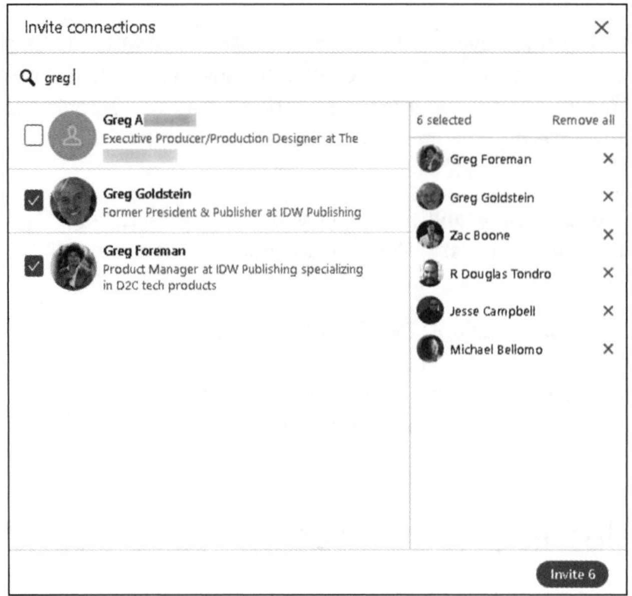

FIGURE 16-14: Invite new people to your LinkedIn group here.

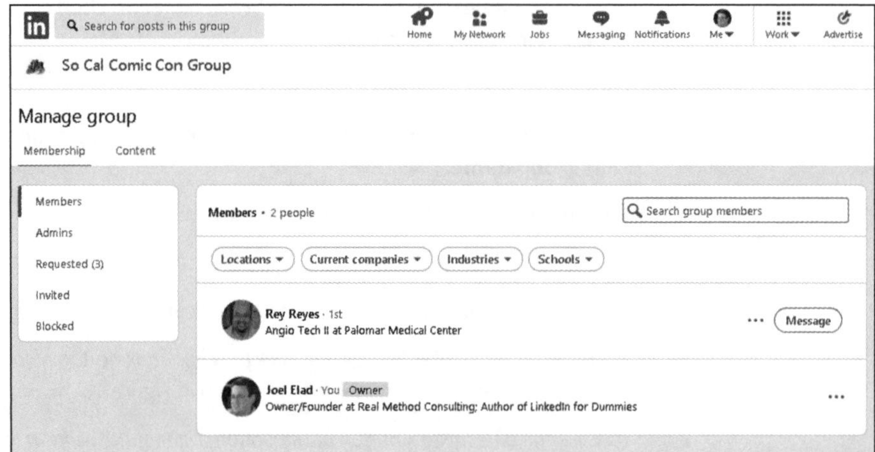

FIGURE 16-15: Manage your LinkedIn group from this page.

Crafting your invitation email

LinkedIn allows you to invite connections to your group. However, if you want your invitation to come with more information, you can send your own invitation from your own email program. Here are a few do's and don'ts to keep in mind as you craft your invitation:

» **Do relate the purpose and benefits of the group.** People are busy and need to understand why they should join this group. Explain the benefits of being connected to other people, the ability for professional development or advancement, and what you hope to accomplish with this group. Remember, you're sending this to LinkedIn members, so don't worry about explaining LinkedIn; just explain your group.

» **Don't go on forever.** Make your invitation no more than one or two paragraphs. Introduce yourself, introduce the group name, tell people the benefits of joining, encourage them to join, include the link to the group page, and then sign off. No one will read a long diatribe or laundry list of reasons to join. Use bullet points and short sentences whenever possible.

» **Don't put other offers in the email.** Some people use the group invitation as an opportunity not only to encourage folks to join one group but also to push a second group invitation or highlight a link to the group's non-LinkedIn website. The moment you start presenting multiple options for people, you lose their attention and they are less likely to sign up.

In your email, provide a direct link to your group home page. Simply bring up the page on your computer screen and then copy the URL from the location bar in your web browser. Typically, the URL will look like this: `www.linkedin.com/groups/idnumber`, where *idnumber* is the numerical ID for your group that LinkedIn created.

As members respond to your invitation, they're moved from the Invited list to the current list of your group, and a small group logo appears in their profiles.

Approving members to your group

As more and more people find out about your new group and as members start joining, you may find that some of the people who have clicked the link to join aren't on your Invited list. Perhaps you didn't realize that they were on LinkedIn or maybe they clicked the wrong link and don't belong in your group.

REMEMBER

It can be helpful, from an administrative standpoint, to develop criteria or guidelines for people to join your group, so you can evaluate each request as it comes in. Consider talking to any governing members of your group (in case you are just the LinkedIn group administrator, but not the actual day-to-day person in charge of the organization) to develop criteria for joining the LinkedIn group in the early days of establishing it, so you don't have to worry about this later on when things get busy.

Regardless, you need to either approve or reject people's membership requests. Follow these steps:

1. **From the top navigation bar, click the Work icon, and then click Groups in the drop-down list that appears.**

   The list of groups you belong to appears.

2. **Scroll down (if necessary) until you see the name and logo of the group you're maintaining, and click that group name.**

   The home page for your group appears.

3. **Click the Manage group link in the top-left corner to display your Manage page.**

4. **Click the Requested link below the Membership header.**

   A list of the people waiting to be approved for your group appears, as shown in Figure 16-16.

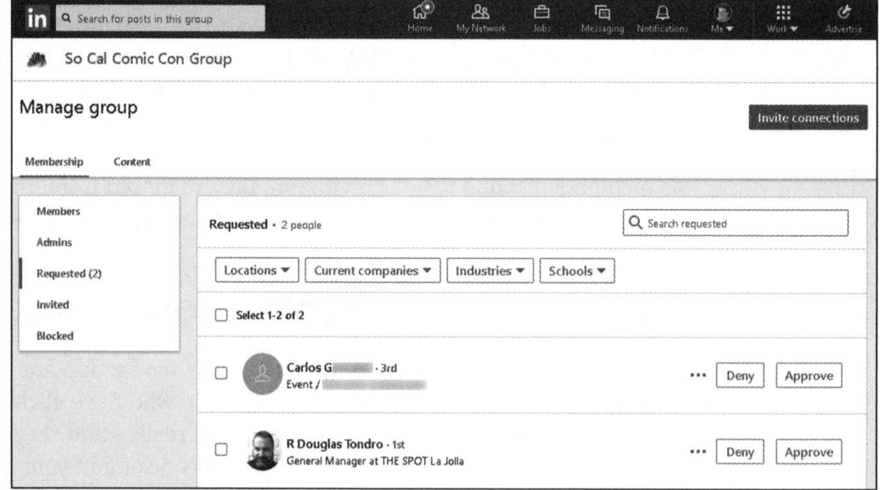

FIGURE 16-16: See who is waiting to be approved to your LinkedIn Group.

5. **To find more information about a person before accepting or denying membership, click the person's name to display his or her profile.**

   In addition to reading the profile, you can also send the person a message through the profile page.

6. **To accept someone, deny someone, or send a message:**

   - *To approve membership, click the Approve button.*
   - *To refuse membership, click the Deny button.*
   - *To permanently block someone from trying to join, click the 3 dots and then click the Block from Group link.*
   - *To send someone a message, click the 3 dots next to the Deny button, and then click the Message link.*

   When you click Approve or Deny, the user's name disappears from the page.

You can approve or deny more than one person at a time by simply selecting the check boxes next to their names first. To select everyone, click the Select X-Y check box at the top of the list.

You can remove someone from the group at any time after you initially approve that person, by going to the Members page and clicking the Remove link to the right of the person's name in the Members list.

If you're going to decline someone, you may want to send a Message first and let him know why you're denying his request. After you deny that person, the only way you can send him a message is through the InMail system.

through LinkedIn

» Marketing your business using online strategies

» Getting to know your prospects

» Following up on LinkedIn with future prospects in mind

Chapter 17

Implementing Sales and Marketing Techniques

In this part of the book, you find out how to start applying everything the previous parts cover about how to use LinkedIn for specific situations and needs. After all, every great invention needs to fulfill some sort of purpose, and LinkedIn is no exception. Its value is not just in how it allows you to network and build your brand, but also in how you can use LinkedIn to handle other tasks more easily and effectively.

In this chapter, I discuss the age-old disciplines of sales and marketing, including how to generate sales and how LinkedIn can affect your entire sales cycle. LinkedIn can help you spread the gospel of your business mission by serving as a vehicle for positive and rich marketing messages about both you and your business, whether it's a start-up, personal service provider, or a Fortune 500 company. Part of the power of LinkedIn comes from involving others in your marketing initiatives, so I cover some ways for you to do that as well.

Marketing Yourself through LinkedIn

When it comes to maximizing the benefit you receive from LinkedIn, you are your biggest advocate. Although your network of connections is instrumental in helping you grow, much of your marketing happens without your involvement. After you create your profile, that and any other LinkedIn activity of yours are read and judged by the community at large — on the other members' own time and for their own purposes. Therefore, you want to make sure you're creating a favorable impression by marketing the best traits, abilities, and features of you and your business. Because of the nature of LinkedIn, this marketing occurs continually — 24/7 — so you should look at LinkedIn as something to check and update on a continual basis, like a blog. You don't have to spend hours each day on LinkedIn, but a little time on a consistent basis can go a long way toward creating a favorable and marketable LinkedIn identity.

The following sections look at the different ways you interact with LinkedIn, and what you can do to create the most polished, effective LinkedIn identity possible to further your marketing message.

Optimizing your profile

In Chapter 3, I discuss building your professional profile on LinkedIn, which is the centerpiece of your LinkedIn identity and your personal brand. I refer to your profile throughout this book, but here, I focus on ways for you to update or enhance your profile with one specific goal in mind: marketing yourself better or more consistently. As always, not every tip or suggestion works for everyone, and you might have already put some of these into action, but it's always good to revisit your profile to make sure it's organized the way you intended.

To make sure your profile is delivering the best marketing message for you, consider these tips:

- **Use the professional headline wisely.** Your professional headline is what other LinkedIn users see below your name even when they're not looking at your full profile. I've seen some users stuff a lot of text into this field, so you should have enough space to communicate the most important things about yourself. If you have specific keyword phrases you want associated with your name, make them part of your headline.

  A standard headline might read something like "Software Development Manager at XYZ Communications," but you can write entire sentences full of great keywords for your headline. My client Liz Goodgold's headline used to read

Branding and Marketing Expert, Author, Coach, and Motivational Speaker

She refined it to

Maximizing Brand Results * Boosting Lifetime Value of Customer * Creating Unforgettable Experiences * Keynote Speaking * Virtual Presenter

Think about how many people would want to connect with her! The headline is not always just about what you are doing. It can be used also to demonstrate what you are capable of doing. Remember, let your audience know what you can do for them!

- **Make sure you use keyword phrases that match popular keywords for you or your business.** The first step, as I just mentioned, is to put these phrases in your headline. The second step is to make sure these phrases are reflected in your Summary, Experiences, and Interests sections.

WARNING

Be careful not to overuse your main keyword phrases. The search engines call this practice *stuffing,* which is cramming as many instances of a phrase into your site as possible in hopes of achieving a higher ranking. If the search engines detect this, you'll experience lower ranking results.

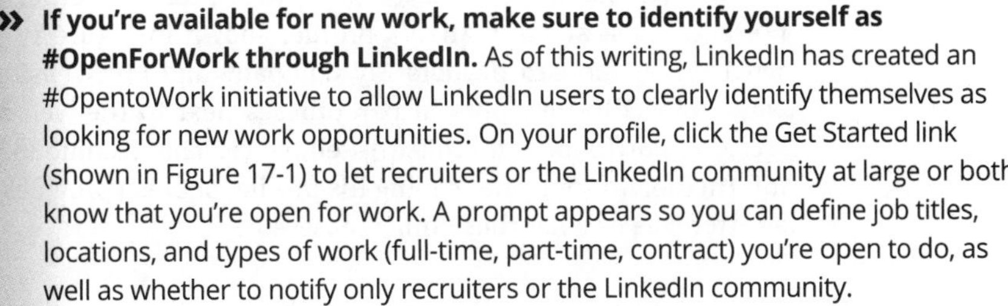

- **If you're available for new work, make sure to identify yourself as #OpenForWork through LinkedIn.** As of this writing, LinkedIn has created an #OpentoWork initiative to allow LinkedIn users to clearly identify themselves as looking for new work opportunities. On your profile, click the Get Started link (shown in Figure 17-1) to let recruiters or the LinkedIn community at large or both know that you're open for work. A prompt appears so you can define job titles, locations, and types of work (full-time, part-time, contract) you're open to do, as well as whether to notify only recruiters or the LinkedIn community.

WARNING

When you use the #OpenForWork functions, there is no guarantee that your current employer (if you have one) won't see that you're open for work.

- **Use the additional sections in your profile to include any relevant information that reinforces your marketing message.** For example, if you want to be seen as an expert in a given field, add the SlideShare application to upload presentations you've given, or update the Publications section of your profile to include the articles or books you've written, articles you've been quoted in, focus or advisory groups you belong to, and any speaking engagements or discussions you've participated in. LinkedIn has created sections such as Projects, Patents, and Certifications for you to display specific accomplishments that are an important part of your professional identity.
- **Make sure your profile links to your websites, blogs, and any other part of your online identity.** Don't just accept the standard "My Company" text. Instead, select the Other option, and put your own words (up to 30 characters) in the website title box, such as *Joel's E-Commerce Education.* (See Chapter 3 for more information on linking from your profile to other websites.)

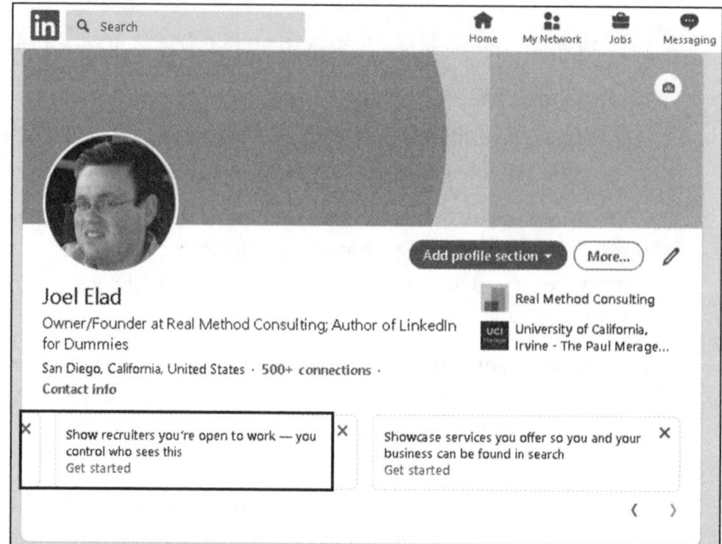

FIGURE 17-1: Let people on LinkedIn know that you're available.

For an example of effectively linking your profile to other areas of your online presence, look at Scott Allen's profile, shown in Figure 17-2. His website links replace the standard headers My Company and My Website with his own text, which LinkedIn now puts in parentheses next to the web address — Company Website, Portfolio, and Linked Intelligence. This technique not only gives more information to someone reading his profile, but also provides search engines with a better idea of what those links represent.

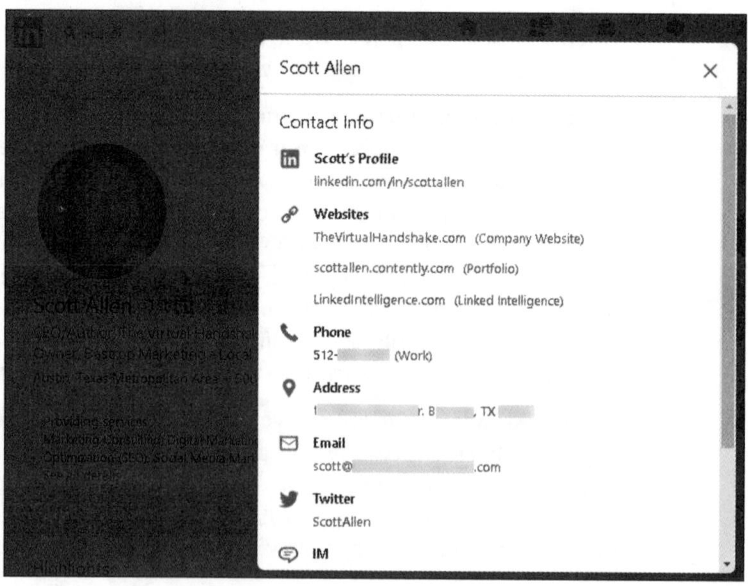

FIGURE 17-2: Give your website links meaningful names.

Marketing yourself to your network

Optimizing your profile in the ways described in the previous section is one of the best ways to market yourself effectively using LinkedIn. Another is to be alert to how well you're communicating with your LinkedIn connections. Whether it's automatic (like when you update your profile and LinkedIn automatically notifies your network, assuming you enabled this option in your Settings) or self-generated (when you use LinkedIn InMail or Messages to send a note to someone else, which I cover in Chapter 6), this communication becomes your ongoing message to the members of your network and keeps you in their minds and (you hope!) plans.

The most effective marketing occurs when people don't realize you're marketing to them. After all, the average American sees all kinds of marketing messages throughout their day. Your goal is to communicate often but not be overbearing about it so your message subtly sinks into people's minds. If you do that, people will think you're grrrr-*eat*! (Hmm, why am I suddenly hungry for cereal?)

So when you're contemplating how to effectively communicate with your network connections, keep these points in mind:

- **Update your profile when appropriate.** Updating your profile means that you're sending an update of your newest projects to your network so that your connections can consider involving you in their own current or future projects. You don't need to update your profile as often as you update a blog, but you certainly don't want to leave your profile untouched for months on end, either. Useful times to update your profile include the following:
  - Getting a new job or promotion
  - Starting a new freelance or contract job
  - Launching a new company or venture
  - Adding a missing piece of your Experience section, such as adding a new position, updating the description of an existing job, or clarifying the role of a group or interest in your profile
  - Receiving an award or honor for your professional, nonprofit, or volunteer work
  - Being appointed to a board of directors or elected to a professional association board
  - Taking on new responsibilities or duties in any of your endeavors

» **Take advantage of the ability to write posts.** When you specify your current endeavors or share your thoughts or observations, several things happen. Your profile reflects what you enter here, your network connections see what you enter here when they read their LinkedIn feed about you (see Chapter 7 for more on network updates), and you start to build your own microblog, in a sense, because people can follow your natural progression.

TIP

A similar example of a microblog is Twitter. As you update your Twitter profile with 280-character messages, other people can follow your activities and even subscribe to these updates. Tie your Twitter updates to your LinkedIn account, so if you tweet on Twitter, those updates are automatically reflected on your LinkedIn profile.

Some people use the Start a Post feature to let people know, for example, that "I am getting ready for my next project" or "I'm finishing up the sixth edition of *LinkedIn For Dummies.*" Other people use posts to show the progression of a certain task, such as "I'm currently conducting interviews for an Executive Assistant position I am trying to fill," then "I've narrowed down my choices for Executive Assistant to two finalists," and finally "I just made an offer to my top choice for Executive Assistant." See Chapter 7 for more on how to use this feature.

» **Search for, and join, any relevant LinkedIn groups that can help you reach your target audience.** It's a good idea to participate in these groups, but whatever you do, don't immediately start conversations just to spam them with LinkedIn messages. When you join the group, you're indicating your interest in that group because your profile now carries that group logo. Membership in such groups gives you access to like-minded people you should be communicating with and adding to your network. Spend some time every week or every month checking out LinkedIn groups and networking with group members to grow your network. See Chapter 16 for more about LinkedIn groups.

» **Participate on a regular and consistent basis.** The easiest way to ensure a steady stream of contact with as many people as you can handle is to dedicate a small but fixed amount of time to regularly interact with the LinkedIn community. Some members spend 15 to 30 minutes per day sending messages to their connections, reading through their news feed, the Groups, Companies, or Influencers page, or finding one to two new people to add to their network. Others spend an hour a week, or as long as it takes to create their set number of recommendations, invite their set number of new contacts, or reconnect with their set number of existing connections. You just need to establish a routine that works with your own schedule.

Marketing Your Business through LinkedIn

LinkedIn can play a significant role in the effective marketing of your business. LinkedIn's value as a marketing tool gets a lot of buzz from most companies' finance departments, especially because they see LinkedIn as a free way of marketing the business. Although you don't have to pay anything in terms of money to take advantage of most of LinkedIn's functions, you do have to factor in the cost of the time you put in to manage your profile and use LinkedIn to the fullest.

Currently, LinkedIn offers your company promotion through its Company pages section. LinkedIn ties status updates, job titles, and other pertinent information from company employees' profiles directly into the Company page. From each page, you can see those people you know in the company, open career positions, recent updates from their employees, and other pertinent facts.

If you own a business, you can create your own Company page. You need to have your company email address in your LinkedIn profile and be established as a current employee, manager, or owner of that company in your profile as well. I discuss how to build a Company page in Chapter 15.

Using online marketing tactics with LinkedIn

Marketing your business on LinkedIn involves working through your own network, employing both your current list of contacts as well as potential contacts in the greater LinkedIn community. Your efforts should also include making use of links from your online activities to your LinkedIn profile and promoting your business online from your LinkedIn identity. Here are some things to keep in mind as you develop your LinkedIn marketing strategy:

- **Encourage every employee to have a LinkedIn profile and to connect to each other.** Extending your network in this way increases your exposure outside your company. And if someone in your organization is nervous about preparing her profile, just tell her that LinkedIn can be an important asset in her professional or career development. You can mention that even Bill Gates has a LinkedIn profile. That should do the trick! (And then buy her a copy of this book to get her started.)
- **Make sure your business websites and blogs contain a direct URL link to your LinkedIn profile.** By offering your website visitors a direct view to your LinkedIn profile, you're allowing them to verify you as an employee of the company because they can see your experience and recommendations from

other people. They might also realize they share a bond with you and your business that they never would have discovered without LinkedIn.

- **Make sure your LinkedIn profile links back to your business website and blog.** You not only want your visitors and potential customers to be able to verify who you are, but you also want them to go back to your website and do some business with you! Make sure that you, and every employee of your company who's on LinkedIn, include a link to your business's website and, if there is one, the company blog.
- **Make sure that your most popular keyword phrases are in your company or personal profile.** Use sites such as Wordtracker (`www.wordtracker.com`) or Moz Keyword Explorer (`www.moz.com/explorer`) to find the hottest keyword phrases in your field. If your business is doing any online ad campaigns, make sure those keyword phrases are the same as the ones in your profile. Presenting a consistent image to potential customers makes you and your company look more professional.
- **Develop relationships with key business partners or media contacts.** When you search for someone on LinkedIn, you can be precise about whom you want to reach. So, for example, if you know that your business needs to expand into the smartphone market, you can start targeting and reaching out to smartphone companies such as Apple, Samsung (maker of the Galaxy and Note), and Huawei (maker of the P20 and P20 Pro). If you want to increase your visibility, start reaching out to media members who cover your industry.

Mining for Clients

It's a big world out there. In terms of clients, you need to ask yourself whom you're looking for. Is everyone a potential client, or do you have a specific demographic in mind? A specific skill set? Maybe you've written the greatest plug-in tool for accountants who work in the financial services industry, and you want to sell this tool directly to your likely users. With LinkedIn, you can conduct a search to find people who match your criteria. Then after you locate those people, it's up to you to approach them and close the sale, which I talk about in "Closing the Deal," later in this chapter.

Before you start your search, ask yourself some questions that can help you with generating your leads:

- Are you looking for people with a specific title or in a particular industry?
- Are you looking for high-net-worth or well-connected donors for your nonprofit organization?

» Are you looking for decision-makers in a company, or are you seeking a general audience? (That is, are you trying to sell into a company or directly to people?)

» Besides your main target industry, can you approach related industries, and if so, what are they?

» Does the location of your potential contact matter? Does making the sale require an in-person visit (which means that the contact needs to live near you or you have to be willing to travel to this person)?

With your answers to these questions in mind, you're ready to start searching LinkedIn for your leads.

Generating leads with the Advanced People search

When you're ready to start looking for leads, I recommend jumping right in with the LinkedIn Advanced People search, which allows you to search the database consisting of hundreds of millions of LinkedIn members based on the criteria you've established for the leads you want to generate.

To start a search, enter a keyword in the Search box at the top of any LinkedIn page and press Enter. Say you need accountants who work in the financial services industry. To start such a search, type *accountants* and press Enter. When the results screen appears, click the All Filters link, and then click the Financial Services check box under the Industry field, as shown in Figure 17-3. Click Search to add this new filter to your search request.

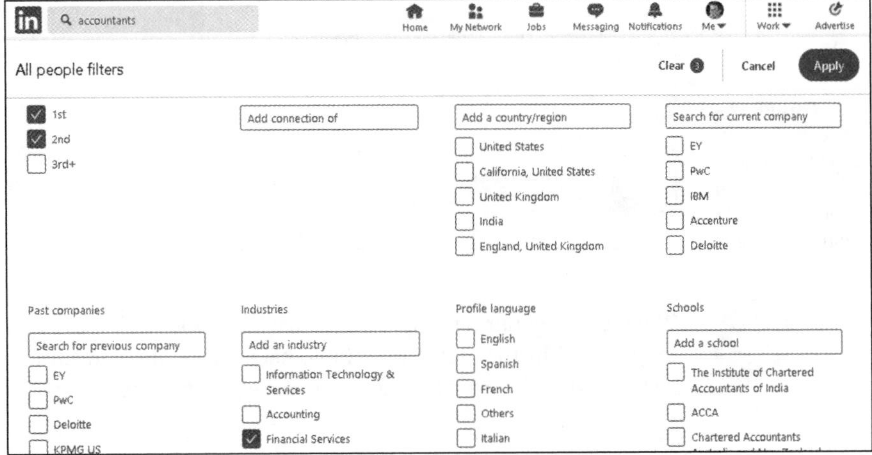

FIGURE 17-3: Use the Advanced People search to find potential clients.

I also selected the 1st and 2nd Connections check boxes. Why? When you search the LinkedIn database, your own network can help you identify your *best leads* (people only two degrees away from you whom you can reach through a first-degree connection introducing you) if you make sure those options are selected. When you see your search results with those options selected, you first see which results are closely connected with you via your connections. You can click each person's name to read his or her full LinkedIn profile, see how you're connected, and decide whether you have a potential lead. (This method usually gives you much more information than a simple Google search, which would provide only a LinkedIn member's public profile, not the full profile.)

After you identify your best leads, you can use LinkedIn to find out what connections you have in common: Simply click the name for each search result to see the shared connection. For example, suppose I see the 1 Mutual Connection link for someone in my search result, such as Bobbi K. When I go to Bobbi K's profile page, I see that my friend Doug (R Douglas Tondro) is the shared connection between me and Bobbi, as shown in Figure 17-4. That information helps me approach Bobbi, because I can ask Doug for an introduction or for more information about Bobbi.

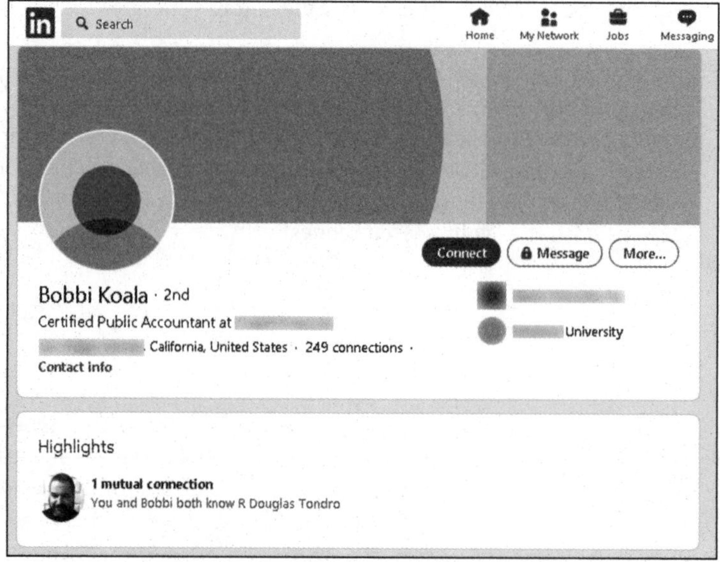

FIGURE 17-4: See who in your LinkedIn network is a shared connection with your target lead.

TIP

When doing general prospecting, surveying the market for that perfect lead (or at least a lead in the right direction), keep these ideas in mind while filling in the appropriate Advanced Search fields for each strategy:

- **Generalize your search.** If you're looking for your ideal contacts independently of the company they work for, focus primarily on the Title field and the options present under the Industry header to find your leads.
- **Narrow your search.** Use the Keywords field to narrow your results list when you need to reach people within a certain niche of an industry or job.
- **Target specific people.** Use either the Company or Keywords field, plus the Title field, to help you find specific employees in your target companies.
- **Help your product or service sell itself.** Search for the customers of your customers to get those people excited about your product or service, so that they'll demand it from *your* customers! This strategy is also known as *pull marketing.*

Finding the decision-maker

Although generating a list of potential leads is a great first step in marketing your product, being an effective salesperson often comes down to finding that right person with whom you can present an offer to buy something. This person is the *decision-maker* (or the *final authority*, or even just *da boss*). You can talk to as many administrative assistants and receptionists as you'd like, but your sales effort will be stalled without the name or contact info of the person who makes the purchasing decisions.

LinkedIn can help you reach that decision-maker in the following ways:

- **Include words such as *Account Manager, Director,* or *Vice President* in the Keywords field when you perform an advanced search.** If your results show someone who's in your extended network, now you have a specific name to mention when you call the company. I recommend you approach that person via LinkedIn and your mutual connections first, thereby making your first contact with her more of a "warm call" than a cold one.
- **Access the LinkedIn Company page to find out specific information about your target company.** If you're trying to reach someone in a company, see whether that person shows up as an employee on the Company page. To do so, start typing the name of the company in the top Search box. As LinkedIn generates a drop-down list of options, click the company name in the Companies section of the list. For example, suppose that you need to reach someone at Wiley. When you bring up Wiley's Company page, as shown in Figure 17-5, you get some specific information right away.

You immediately see who in your network works for this company, so you know whom to approach to pass along your request to the decision-maker, or to tell you who that decision-maker is. Scroll down the page to view other useful information, such as recent updates from the company, similar companies or topics to this company, and Showcase pages. You can then follow that company (by clicking the Follow button) to see all its new updates and information as part of your LinkedIn news feed.

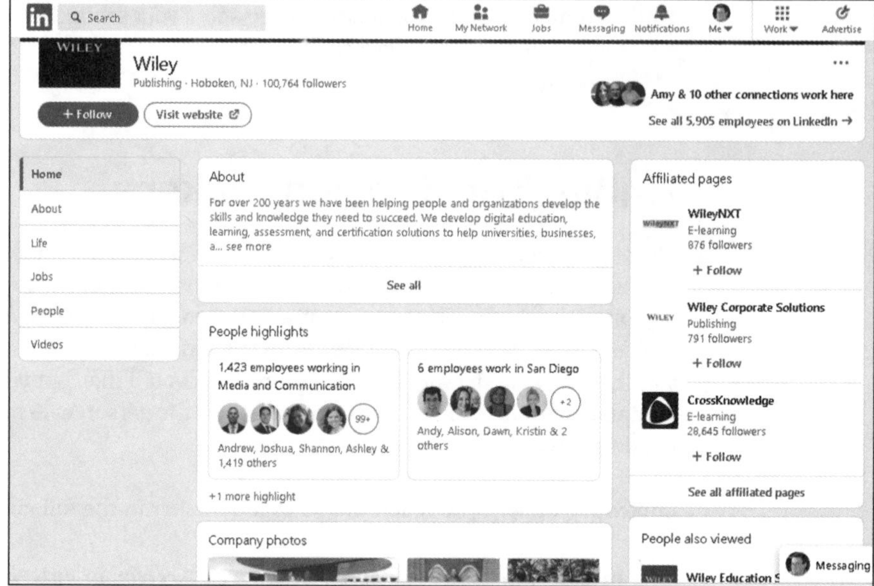

FIGURE 17-5: Get specific information about your target company through its profile.

- **Take advantage of your existing network to ask for an introduction, to seek out advice, or to be pointed in the right direction.** Using your network in this manner was basically the original intent of LinkedIn: You contact someone who works at your target company and ask that contact to introduce you to the decision-maker. The decision-maker is much more likely to be receptive to an introduction than a cold call. Your network connection might also recommend you to the decision-maker, which carries some weight when you try to close the deal. In addition, you may have a select group of people in your own network who can provide advice on whom to connect with, as well as advice or ideas on selling your product, service, or nonprofit organization.
- **Use InMail to contact the decision-maker (if she is on LinkedIn) or someone close to the decision-maker.** You may not have the time or opportunity to get introduced to your decision-maker, and if you're using

InMail to approach the decision-maker, why not just go for the gusto and introduce yourself directly? This is a faster option than waiting or asking for an introduction, but there's the chance the decision-maker will ignore your message. (In the case where the decision-maker isn't on LinkedIn, use LinkedIn to find the closest person and ask that person for help, for a connection, or for information to help you reach the next level.) You have to decide what's best for your situation.

WARNING

There's one big "not to do" when mining for client: Do not send a connection request to someone and then immediately start pitching the person if he or she accepts the connection request. Not only is this is a giant turn-off for the person who gets the unwanted pitch, it's nowhere near the point of LinkedIn connections.

Closing the Deal

Establishing a connection with the right person (the one who makes the purchasing decisions) is half the battle in getting your product sold. However, you still have to convince the person and close the deal. In this section, I give you some pointers on how to put LinkedIn to work for you for the final phase of a sales effort: completing it successfully!

The key to getting the most out of LinkedIn for closing the deal is knowing that LinkedIn has not just names but also detailed profiles of its hundreds of millions of users, millions of news articles and comments, associations made through LinkedIn groups, and corporate information through LinkedIn Company pages.

Preparing for the client meeting

Suppose that your initial conversations with your prospects have gone well and you've been granted a meeting with a potential client to make your pitch. Whereas you may have already used LinkedIn to gain more information about the specific person, you can now get details about the specific industry, the company, and the company's potential response to your business pitch. Here are some tips on gathering information about the people you are meeting and the company:

» **Read the client's *full* profile to discover all you can about his or her interests, likes, dislikes, and so on.** You can do far more than simply scan a person's profile looking for past jobs and view her education to see whether she shares an alma mater with you. A person's LinkedIn profile can be a gold mine of information about that person. For example, people may include links to their own websites, blogs, or company websites. Follow those links, especially to blogs or personal websites, and see what you can find out. In the prospect's profile, look over the Interests section, their status updates, and the Additional Information section. And don't forget the Contact Settings section — this is where you can find out under what circumstances this person wants to be contacted. Be sure to respect those wishes.

- **Read your client's recommendations for other people.** You can gain a lot of insight by seeing what qualities a person likes to praise in other people, especially if your prospect has left multiple recommendations. In this way, you also gain insight into the people he trusts, so check those people who received a recommendation to see whether you have a connection to any of *them.* If so, ask that person first for an introduction to your prospect.
- **See the activity your client (and the company) has on LinkedIn.** If you pull up someone's profile, look for a section in his profile page below the summary box called <someone's> Activity (or <someone's> Articles and Activity) and click the See More link to see articles and posts that the person made, and also click the All Activity link for status updates, articles he liked, commented, or shared, and topics he follows, as shown in Figure 17-6. When you read these items, you might gain some insight into this person's preferences and hot button issues — what motivates or annoys him.

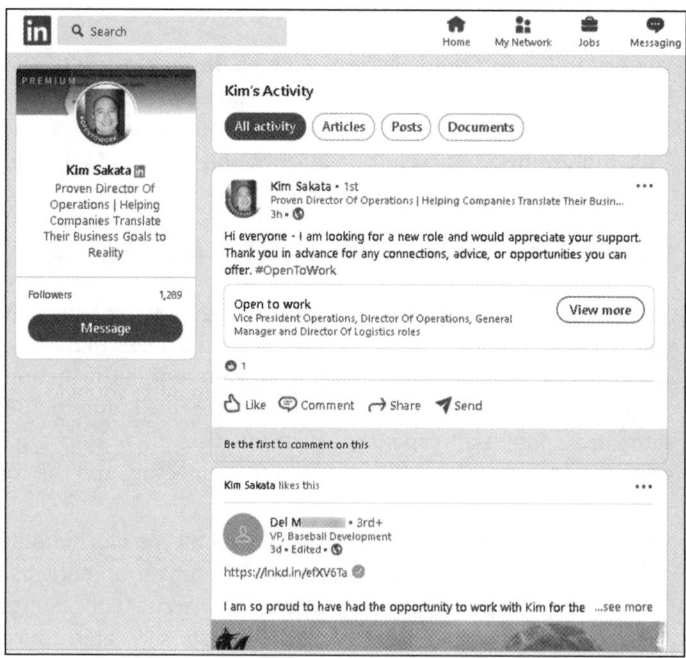

FIGURE 17-6: Read through the activity of your prospect on LinkedIn.

Also, look at the Company page, and pay attention to recent company updates. You will get a sense of what the company is promoting, its top focuses, and key company announcements. Doing so gives you more background information and therefore more confidence; also, this type of knowledge helps you identify interests or commonalities to enhance your sense of connection with your buyer (and hers with you).

REMEMBER

All these efforts are meant only to prepare you and get you closer to your prospect or target company so that you can make your pitch. Obviously, to complete the sale, you still need to have a compelling product, pitch, and offer for this company. Have everything ready *before* you approach your prospect. Take the information you've learned and organize it around the company, the person you're meeting, and the opportunity you're trying to gain. Also prepare any potential questions (along with your answers to those questions) that may come up during the meeting.

Reporting a positive sale

Reporting the completion of a sale is my favorite part of the business sales process. You made the sale, developed the solution, and delivered it to the customer. At this point, many people think, "Whew, I'm done. Nothing to do now but enjoy happy hour!" This response is common and natural, but as a member of the LinkedIn world, your job isn't really done. You want to demonstrate your growth (and your company's growth) that resulted from handling this project to encourage future contracts to come your way. Here are some actions to consider after you complete the sale and deliver the solution:

- **Invite your customer to join your network.** You worked hard to earn this customer's trust and to meet (or exceed) his expectations by completing the sale. As a result, you should feel comfortable enough to send him an invitation to join your network. Doing so could keep you in contact with this customer for future opportunities. Studies have shown that it's six times cheaper to sell to an existing customer than to acquire a new customer.
- **Leave your customer a recommendation.** After you add a customer to your network, post a recommendation for him on the system if you feel it's deserved. For example, the customer was easy to work with during a difficult project and was an active, positive partner in the project. Doing so gives your customer a sense of reward for being a positive contributor, but more important, it informs the community that you did a project for this person, which can help you in the future. Also, the customer may reciprocate by leaving you a recommendation, which strengthens your profile and makes you more appealing to future prospects.

- **Stay in touch with your customer.** You can keep track of your customer's activities by monitoring your network updates (if he is a part of your network). Routinely keep in touch about the solution you delivered, perhaps to open the conversation for selling additional products or services or maintenance contract work.
- **Update your profile with the skills you acquired or demonstrated through this sale.** To be ready for future prospects who search the LinkedIn database, it's important to have the right keywords and skill sets in your profile so that these prospects can identify you as someone who can provide a similar solution for them. If you're a consultant or a freelance worker, you can add the project you just completed as experience in your profile as well. (See Chapter 3 for tips on how to update your profile.)
- **Tap the customer's network by asking him for referrals.** After you connect with your customer, keep an eye on his network. If you think you see a future prospect, consider asking your customer for an introduction or a recommendation. Usually, if you provided a quality solution, the customer may readily oblige your request, if they don't feel there is a conflict or a sense of uneasiness.

IN THIS CHAPTER

» Understanding the types and benefits of LinkedIn Ads

» Checking out filtering options

» Creating an ad

» Measuring the effectiveness of your ad

Chapter 18
Using LinkedIn Ads

With so many options on the Internet to occupy your viewing time, even in the LinkedIn website itself, it's easy to wonder how you can capture a person's attention. You can engage, present, and connect with other professionals in lots of ways, but sometimes, an extra strategy is needed to bring your message home. In LinkedIn's case, you can create targeted messages to reach your community.

LinkedIn Ads allow businesses and entrepreneurs to create and manage their own self-service advertising and create a targeted, specialized message to reach a portion of the overall LinkedIn network.

In this chapter, I discuss the types of LinkedIn ads and some basic restrictions and guidelines to keep in mind. I walk you through the creation of an ad and describe some analytics and reports available for judging the efficacy of your ad campaign.

Understanding LinkedIn Ads

The first thing you should consider about any advertising system, including LinkedIn ads, is whether that system can help you reach your target audience. So ask yourself, could you benefit from a network of over 722 million working professionals and business owners around the world? If the answer is no, perhaps you should flip to the next chapter. But if the answer is yes, keep reading.

One of the powerful aspects of LinkedIn ads is that you can really target your target audience. Given that LinkedIn knows a lot about its members, it can help deliver your ad to a specific audience, depending on your needs. Perhaps you're targeting only business owners who live in the Pacific Northwest and have more than five years of experience. Maybe you're marketing a financial software package for accountants who work in large companies. Then again, you could be trying to reach all company presidents or CEOs of small, medium, or large companies. With LinkedIn, you can set one or more filters to target the most relevant audience for your ad, which should increase the participation and effectiveness of your ad.

When you look at your LinkedIn home page (an example is shown in Figure 18-1), you can see two of the three types of ads that LinkedIn promotes to its members:

- **Text (and image) ads:** Just as they sound, text ads offer you the ability to create a basic ad message, which is typically displayed along the top of the screen or on the rightmost column of the home page or your message inbox, sometimes with a designated image. You can set a specific URL that, when clicked, takes the user to a specific destination or results website, either on or off LinkedIn.
- **Sponsored updates:** These updates are included in the news feed of LinkedIn users, but are clearly labeled *Sponsored* or *Promoted* so that the users know it's not coming from a connection. Sponsored updates typically contain a link to an article, a destination website, or a LinkedIn Company page, and give the user the ability to interact with your company through like and comment links connected to the update.

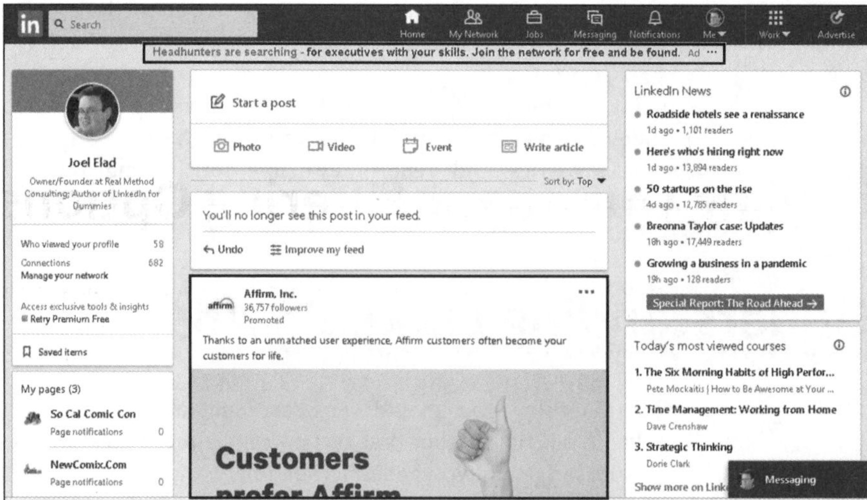

FIGURE 18-1: LinkedIn includes text ads and sponsored updates on its pages.

» **Sponsored InMail:** The third type of advertisement, sponsored InMail, isn't shown in the home page. These ads are sponsored email messages that you can write and send directly to members based on the demographic filters that you set. Only active members will receive these messages. LinkedIn has controls that prevent sponsored InMail from flooding its members' LinkedIn inboxes, so members are more likely to open the messages they receive this way. Your messages are customized to display well on a desktop or a mobile screen, and you can include call-to-action buttons as part of your InMail.

These ads enable you to drive qualified professionals to your business or LinkedIn landing page, because LinkedIn offers you a variety of targeting options to choose the right audience. You can control your ad budget and choose between two cost models: pay-per-click (PPC), where you pay every time a potential customer clicks the link in your ad, or cost-per-impression (CPM), where you are billed for every 1,000 times your ad is displayed on a potential customer's screen (that display is also known as an *impression*), regardless of whether the link was clicked.

TIP

If your ad budget is more than $25,000 per month, you can have access to your own account manager and more advertising options. Visit the LinkedIn Business Solutions page for more information at `https://business.linkedin.com/marketing-solutions`.

Elements of LinkedIn Ads that will seem familiar to anyone who is engaged in some online advertising, especially if you've used sites such as Google Ads or Facebook Advertising. Beyond the targeting filters, LinkedIn Ads also lets you control the bidding amount you're willing to spend per click or impression; run multiple variations of ads to test for the highest conversion rate; design your ad through its website by choosing text, images, and destination URLs; and budget your spending to control daily and total ad expenditures. You get to study the results of your ad campaign to help gauge measurable results, just as you do in other platforms.

Finding Out about Filtering Options

Other advertising networks allow you to filter your target audience by a few known attributes of the person who will see your ad — age, gender, and location of the audience member. LinkedIn allows you to go one step further by allowing you to search for specific criteria.

You can use filters in LinkedIn ads to segment your audience by these factors:

- **Company name, industry, and size:** Although you can make the argument that people's employers doesn't define who they are as people, employers may make a difference in whether your ad (and your product or service, by extension) would be relevant to them. You can specify a filter for a company name (let's say you want only companies that include or exclude a particular word), the company's industry (perhaps you want to target only transportation or high-tech companies), or the company's size as defined by the number of employees (this means you could target companies with, say, fewer than 50 employees or 5,001 or more employees).
- **Job title and job function:** If you're trying to reach all the software developers or Six Sigma consultants out there, you can create a job title filter and look for specific titles you provide. Going up one level, the job function filter allows you to target an audience where their job falls under a specific function, such as information technology, marketing, operations, purchasing, or sales.
- **Job seniority:** Okay, you've targeted your audience by job title, but is that enough information? After all, someone who's been doing that specific job for 1 or 2 years will have different needs than someone who's been a manager at that job for 10 to 15 years. You can specify someone's job seniority (years of experience) by different levels, from training and entry (think entry level) to senior, manager, director, VP, and CXO (which is shorthand for any chief officer, such as CEO, CFO, or CTO).
- **Member schools, fields of study, and degrees:** Let's say you are a recruiter and are trying to reach people based on their higher education. You can target your audience by specifying one or more names of schools, as well as specific fields of study or degrees, to include or exclude. (For example, maybe you want to reach people with Electrical Engineering degrees but not people with Mechanical Engineering degrees.)
- **Member skills:** You can specify one or more specific skills that members have identified in their profile.
- **Member groups:** Someone once said that you're judged by the company you keep, and LinkedIn ads is no exception to that concept. You can target your audience based on the group memberships that people have. This way, your ad can target people who belong to groups that match the goal of what you have to offer.
- **Years of experience:** Instead of searching for job title or seniority, you can target your audience by years of experience they have in their LinkedIn profile.

» **Company followers:** If you have a LinkedIn Company page, you can now target your LinkedIn ads two different ways. You can display your ad only to people who are following your LinkedIn Company page, or only to people how are not following your Company page.

» **Company connections:** You can target the first-degree connections of employees at companies that you specify. If you're trying to reach people who know someone at your target company, for example, this filter is for you.

The best use of filters comes when you combine two or more elements to qualify the audience you need to reach. Although it may seem that targeting project managers, for example, is good enough, you may really need project managers with specific skills, or project managers who have done the job for five or more years. When deciding which filters to use, think carefully about your target audience.

Creating an Ad Campaign

When you are ready to create a new ad campaign, follow these steps:

1. **Click the Work icon on the right side of the top navigation bar, and then click Advertise from the drop-down list that appears.**

   The advertising start page shown in Figure 18-2 appears. After you set up your account information, this page will describe the features and operation of the different ads available.

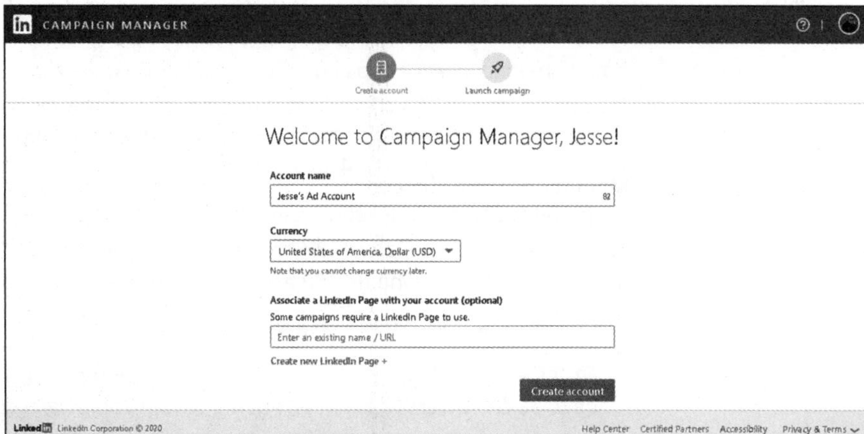

FIGURE 18-2: Start building your ad campaign here.

2. **If this is the first time you're creating an ad, do the following:**

   a. *Define your ad account name.*

   b. *Select your currency.*

   c. *(Optional) Specify whether you have a Company or Showcase page to associate to your account.*

   d. *Click the Create Account button to start your ad account.*

   The screen shown in Figure 18-3 appears.

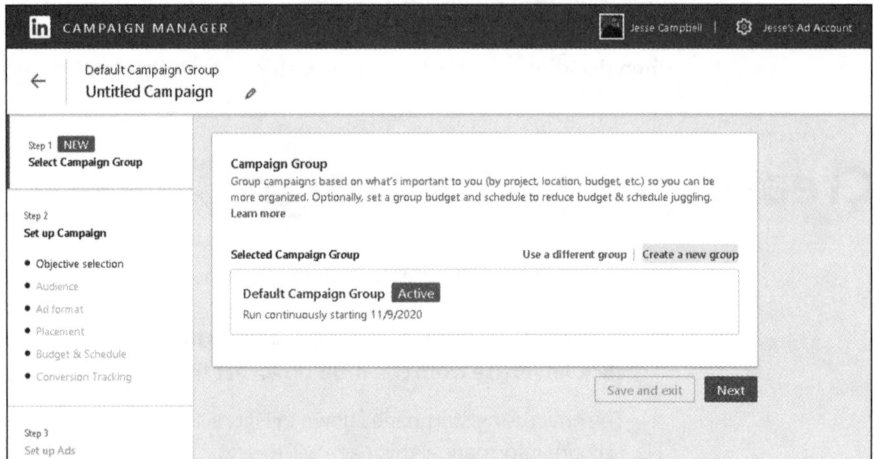

FIGURE 18-3: Establish your campaign group for this ad.

3. **Select Create a New group. If this is your first ad campaign, click the Create Campaign Group button from your Campaign Manager page to continue.**

   You're creating a new campaign, so select either Create a New Group (refer to Figure 18-3) or Create Campaign Group (if you see a list of existing campaign groups on your screen) to create a specific ad campaign group. The pop-up window shown in Figure 18-4 appears.

   If you wanted to use an existing campaign, you would select the name of your existing campaign from the list below the Selected Campaign Group header, click Next, and go straight to Step 5 to continue with this process.

4. **Define your new ad campaign group:**

   a. *Enter the name of your campaign group in the text box provided.* You can use up to 90 characters to define the name of your campaign group, so try to create a name that summarizes the goals or target audience of your ad campaign. Add some detail in the name in case you decide to run multiple campaigns to test the effectiveness of your message (for example, Sample Campaign A, B, and C).

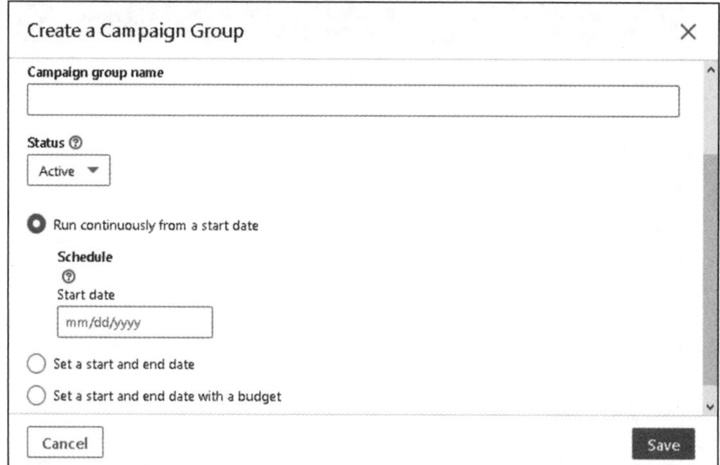

FIGURE 18-4: Give your campaign group a meaningful name.

b. *Set the status of your group as Active or Draft.* Draft is recommended only if you want to build out your ad campaign without the risk of ads running before you're ready.

c. *Decide when your ads will run. You have the following choices:*

- *Run Continuously from a Start Date:* Ads will start running on the date you assign in the next field and will keep running until you stop the campaign.
- *Set a Start and End date:* Ads will start running on the designated start date and finish running on the designated end date, regardless of the ad budget.
- *Set a Start and End Date with a Budget:* Ads will start running on the designated start date and finish running either on the designated end date or when the ad budget is depleted.

d. *Click Save to create your new campaign group.* You return to the Campaign Manager page.

e. *Click the Ad Campaign Group you want to use and then click the blue Next button.* The Set Up Your Campaign page appears, as shown in Figure 18-5, where you define the core of your ad campaign.

5. **Define your ad campaign objective by clicking your chosen objective name.**

   LinkedIn provides a number of options for setting up an ad campaign, such as building brand awareness, gaining user consideration (through website visits, engagement, or video views), and generating conversions (through lead generation, website conversions, or job applicants).

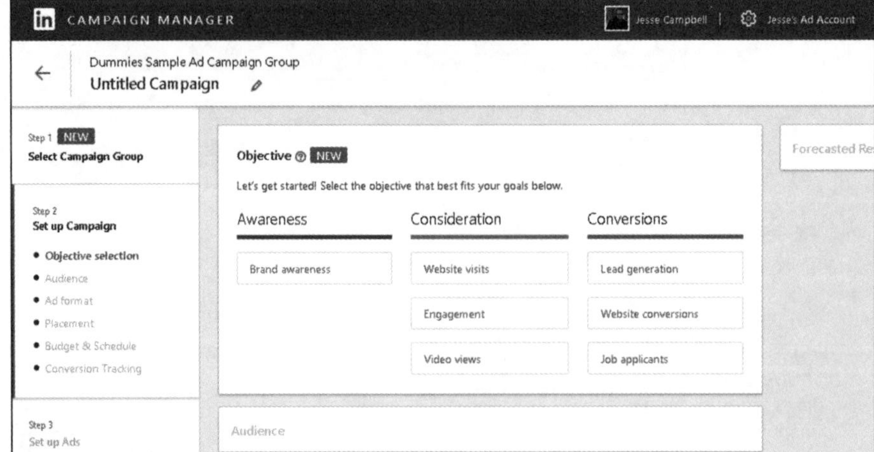

FIGURE 18-5: Choose the objective for your ad campaign.

TIP

If you're unsure what objective is for you, roll your cursor over each objective name in Figure 18-5, and you'll see a pop-up window explaining that objective with more information and examples.

6. **Use the targeting filters (see Figure 18-6) to come up with your ideal target audience for your ad.**

   You can target potential ad viewers using the information LinkedIn has for their account. You can target based on location, job title, company name, company size, and other elements including field of study, skills, degrees, group affiliations, or demographic information such as gender or age.

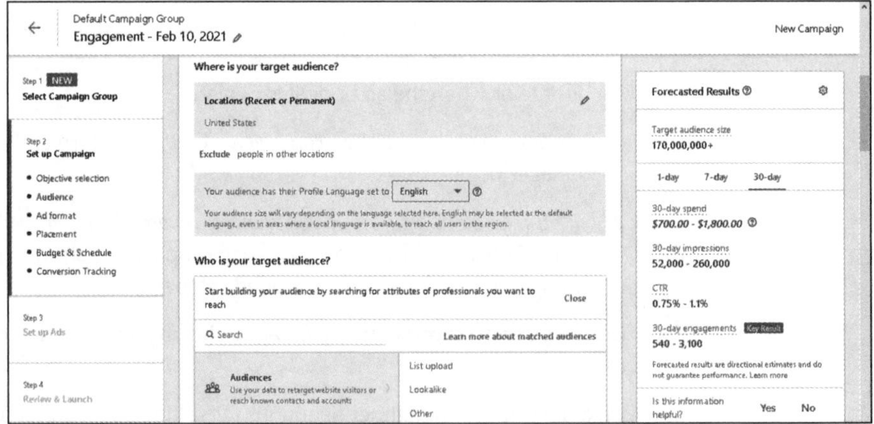

FIGURE 18-6: Start defining the audience for your ad.

LinkedIn separates their filters into two categories: location ('Where is your target audience?') and attributes ('Who is your target audience?'). Click the pencil icon to the right of the Locations header, and use the Search box that appears (see Figure 18-7) to choose one or more locations where your target audience resides. Then click the Close link.

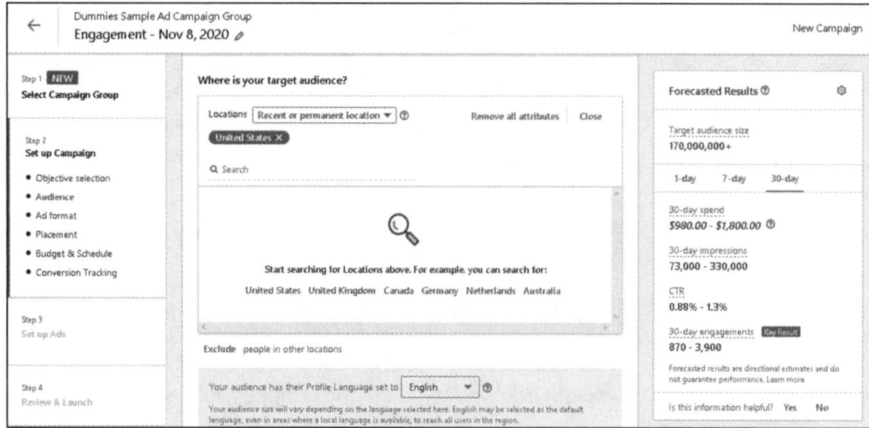

FIGURE 18-7: Set up location targets for your ad audience.

Next, scroll down to the "Who is your target audience?" section. You can use the Search box in that section to find attributes of your target audience, or click Audience Attributes to display a list of the most common attributes (see Figure 18-8): Company, Demographics, Education, Job Experience, and Interests and Traits. Click any of those attributes to set your target audience criteria. As you add criteria, the target audience size is updated on the right side of the screen. Repeat the process until you've defined all your criteria.

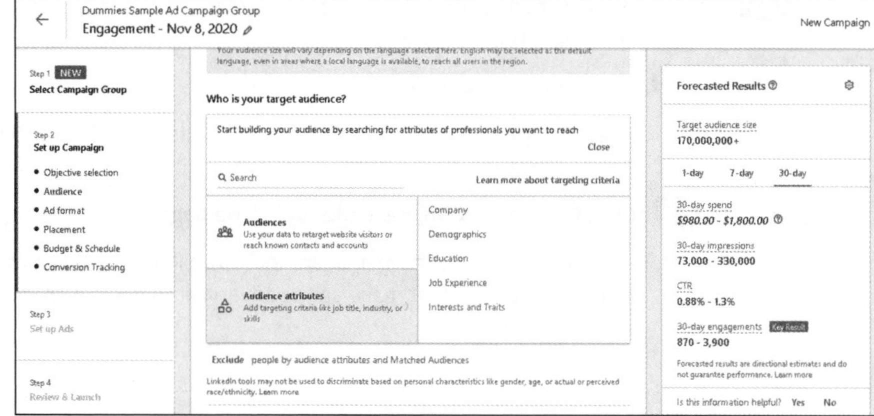

FIGURE 18-8: Define your target audience attributes with built-in filters such as Demographics.

WARNING

As of this writing, a location filter is required and LinkedIn will assign the default of your country as the first location; you can target up to 10 regions, subregions, or countries; and your ad must be able to target at least 1,000 potential viewers, so you can't use too many precise filters.

7. **Scroll down the page and finalize the format type and, optionally, LinkedIn page promotion:**

   a. *Click the button for the ad format type you want to create.* The ad options include single image ad, carousel image ad, video ad, Follower ad, and conversation ad. (The objective you select helps set your ad format options.) For this example, you walk through creating a single image ad. The conversation ad is basically a targeted email campaign that appears in the inbox of LinkedIn users; the rest of the ads show up in the users' news feeds.

   b. *When LinkedIn asks for the targeted Company or Showcase page that the ad will promote, enter that information in the box provided.*

8. **Scroll down and set the budget and schedule for your campaign.**

   You can set a daily budget, a lifetime budget, or a combination of both. LinkedIn asks you to define the budget(s) in the boxes provided.

   As for schedule, depending on your budget choice, you can run the campaign continuously from a start date that you designate or you can choose a custom start date and end date. Then scroll down and set a manual bid amount that you want to spend. You're bidding against other advertisers; LinkedIn gives the highest bidder the best opportunities to show his or her ad to LinkedIn users. Bid appropriately: Too low of an amount means very low visibility, but too high of an amount means your budget will be depleted too quickly. LinkedIn prompts you with suggested amounts based on what similar advertisers paid.

TIP

You can also install a tracking tag in your ad at this phase of the ad creation process to track conversions. Click the Add Conversions link and follow the prompts to measure your conversions, which you can analyze after your campaign runs on LinkedIn.

9. **Click the Next button.**

   The Ads page for your campaign appears, as shown in Figure 18-9, where you design the ad layout and copy for your campaign.

10. **Click Create New Ad, near the top of the page.**

   The Create a New Ad page appears, as shown in Figure 18-10, where you can provide the details that make up the advertisement you plan to run.

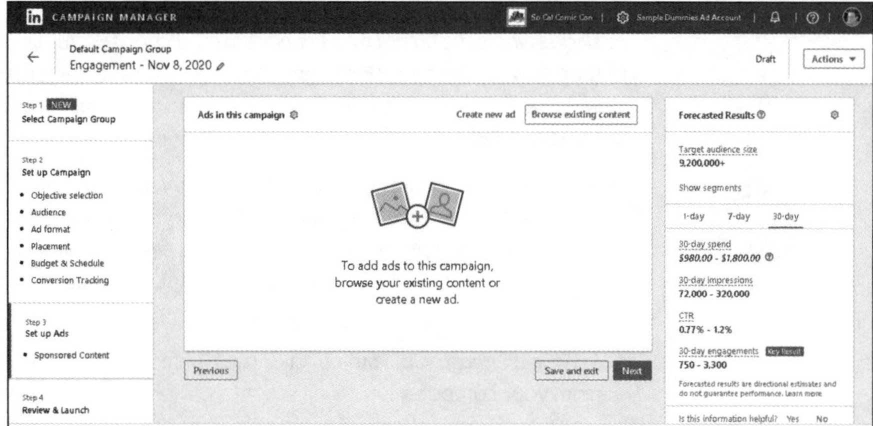

FIGURE 18-9: Create specific ads for your campaign.

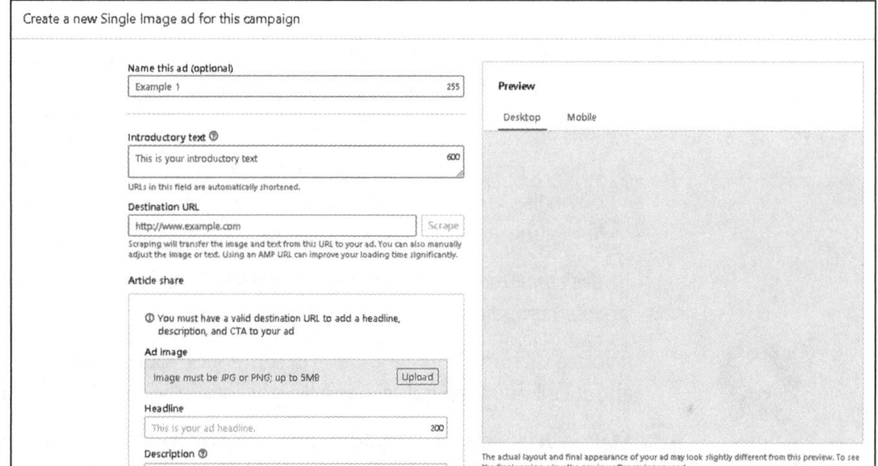

FIGURE 18-10: Build the details of an individual ad.

11. **Define the following, while seeing a preview of your ad as you write it:**

    a. (optional) *Enter the name of your ad.* You are limited to a 255-character name, which is used only so you can keep track of your different ad creations. The ad name will never be visible to your ad customers.

    b. *Enter the message copy in the Introductory text box*. The recommended length is no more than 150 characters, to avoid a user's device automatically truncating your ad. Therefore, choose your words carefully. LinkedIn will automatically shorten URLs for you to make the ad copy more efficient. You can write up to 600 characters if you need to, but just realize that not everything will be visible on some devices.

c. *Decide where the ad will take people.* You can choose your LinkedIn page (and then define which specific page, such as a Company page) or an external website. For the latter, define the exact URL in the Destination URL text box provided.

TIP

If you click the Scrape button after entering your external URL, LinkedIn will go out to that website and scrape its primary image and text and prefill the Image and Description part of your ad. You can still edit any of those fields, but if the website text mirrors what you want, this feature can help save time in data entry.

d. *Provide an image with your ad.* Click the Upload button to upload the image from your computer.

e. *Enter the headline of your ad.* You are limited to a 200-character headline.

f. *Enter the ad description*. You have 600 characters for the full description, which gives more information to users who will view your ad. The description may not be fully visible to all LinkedIn users, so the Introductory Text box should have the core message that any viewer needs to see. That said, having a full description can only help your ad conversion results.

g. *If you're designing a call to action ad, choose a call to action.* From the drop-down list, choose a call to action that matches your goals for the ad, such as lead generation, website conversion, or job applications.

h. *Click the Create button at the bottom right of the screen to save this ad to your campaign.*

TIP

If you're unsure about whether the content of your ad will be allowed, read about LinkedIn's ad guidelines at `www.linkedin.com/legal/ads-policy`.

12. **Make variations of your ad to test the effectiveness of different text messages or images or both.**

    You can create up to 15 variations of the same ad to see which combination of text and image gets the most attention. Simply click the Create New Ad link again, near the top of the page (refer to Figure 18-10) and repeat Step 11.

13. **When you're satisfied with the number of ad variations for this campaign, click Next.**

14. **If you are a first-time user, provide a credit card for LinkedIn to bill when your ad campaign is live.**

    LinkedIn provide a summary and asks you to enter a valid credit card so it can bill your card after people start clicking your ad or LinkedIn displays your ad with enough impressions to incur a charge on your ad campaign. After you enter your payment method, scroll down and click the Review Order button so LinkedIn can store that payment information. After your ad account is established with LinkedIn, you won't see this step again when you build an ad.

15. **Review the details of your ad campaign as presented to you on the Review & Launch screen. Then scroll down and click the blue Launch Campaign button to start your ad campaign.**

 That's it! You will see a screen confirming your campaign. LinkedIn reviews your ad to make sure you're complying with its ad guidelines, a process that takes an average of 12 hours or less, depending on the day and time you submitted the campaign. You'll receive a notification after the ad is approved and running.

Managing Your Ad Campaign

After your ad campaign is approved and starts appearing on your audience's LinkedIn web pages, the LinkedIn Campaign Manager will be able to start displaying relevant information about the performance of your ad campaign.

The Performance page summarizes the following aspects of your campaign:

- Money spent
- Number of impressions
- Number of clicks
- Number of leads (LinkedIn members who submit their information in response to your ad)
- Number of social actions (likes, comments, shares, and follows)
- Number of conversions (people who clicked your ad and performed your desired action)

You can also choose a metric, such as Clicks, Impressions, or Average CPC, by looking for the Show Graph For header and then clicking the drop-down arrow to its right to choose your metric. You'll see a line graph showing the data as far back as the most recent day, week, or month of the campaign, or the life of the campaign.

LinkedIn also provides a Click Demographics screen, available by clicking the Demographics link under your LinkedIn Ad Account name on the Performance screen. This screen aggregates the data for each person who clicked on your ad in terms of job function, industry, title, seniority, and other factors. This way, you can see if your ad is appealing to a specific demographic. This data is especially useful if you decide to revise your campaign.

At any time, you can go back and edit your existing ad campaign by clicking the LinkedIn Campaign Manager logo at the top of the screen and scrolling down to your ad campaign list. Then change the ad elements (the image and text of your ad), the audience (the targeting filters you defined), the bid amount and budget for your ad, and more. After you save your changes, your ad campaign is updated with the newest choices you made.

When you look at these metrics and think about how to improve your results, keep these points in mind:

- **Drop the worst performing variations.** If you created multiple variations of your ad, go back and delete or disable the ones providing the lowest click-through rates. This will raise the effectiveness of your overall campaign and increase the impressions because LinkedIn's algorithms will be more likely to serve up a higher-performing campaign so it earns more money for that advertising slot.
- **Change your destination URL.** The problem may be not with your ad but with the conversion page the potential customer reaches after clicking your ad. If you use analytic software on your own website, you can see whether people are leaving your destination URL without acting on your call for action.
- **Consider using a face as your ad image.** Other advertisers have mentioned that the best-performing ads they've experienced were ads that used a picture of someone's face as opposed to a logo or product image. You're limited to a 50 pixels-by-50 pixels image, so don't use a complex or text-laden image. You can best connect to your audience with a visual image that's inviting and personal, such as someone's face.
- **Ask for the click.** Although you're limited to only 75 characters, you should specify for readers to click the link, not just describe what you're offering. At a minimum, give readers a good idea of what they are receiving or how your offer can improve their life with a tangible benefit.
- **Test out new content.** After you've been running a campaign for a while, try out new content in your ad. It'll catch the attention of people who have already acted or dismissed your previous ad and raise interest and interaction.
- **If you run a sponsored update, pay attention to the comments it receives.** If you want your sponsored update to perform better, be sure to like the update yourself, have your employees engage with the update, and answer any comments from customers. That interaction and involvement will raise the update's visibility and, I hope, gain you further engagement and a positive brand image.

TIP

As you progress with your LinkedIn ad campaigns, you can also utilize tools such as AdStage's All in One Advertising platform to help you with all your online ad campaigns. Go to `www.adstage.io` for more information. You can see AdStage's home page in Figure 18-11.

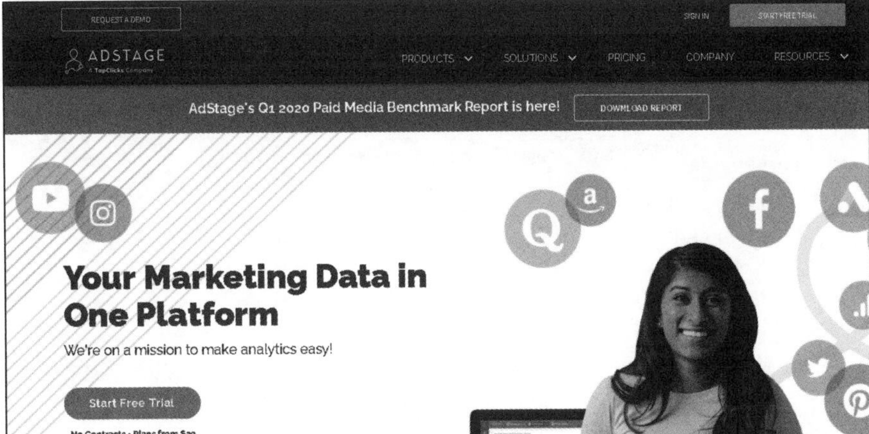

FIGURE 18-11: Use advanced tools such as AdStage to help manage your ads.

LinkedIn

» Creating a focus group to gain knowledge and expand opportunities

» Using LinkedIn to smooth the way when relocating

Chapter 19

Discovering Creative Uses of LinkedIn

When you think of a business networking site such as LinkedIn, the most obvious applications spring to mind pretty quickly: finding a job, finding an employee, meeting new people, building a new business, getting funding and partners for that new business, and so on. But LinkedIn has even more uses than the obvious ones. The power of the Internet and hundreds of millions of LinkedIn members have encouraged people to use this large community to accomplish other goals, both close to home and around the world.

In this chapter, you look at some of the creative uses people have found for LinkedIn. Some people use LinkedIn with other services, such as Google Alerts. Other people use LinkedIn as a gathering place to find recruits to help mold a new venture. Yet others have been using LinkedIn to meet each other in person! I describe these endeavors as well as provide several case studies with some points to keep in mind if you feel like doing something similar.

Mashing LinkedIn with Other Services

One of the trends on the Internet has been the creation of mashups. No, I'm not talking potatoes here. A *mashup* is created when somebody puts together data from two or more applications into a single new and useful application.

For example, say you combine real estate sales data from a database application with the Google Maps application, enabling a search result of the real estate data to be mapped onto a satellite image on Google. The satellite image represents a mashup because it's a new, distinct service that neither application provided on its own.

Something similar to the concept of mashups occurs with creative uses of LinkedIn. As LinkedIn continues to evolve and its members use more and more of LinkedIn's functionality, new uses for LinkedIn emerge, especially as part of a user's Internet exploits. The following sections describe a smattering of these mashups.

LinkedIn and Google Alerts

LinkedIn + Google Alerts = better-informed communication

I got this tip from Liz Ryan, a workplace expert, author, and speaker, as one of her top ten ways of using LinkedIn. It has to do with using both sites as a business tool when you're trying to reach out to an important potential business contact whom you do not know. It works as follows:

1. **In the Search box at the top of any LinkedIn page, type the name of a person at a company who is relevant to your situation and with whom you'd like to connect, and then press Enter.**

   The Advanced People Search page appears.

2. **Make sure the People filter/header is selected near the top of the page, and then fill in any other appropriate fields to search for that person at a company with whom you would like to connect.**

3. **Armed with the name that turned up in the results, set up a Google Alert (by going to `www.google.com/alerts`) with the person's name and the company name.**

   Google will notify you when that person is quoted or in the news.

When you go to Google's Alerts page (as shown in Figure 19-1), you simply enter the person's name and company name in the search query box, and then configure how you want Google to alert you by clicking the Show Options link and then setting the How Often, Sources, Language, Region, and How Many filters. Finally, you set the email address you want the alerts sent to. Click the Create Alert button, and you're good to go!

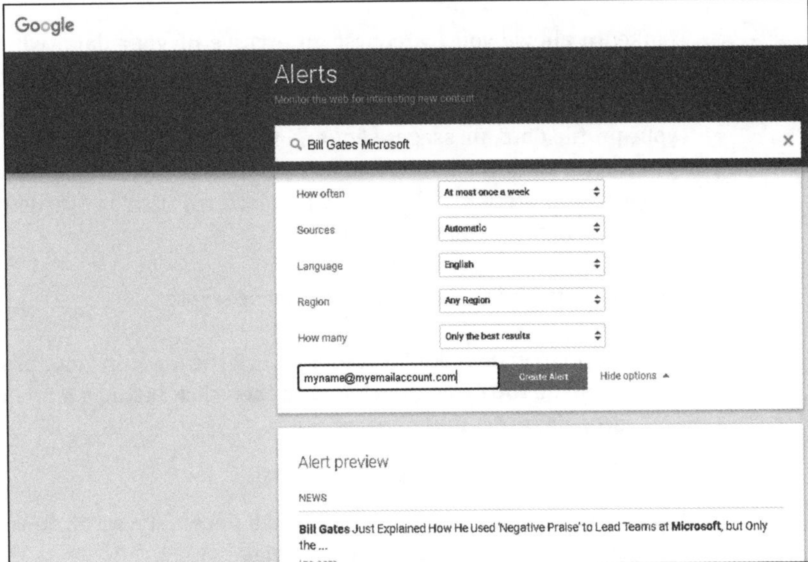

FIGURE 19-1: Google can automatically send you specific alerts.

When you receive a notice from Google Alerts, you have a much better idea of what the person is working on. This knowledge gives you an icebreaker for striking up a conversation. Rather than send a random connection request, you can reference the person's speech at the last XYZ Summit or agree with his last blog post. You show initiative by doing the research, which can impress or flatter the contact and give you something to refer to when you talk about his accomplishments or innovations.

WARNING

Don't overuse all the information you get when you contact the person, or, as Liz Ryan warns, he might think you're a business stalker.

LinkedIn Archives and Data Syncing

LinkedIn archives + data syncing = ready-to-build Rolodex

There is a wealth of information contained in your LinkedIn account — from your list of connections to your experience, education, skills, and other profile information, to your status updates, long-form publisher posts, and publications posted through LinkedIn. As time goes on, the information from this account may contain more up-to-date info than your email or contact information systems. Especially if you're in a sales position, contacts and daily information are crucial to your ongoing survival. Today, there's an easy way to capture that data and use it for other programs to help you manage your life.

LinkedIn allows you to request an archive of your data, which means you can download files that contain all your account activity from the moment you joined LinkedIn to today. This activity includes all connections and contacts, as well as your profile data, messages sent and received, and recommendations written and given. This data is downloaded as comma separated value (CSV) files, which can be easily imported to a data-syncing platform such as Evernote, so your data can be available across all your devices.

To benefit from this feature, follow these steps:

1. **Log in to your LinkedIn account. Click the Me icon (your profile picture) from the top navigation bar, and then click Settings & Privacy from the drop-down list that appears.**

   The Settings & Privacy page appears.

2. **Click the Data Privacy header, and if necessary, scroll down until you can see Get a Copy of Your Data (see Figure 19-2).**

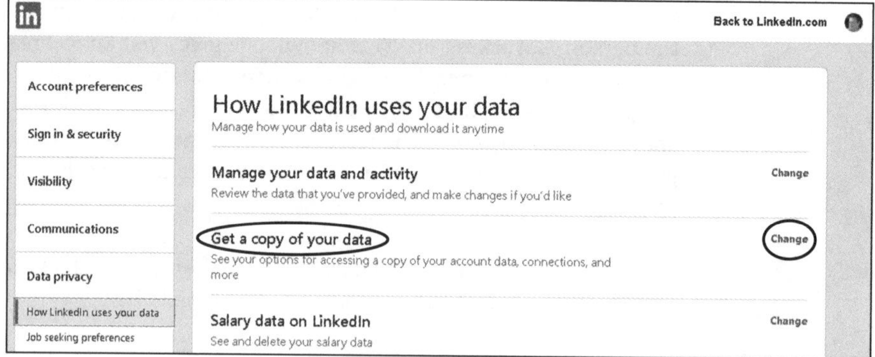

FIGURE 19-2: Go to your LinkedIn account settings to download data.

3. **Click the Change link next to Get a Copy of Your Data to see its options, as shown in Figure 19-3. Then do one of the following:**

   - *To download everything, click the first option, Download Larger Data Archive.*
   - *To specify the data to download, click the second option, Want Something In Particular? and then select the check boxes corresponding to the what you want to download.*

4. **Click the Request Archive button to start the LinkedIn data download process.**

   The data archive comes in two pieces. A short time after you click the button, you get an email with instructions on how to return to LinkedIn to download your data archive, such as messages, connections, and any contacts you imported to LinkedIn.

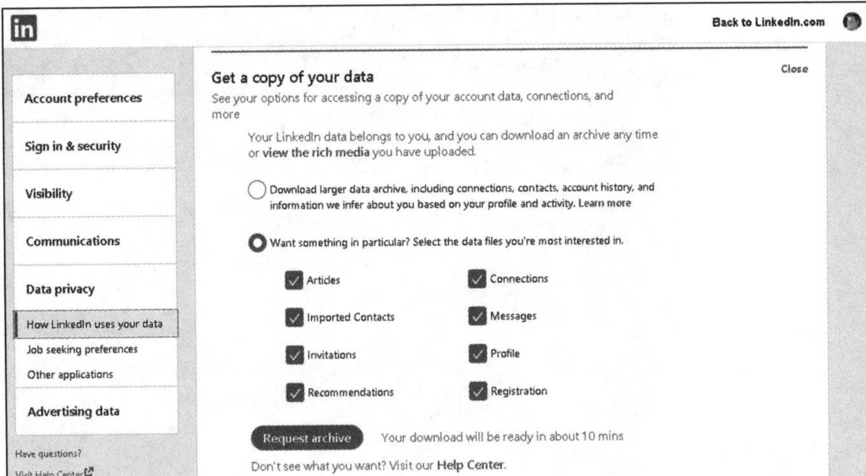

FIGURE 19-3: Request an archive of all your LinkedIn data to date.

After all the data is downloaded to your computer, use your favorite information storage program to upload this archive and keep track of your LinkedIn connections and activity.

LinkedIn and WordPress work together

LinkedIn + WordPress = easier sharing of WordPress blog posts

If you use WordPress to manage your blog, integration plug-ins can make your content publishing life much easier. A WordPress plug-in called WP to LinkedIn Auto Publish enables you to automatically send WordPress blog posts to LinkedIn for posting. You can have your posts sent to your personal LinkedIn news feed or a company news feed where you are a LinkedIn company administrator. You can also choose the feature image to use with your LinkedIn post, regardless of the feature image used for the post on the WordPress blog.

Figure 19-4 shows the WP to LinkedIn Auto Publish app download. To add the plug-in to your WordPress site, simply click the Download link and follow the instructions. After the plug-in is enabled, when you create a blog post, options will appear for determining whether a personal or company page post will be made on LinkedIn and what image (if any) will be associated with the LinkedIn post that WordPress creates for you. You can also customize various settings for your post, including whether the post will be visible to the public or just to your connections.

WARNING

You need to run WordPress 3.0 or newer and PHP+ version 5 or newer if you want to install and use the WP to LinkedIn Auto Publish plug-in.

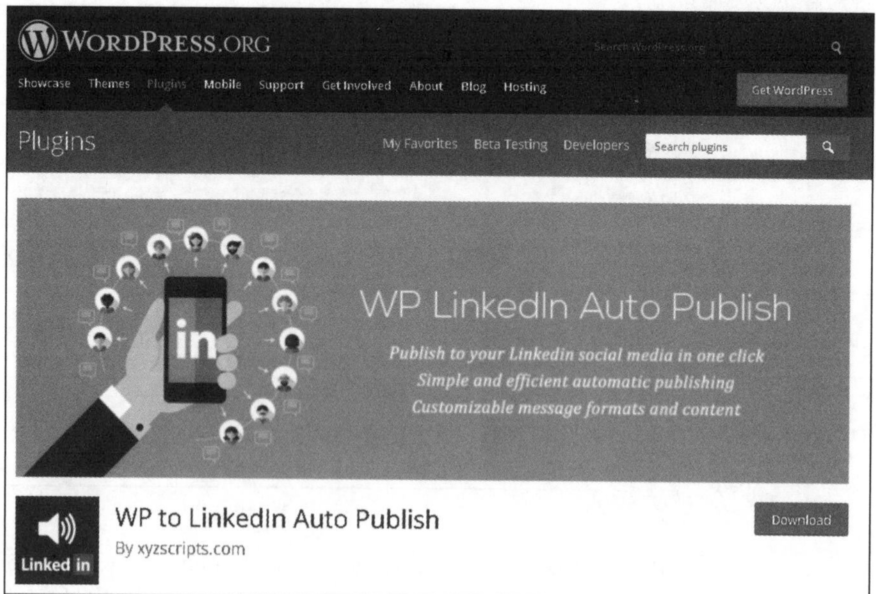

FIGURE 19-4: WordPress integrates your LinkedIn news feed with your blog posts.

Building Your Focus Group

In other chapters, I tell you about the potential for finding qualified employees and customers using LinkedIn, and how LinkedIn can help you perform market research and gauge reactions to a product using advertising. Here, I want to take these ideas one step further and discuss how LinkedIn can help you build a focus group for your new or next project.

Here are some ideas to keep in mind if you want to build your own focus group using LinkedIn:

- **Start by building your network.** Your best participants in this group are first-degree connections of yours (or of another employee of your company) because those people are most likely to join based on your recommendation and how well they fit your group's purpose. Try to network and invite potential candidates right away.
- **Build your accompanying website before building the group.** Your focus group participants will want to see something before deciding to join and participate, so make sure you've spent some time building an informational web page, email, FAQs, or another system that is available for viewing before you start to build your group.

» **Use your first-degree connections to expand your network.** After you've rustled up some involvement there, expand your group by asking for referrals or introductions to potential second- and third-degree network members or general LinkedIn members who might add some value and insight to your process.

REMEMBER

Odds are your focus group will be closed, or invisible to searches, so you need to rely on invitations or word-of-mouth to gain a targeted and screened audience for your focus group.

» **Continually send out updates.** You should always be sending out some form of update, whether you do so by filling out the status update option, using LinkedIn Messages, or going through your own email system. Don't deluge people with messages — but also don't ask them to sign up and then be silent for weeks or months. Keep your group members informed and ask for input when needed.

HOW LINKEDIN GOT KRISTIE THE PEOPLE SHE NEEDED

Kristie Regier was facing a dilemma. She started a business that teaches music enrichment classes to young children. She was looking for a company that could help with both website and logo design, but was having trouble. "I was quite disheartened to learn that no one could address my initial needs because of my daunting preliminary budget."

Enter LinkedIn. Regier got a LinkedIn email update announcing that one of her contacts had connected with a mutual friend from her high school. This shared connection had just opened a consulting business, Regier learned through LinkedIn. "I reached out to him, and he was enthusiastically eager to work with me despite my own start-up woes."

Three months later, Regier received a "beautiful website and dazzling logo." The best part? "It was for a reasonable fee that fell within my price range." The consultant friend added some complementary business cards and letterhead stationery as appreciation for her business. "He was so appreciative of getting my business and that I believed in him and his latest endeavor."

One year after the website launched, Regier's company is thriving. "Most of my success is due to that informative website and prominent logo. I get almost as much praise for my website and logo as I do the music classes themselves!" Without LinkedIn and the power of networking, Regier could still be looking for a cost-effective solution. "Instead of singing the blues, I have happy harmony, all thanks to LinkedIn!"

» **Post articles or long-form posts related to what you need your focus group to weigh in on, and add a few sentences when posting (or reposting) this information, asking for people's input.** When you put out these articles and gather people's input, you'll begin to see who is passionate and knowledgeable about the subject material, or who wants to learn more and contribute more. Both sets of people could make excellent focus group members.

» **Ask for recommendations.** As group members get introduced to your product, ask them for a recommendation in your profile if they liked or approve of the product. Getting their feedback or recommendations helps build future involvement when your product is live and ready for the mass market.

Using Location-Based LinkedIn Ideas

It's easy to forget the importance of location when you have easy access to such a resource-rich community as LinkedIn. After all, you can communicate with your contacts through LinkedIn Messages, send recommendation requests or post questions, and grow your network without leaving your computer. When you're finished using your computer, however, you need to interact in the real world, whether your interaction amounts to shoveling snow or catching a plane to a far-flung convention. When it comes to location-based situations, meaning that the problem or situation is tied to a physical spot, you can discover solutions with the help of LinkedIn.

The best use of LinkedIn for location-based problems is this: Your network is typically spread out across the country and across the world. Therefore, you can tap not only someone's professional experience, but also her knowledge or presence in a specific geographical area to help you solve a problem. In this section, you look at three location-based situations.

Building your network before moving to a new city

These days, when you have to move to a new city, you can do a lot of planning for it on the Internet. You can research the neighborhoods, look into the school systems, and shop for homes online. You can take this process one step further if you plan to move to a different country, and you need information on local customs, cultures, and practices. But what about the questions you can't seem to answer through a web browser? What about the local knowledge of places to go and places to avoid? LinkedIn can help.

HELLO? ANY OPPORTUNITIES OUT EAST?

Chuck Hester had a problem. He had to relocate his family from California to Raleigh, North Carolina, and he didn't have a job for himself when he would arrive. In fact, he didn't know anyone in Raleigh — but what he *did* have was a rich LinkedIn network. Hester quickly saw the value of LinkedIn and started contacting people and building relationships, driving his number of connections into the thousands.

Hester started networking with everyone he could who was located in Raleigh. He tapped his existing network to put him in touch with like-minded individuals who lived in the area and kept searching for contacts. One of the contacts he made was the chief executive of iContact, an email marketing company. Hester turned this contact into a job interview, and became the corporate communications manager for iContact. Even virtual persistence can pay off! Today, Hester continues to grow his LinkedIn network, and help others learn the power of LinkedIn.

Every LinkedIn user has defined her location, so you can do a search and figure out which LinkedIn users live in your target area. If nobody in your network is from your target area, start networking and expand that network to include people who reside (or used to reside) in that area who can help.

Here are some specific actions you can take through LinkedIn to help you with the big move:

- **Use LinkedIn groups to find your community.** Not every group on LinkedIn is directly related to software development or venture capital. You can look for specific groups of people who share a common skill through LinkedIn groups (see Chapter 16 for more information), join the group and start a discussion topic with your question, and see what the community says in response. Take a look at Figure 19-5, which shows how a search for a specific city (New York City) yields thousands of possible groups. You can narrow your search by adding a specific profession or interest, and then click Join to access the group.
- **Start as early as possible.** Building a region-specific network takes time as you recruit new members, ask your existing contacts for referrals, and search for specific people who match the location and either an industry or a job title. As soon as you sense that a move is necessary, or maybe when you're mulling over whether to move, start building your network so that you can tap those people for location-specific information before you move.

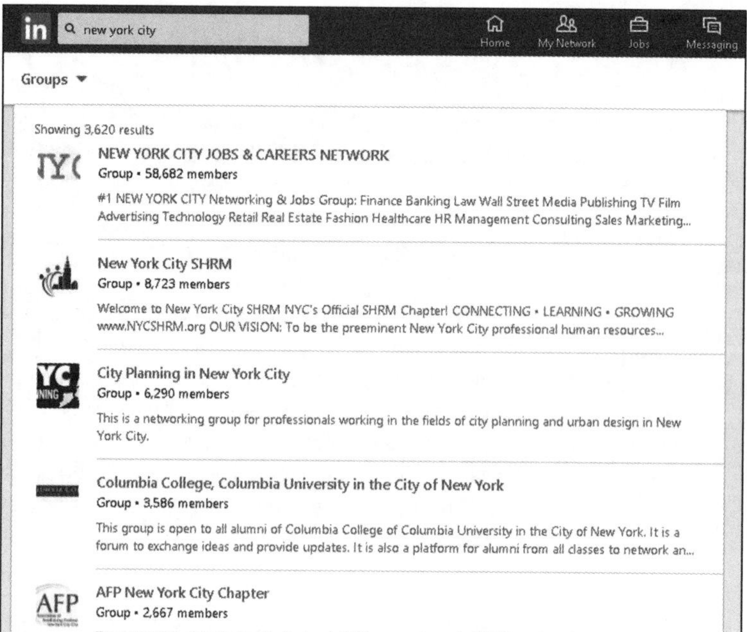

new york city
Home
My Network
Jobs
Messaging
Groups
Showing 3,620 results
NEW YORK CITY JOBS & CAREERS NETWORK
Group • 58,682 members
#1 NEW YORK CITY Networking & Jobs Group: Finance Banking Law Wall Street Media Publishing TV Film Advertising Technology Retail Real Estate Fashion Healthcare HR Management Consulting Sales Marketing...
New York City SHRM
Group • 8,723 members
Welcome to New York City SHRM NYC's Official SHRM Chapter! CONNECTING • LEARNING • GROWING www.NYCSHRM.org OUR VISION: To be the preeminent New York City professional human resources...
City Planning in New York City
Group • 6,290 members
This is a networking group for professionals working in the fields of city planning and urban design in New York City.
Columbia College, Columbia University in the City of New York
Group • 3,586 members
This group is open to all alumni of Columbia College of Columbia University in the City of New York. It is a forum to exchange ideas and provide updates. It is also a platform for alumni from all classes to network an...
AFP New York City Chapter
Group • 2,667 members

FIGURE 19-5: Look for groups based in your target city.

» **Consider Chamber of Commerce groups.** Do an Internet search for Chamber of Commerce groups in your new area and see if they have a LinkedIn group or their own website. These groups often have excellent resources for people who are relocating and looking to learn more about the area, especially for local businesses.

» **Look for contacts who used to live in your new city.** You might try entering the location of your new city in the Keyword search field rather than the Location field. By doing so, you might find first-degree connections or second-degree network members who used to live in your target area but have since moved; they might reference their past locations in their profiles. Contact those people and see whether they can introduce you to any contacts they may still have in that target area, regardless of whether those contacts are on or off LinkedIn.

Arranging face-to-face meetings when traveling

LinkedIn can serve as a wonderful resource even when you are not moving to another city but are simply traveling for business or personal reasons. Suppose that you know you have some extra time on your trip, or you want to make some local connections to reinforce your business trip. Why not tap your LinkedIn network and visit your contacts in person?

A growing practice of busy LinkedIn professionals who travel is to arrange face-to-face visits with other LinkedIn members during a business trip. This way, the traveler can meet with someone she is familiar with who could share similar interests and goals. Also, both people get a chance to expand their networks by creating a stronger connection. To bring about in-person meetings, most people either post something to LinkedIn groups or send a message to targeted members of their networks.

If you're interested in making your next trip more of a LinkedIn adventure, keep these tips in mind:

- **Provide enough notice to attract people's attention.** If you're putting up a post on Monday night that you're available for Tuesday lunch, you probably won't get many responses in time to set up anything meaningful.
- **Don't give too much notice, or your visit will be forgotten by the time you arrive.** Some notice is necessary to get on people's calendars, but too much notice will make people forget as your visit gets closer. More than two to four weeks in advance is probably too much notice.
- **Be specific about your availability.** It's great that you want to get together, but you probably have other plans when you're visiting. Therefore, when you contact other members, offer a few choices of when you can get together — and be specific. For example, you could say, "Hey, I'm going to be in San Jose for most of next week. Who's available either Monday night or Wednesday lunchtime to get together?"
- **Use your get-together to help prepare for business.** Your get-togethers with people in other cities don't have to be purely social. Suppose that you're traveling to that city for an interview. Perhaps you want to send a targeted message to a few contacts who used to work for your target company and ask to meet them in person before your interview so that they can help you prepare. Or maybe you want to practice your sales presentation on a knowledgeable person before you go into someone's office to do the real thing.

Networking with LinkedIn . . . in person!

Social networking is a great way to stay connected, grow your personal and professional contacts list, and learn about new opportunities. But after lots of emails, instant messages, and discussion boards, sometimes you just want the experience of meeting someone face to face. Many LinkedIn members feel this way and use the virtual power of LinkedIn to bring together people in the real world. Although online methods can expedite the process of finding the right people, they can't replace the power of face-to-face networking.

To enable face-to-face networking, LinkedIn has added LinkedIn *events.* On the home page, look for the Events header in the left side navigation options, below your Groups header. Click the + sign next to Events, and a pop-up window appears for entering details to create a LinkedIn event, as shown in Figure 19-6. Fill in the details, from event name, organizer (either yourself or any company where you're the company page administrator), date, time, location, and a description. (You have 5,000 characters to describe your event to the LinkedIn community.) Then click the Create button to create an event.

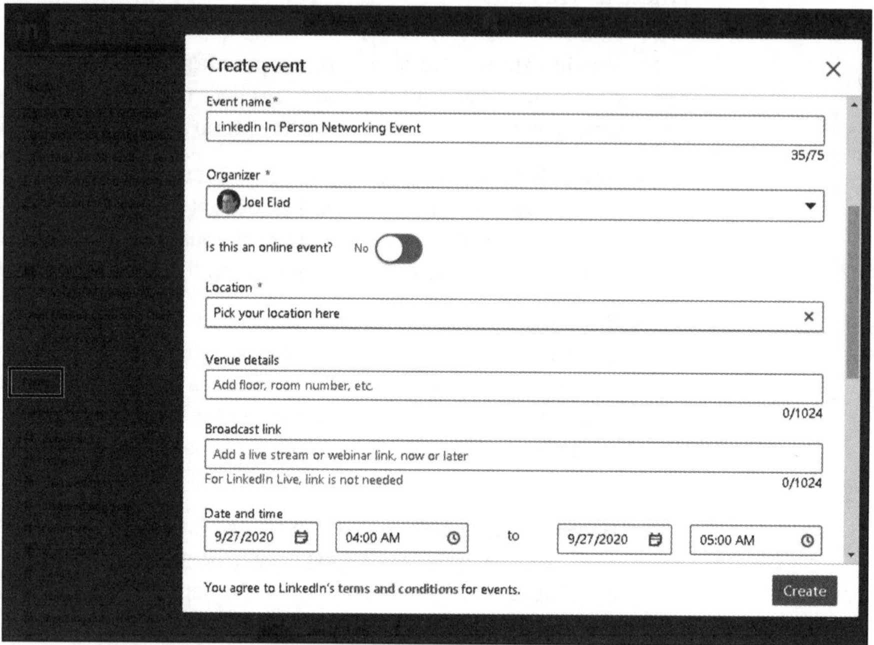

FIGURE 19-6: Use LinkedIn to create an Event for in-person networking.

One of my connections, Andrew, turned to LinkedIn years ago to help find interest for a regular get-together of technology folks, in which companies involved in newer web-based technologies open their doors to hungry technology workers who then learn about their host company over lunch. He posted a question on LinkedIn to find a host company and received several responses, which led to some great meetings!

An app called LetsLunch (shown in Figure 19-7) helps entrepreneurs find each other and set up networking meetings during lunch. In addition, companies are using LetsLunch to recruit potential new hires, so you can not only meet fellow employees in other companies but also meet hiring managers and decision-makers and get exclusive office tours.

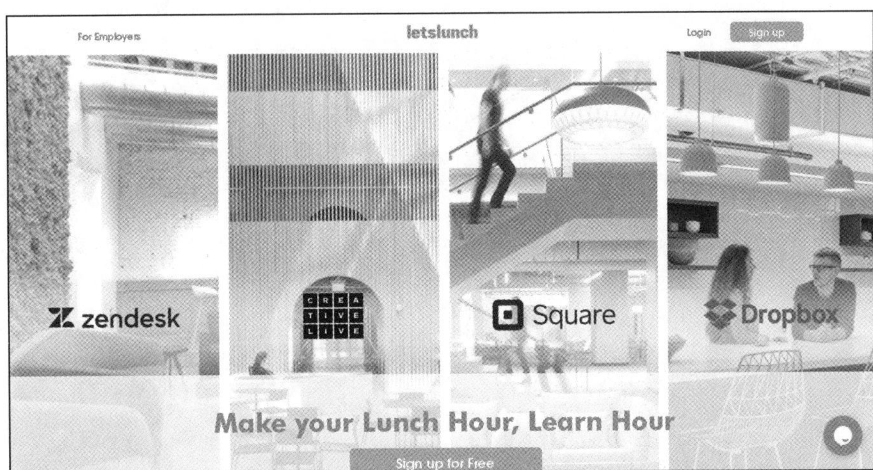

FIGURE 19-7: Use LetsLunch to set up lunch meetings with fellow workers and companies.

LetsLunch hopes to build communities of like-minded people, and it can't do that without interfacing with your LinkedIn profile data to learn more about you instantly. That information is used to help tailor potential connections and recommendations for meetings. Because the company strives to get people away from their keyboards at lunchtime to do some networking, their motto has evolved to "Make Your Lunch Hour, Learn Hour."

6

The Part of Tens

IN THIS PART . . .

Discover ten essential do's and don'ts for getting the most value out of LinkedIn.

Find ten popular online resources to help you with your LinkedIn activity.

» Following netiquette to keep from alienating contacts

» Keeping your LinkedIn activity more personal and less mechanical

Chapter 20
Ten LinkedIn Do's and Don'ts

I cover a lot of ground in this book — so much that it might be hard to remember it all as you're going about your daily use of LinkedIn. So here are ten essential do's and don'ts to help you build relationships and get the most value out of LinkedIn.

Do Keep Your Profile Complete and Current

Even though LinkedIn has many features, your profile is still one of the most compelling reasons to use the website, which is why LinkedIn is one of the best searchable databases of businesspeople available. And if you want other people to find you, you need to make sure that your data is complete and current. Here are a few ways to do that:

» **List all your former employers and schools.** Including your complete work and educational background in your profile can help you reconnect with former colleagues and classmates.

If you've had a lengthy career, you don't necessarily need to include details about positions early in your career — just the companies and titles will suffice. A good guideline is to include details on just the past 7 to 10 years. Additionally, consider including only those positions relevant to your current work. For example, I seriously doubt that my first job at a McDonald's is relevant to my current work as an author (unless I want to write the sequel to *Fast Food Nation*). I've also grouped a lot of my contract work under one experience heading with my own consulting company name, because many of the consulting jobs were similar in nature. It's up to you how you want to present your experience to the LinkedIn community.

- **Take advantage of the rich sections you can add to your profile.** In the early versions of LinkedIn, you could highlight your work experience and education and a few other elements of your identity. Today, LinkedIn allows you to add many sections that could apply to your overall work experience, such as presentations or publications you wrote, courses you've taken, patents you've earned, or projects you're working on. In addition, you can add documents, videos, photos, web links, and presentations to any job you list in your Experience section. One of the most popular elements that people add to their profiles is video, which is now hosted natively on LinkedIn's site.
- **Update your profile (and headline) any time you achieve a new position, complete a major side project, or receive a special award or recognition.** Your direct connections will be notified of the change (assuming neither they nor you haven't turned off the feature). This is a subtle, unobtrusive way to notify your network of your career changes. And you never know when someone is going to be looking for what you have to offer. Make sure that if you have a new position, you update your email address so people can still reach and invite you. You should also provide status updates that go out to your network. Many people share their status update but forget to go back and update their profile, so be sure to do both tasks regularly basis.

Don't Use Canned Invitations

When you send someone an invitation to join your network, don't use a LinkedIn default invitation text message. Nothing says "You're not really worth a few extra seconds of my time" quite like the all-too-familiar "I'd like to add you to my professional network" message.

That doesn't mean every invitation has to be a lengthy personal epistle. Here are a few tips for keeping invitations efficient but personal:

- **Keep it short when you can.** With people you know well and have been in recent contact with, canned messages are too long. The message can be as simple as "Great to see you last night, Jerry — let's connect."
- **Make sure to mention how you know the person, especially for contacts you haven't spoken to recently.** Although you may remember the person you're hoping to connect with, that person may not have the same recollection. If you haven't spoken to the contact in a while, start the invitation with an indirect reminder or reference of the last time you two interacted. For example, "Hey, I know it's been 10 years since we went to UCLA and had Computer Science classes together, but I thought we could stay connected via LinkedIn."
- **If the contact isn't already a member of LinkedIn, offer to help with the registration process.** You can try to explain the benefits of joining LinkedIn in an email, but no matter what you do, it's going to come across as a sales pitch or at least a bit evangelistic. The best way to persuade people is to offer to spend a few minutes on the phone explaining LinkedIn and how you're using it. That also turns the invitation into an opportunity to strengthen your relationship with that person by offering your time to bring something of value.
- **You can still personalize a batch of invitations.** You can give an invitation a personal touch even if you're sending it to multiple people. For example, you can send the same invitation to all the people you met or ran into at an event. Or you can send one invitation to everyone in your chamber of commerce. Just remember to write it as if it were going to one person, not the entire group.

For more on invitations, see Chapter 5.

Don't Expect Everyone to Network as You Do

Setting rigid networking expectations can be a source of needless frustration and can prevent you from building relationships with some great people. Here are some of the common issues that arise:

- **Different people have different standards for connecting.** Some people use LinkedIn to connect only with people they know well or with whom they share common points of interest. Others connect with anybody. None of these approaches is wrong. If some people don't have the same standard for a connection that you do, don't take it personally and don't judge them — they're doing what's right for them.

» **People might have good reasons to not allow other people to browse their connections list.** Don't hold anything against people who don't enable connections browsing. People may be concerned about client confidentiality and be required to keep their connections private. Or they may be connected to a competitor and not want their bosses and co-workers to know about it. Or they may just be concerned about their time commitments and not want to handle the potential growing number of requests to meet other people in their network, if all their friends see their long list of connections. However, even if a person has disabled connections browsing, you can still ask for introductions to people that person knows. Frankly, if you're just browsing other people's networks, maybe you should think about a more focused approach.

» **Not everyone responds in a timely manner.** If your message doesn't get a reply or you haven't received a reply to your InMail after a few weeks, don't take it personally. It doesn't mean that you're unimportant; perhaps the people you're trying to contact with are busy or infrequent LinkedIn users. If your request is urgent, pick up the phone or consider sending another email acknowledging that the other person is likely very busy but you were checking in one more time to see whether he or she would be willing to set up a time to talk or converse online. Don't underestimate the power that a friendly and understanding note can have on the other party.

» **Some people are bad with names.** Just because you remember somebody's name doesn't mean that she remembers yours. Unless you're 100 percent certain that she will recognize your invitation, contact her via email, phone, or a LinkedIn message before sending a connection request. Otherwise, don't be surprised if she declines your invitation or clicks the I Don't Know This Person link.

» **Relationships aren't always reciprocal.** For example, if you were someone's client, you might be able to provide a great recommendation for him. That doesn't mean he can do the same for you, so don't expect it.

» **Not everyone networks just to network.** Some people are extremely busy and not receptive to "I'd just like to meet you" requests. It's nothing personal, and it doesn't mean they're bad networkers. It just means that the demands on their time exceed the supply.

Do Your Homework

People provide you with all kinds of guidance, both direct and implicit, regarding what to contact them about and how. If you're the one initiating the communication, it's your responsibility to communicate on their terms. And showing that you took the time to do your homework about them demonstrates a certain level of commitment to the relationship from the outset.

The most basic rule of good conversation is to listen. In the context of LinkedIn, that rule means simply this: Pay attention to what's in a person's profile. Any time you contact somebody, review his or her profile.

When you send an introduction request message or an invitation to someone you don't know very well, don't put the burden on her to figure out what your common areas of interest or potential opportunities. You took the time to read her profile and determine that it's a worthwhile connection. Save her the trouble of figuring out what you already know and put your common areas of interest in your introduction request or invitation.

Do Give LinkedIn Messages Equal Importance

Many people have a tendency to treat LinkedIn communications as less important or less time-sensitive than an official email or phone call.

Nothing could be further from the truth. People get jobs, hire employees, gain clients, and make deals as a result of LinkedIn-based communications. They are as much a part of your essential business correspondence as the rest of your email. (If they're not, you're connecting with the wrong people!)

Here are some tips for managing your LinkedIn communications:

- **Don't turn off email notifications.** Missing time-sensitive communications is one of the worst things you can do. If the volume of email seems overwhelming, you can use email rules to move LinkedIn requests into a separate folder, but as a general productivity practice, you want as few different inboxes as possible.

  To make sure your email notifications are set up correctly, log in to your LinkedIn account and either visit the Communications section of the Settings page or go to `www.linkedin.com/psettings/communications-controls/email`.

  You see the Email Frequency screen, as shown in Figure 20-1.

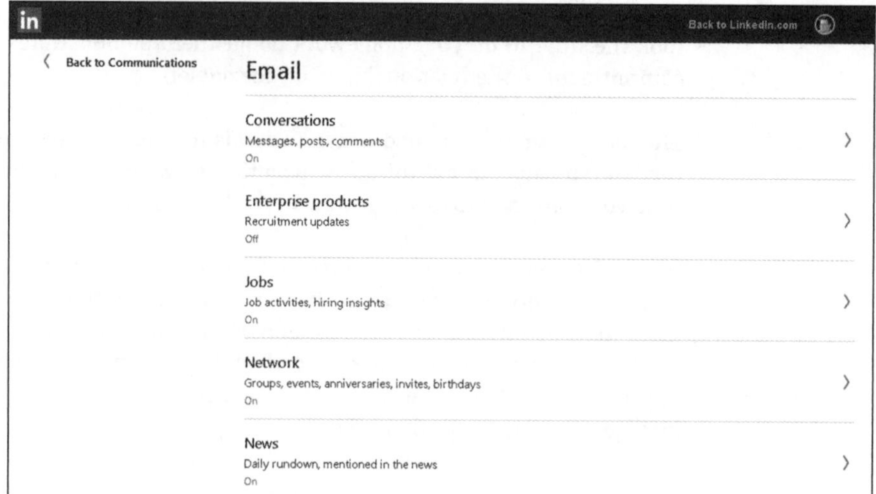

FIGURE 20-1: Set your email notification frequency so you don't miss an important message.

By clicking the link for each category — such as Conversations, Messages, Mentions or Tags of You in Posts, and Responses to Your Updates and Posts — as shown in Figure 20-2, you can set up what you receive in an individual email and in a weekly digest email as well as set a Recommended frequency that shows only messages you might have missed. (In some categories, a daily digest email option is also available.)

- **Check your LinkedIn inbox every day.** Or check it at least every few days. You wouldn't go a week without checking your email at work, so don't treat LinkedIn messages any differently. (See Chapter 6 for more on how to manage your LinkedIn inbox.)

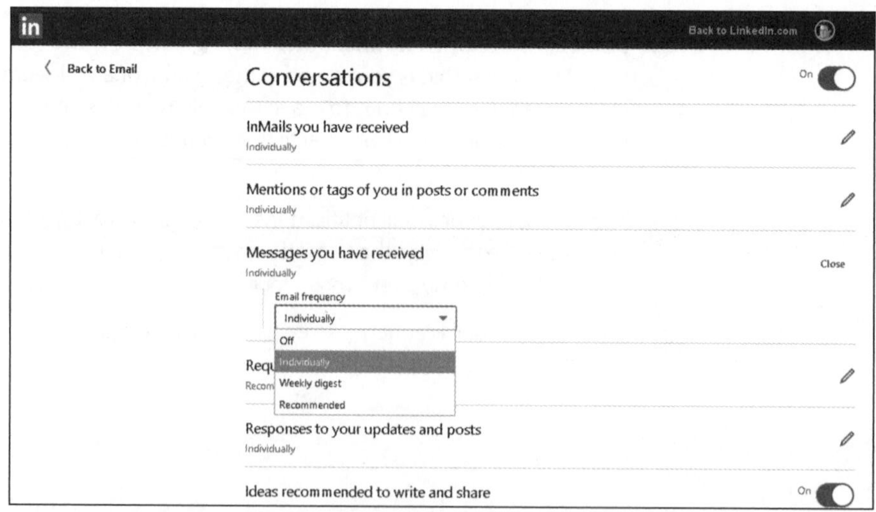

FIGURE 20-2: Decide how often you want to be contacted.

» **Use the automated responses to reply more quickly.** LinkedIn now offers canned responses to incoming messages, so you can click a button and add replies such as "Thanks," "I'll get back to you," or the ever-popular thumbs-up emoji instead of banging out a response. This feature is handy when you use your mobile device to communicate with others via LinkedIn.

» **Do it, delegate it, defer it, or delete it.** This technique from David Allen's book *Getting Things Done: The Art of Stress-Free Productivity* (Penguin, 2015) will help you keep your inbox organized. As you're going through your inbox, if you can handle a request in less than two minutes, go ahead and do it. Or you can delegate it by sending the message to another contact or recommending one of your contacts as an expert to answer the person's question. If something in your inbox will require more time, defer it by putting it in your work queue to handle later.

For additional tips on email organization and productivity, check out David Allen's book *Getting Things Done*, and also take a look at 43 Folders' Inbox Zero collection at `www.43folders.com/izero`.

Don't Spam

One person's networking is another person's spam. Better to err on the side of caution. You can use LinkedIn productively in plenty of ways without getting a bad rep as a spammer. Here are some basic rules of etiquette:

» **Don't post marketing messages or connection-seeking messages as your status updates.** All of these will get your message flagged and removed fairly quickly. A fine line exists between market or product research that calls attention to your company and an advertisement.

» **Don't automatically subscribe your connections to your newsletter.** This is admittedly a gray area. Connecting with someone indicates a certain level of receptivity to receiving communication from that person, and it's reasonable to assume that should include something more than just LinkedIn messages. After all, he's supposed to be someone you know and trust, right? Well, that's not necessarily the same thing as signing up for a regular bulk newsletter.

  I think it's better to be safe than sorry, so I don't recommend auto-subscribing folks to your newsletter. People can get ticked off if they suddenly start getting a newsletter they didn't subscribe to. The best approach is to ask permission to subscribe individual contacts to your newsletter. If you get their permission and they complain later, you can politely point out that you asked first.

- **Don't send connection requests to people you don't know.** Unless they've given some kind of explicit indication that they're open to receiving invitations (for example, announcing it in a LinkedIn group, stating it in their profiles, or being a member of an open networking group), you have to assume that most people don't want to receive connection invitations from strangers. Such rampant inviting behavior will get you suspended soon enough. Again, the solution is simple: Ask permission first. Send a message to get introduced through a common connection, or contact the person via email or his or her website, and ask whether it would be okay for you to send a connection invitation.

Do Make New Connections

You're setting yourself up for disappointment if you set up a profile, connect with a few of your contacts, and then expect business to come your way. That's not to say that it can't happen, but being proactive goes a long way:

- **Search for people who can help you with your goals.** If you want to meet people in a particular city, industry, or target market, search for them and send messages to start a conversation. Some people are receptive to corresponding or talking just for networking purposes, but you'll get a better response if you have a specific need or opportunity as the basis of your contact.
- **Introduce people to each other.** LinkedIn's basic introduction paradigm is reactive. For example, an introduction is made when person A wants to connect with person C via person B. But an essential practice of a good networker is identifying possible connections between people in your network and introducing them to each other. You can do this by sharing one person's profile with the other and copying the first person (see Chapter 5). Or you can send a LinkedIn message to both connections introducing them and telling them why you think they should get to know each other. That said, you should give each party a head's-up first, so they know what to expect.
- **Get involved.** The Groups section is the main form of public group interaction on LinkedIn. You can come together with other people to talk about a shared interest, or as alumni of a school or university, or as former or current employees of a given company. After you join a group, you have access to the other group members just as you do a first-degree connection or second-degree network member. Group involvement is a great way to expand your network and further your education.

Do Cross-Promote

Your LinkedIn profile is just one web page of your total web presence. It should connect people to your other points of presence, and you probably want to direct people to your LinkedIn profile from other venues as well. Here are some good cross-promotion practices:

- **Customize your LinkedIn profile links.** As described in Chapter 3, you can create up to three links in your profile that you can use to lead people to, for example, your business site, personal site, blog, book, or event.
- **Include a link to your LinkedIn profile in your email signature.** You can use the link both in your email signature and also on discussion forums. If you don't have a centralized personal professional website, your LinkedIn profile is a good alternative.
- **Link to your LinkedIn profile in your blog's About page.** Why rehash your entire bio? Include a few paragraphs that are relevant to the blog and then refer people to your LinkedIn profile for more details.
- **Install the LinkedIn app for your smartphone or tablet or both.** LinkedIn has added a lot of functionality to its mobile app, which is available for the iOS or Android operating system. Using the LinkedIn mobile app will allow you to access the site when you're out and about, networking in person. I cover the main LinkedIn app in Chapter 10.
- **Put your LinkedIn URL on your business card.** More and more people are starting to do this, because your LinkedIn profile is a good home page for business contacts. You can put contact information, your experience history, and many other vital details on your LinkedIn profile. When someone connects with you via LinkedIn, that person will always be able to reach you. Whereas phone numbers and email addresses can change, your LinkedIn connection will never change unless you want to remove someone as a connection.

Do Add Value to the Process

LinkedIn is based on the idea that existing relationships add value to the process of people meeting each other. If you are just passing the introduction "bucket" down the virtual bucket brigade, you're getting in the way of communication, not adding value.

To add value, you have to give those request messages for an introduction some thought. Is it an appropriate fit for the recipient? Is the timing good?

Add your comments to any message you forward to help facilitate an introduction. How well do you know the sender? Saying "I worked with Michael Bellomo for several years as a co-author, and he was hard-working, trust-worthy, and ambitious" goes a lot further than saying "Hey, Francine, here's this guy Michael to check out." For additional guidance on how to handle this tactfully, see Chapter 5.

Don't Confuse Quantity with Quality

Just because you're doing a lot of something doesn't mean you're doing something well. And when you think about it, is *more networking activity* what you really want? Or do you really want *more results with less activity*?

If you want to track your progress using LinkedIn, don't measure it by meaningless metrics such as the number of connections, endorsements, or questions answered. Use metrics that you know directly tie to business results, such as these:

- Leads generated
- Joint venture or strategic partner prospects generated
- Qualified job candidates contacted
- Potential employers successfully contacted
- Interviews scheduled
- Speaking opportunities garnered
- Publicity opportunities created

These do's and don'ts are a basic list for you to keep in mind as you use LinkedIn. The best rule to consider is the Golden Rule: "Do unto others as you would have them do unto you." Be open, accommodating, honest, and respectful, and the power of LinkedIn should become more evident every day you use it.

» Helpful webinar and video channels

» Information repositories and podcasts

» Aggregation and website tools

Chapter 21
Ten LinkedIn Resources

As you continue building your LinkedIn presence, you might want to take advantage of additional websites that keep you up to date on new features and possibilities on LinkedIn. These sites explore common and uncommon uses for the website and make you think about how to take advantage and enjoy the benefits of LinkedIn and social networking in general. I've rounded up a list of ten Internet resources that can provide extra information or functionality regarding your LinkedIn activities. Most of these resources are free, but some sites such as Buffer offer more powerful features for a monthly fee. Whether you use one or use them all, I'm sure you can find the resources that best match the way you like to learn and grow online.

The Official LinkedIn Blog

`blog.linkedin.com`

Years ago, Mario Sundar, previously a LinkedIn evangelist who promoted the company on his own blog, was hired by LinkedIn to start its official company blog. Today, various LinkedIn employees put up fun, informative, and timely blog posts about new functions or changes to the site as well as success stories, case studies, and practical information to make your LinkedIn experience that much more rewarding. In addition, a targeted blog for LinkedIn Marketing Solutions with helpful posts and articles that apply more to marketing yourself is available at `https://business.linkedin.com/marketing-solutions/blog`.

Overall, the blog posts live on forever, and you can search them to find out valuable information or post your own comments to give feedback!

You can also follow the official LinkedIn Twitter feed (@LinkedIn), the LinkedIn Help Desk Twitter feed (@LinkedInHelp), or follow LinkedIn on Facebook at `www.facebook.com/linkedin`.

LinkedIn Integrations with Zapier

`https://zapier.com/apps/linkedin/integrations`

As more apps and websites become part of your daily routine, it's more important than ever to connect your LinkedIn activity with every other facet of your online life so you don't repeat efforts to share information that you create on LinkedIn and vice versa. With Zapier's LinkedIn Integrations, you can connect your LinkedIn account to over 2,000 other apps. This way, you can automatically share content from your Facebook pages, Mailchimp email newsletters, WordPress blog posts, and lots of other services to your LinkedIn account and feed. Conversely, any content you create or share on LinkedIn can be pushed to your other social media accounts, without logging into each service individually.

When you sign up with Zapier, they'll offer tutorials on how to best use their service and how they can help automate and save you time as you build your cohesive social media strategy. Zapier creates customized content targeted to users who want to apply this power to their LinkedIn account.

LinkedIn Marketing Solutions

`www.slideshare.net/LImarketingsolutions/`

In 2012, LinkedIn acquired a company called SlideShare, which allowed people to store, display, and collaborate on their presentations using the SlideShare website. LinkedIn then incorporated SlideShare into its overall business, allowing people to display SlideShare presentations from their LinkedIn profile. The Marketing Solutions team has created a hub of fascinating presentations on the SlideShare website, grouping together actual presentations they give at industry conferences, case studies of companies and people who use LinkedIn and their various marketing elements, and insights and infographics that LinkedIn has generated.

The result is the LinkedIn Marketing Solutions hub on Scribd (which recently acquired SlideShare) now hosts hundreds of presentations and thousands of followers on the hub. You can follow this account to be notified of the newest uploads, and watch videos and download presentations in a number of areas.

LinkedIn YouTube Channel

`www.youtube.com/LinkedIn`

The explosion of video clips available on the Internet is best signified by looking at one of the most popular websites on the Internet — YouTube. Today, people use YouTube as a search engine, looking for a video clip that can answer their question instead of a text result from a search engine such as Google. Because of this, companies such as LinkedIn have their own channels, or collections of videos about their subject matter, that are organized and cataloged for quick viewing.

LinkedIn's YouTube channel offers a wealth of information, from the informational videos about products such as LinkedIn Mobile or Company pages, to LinkedIn influencers who share their knowledge with the worldwide community, to a LinkedIn Speaker Series that shares knowledge catered to working professionals who use LinkedIn. You can subscribe to this channel to be informed of any new additions to the channel, as new content is always being added.

Today, LinkedIn now has specialized YouTube channels focusing on the following:

- LinkedIn marketing solutions
- LinkedIn talent solutions
- LinkedIn sales solutions
- LinkedIn engineering
- LinkedIn help

Linked Intelligence

`http://linkedintelligence.com`

When LinkedIn was growing in size and popularity during its early days, blogger Scott Allen put together the Linked Intelligence site to cover LinkedIn and its many uses. Over the years, he built up a healthy amount of blog posts, links, and valuable information from himself and other bloggers regarding LinkedIn and how to use it.

One of his more ambitious projects is simply dubbed 100+ Ways to Use LinkedIn. Allen had bloggers compete to provide valuable information and tips across all of LinkedIn's functions, and he created a table of contents of the best entries on his blog site. You can still find this handy resource at `www.linkedintelligence.com/smart-ways-to-use-linkedin`.

The large repository of links and information can be helpful to new, intermediate, or power users of the site. Today, Linked Intelligence has its own LinkedIn summits, webinars, and numerous topics of information.

LinkedIn Speaker Series Podcast

`https://podcasts.apple.com/us/podcast/linkedin-speaker-series/id911570278`

The staggering popularity of the Apple iPod gave rise to a new way of broadcasting audio information to eager listeners — the podcast. Think of the podcast as a recorded audio broadcast that you can download to your iPod, smartphone, iPad, computer, or other device. You can subscribe to engaging and unique podcasts, regardless of where in the world they're recorded and played.

With the LinkedIn Speaker Series, LinkedIn employees use their connections to attract different speakers to come talk about their specialties and to help users become more productive and, therefore, more successful. This podcast series also has a wealth of archived shows available for download, so you can listen to success stories and get all sorts of inspiring ideas and advice from influential professionals. You can subscribe to this podcast series and hear great interviews, tips, and stories.

LinkedIn Plugins

`https://developer.linkedin.com/plugins`

Add LinkedIn functionality to your website without knowing lots of special programming codes. LinkedIn's developer network offers people the chance to insert prewritten blocks of code (usually in JavaScript) on their websites to share company information from a LinkedIn company page or automatically fill in LinkedIn information on your website.

Social Media Examiner

`www.socialmediaexaminer.com`

Social Media Examiner, which started in 2009, provides all sorts of articles, guides, podcasts, interviews, and information about top social media sites, including LinkedIn. It recommends different ways to market yourself on all these sites, and provides targeted analysis on different features as LinkedIn rolls them out. It offers an email subscription of daily articles, and different industry reports that you can download and use for yourself or your business.

TextExpander

`https://textexpander.com`

As you use LinkedIn, you might notice that you write several types of messages that could be saved as scripts. For example, every time you apply for a job, or reach out to connect to a second-degree connection them, or follow up with a new prospect, your responses might become more standard. Imagine if there was a service that enabled you to easily bring up a stored repository of standard responses that you could quickly customize and send. That service exists, and it's called TextExpander.

You can install TextExpander on Windows, on Mac, or as a Google Chrome extension. Store a series of responses, creating a shortcut for each. Then simply type a shortcut, and TextExpander will replace it with the stored response, which you can then customize with someone's name or other details and send. In this way, you can follow up more quickly and efficiently. In addition, TextExpander works for many other websites besides LinkedIn.

Buffer

```
https://buffer.com
```

If you're active on LinkedIn and other social networking sites (Facebook, Twitter, Pinterest, and others), you probably hop from site to site to provide up-to-the-minute information about what you're doing and what you want others to know. Well, instead of site hopping, you can use one function to update your status across all your social networking pages and microblogs: Buffer.

It works like this: You log in to the site and enter your message in the dashboard. You then select the sites you want to update with your new status message, and choose the day(s) and time you want the updates to be posted. Buffer does the rest, reaching out to your various pages to add your new status message. It's a great centralized way to keep all your various profiles as up to date as possible, and it's designed to update your LinkedIn status by answering the question, "What are you working on?" As of this writing, Buffer offers a free plan that allows you to schedule up to 10 posts at one time.

Index

Symbols and Numerics

A

B

C

D

E

G

H

K

L

M

N

O

P

Q

R

S

T

U

V

W

Y

Z

About the Author

Joel Elad, MBA, is the head of Real Method Consulting, a company dedicated to educating people through training seminars, DVDs, books, and other media. He holds a master's degree in Business from UC Irvine, and has a bachelor's degree in Computer Science and Engineering from UCLA. He also operates several online businesses and co-founded and operated the So Cal Comic Con for six years.

Joel has written seven books about various online topics, including *Facebook Advertising For Dummies, Starting an Online Business All-in-One For Dummies, Starting an iPhone Application Business For Dummies,* and *Wiley Pathways: E-business.* He has contributed to *Entrepreneur* magazine and Smartbiz.com, and has taught at institutions such as the University of California, Irvine, and the University of San Diego. He was an Educational Specialist trained by eBay and a former Internet instructor for the Learning Annex in New York City, Los Angeles, San Diego, and San Francisco.

Joel lives in San Diego, California. In his spare time, he hones his skills in creative writing, Texas Hold 'Em poker, and finance. He is an avid traveler who enjoys seeing the sights both near and far, whether it's the Las Vegas Strip or the ruins of Machu Picchu. He spends his weekends scouring eBay and local conventions for the best deals, catching the latest movies with friends or family, and enjoying a lazy Sunday.

Dedication

I want to dedicate this book to my amazing mother, Hanna, for her strength, pride, joy, confidence, flair, and utter deep love for everything I set my heart to doing. She was unique and fearless, speaking her mind whenever possible, and loved life, her family, and her hobbies. Her support sustained and guided me, and will continue to inspire and guide me always. I love ya, Mom. Say hi to Dad for me!

Author's Acknowledgments

First and foremost, I have to give the BIGGEST thanks to the great team at Wiley who made this book project possible. Thanks to Steve Hayes and Kristie Pyles for pushing this project forward and keeping me in place. An absolute, huge, bear-hug thanks to Susan Pink for putting up with my fast and furious submissions; she definitely kept me on track to make this book happen and made me sound so clear and grammatically correct! Thanks go out to my technical editor, Michelle Krasniak, for catching the points I missed and making every step along the way go correctly.

I have to give a special thanks to Scott Allen, who was instrumental in getting this book project started. Scott, I appreciate your help and support, as well as your infinite knowledge on the subject.

Thanks, as always, go out to my friends and new LinkedIn contacts who provided me with stories, examples, and endless encouragement. I especially want to thank Michael Bellomo, Jesse Campbell, David and Cherie Conde, Keith Davidsen, Lynn Dralle, Greg Foreman, Greg Goldstein, Steve Hayes, Chuck Hester, Doug Johnson, Sarah Lundy, David Nguyen, Kristie Spilios, Denton Tipton, and Doug Tondro. I normally thank my local Starbucks, but I wrote this edition in 2020 while sheltering in place.

Lastly, thanks to my support network for putting up with my late-late-night writing sessions and frequent seclusion to get this book ready for publication. Your support is always invaluable.

Publisher's Acknowledgments

Executive Editor: Steve Hayes

Project Editor: Susan Pink

Copy Editor: Susan Pink

Technical Editor: Michelle Krasniak

Proofreader: Debbye Butler

Production Editor: Tamilmani Varadharaj

Sr. Editorial Assistant: Cherie Case

Cover Image: © metamorworks/iStock/ Getty Images Plus/Getty Images